# BTEC Level
## *Building Better Results*

endorsed by

# BTEC National
# Business

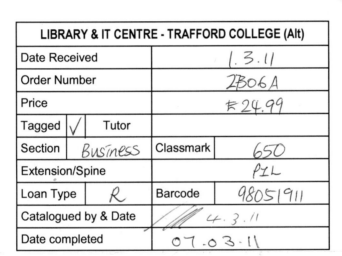

Editor: Lin Pilling
Naomi Birchall

With contributions from
Karen Hough and Richard Cotterill

DYNAMIC
LEARNING

HODDER
EDUCATION
AN HACHETTE UK COMPANY

This material has been endorsed by Edexcel and offers high quality support for the delivery of Edexcel qualifications.

Edexcel endorsement does not mean that this material is essential to achieve any Edexcel qualification, nor does it mean that this is the only suitable material available to support any Edexcel qualification. No endorsed material will be used verbatim in setting any Edexcel examination and any resource lists produced by Edexcel shall include this and other appropriate texts. While this material has been through an Edexcel quality assurance process, all responsibility for the content remains with the publisher.

Copies of official specifications for all Edexcel qualifications may be found on the Edexcel website – **www.edexcel.com**

Orders: please contact Bookpoint Ltd, 130 Milton Park, Abingdon, Oxon OX14 4SB. Telephone: (44) 01235 827720. Fax: (44) 01235 400454. Lines are open from 9.00–5.00, Monday to Saturday, with a 24-hour message answering service. You can also order through our website **www.hoddereducation.co.uk**.

If you have any comments to make about this, or any of our other titles, please send them to educationenquiries@hodder.co.uk

*British Library Cataloguing in Publication Data*
A catalogue record for this title is available from the British Library.

ISBN: 978 1 444 11187 3

First Edition Published 2010
Impression number    10 9 8 7 6 5 4 3 2 1
Year                          2014  2013  2012  2011  2010

Copyright © 2010 Naomi Birchall, Karen Hough, Richard Cotterill

Hachette UK's policy is to use papers that are natural, renewable and recyclable products and made from wood grown in sustainable forests. The logging and manufacturing processes are expected to conform to the environmental regulations of the country of origin.

Cover photo © Kelly Redinger/Design Pics/Corbis
Typeset by Pantek Arts Ltd, Maidstone, Kent
Printed in Italy for Hodder Education, an Hachette UK Company, 338 Euston Road, London NW1 3BH

# Contents

Introduction                                                                                      v
Acknowledgements                                                                                vii

Unit 1: The business environment                                                                  1

Part 1: Different types of business and their ownership                                           2
Part 2: Business organisation and planning                                                       14
Part 3: The impact of the economic environment                                                   24
Part 4: The impact of political, legal and social factors                                        32

Unit 2: Business resources                                                                       39

Part 1: How human resources are managed                                                          40
Part 2: Know the purpose of managing physical and technological resources                        51
Part 3: Know how to access sources of finance                                                     56
Part 4: Interpreting financial statements                                                        60

Unit 3: Introduction to marketing                                                                75

Part 1: The role of marketing in organisations                                                   76
Part 2: Using market research and marketing planning                                             91
Part 3: Targeting customer groups                                                               100
Part 4: Developing a coherent marketing mix                                                     107

Unit 4: Business communication                                                                  121

Part 1: Different types of business communication                                               122
Part 2: Presenting business information effectively                                             127
Part 3: The issues and constraints relating to the use of business information in organisations 133
Part 4: Communicating business information using appropriate methods                            139

Unit 5: Business accounting                                                                     149

Part 1: The purpose of accounting                                                               150
Part 2: Cash flow forecasting                                                                   157
Part 3: Profit and loss accounts and balance sheets                                            166
Part 4: Reviewing business performance using ratio analysis                                     174

Unit 9: Creative product promotion                                                              183

Part 1: Constituents of the promotional mix                                                     184
Part 2: The role of promotion within the marketing mix                                          193

Part 3: The role of advertising agencies and the media          200
Part 4: Creating a simple promotional campaign          205

## Unit 10: Market research in business          211

Part 1: The main types of market research used to make marketing decisions          212
Part 2: Planning market research          222
Part 3: Carrying out market research          225
Part 4: Interpreting market research findings          234

## Unit 13: Recruitment and selection in business          245

Part 1: The process of recruitment planning          246
Part 2: Regulations affecting the recruitment process          254
Part 3: Key recruitment documentation          259
Part 4: Interviewing and selection          264

## Unit 36: Starting a small business          277

Part 1: The initial business idea          278
Part 2: The skills and development required to run a business successfully          287
Part 3: Legal and financial aspects of business start-up          293
Part 4: Producing an outline business start-up proposal          305

Index          310

# Introduction

From September 2010 all learners registered on a BTEC Level 3 will be enrolled on the new specifications which sit on the Qualification Credit Framework (QCF). These new BTECs can act as stand-alone qualifications, form part of the Additional Specialist Learning alongside Diplomas or Technical Certificates within Apprenticeships.

As at present, the BTEC qualifications are made up of units, but the big change is that each unit is now allocated 'credits'. These credits, as well as building the BTEC qualification, form part of the Awards, Certificates and Diplomas of the Qualification Credit Framework (QCF) introduced as a way of rationalising and understanding the different types of qualifications that learners hold, what level they are and how they compare to other qualifications.

BTEC National qualifications on the new framework will become Level 3 BTEC Nationals (QCF) and will be named as follows:

| | | |
|---|---|---|
| Level 3 BTEC Certificate (a new qualification) | consisting of 30 credits | equivalent to 1 AS Level |
| Level 3 BTEC Subsidiary Diploma (previously called BTEC National Award) | consisting of 60 credits | equivalent to 1 A Level |
| Level 3 BTEC Diploma (previously called BTEC National Certificate) | consisting of 120 credits | equivalent to 2 A Levels |
| Level 3 BTEC Extended Diploma (previously called BTEC National Diploma) | consisting of 180 credits | equivalent to 3 A Levels |

## What does this mean for teachers?

The features of the revised QCF BTEC Level 3 National are that they retain the qualities of a current BTEC in that they are highly work-related. This book relates to the qualification by providing detailed work-related underpinning knowledge that supports learning and leads learners confidently towards assessment.

- Chapters have a common format linked to the unit's learning outcomes and content.
- Focussed areas of learning are provided by up-to-date case studies.
- Learners are encouraged to apply their knowledge and understanding through a range of well-designed and relevant activities.
- Learning is enhanced by reflective recap questions encouraging practice on what has been learnt.
- Each chapter has a valuable resource bank of Key Terms for each learning outcome.
- The end of learning outcome assignments assist teachers in ensuring their learners complete assignments that cover the unit's requirements.

## What does this mean for learners?

BTECs are work-related and this book gives you information, advice and guidance that is up-to-date on how to achieve a Level 3 BTEC in Business at pass, merit or distinction.

- The topics chosen for study are up-to-date, interesting and relate to the assessment of the unit.
- Learning is provided for each learning outcome that gives you the knowledge you will require before answering assignments.
- On many of the units you are given the chance to work with others or work individually.
- The units chosen have been very popular with previously successful learners.
- This book provides an exciting avenue to achieve your BTEC and move on to higher education or employment.

Lin Pilling
August 2010

# Acknowledgments

Every effort has been made to trace the copyright holders of quoted material. The publishers apologise if any sources remain unacknowledged and will be glad to make the necessary arrangements at the earliest opportunity.

The authors and publishers would like to thank the following for permission to use copyright photos:

© Chris Martin Bahr/Rex Features, p3; © Mango Productions/Corbis, p4; © VIEW Pictures Ltd / Alamy, p7; © Adrian Sherratt/Rex Features, p10; © Per Lindgren/Rex Features, p17; © Keith Leighton / Alamy, p20; © PjrTravel / Alamy, p33; © Frederic Cirou/PhotoAlto/Corbis, p41; © Wildscape / Alamy, p43; © locs / Alamy, p44; © Digital Property / Getty Images, p48; © PhotoStock-Israel / Alamy, p51; © Jochen Tack / Photolibrary, p52; © Mar Photographics / Alamy, p53; © Corbis Premium RF / Alamy, p60; © PHILIPPE PSAILA / SCIENCE PHOTO LIBRARY, p61; © Corbis Super RF / Alamy, p62; © David Franklin/ iStockphoto.com, p64; © Alex Segre / Alamy, p76; © David Lee / Alamy, p79; © Art Directors & TRIP / Alamy, p84; © Innocent Drinks, p92; © Simone van den Berg – Fotolia.com, p103; © Chloe Johnson / Alamy, p108; © Hugh Threlfall / Alamy, p110; © Moonpig, p114; © Sean Locke/ iStockphoto.com, p116; © Pixtal Images / Photolibrary, p127; © OLIVEIRA Sylvain / Sunset/Rex Features, p129; © Carl Skepper / Alamy, p130l; © Google, p130r; © Action Press/Rex Features, p134; © green stock / Alamy, p140; © Jeff Morgan 03 / Alamy, p144; © Rex Features, p151; © PETER COOK / Photolibrary, p153; © Alexander Raths – Fotolia.com, p154; © Nick Koudis / Getty Images, p162; © British Tourist Authority, p168; © Andersen Ross / Getty Images, p178; © Marks and Spencer, p188; © innocent drinks, p190; © Lourens Smak / Alamy, p194; © Action Images, p202; © MM Productions/ Corbis, p206; © Steve Meddle/Rex Features, p208; © Winston Davidian / istockphoto.com, p213; © Clive Streeter / Getty Images, p215; © kasayizgi / iStockphoto, p228; © Freefall Images / Alamy, p250l; © Peter Titmuss / Alamy, p250r; Library photos posed by models/www.JohnBirdsall.co.uk, p254; Glenn Copus / Evening Standard /Rex Features, p261; © Alexander Raths / iStockphoto, p266l; © vm / iStockphoto, p266r; © g_studio / iStockphoto, p270l; © Catchlight Visual Services / Alamy, p270r; © microgen / iStockphoto, p279; courtesy of Fraser Doherty, p281; © RICHARD YOUNG/Rex Features, p283; © Tony Kwan / iStockphoto, p296l; © Getty Images, p296r.

Key: l = Left; r = Right

The business environment is made up of hundreds of thousands of different types of firms operating within the economy. Many of these businesses, such as Tesco, Ryanair, Virgin and McDonald's, operate around the world and have become familiar to most of us. Many thousands more are tiny and consist of one or two people, operating on a very small scale. Some businesses make goods, others provide services. Some sell their products direct to the final consumer and some firms sell to other firms. Businesses are set up for many different reasons, and what they aim to achieve is likely to change over time. Despite these differences, businesses have a great deal in common – they all aim to satisfy their customers' needs and wants by organising and managing resources, such as materials, labour and finance, turning them into products and selling them on.

Many businesses concentrate on selling goods or services on a local basis, particularly when they are first set up. There are a number of reasons why this might be the case. It is quicker and cheaper to find out about the local market and the needs and wants of the customers in it than to research a wider area. New businesses are also likely to lack the financial resources to invest in the production facilities needed to operate on a large scale. They may also be unwilling to take the risk of doing so until they have become established. Some businesses choose to continue to operate on a small-scale, local basis rather than expand. This may be because their owners wish to keep control and make all the decisions themselves or to maintain a close relationship with their customers. However, staying small and relying on a relatively small number of customers limits the amount of sales and therefore profit that can be generated. Small businesses are also more vulnerable. If they depend on one market and sales begin to fall, perhaps because of new competition, they may struggle to survive.

The first step taken by firms attempting to grow is often to expand operations on a regional or national basis. For example, a successful restaurant may become a chain by opening up new outlets in other towns and cities in the UK. Customers across the country may have differing tastes and expectations. This means that operating on a national basis will involve more risk and require careful research into market conditions. However, it can make firms less dependent on any particular group of customers. It should also lead to increased sales volume, creating opportunities for increasing profit.

Once established on a national level, the next step forward for many businesses is to expand internationally by selling their products in different markets around the world. This strategy involves more risk, as the tastes and requirements of customers overseas may differ significantly from those in the home market. Legislation affecting business operations is also likely to be different in other countries, forcing changes in the way firms produce and market their products. However, operating on an international basis should mean much higher sales and can help to maintain growth when the domestic market becomes saturated. It may also offer some protection against the effects of recession at home.

The development and increased use of the internet have made it easier for businesses to become international. Relatively few, however, can claim to have a global presence. Companies such as Coca-Cola, McDonald's and Nike produce and sell in most countries and their brands are instantly recognisable. Such companies are referred to as multinational corporations. These are businesses that not only sell their products in many different countries but also have production facilities there.

## Public or private sector

The vast majority of businesses in the UK, both large and small, operate in what is known as the **private sector**. This is the term used to describe organisations within the business environment that are owned and controlled by private individuals or other businesses. The private sector dominates most major economies including the UK. However, the **public sector** too is responsible for a great deal of the country's economic activity. This sector consists of organisations that are controlled and funded by central or local government. These include public services such as education and health care, nationalised industries and public corporations such as the BBC.

Global brands are instantly recognisable around the world

## Not-for-profit/voluntary organisations

One of the main objectives of most businesses is to make a **profit** – i.e. a surplus of revenue over costs – for its owners as a reward for being prepared to take a risk and as a return on their investment. However, some organisations are set up with the aim of purely providing a service. They are run by individuals who volunteer to work, i.e. do not get paid. Such organisations usually operate at a local level, running youth clubs or providing support for the unemployed, the homeless or the elderly.

## Sectors of business activity

Businesses can also be classified by the economic sector into which they fall:

- **The primary sector** – This consists of organisations that produce unprocessed materials from the earth or the sea, including farming, fishing, forestry, or the extraction of oil and minerals such as coal. These raw materials represent the start of the production process of all goods and services; for example, farming and fishing provide the materials used in the food processing industry.
- **The secondary sector** – This consists of organisations that process raw materials taken from the primary sector and turn them into semi-finished or finished goods. This includes construction, oil refining and manufacturing. A typical example of this is car production, which brings together and assembles parts produced by a number of different businesses.
- **The tertiary sector** – This consists of organisations that provide finished goods or services to other businesses or the consumer. Examples include retailing, leisure, transport, tourism, education and health care, and financial services such as banking and insurance.

In the post-war period, the tertiary sector has expanded in most Western economies, including the UK, while the relative importance of the other sectors has declined.

## Business purposes

The purpose of a business is the reason or reasons why it exists. These reasons depend, to a large extent, on the aims and objectives of those responsible for setting the business up and managing it.

- **The supply of products** It could be argued that this is a common purpose for all businesses. The term 'product' refers to both goods (tangible items such as cars, microwave ovens and laptops) and intangible services, such as insurance, health care and hairdressing. By specialising in a particular area of production, businesses can develop the expertise to produce goods and services quickly and cheaply. Consumers also have access to a much wider range of products than would be possible if they had to satisfy their wants and needs themselves by being self-sufficient. Many businesses take the goods or services of other firms and **add value** by processing them in some way. A restaurant, for example, takes basic food ingredients and turns them into a range of starters, main courses and desserts, offering the convenience of a ready-made meal in pleasant surroundings to its customers. A travel agent may search for the hotel with the most suitable facilities in a particular resort and the cheapest, most convenient flights, saving customers time and money. The price that businesses charge for doing this is a reflection of the additional value created for the consumer.
- **The difference between profit and not-for-profit organisations** Profit is the difference between the income generated from a business from sales (known as **revenue**) and other activities and the costs it incurs in doing so over a given period of time. Few, if any, businesses can afford to make a **loss** (i.e. incur costs that are greater than revenues) indefinitely, as this would eventually use up all of the finance invested in

the business. A key objective for most businesses is to generate profits in order to provide income for their owners. For example, an accountant might choose to become self-employed because he or she believes that they can generate more income running their own business than working for another company. Large companies such as Tesco pay a proportion of the profits generated each year to their owners, the **shareholders**. However, many businesses that have been set up in recent years aim to use any profits made to tackle issues in society, such as homelessness or promoting fair trade for farmers in developing countries. These organisations aim to keep their operating costs very low indeed, in order to ensure that as much money as possible can be raised (see **charitable trusts** and **social enterprises** on pages 6–7).

There are a number of reasons why people may choose to set up their own business, in addition to those outlined above. For instance, someone may have a hobby or interest that they are able to turn into a business venture. Others may prefer the independence of working for themselves, and enjoy the challenge, responsibility and greater control of making all of the decisions.

## Types of business

### Private sector businesses

Within the private sector, there are many forms of ownership or **legal structure** that a business can take. The main types of private sector businesses are outlined below.

### Sole trader

A **sole trader** business is owned and controlled by one individual. This individual is responsible for making all of the decisions about how the business is run and receives any profit made as a result. Although sole traders may employ others to work within the business, many owners also carry out the work themselves. Sole traders are the most common type of business within the UK, particularly in the provision of services; examples include plumbers, electricians and small independent newsagents or convenience stores. They require little paperwork and finance, so are relatively easy to set up and run. The accounts of sole traders, unlike those of many other types of business, do not need to be published, reducing administration costs and helping to maintain confidentiality.

However, there are a number of disadvantages in operating as a sole trader. Having to carry all

A sole trader

of the responsibility for running the business can become a burden. This can lead to stress, especially as one person is unlikely to have all the business skills, such as marketing and accounting, to do so. The business may not be able to operate for any length of time without the owner, making it difficult to take time away for holidays or as a result of illness. If either occurs, the business may have to shut down, at least temporarily, leading to a loss of income. Sole traders may also find it difficult to raise the funds to expand. Finance may be limited to the owner's savings and any profit made, as banks often view such businesses as high risk and may therefore be reluctant to lend money.

Possibly the greatest potential drawback to being a sole trader is having **unlimited liability**. From a legal viewpoint, there is no difference between the business and its owner. This means that the sole trader is personally liable for any debts incurred by the business and could be forced to sell their own possessions, such as a house or car. The sole trader may even face bankruptcy if they are unable to raise the money needed to cover the business debts.

### Partnership

This is formed when two or more people are in business together, without having set up a limited company. Although they are not legally required to do so, many partnerships produce a document known as a **deed of partnership**. As well as giving basic information, such as the partnership's name and the type of business, the deed sets out the rights and duties of each of the partners within the business, the amount of capital they are to contribute and their share of any profits or losses that might be made. Once it is produced, the deed is legally binding and can help to resolve any disputes or misunderstandings that may arise. If a deed of partnership does not exist, the partnership is governed by the terms of the **Partnership Act 1890**.

There are a number of advantages to choosing to operate as a partnership, particularly in comparison with a sole trader business. Each of the owners may bring different ideas, skills and experience into the business, improving the quality of decision making and allowing the business to operate more effectively. The finance available within a partnership is likely to be greater, as each partner is required to invest. Having a number of owners within the business can also mean less stress, as the responsibility of running the business can be shared and partners can cover for each other.

Partnerships also have a number of potential disadvantages. Unlike the owner of a sole trader business, partners have to share any profits generated. However, given the greater level of finance involved and the scope therefore available for producing greater profits, each individual partner's share may still be a significant amount. Disputes between partners may occur and trying to reach agreement may take time, affecting business performance, although rules and procedures for resolving disputes may be included in the deed of partnership. Ineffective decision making or the poor work ethic of one partner is likely to have an impact on the whole business, counteracting the efforts of others. Ordinary partnerships also suffer from unlimited liability and this can be particularly problematic given that all partners may suffer as a result of the negligence or misconduct of one individual. This can be overcome to some extent by setting up a **limited liability partnership** (LLP). In such cases, the personal liability of most of the partners is reduced because the business, rather than its owners, is responsible for any debts incurred. However, at least two partners are required by law to accept additional responsibilities as a result of this.

## Limited company

Unlimited liability often acts as an obstacle to growth for sole traders and partnerships. Because of the risks involved, owners may choose to avoid borrowing funds or taking on high levels of trade credit in order to expand. However, this means that they may also miss out on opportunities to generate more sales and higher levels of profit. In order

to overcome this, many businesses go through the process of incorporation in order to become a **limited company**. This creates a separate legal identity for the business, separate from that of its owners, meaning that it can own assets and run up its own debts. The owners of the business, usually referred to as **shareholders**, enjoy **limited liability**, meaning that they stand to lose only the amount they have invested in the business if it gets into difficulty, and will not be held responsible for all of its debts. This encourages individuals to invest because their risk is limited.

A number of steps need to be taken in order to create a limited company with its own legal status. The business has to be registered with the Registrar of Companies and two key documents need to be provided:

- The **Memorandum of Association** – This gives basic details about the company, including its name, its objectives, the maximum amount that can be raised by selling shares (known as the authorised share capital) and the voting rights of the shareholders.
- The **Articles of Association** – This contains information on how the business will be run, including shareholders' rights and the role of directors.

Preparing and providing this documentation means that setting up a limited company is more complicated than some other types of business, such as sole traders and partnerships. Limited companies must have their accounts audited and provide a great deal of information on their financial performance annually to Companies House. They are also required to hold an annual general meeting (AGM) for their shareholders to approve company accounts, question the company chairman and elect the board of directors. These regulations add to the operating costs of setting up and running this type of business.

Limited companies can be set up as either **private limited companies** or **public limited companies**.

## Private limited company

A private limited company can be set up by an individual with relatively little capital. The company name usually contains the word 'Limited' or the abbreviation 'Ltd'. Shares in a private limited company cannot be bought or sold without the permission of the existing shareholders and they cannot be made available for sale on the stock market. This allows the original owners to maintain

**Figure 1.1** Organisations in the private sector

control of the business, rather than have their influence watered down each time new shares are issued to other investors. However, it may mean that finance is more difficult to obtain and the business is only able to grow relatively slowly.

### Public limited company

A business needs a minimum share capital of £50,000 in order to become a public limited company (plc). Most large organisations within the private sector, including banks such as Barclays and Santander and retailers such as Tesco and Marks and Spencer, are public limited companies. Unlike a private limited company, the shares of a public limited company can be freely bought by and sold to the general public. This makes it much easier for such businesses to raise finance but it can make it difficult for the original shareholders to keep control and may even lead to a takeover by another company. There may also be conflicts between the objectives of the shareholders and the board of directors who are appointed to run the business on their behalf. A public limited company may have thousands of shareholders, many of whom know little, if anything, about running a business. Often shareholders are interested only in making as much money as quickly as possible – known as short-termism. This forces directors and managers to pay out a great deal of any profit made as dividends to shareholders and to invest in projects that will bring quick returns, rather than taking a more long-term view.

## Public sector businesses

The public sector consists of activities and services that are provided and funded by the government on behalf of the public. There are a number of different ways in which this is done, including:

- **Government departments** – There are a large number of departments within central government, including the Department of Health, the Department of Transport and the Department of Children, Schools and Families. These departments are not driven by the objective of making a profit, but are required to carry out their activities efficiently and cost effectively.
- **Government agencies** – These are set up to take responsibility for a particular service or function. Agencies can be created by the UK Parliament, the Scottish Parliament or the Welsh National Assembly. They are more independent than government departments but they are accountable for their actions to the executive that created them.

**Figure 1.2** Organisations in the public sector

## Other types of business

### Worker cooperative

Worker cooperatives are organisations that are owned and controlled by their worker-owners. They are sometimes referred to as producer cooperatives. Cooperatives are set up and run by a group of people or businesses for the mutual benefit of those who own it (known as its **members**). They are based on the principles of democracy, equality and self-help. Members have an equal say as to how the cooperative is run and get a share of the profits. This can be very motivating, as employees work harder to make their decisions successful and benefit directly from the results. However, workers may lack management experience, leading to ineffective decision making.

### Charitable trust

A **charity** is a non-profit-making organisation set up to support a cause by collecting money from the public. Charitable causes are very wide-ranging in their nature and include the relief of poverty, illness, cruelty to animals, the promotion of religion, education, environmental awareness and political freedom. Charities aim to make a surplus, rather

## The John Lewis Partnership

The John Lewis Partnership is one of the UK's leading retailers. The business, set up in 1864, now controls 28 department stores, 227 Waitrose supermarkets and a John Lewis at Home store. It is also the UK's largest fully employee-owned company. Its 70,000 permanent employees are known as 'partners' and the co-ownership structure of the company gives each one a voice in how it is run. The management structure of the Partnership consists of the Chairman, the Partnership Board, the divisional Management Boards, the Group Executive, and the Business Strategy Group. However, John Lewis also has a number of councils and committees that give employees control over the running of the company. The Partnership Council elects five Partnership board directors, which gives them a voice and a means of holding management to account. There are also divisional councils, with at least one elected councillor to represent each branch. Each John Lewis selling branch has a Branch Forum (known as PartnerVoice Forums in Waitrose stores), where elected members question management and raise issues.

### Activity

Examine the key benefits and drawbacks for the John Lewis Partnership from operating as an employee-owned company.

than a profit, from public donations, once their running costs have been deducted. This surplus must be used to support the purpose or cause for which the charity was set up. Some charities, such as Oxfam, Friends of the Earth and Greenpeace, have grown very large and operate on an international scale. Many of the people involved in setting up and running charities provide their services voluntarily. However, unlike voluntary organisations, they also employ paid managers and staff to work for them. The management of a charity is overseen by a group of trustees – people with business and other relevant experience who provide their services on a voluntary basis.

A **charitable trust** is a charity that has been set up with a trust deed. By contrast, a **charitable company** is established with a memorandum of association and articles of association. Charitable trusts aim to benefit society, either as a whole or by targeting sections of it. For example, the purpose of the Joseph Rowntree Charitable Trust (JRCT) is to give grants to individuals and projects that are aimed at reducing poverty, political equality and social injustice such as racism. Like all charities, the activities of charitable trusts are overseen and regulated by the Charities Commission.

### Social enterprise

Some organisations use any surpluses that they are able to create to tackle problems within society. A **social enterprise** is another type of organisation that aims to make profit to benefit others rather than its owners. It uses business activities such as the production and sale of goods or services to fulfil social aims, such as creating jobs in areas of high unemployment or to improve the quality of life for groups within the community.

# Business stakeholders

In 2008, discount store Aldi announced its intention to open the first of 13 stores in Edinburgh. This decision would have affected those living and working in the city in different ways. The range of supermarkets available to shoppers would have increased, improving customer choice. The decision would have helped to create jobs, providing work and incomes for the people recruited to work in the stores. In addition, many local businesses, such as shops, restaurants and bars, would have benefited from increased trade, as newly employed Aldi workers have more income to spend. However, the Aldi expansion into Edinburgh is likely to

## Making a difference

Global Ethics is the organisation behind the One brand – a range of products including bottled water. Although it is not a charity, all of the profits generated by Global Ethics are used to finance humanitarian projects in developing countries. For example, money raised from selling One Water is used to purchase and install PlayPumps. These are roundabouts that pump clean water from beneath ground each time a child plays on them. The water is then stored in tanks, providing safe and convenient supplies to nearby villages. The profits generated from selling One Condoms are used to provide HIV/AIDS screening, counselling and training for medical staff in South Africa.

**Source: www.onedifference.org**

### Activity

There are thousands of social enterprises currently operating in the UK. Carry out research, individually or in pairs, and produce a short presentation on one of them, outlining its business activities and the cause(s) it supports.

have caused problems in other areas. Some retailers may have struggled to compete with Aldi's low prices, resulting in a loss of sales, and possibly even closure for some smaller, independent stores. Increased levels of traffic from customers' cars and delivery lorries may have increased congestion in certain parts of the city.

This highlights the fact that business activities can affect a wide range of groups – benefiting some and creating problems for others. An individual or group that is interested in or affected by a firm's behaviour is known as a **stakeholder**. The needs or concerns of each stakeholder will vary, but failing to take these needs into account can lead to problems for a business, even if it is operating within the law. Many managers attempt, therefore, to identify who their stakeholders are, what needs they have and the extent to which they should be taken into account in the decision-making process.

There are a number of key stakeholder groups, which are outlined below.

## Owners

The owners of a business are the individuals (or, in some cases, other firms) who have invested the finance required to set it up, keep it running and allow it to grow. In theory, any profits made by the business belong to the owners as a return for their investment, but they risk making nothing and even losing their money if the business does badly. They will therefore want the business to be run as efficiently as possible, in order to keep costs down and increase the profits made.

A small business may have only one owner, who is also often responsible for managing it and carrying out much, if not all, of the work. In such situations, the owner has a great deal of influence over the business, its strategies and performance. The **shareholders** of small and medium-sized limited companies often also act as directors, allowing them to have a great deal of day-to-day control. Large limited companies, on the other hand, often have thousands of shareholders and so a **board of directors** is appointed to run the business on their behalf. The shareholders are invited to attend an annual general meeting (AGM), where they can choose to dismiss the board if they are not happy with the way the company is being run. In practice, however, only shareholders with a large proportion of shares are likely to have any real influence.

## Employees

These are the people who provide the labour and skills needed by businesses in return for the payment of wages or salaries. They may also receive fringe benefits, such as company cars, private medical insurance and contributions to pension schemes. Employees are also likely to expect rates of pay and benefits to be competitive, i.e. comparable with those paid by other firms for similar jobs. They have a legal right to work in an environment that is safe and free from bullying, harassment and discrimination. They may also wish to have a large degree of job security, allowing them to plan for the future more easily.

The extent to which any individual employee can influence business activity depends on how much their skills and expertise are required by it. Key employees are likely to be able to negotiate better terms and conditions than workers with more general skills in less important roles. The latter group may therefore choose to join a trade union in order to act collectively to influence business policy (see page 9).

**Figure 1.3** Business stakeholders

# Customers

Customers demand the goods and services produced by businesses, usually – but not always – in exchange for payment. A firm's customers may consist of other businesses who buy its goods or services in order to assist their own operations. In some cases, the organisation acting as customer may be the government, buying in goods and services for areas such as education or health care. Many other firms sell directly to customers buying products for their own consumption. Value for money is a key expectation for most customers. This does not necessarily mean that they expect to pay the lowest prices possible, but prices that reflect the product's quality, via factors such as design, durability and convenience of use.

Businesses need customers to generate income from sales. Because of this, most businesses recognise the need for and take steps to achieve high levels of customer satisfaction, beyond those required by the law. Although this uses up resources and adds to costs, retaining existing customers is usually cheaper and easier to do than having to constantly attract new ones. The degree of influence that an individual customer may have over the way a business is run will depend, to some extent, on the value of its sales. Many of the large supermarket chains have been successful in using their dominance of the UK grocery market to put pressure on their suppliers to cut prices.

# Suppliers

These are the businesses that provide the materials and services required by a firm's operations.

For example, a restaurant will need regular supplies of ingredients, less frequent supplies of tableware, and a constant supply of power for heating, lighting and the use of equipment. Suppliers will have a number of expectations, including regular orders, prompt payment and prices that reflect the quality of the goods or services they provide.

Large suppliers may also attempt to influence business behaviour in certain ways. For example, the producer of a leading brand may threaten to withdraw supplies unless a retailer gives its products prominent shelf space or agrees not to stock rival brands. Smaller suppliers are unlikely to have the same degree of influence over their customers, particularly if they are competing for orders with a large number of rivals.

# Trade unions

A trade union is an organisation that is set up to represent the interests of the workers that join it. Modern trade unions offer their members a wide range of services, including legal advice, education courses and discounts on mortgages and insurance. However, their principal purpose is to protect workers' rights and improve pay and working conditions. Trade union representatives negotiate with employers on behalf of their members and may take industrial action, including overtime bans and strikes, in order to achieve their goals.

The ability of trade unions to influence business activity was reduced to some extent by the introduction of legislation by the UK government during the 1980s and early 1990s. However, trade unions remain influential in many industries. There are a number of factors that might affect the ability of a trade union to influence business activity, including the rate of membership among the workforce and the level of support received from the general public for any action taken.

## Employer associations

These are bodies that are set up to represent the interests of employers, usually in a particular area or sector of the economy. They lobby the government and put pressure on it to pass legislation and create favourable economic conditions for firms to operate in. They also support members by carrying out research into issues affecting business.

## Local and national communities

The impact of business activity can often be felt in the local or wider environment by those with no direct connection. Many businesses provide sponsorship for local or national sports teams or fixtures as a means of promotion, benefiting all those that participate. They may also sponsor projects that support groups and tackle issues within the community. For example, in the last ten years, cereals producer Kellogg's has invested £10 million, working alongside charity ContinYou to promote the benefits of breakfast clubs for children. However, business activity can also have a number of negative effects on the community, including damage to the environment caused by increased pollution on a national and even an international scale. For some years, concern has been growing about the effects of burning fossil fuels, such as coal and gas, on the world's climate. These fuels have traditionally been used to generate much of the electricity needed for both domestic and industrial use. However, they are also responsible for releasing greenhouse gases that are believed to be a key cause of increasing global temperatures and rising sea levels, damaging the livelihoods of many communities, particularly in developing countries.

Pressure group activity is often concerned with attempting to influence business behaviour, in order to protect community interests. The extent to which pressure groups are successful may depend on their ability to attract public support, particularly from customers who may threaten to stop using a business unless it changes its behaviour.

## The cook versus the supermarket giant

TV cook Hugh Fearnley-Whittingstall has been campaigning to improve welfare standards for chickens for a number of years. He has appeared in a number of programmes that have highlighted the conditions endured by chickens raised in intensive indoor battery farms. According to him, the supermarkets are partly to blame for this by selling chicken products too cheaply.

In 2008, Mr Fearnley-Whittingstall attempted to bring about changes in the way that Tesco – the UK's largest supermarket – sources its chicken products. As a Tesco shareholder, he tabled a motion asking investors to adopt higher standards for rearing birds at the company's annual general meeting. These standards have been drawn up by the RSPCA and affect the way birds are fed, exercised and transported. Farms meeting the standards are allowed to carry the Freedom Food logo on their products. The motion needed 75 per cent of shareholder votes in order to be adopted, but actually got less than 10 per cent. Mr Fearnley-Whittingstall claimed that his actions had, nevertheless, drawn public attention to the issues and the real cost of cheap food.

Tesco is responsible for more than 20 per cent of intensively reared chicken in the UK. According to the company, its welfare standards are among the highest in the world, but it admits that it is making changes to increase the amount of higher-welfare chicken sold in its stores.

**Source: BBC news**

## Questions

a) To what extent do you believe Hugh Fearnley-Whittingstall's actions were a failure?

b) Examine the possible consequences for Tesco from switching to only selling more expensive, higher-welfare chicken in the future.

## The government

The government is interested in businesses for a number of reasons. They produce the goods and services that add to the nation's wealth – many of which are consumed directly by government departments and agencies. They create jobs, giving their employees incomes, and pay taxes, providing revenue to fund public services. The government is also keen to ensure that businesses operate within the law by competing fairly, maintaining the safety of workers and respecting the rights of consumers.

The government has a great deal of influence on business activity. It passes legislation that can directly affect the types of goods and services produced, the ways in which they are produced and the methods used to sell them to the public. For example, a ban on advertisements for foods that are high in fat, salt and sugar during children's television programmes was introduced in the UK in 2008, in an attempt to reduce childhood obesity. The government's economic policies can also have a major effect on business activity, by influencing economic variables such as interest rates, the exchange rate, and the levels of unemployment or inflation.

## Key terms

**Articles of Association** One of two key documents required to set up a limited company (see also Memorandum of Association), containing information on how the business will be run, including shareholders' rights and the role of directors

**Charitable trust** A charity that has been set up with a trust deed, rather than with a Memorandum of Association and Articles of Association, and with the aim of benefiting society in some way

**Deed of partnership** A document that is often produced when setting up a partnership. It contains the business name and other basic details, but also sets out the rights and duties of each of the partners within the business, the amount of capital they are to contribute and their share of any profits or losses that might be made

**Limited company** A business that has gone through the process of incorporation, giving it a separate legal identity from that of its owners, and meaning that it can own assets and run up its own debts

**Limited liability** This means that the owners of a business stand to lose only the amount they have invested if it gets into difficulty and will not be held personally responsible for all of the business's debts

**Memorandum of Association** One of two key documents required to set up a limited company (see also Articles of Association), giving basic details about the company, including its name, its objectives, the maximum amount that can be raised by selling shares (known as the authorised share capital) and the voting rights of the shareholders

**Partnership** A legal form of business organisation, set up by two or more owners (known as partners). The partners usually have unlimited liability

**Primary sector** The sector of the economy concerned with producing unprocessed materials from the earth or the sea, including farming, fishing, forestry or the extraction of oil and minerals, such as coal

**Private sector** The part of the economy made up of business organisations that are owned and controlled by private individuals or other businesses

**Public sector** Part of the economy made up of organisations that are controlled and funded by central or local government, including public services, such as health care, nationalised industries and public corporations such as the BBC

**Secondary sector** The sector of the economy concerned with processing raw materials taken from the primary sector and turning them into semi-finished or finished goods, for example construction, oil refining and manufacturing

**Shareholder** The owner of a limited company

**Stakeholder** An individual or group with a direct interest in the activities of a business and how it is run. Examples include owners, employees and customers

**Tertiary sector** The sector of the economy concerned with providing finished goods or services to other businesses or the consumer, for example retailing, tourism, education and health care

**Unlimited liability** Where the owner of a business is personally liable for any debts incurred by it

**Worker cooperative** A type of business organisation that is owned and controlled by its employees

## Q Re-cap questions

1 Explain one potential benefit and one potential drawback in expanding from operating on a local to a national scale.

2 Explain what is meant by a multinational company.

3 Outline the difference between the public sector and the private sector.

4 Using examples, explain what is meant by the following: a) the primary sector; b) the secondary sector; c) the tertiary sector.

5 Suggest two possible reasons why the sole trader is the most common form of legal structure in the UK.

6 Explain what is meant by a deed of partnership.

7 Suggest one reason why: a) a sole trader might be turned into a partnership; b) a partnership might be turned into a private limited company; c) a private limited company might be turned into a public limited company.

8 State two types of business that do not pay out to their owners the profits that they make.

9 'A stakeholder is the same as a shareholder.' True or false? Justify your answer.

10 Identify two stakeholder groups for budget airline Ryanair; describe the needs of each group and suggest any possible conflicts between these needs.

**P1** Describe the type of business, purpose and ownership of two contrasting businesses.

According to the specification, you need to choose one private sector organisation and one public sector organisation (it could be useful to use your school or college for this). You also need to comment on the extent of the owners' liability. Public sector organisations are controlled on behalf of the public by the government, which is, therefore, liable for any losses they make. For the private sector organisation, you must be clear as to the legal structure of the business in order to find out whether its owners have limited or unlimited liability.

**M1** Explain the points of view of different stakeholders seeking to influence the aims and objectives of two contrasting businesses.

You need to have a clear idea of the views, needs and expectations of the stakeholders for both businesses, as well as each organisation's key aims and objectives, in order to link the two together.

**D1** Evaluate the influence different stakeholders exert in one organisation.

This requires you to make judgements as to which stakeholders exert most influence. This should not merely be your view, but backed up with evidence, so choose the organisation most likely to provide some good examples that you can use.

**P2** Describe the different stakeholders who influence the purpose of two contrasting businesses.

You need to choose a number of stakeholders that are identified in the unit specification and relevant to the business. For this criterion, you need to describe the stakeholders themselves, rather than giving a detailed account of their needs. Make sure you use appropriate business language, e.g. refer to the owners of a limited company as shareholders. You could also include details such as the number of owners, employees and customers (or an estimate for larger businesses) and the names of key suppliers.

See page 37 for suggestions for Assignments for Unit 1.

## Organisational structures

The structure of an organisation refers to the way in which it organises its resources internally, in order to carry out its activities. This internal structure is sometimes referred to as a **hierarchy**.

Very small businesses may have little, if any, need for a formal structure, given that only one or two persons will be responsible for carrying out all of the roles and duties. However, as a business begins to grow, the lack of any formal structure can lead to confusion as to what needs to be done and by whom. This can mean that the same tasks are performed needlessly by more than one person, leading to a waste of resources, while other essential activities are overlooked. In large organisations, employing hundreds or thousands of staff, a clear structure is essential if the business is to function effectively.

Establishing a clear internal structure for an organisation serves a number of purposes:

- **Division of work** – An organisation's structure sets out the roles of all the different employees within a business, from those at the top of the organisation to those on the shop or factory floor. Employees are often organised into functional areas, such as production or marketing, and, within these areas, are given a specific role involving a number of different duties. For example, within a firm's accounting and finance department, some employees will be responsible for dealing with payments to suppliers of goods and services bought by the business, while others will focus on ensuring that payments are received from customers. Although these tasks may represent only a small part of the overall process, failure to carry them out may cause delays or affect quality.
- **Lines of control** – The internal structure of a business also needs to clarify for whom employees are responsible and to whom they are accountable. The chain of command within an organisation shows the pattern of authority and control within an organisation. In a call centre, for example, a customer services assistant would be accountable to his or her section supervisor. The supervisor would act as the assistant's line manager, with specific authority over them. Managers may choose to delegate tasks to their subordinates, but they still retain overall responsibility for ensuring these tasks are completed successfully.
- **Communication routes** – This involves the transfer of information between different levels within a business. For example, strategies that are formulated by senior managers have to be communicated to marketing, finance, production and human resources managers further down the hierarchy. These managers decide how to implement the strategy within their own areas, then pass on appropriate instructions to the various members of their teams. Messages may also need to travel up through the business. For example, sales staff may have valuable information about changing customer trends that need to be communicated to decision makers at the top of the business. The speed and effectiveness of communication from the top to the bottom of an organisation (and vice versa) are affected by the number of levels within the hierarchy. The more levels there are, the slower is the speed and the greater the possibility that messages will become lost or distorted.
- **Span of control** – This refers to the number of employees (known as subordinates) who report directly to a manager. A **narrow span** of control exists when a manager is directly responsible for a relatively small number of subordinates. Typically, a narrow span would be less than six. This allows managers to have frequent contact with their workers and, therefore, supervise them closely. It also means more levels in the hierarchy, increasing the costs of management salaries, lengthening the chain of command and slowing down communication. A **wider span of control** – typically around twelve – means more subordinates to manage. This requires subordinates to work more independently because managers have less time to supervise them. However, it also means that there are fewer internal levels, speeding up communication within the organisation. Generally, senior managers have narrower spans of control because the employees they are managing have more diverse and complex roles, making them more difficult to oversee.

## Organisational charts

An organisation's internal structure or hierarchy can be illustrated by using an organisational chart. This is a diagram that shows the different levels or layers within the hierarchy. Employees on each level will have different amounts of authority. **Organisational charts** can also be used to identify lines of control and communication routes within a business, as well as the span of control of individual managers.

At the very top of a typical company's hierarchy are the most senior managers or directors. They have the most power authority, and are responsible for formulating the organisation's overall strategy. They are directly accountable to the owners of the business, the **shareholders**.

Underneath the directors, there are likely to be a number of levels of management. These managers usually operate within a specific functional area, such as production, marketing or human resources. They are responsible for ensuring that their areas operate effectively, by controlling and coordinating different resources, including employees at lower levels.

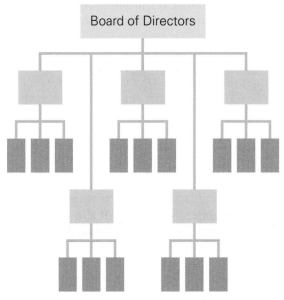

**Figure 1.4** A simple organisational chart

## Types of organisational structure

The exact structure adopted will depend on the needs of the individual organisation and the environment within which it operates. The structure is also likely to change over time as the business reorganises in response to internal or external changes, in order to maintain or improve the efficiency of its operations.

Common types of structure adopted by businesses include:

- **Functional** – This involves organising employees into departments representing the main functional areas of business, such as marketing, production, human resources and finance. Employees have clearly defined roles and responsibilities within each department.
- **Geographic** – Businesses that operate on a national or international scale may structure themselves in terms of geographic areas or regions, in order to reflect different market conditions. For example, electronics giant Sony has five business divisions – America, Europe, Japan (including Taiwan and South Korea), East Asia (mainland China and Hong Kong) and Pan Asia (consisting of Southeast Asia, the Middle East, Africa and Oceania).
- **Product** – A business selling a number of products may structure itself along these lines. For example, a large financial services company may be divided into different areas specialising in insurance, pension and investment products.
- **Type of customer** – Some businesses may have distinct customer groups with specific needs and therefore be structured along these lines. For example, computer manufacturer Dell groups its customers into home buyers, small and medium businesses, large enterprises and the public sector.

## Key functional areas of business

There are a number of functions that are common to all businesses, regardless of their size or the products that they sell. These functions are necessary for a business to operate effectively. Larger organisations may be structured into departments that specialise in carrying out these functions (see Types of organisational structure, above).

Key business functions include:

- **Production** This is at the heart of all businesses. The term 'operations' is often used to recognise that many businesses provide services rather than produce goods. Decisions must be made regarding what exactly is to be produced, in terms of design and quantity, as well as how, when and where to produce it. Materials required by the production process need to be ordered and stored, machinery needs to be purchased and maintained and the right number of suitably skilled production workers need to be in place. Control systems need to be put into place to ensure that agreed standards of quality are achieved. Production may also involve the research and development of new products and the modification of existing ones, in order to keep the business successful.

- **Finance** This function involves recording all the financial activities that take place. Accurate financial records are important for a number of reasons. Details of all the revenue generated and the costs incurred allow a firm to calculate how much profit (or loss) it has made over a period of time. Businesses are required to pay tax on the profits they make, as well as pass on VAT charged to customers. Accurate records should ensure that the problems that would result from either paying too much or too little tax are avoided. Limited companies are also required to publish their financial accounts at the end of every year. Within the business, managers require financial data to inform their decisions. Such data helps them to set realistic targets and then monitor performance to try and ensure that these targets are met. Financial data can not only show the level of profit or loss but how it was made, informing managers and helping them to decide on what to do next.

- **Marketing** This function is concerned with understanding the customer and attempting to ensure that products match customer needs as closely as possible, while still generating acceptable profits. Market research is required to identify customer needs. This function is also responsible for producing an appropriate marketing mix, in terms of a range of appropriately priced products that are effectively promoted and distributed to customers. The marketing function needs to work closely with operations to ensure that the goods and services produced are those required by customers.

- **Sales** This function is concerned with getting customers to buy the products produced by a business by generating orders. This may involve personal contact with customers from sales reps, particularly if customer requirements are likely to be varied and need to be carefully assessed. Other firms may rely heavily on telephone sales staff to generate orders. The sales function is closely linked to marketing. Some businesses may not employ any sales staff but use promotional techniques, such as advertising.

- **Human resources** This function is responsible for managing the people within a business. Its purpose is to ensure that the right number of workers, with the right skills, are employed to allow the firm to operate effectively. Human resources cover a wide range of activities, including recruitment and selection, training and development and industrial relations. Human resources staff are required to work closely with managers in other areas of the business, offering support and specialist knowledge.

- **Customer service** This function covers all of the activities carried out by a business when dealing with its customers, to try and ensure that their expectations are met or even exceeded. Market research is needed to identify these expectations in the first place, then goods and services need to be produced that deliver what

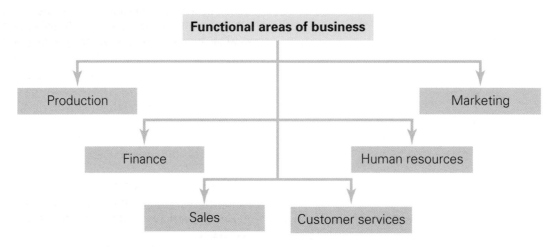

**Figure 1.5** Functional areas of business

they promise, at a time and a place that are convenient to the consumer. Workers need to be trained to deal with customers effectively. The provision of customer service therefore draws on all areas of a business.

## Strategic planning

The term **strategy** refers to the medium- to long-term plans drawn up by senior managers, which are designed to meet the overall objectives of a business. A firm's strategy identifies the actions that will be taken so that these goals can be achieved. It should also outline the impact of doing so on the key areas of the business, i.e. operations, marketing, finance and human resources. For a strategy to be effective in achieving the objectives set, the business needs to operate in an environment that is suited to its key strengths. These strengths – sometimes referred to as core capabilities – develop over time and may include knowledge and understanding of particular markets or a reputation for innovation and quality.

## Mission and values

The phrase 'being on a mission' is often used to describe someone who pursues their goals with great passion and enthusiasm. They are clear about the direction they are going in and determined to get there. A **business mission** performs the same function. It conveys the values and overall aims of the business, highlighting what it was set up to achieve, and communicates this to the business's stakeholders including its owners, employees and customers. Many businesses attempt to convey these values by publishing a **mission statement**. This summarises the firm's values and objectives into a sentence or two, providing a clear focus and direction to motivate employees and inspire them to work together. However, writing and publishing a mission statement can be a meaningless exercise if the objectives and values contained in it are not shared, or at least supported, by the managers and employees within the business.

## Strategic aims and objectives

**Strategic aims** are general statements that describe the overall direction in which a business wants to go in the medium or long term. For example, the strategic aim of discount retailer Aldi might be to eventually be within the top five UK supermarkets. Strategic aims affect the whole organisation, rather than certain parts or areas. Having a clear idea about exactly what the business wishes to achieve does not necessarily guarantee success, but it makes it more likely that the actions and activities chosen are appropriate and more likely to be successful.

**Strategic objectives** are the targets or goals that are set out by the senior managers of a business. They are based on the general aims of the business but are more specific in nature. They are designed to give direction and make it clear

---

## easyJet

easyJet's mission statement is:

> '... To provide our customers with safe, good value, point-to-point services ... To effect and to offer a consistent and reliable product and fares appealing to leisure and business markets on a range of European routes ... To achieve this we will develop our people and establish lasting relationships with our suppliers.'

### Questions

a) Outline the general aims of easyJet, as suggested by the company's mission statement.

b) Describe the likely reaction of three of easyJet's stakeholder groups to the company's mission statement.

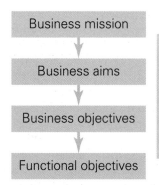

The business mission is expressed in terms of general aims and more specific objectives. These are then cascaded throughout the organisation by creating functional objectives that are coordinated and designed to support overall business

**Figure 1.6** Cascading a business mission

to everyone what needs to be achieved. For example, one of Aldi's objectives based on the strategic aim of being one of the UK's top five supermarket retailers could be to grow sales by at least 15 per cent per year over the next ten years in the UK market. Once a firm's strategic objectives have been set, they are then used to create functional objectives for different areas, such as production, marketing and human resources. Doing this allows that the overall strategic objectives are cascaded effectively throughout the organisation, in order to ensure that all areas of the business (and the departments and individual employees within them) are coordinated and working to achieve the same goals.

In order to be as effective as possible, managers need to set SMART objectives. SMART stands for:

- **Specific** Objectives should be focused on a particular area of performance, such as profit, sales turnover or market share.
- **Measurable** Objectives should be quantifiable and expressed in numerical terms, making it easier to see whether they have been achieved, or how much progress has been made.
- **Achievable** Objectives need to be sufficiently ambitious to provide a challenge and move the business forward. However, they need to be realistic, given the resources of the business and the external environment in which it operates, as repeatedly failing to meet targets can lead to demotivation.
- **Resourced** Objectives need to be supported by an adequate level of resources, including sufficient finance and the right number of appropriately skilled employees, in order to have a realistic chance of being achieved.
- **Time-bound** Objectives need to have a deadline in order to motivate employees and measure progress.

## The strategic planning process

Once a business has set its objectives, it can begin to draw up detailed plans in order to achieve them. The first step in doing this involves gathering and analysing information about the market within which the firm is operating. Useful data might include, for example, the sales forecasts, trends in consumer expenditure, the level of competition and the state of the economy (see Section 1.3). Markets are prone to change and this change can be sudden and dramatic. Unless managers have a clear idea of the conditions that the business is likely to be operating in, both now and in the future, its objectives and strategies may be unrealistic. Managers must also have a detailed understanding of the resources that will be available to support any strategies that are implemented. This will include the level of finance and the size and quality of the workforce.

The next step in the planning process is to devise a number of potential strategies, based on the information gathered. Given that there is usually more than one way of achieving an objective, it is useful to consider the benefits and drawbacks of a range of options. This encourages managers to adopt a more scientific and rational approach, rather than simply acting on hunch or instinct. It increases the chances of choosing the strategy that is most appropriate to the organisation's needs and therefore most likely to succeed. Once the chosen strategy is implemented, it needs to be monitored regularly. Setting interim targets can help to keep a strategy on course, by checking progress and alerting managers to take corrective action quickly if problems occur or the environment changes suddenly. Finally, strategies should be reviewed to establish the extent to which they have been effective in achieving the objectives set at the beginning of the process.

**Figure 1.7** The strategic planning process

## Influencing factors

The managers of a business are rarely able to set objectives and draw up strategy without having to take into account a number of influencing factors. These influences can act as a constraint on business plans or provide opportunities that act to increase the likelihood of success. Key influences include business type and ownership, stakeholders and the business environment.

## Business type and ownership

The objectives and strategies adopted by a business are likely to depend, to some extent, on the nature of its ownership. Sole traders have one owner and so their objectives are set by this individual. As the business grows, agreement has to be reached between a larger number of owners (either partners or shareholders) regarding the direction that the business will take. The process of strategic planning in large public limited companies is the responsibility of senior managers and directors, who are appointed to run the company on behalf of the shareholders. In practice, however, where there is a divorce of ownership and control within a business, directors and managers may pursue their own objectives, including paying themselves large salaries and building up their own departments. This increases operating costs and reduces the amount of profit available to pay dividends to the shareholders.

## Stakeholders

All businesses have a range of stakeholders who can influence the strategic planning process. The quality and commitment of employees, for example, can have a significant impact on what a business is able to achieve. Customer loyalty and the support and flexibility of suppliers are both valuable assets. However, it is the owners of the business that are likely to have most influence over business objectives and strategy. A business may have been originally set up to generate profit for the owners, and acting to improve **shareholder value** may continue to be the overriding objective. Managers may find that this prevents them from investing in projects that are potentially highly profitable but risky, or those that are only likely to generate significant returns in the long term. Some businesses are set up for other reasons, such as to promote a social cause, which will have a major influence on objectives and strategy. For example, The Body Shop, established by Anita Roddick in 1976, continues to operate as an ethical business, despite being bought by cosmetics multinational L'Oréal in 2006. According to the company's mission statement, its aims include '… the pursuit of social and environmental change [to] meaningfully contribute to local, national and international communities [and to] passionately campaign for the protection of the environment and human and civil rights'.

## The business environment

The **business environment** refers not only to the firms that operate in a market and in many cases compete against each other, but also to the legislative framework and economic conditions that influence business activity. For example, firms operating in markets where competition is very fierce usually have little scope to increase prices and are forced to keep a tight control on their costs in order to make profits. Changes within the economy can also create opportunities and challenges for businesses. An increase in interest rates, for example, can lead to a significant rise in operating costs for businesses with existing debt, as well as leading to a fall in demand from consumers and other businesses affected by the rise. On the other hand, a decline in the value of sterling against the euro could improve the competitiveness of UK firms, in both domestic and foreign markets, as UK goods become cheaper abroad and imports become more expensive in the UK. The introduction of new laws or changes in existing legislation may benefit some businesses but create challenges for others.

## The cider tax

A controversial tax on cider was postponed by the UK government only days after its announcement in the March 2010 Budget. The UK Chancellor, Alistair Darling, had revealed plans to increase the duty on cider by 10 per cent above inflation, which would have led to a price rise of around 15p a pint. The announcement was condemned by consumers and cider manufacturers, and had even resulted in a protest group, called Leave Our Cider Alone, being set up on Facebook. According to the Chancellor, the purpose of the tax increase was to correct the 'long-standing anomaly' under which cider is taxed at a much lower rate than other forms of alcohol. The duty on wine, beer and spirits was increased by 2 per cent.

According to the National Association of Cider Makers, the government's decision to freeze the duty on cider between 2004 and 2008 helped the industry to double in size. By 2010, the retail cider market in the UK was worth £2.1 billion and accounted for 9 per cent of total alcohol sales. The expansion of the industry benefited smaller manufacturers, such as Weston's and Thatcher's, as well as larger brands, including Bulmers and Magners. C&C Group, the Irish company that sells Magners, said it would absorb the rise, if introduced.

However, Roger Jackson, the commercial director at Weston's, claimed the decision to increase cider duty could be 'devastating' for the cider industry. There are around 470 small cider producers in the UK, most of whom make specialist or premium drinks. Changes in the level of production require long-term planning, as it takes some years after planting an orchard before it yields any return. Pub owners also voiced concerns about the impact on their businesses of any decision to go ahead with the tax. The sale of budget-priced alcohol by the large supermarket chains, such as Tesco, is seen as an attempt to poach sales from pub drinkers by encouraging consumers to drink at home. The highly profitable supermarkets have the resources to absorb such tax rises, rather than increase their prices.

**Source: timesonline**

### Questions

a) Explain how changes in the duty on cider sales influence the production of cider in the UK.

b) Identify two groups that are likely to benefit if the proposed increase in duty on cider goes ahead in the UK. Justify your answer.

## Different types of aims and objectives

As we have already seen, the aims and objectives of a business organisation are influenced by a range of factors. This means that they are likely to change over time, in response to the changing circumstances faced by an organisation.

## Private sector aims

- **Break even** There are points in the life cycle of most businesses where generating enough sales revenue to just cover costs is the most realistic target. For example, many newly established businesses have to face a number of **start-up costs**, such as heavy advertising expenditure or the cost of acquiring equipment. They are also likely to generate relatively low levels of **sales revenue** in the early months (and sometimes years) of trading until they become better known, attracting more customers and generating repeat sales. However, most business owners are unlikely to be content to continue to break even in the long term. Generating a surplus of revenue over costs, i.e. profit, creates an important source of finance for reinvestment in the business, as well as acting as a return for the efforts made and risks taken by the owners themselves.

- **Survival** Some businesses may face periods when they are unable to break even. During periods of economic recession, sales revenue may fall sharply but certain running costs, known as **fixed costs**, remain and have to be paid, regardless of the level of production and sales. In such situations, a business will need to take action to survive in the short term until it is able to return to making a profit. It may need to borrow cash or sell off assets in order to raise the finance required to cover temporary losses. However, few private sector businesses can continue to make losses indefinitely and, once their resources have run out, they will be forced to close down.

- **Profit maximisation** A firm maximises profit at a level of sales where the difference between revenue and costs is greatest. The owners of a business may well see profit maximisation as a key business objective, particularly in public limited companies where shareholders are concerned with getting the highest returns on their investments. However, pursuing this objective may damage the long-term prospects of a business. It may discourage managers from committing resources to the research and development of new products or from entering new markets because of the significant costs of doing so.

- **Growth** Firms pursue growth for a number of reasons. Expansion implies higher sales levels, which can lead to higher profits. Growth may also mean that a firm controls a large segment of the market, allowing it to exploit its position by increasing its prices or negotiating better deals with suppliers. Large firms are also less likely to depend on one customer or market, making them less vulnerable to a sudden loss of demand. However, the pursuit of growth is likely to mean lower profits, at least in the short run. Firms may need to charge lower prices than their competitors or spend heavily on advertising and other forms of promotion in order to win sales.

**Figure 1.8** Aims of firms in the private sector

# Public sector aims

- **Service provision** Most organisations in the public sector are set up to provide essential services, such as health care, education, defence and refuse collection. For example, having an educated workforce improves the productivity and competitiveness of UK firms, as well as improving the chances of the individuals involved. Therefore state education is provided to ensure a minimum level of provision for everyone.

- **Cost limitation** Organisations in the public sector are not required to make a profit, as the government provides the finance needed to support their activities. However, keeping the cost of providing public sector services as low as possible allows government revenues to be spread move widely. This means that organisations in the public sector should aim to operate efficiently, eliminating waste wherever possible.

- **Value for money** This does not necessarily require goods or services to be provided at the lowest cost possible, but is rather about matching expectations for quality of provision to the cost of provision. For example, the government may prefer to provide a high-quality system of state health care that may provide more than the minimum possible but lead to better and faster levels of treatment.

- **Meeting government standards** Organisations working within the public sector will set targets relating to operations and performance, in an attempt to ensure efficiency and acceptable standards of customer service. For example, hospital trusts operating within the National Health Service are required to meet 24 core standards, including three that relate directly to hygiene. The Care Quality Commission

(CQC) is the body responsible for checking that these standards are met and has the power to impose sanctions on those trusts that do not, including fines of up to £50,000 and closure. The CQC also has the power to send teams of investigators and patients on unannounced visits into hospitals to ensure that client expectations are being met.

- **Growth of range of provision** Government policy may also include plans to extend and improve the provision of public services in certain areas. For example, from 2006, the entitlement to 12.5 hours per week of free nursery education for three and four year olds was increased from 33 to 38 weeks.

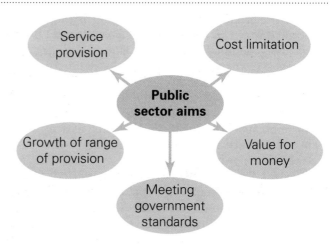

**Figure 1.9** Aims of firms in the public sector

## Key terms

**Aim** General statements that describe the overall direction in which a business wants to go in the medium or long term

**Break even** A level of output where a firm's sales revenue is just sufficient to cover its costs, meaning that neither a profit nor a loss is being made

**Hierarchy** The internal structure of a business showing the various layers of management and responsibility

**Mission** The overall aims and values of the business, i.e. what it wants to achieve

**Mission statement** A written statement of the overall aims and values of a business, which can be used to communicate what the business is attempting to achieve to stakeholders such as employees and customers

**Objective** Specific targets or goals that a business is trying to achieve

**Organisational chart** A diagram used to illustrate the organisational structure or hierarchy of a business

**Organisational structure** The way in which a business organises its resources internally, in order to carry out its activities

**Profit maximisation** The level of output where the difference between a firm's sales revenue and its total costs is at its greatest

**Span of control** The number of employees who report directly to a manager

**Strategy** The medium- to long-term plans of a business that are designed to meet its overall objectives

## Q Re-cap questions

1. Explain two ways in which an expanding business would benefit from establishing a clear organisational structure.
2. 'Communication within a business becomes more effective as the number of layers in its internal structure increases.' True or false? Justify your answer.
3. Examine one advantage and one disadvantage to a business from widening the span of control of its managers.
4. Identify and briefly describe two ways in which a business organisation can be structured.
5. Explain why it is important that the following business functions are coordinated:
   a   Production and marketing
   b   Human resources and finance.

6   Outline one reason why firms publish mission statements.

7   Describe the difference between an aim and an objective.

8   In order to be effective, objectives need to be SMART. Explain what this means.

9   Identify and briefly describe the key stages in the strategic planning process.

10  Outline two likely aims of an organisation in a) the private sector and b) the public sector.

## Grading tips

| | | |
|---|---|---|
| **P3** Describe how two businesses are organised.<br><br>This criterion requires you to describe three aspects of each of your chosen businesses:<br><br>• Their organisational structure, e.g. are they organised by functional area or on the basis of product or geographical area?<br>• The main functional areas, e.g. production, marketing, etc. – what duties are involved and who carries them out?<br>• How strategic plans are made – the employees and the processes involved.<br><br>Note that this criterion is descriptive – you do not need to comment on the success or otherwise of the structures and processes used (see below). | | |
| **P4** Explain how their style of organisation helps them to fulfil their purposes.<br><br>This criterion requires you to take the evidence produced for P3 and link it to the aims and objectives of each business (identified in M1). Try to give as many examples as possible of how each organisation's structure helps it to achieve its objectives. | | |

See page 37 for suggestions for Assignments for Unit 1.

# **Part 3:** The impact of the economic environment

The term **economic environment** refers to all of the factors that affect the behaviour of businesses and consumers. The rate of growth of the economy, the level of unemployment, changes in the level of prices or the cost of borrowing can have a significant influence on demand for products and, therefore, the level of production.

## Changes in the economic environment

A stable economic environment supports business activity, as it allows firms to forecast future conditions with greater confidence, leading to more effective long-term planning. Unfortunately, however, economic stability is not easy to achieve. Although all of the industrialised economies around the world have grown significantly since the Second World War, this rate of growth has been uneven. Regular patterns of fluctuating economic growth are known as the **business cycle** (also referred to as the trade cycle or economic cycle). Business cycles consist of four key stages, which are:

- **Boom** – These periods are characterised by rates of economic growth that are significantly above the long-term average (in the UK, this figure is around 2.5 per cent a year). Low levels of unemployment help boost consumer confidence, leading to high levels of spending and borrowing. Buoyant demand also means that business confidence is high, prompting investment and expansion of production. However, excessive demand may lead to rising prices (known as inflation) and increases in interest rates, increasing living costs and business expenses.
- **Recession** – Technically, this occurs once the economy has undergone two consecutive quarters (i.e. six months) of negative economic growth when output on a national scale is falling. However, the term is also often used to describe an economic slowdown. During a recession, unemployment starts to rise and consumer spending begins to fall. Some firms are unable to survive the loss of sales and are forced to close down. Those that remain in business are likely to postpone any plans for investment. The rate of inflation and interest rates are likely to be beginning to fall.
- **Slump** – National output continues to fall during these periods and unemployment increases to very high levels. The rate of business failures is also likely to be high. Inflation is likely to be very low and prices may even be falling as firms try to generate demand for their products.
- **Recovery** – This stage occurs when the economy begins to move out of recession or slump, and output and demand begin to grow again. Firms increase their levels of investment and begin to take on more workers, in order to increase production. This means that unemployment begins to fall, boosting demand further.

Any initial increase in demand tends to create a ripple effect, spreading through the economy and leading to further increases. For example, a manufacturer will respond to a rise in orders by increasing the level of raw materials it buys. It may also decide to increase its capacity by investing in more machinery. This creates demand for other businesses who, in turn, order more from their suppliers. The overall impact on the economy is, therefore, likely to be much greater than the initial increase in demand and explains why economic growth continues. The impact can also be negative, when the knock-on effects of an initial fall in demand can cause the economy to spiral into recession. This process is known as the **multiplier effect**.

## Inflation

The rate of inflation measures the annual increase in the average level of prices within the economy (an annual fall in the average price level is referred to as deflation). Rising levels of inflation can cause a number of problems for businesses. These include:

- Reduced profit levels if firms are unable to pass on increased costs of materials and power by increasing the prices they charge to their own customers, perhaps because they operate in fiercely competitive markets.
- Worsening industrial relations if managers are unwilling or unable to meet worker demands for wage increases in line with price rises.

- Reduced competitiveness against firms from other countries, both in domestic and foreign markets, if the rate of inflation in the UK is high relative to other major economies.

## The cost and availability of credit

Credit involves acquiring goods and services without paying for them immediately, or borrowing money in order to pay. Both consumers and businesses use forms of credit, such as loans, overdrafts and credit cards, to finance expenditure. Interest rates represent the cost of credit, i.e. the amount that is charged by the lender to the borrower for the use of the borrowed funds. The rate of interest charged varies from product to product. However, all interest rates in the UK relate to the base rate set by the Bank of England. Interest rates are used to influence the level of demand within the economy and keep inflation levels down.

Changes in the cost of credit can affect businesses in a number of ways. For example, an increase in interest rates is likely to have the following effects:

- Firms that have existing debts with variable interest rates, such as overdrafts and some mortgages, experience an increase in costs, thereby reducing profits.
- Firms considering taking out new loans for investment may be discouraged from doing so by the higher cost of credit. A failure to invest may affect future competitiveness.
- Firms selling goods and services that are often bought by consumers using credit, such as cars and foreign holidays, may experience a fall in demand, reducing sales revenue.
- The level of consumer expenditure in general may fall as households have to cut back on unnecessary spending in order to meet the increased cost of existing debts such as mortgages.

The availability of credit can also affect the ability of businesses to finance their activities. Small and new businesses have traditionally found it more difficult to obtain loans, as they are seen as being a greater risk than larger, more established firms. However, the global credit crisis that began in 2008, as a result of excessive lending by banks and other financial institutions around the world, made it much harder for UK businesses and households in general to borrow money.

## Changes in government policy

Government macroeconomic policies are designed to create a stable and supportive environment in which businesses can operate. In recent years, these policies have been targeted in particular at achieving steady economic growth and stable prices. The main types of government policy include:

### Fiscal policy

This refers to the actions taken by the government regarding public spending, taxation and borrowing. Government or public spending includes the funding of state-provided services, such as education, health care and law and order, as well as benefit payments, including the State Pension and the Jobseekers' Allowance. Public spending accounts for approximately 40 per cent of all spending that occurs in the UK, so even small changes in the level of spending can have a significant effect. These changes can affect businesses in the private sector in a number of ways:

- They affect the level of demand for those firms involved in supplying goods and services to the public sector. For example, a decision by the government to increase expenditure on post-16 education could lead to an increase in demand for construction companies, textbook publishers and suppliers of computers and electronic whiteboards.
- They can affect the level of demand in a more general sense by increasing employment in the sectors that are affected. Having more people in work leads to higher levels of consumption for most goods and services, benefiting businesses throughout the economy.
- The money used to finance this expenditure is raised from taxation. The impact on business from changes to the taxation system depends on the type of tax changed and the nature of the change (see below).

Fiscal policy can be used to increase or reduce the level of activity in the economy. The government can attempt to boost demand by using expansionary fiscal policy, where public spending levels are higher than taxation levels. On the other hand, the government may wish to reduce excessive demand that could increase inflation. In such situations, it could use deflationary fiscal policy, where the overall level of taxation is higher than public spending.

# Monetary policy

This type of policy aims to influence the level of demand and output by attempting to influence the amount of money in the economy. Although this can involve either controlling the money supply and/or the level of the exchange rate, in recent years the main instrument for doing this has been the interest rate. An increase in interest rates tends to reduce economic activity, while a cut in interest rates tends to have the opposite effect (see the section of this unit on the cost and availability of credit). The impact of changes in interest rates on individual businesses, however, depends largely on the nature of their products and financial circumstances. For example, a business with large levels of existing debts may be faced with a significant rise in costs from a relatively small rise in interest rates. Businesses selling goods or services that are likely to be bought on credit are more likely to see a fall in sales than a supermarket or petrol station.

## Changes in legislation

The government can also affect business activity directly by passing new laws or making changes to existing legislation (see Unit 1.4).

## Demand

The demand for a product is made up of the desire for customers to have the product and their willingness and ability to pay for it. The demand for a good or service can be illustrated using a demand curve. For most products, the demand curve slopes downwards from left to right, indicating that the level of demand increases as price falls.

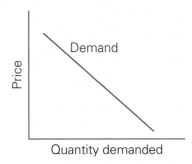

**Figure 1.10** Basic demand curve

There are a number of factors that influence the level of demand for a product. These include:

- **Affordability** This is determined by the price of a product and the incomes of the customers wishing to purchase it. As the price of a good or service falls, more people can afford it and so demand is likely to rise. Falling prices also mean that customers have to sacrifice less in order to obtain the product in question. It is common for newly invented or new versions of electronic goods (such as games consoles and mobile phones) to be launched on the market at relatively high prices, in order to deal with limited supply and to recoup research and investment costs. Prices are then reduced once the market has been tested and production capacity adjusted to deal with increasing demand. Rising incomes also mean that people can afford to spend more, particularly on products that are considered to be inessential or luxury items. For example, leisure club membership and demand for holidays in the Caribbean and the Far East have increased as average incomes in the UK have risen.

- **Competition** and the **availability of substitutes** A substitute good or service is one that performs a similar or identical function to that of another product. It could be argued, for example, that all the various brands of washing detergents are close substitutes for each other. Competition is most fierce in markets where there is little, if any, differentiation between products. Firms that sell products that can be easily substituted for others are particularly vulnerable to changes in price – in such cases, demand is always likely to move to the product with the lowest price. This often leads businesses to invest in developing brand image in order to differentiate their products from those of rival firms.

- **Level of Gross Domestic Product (GDP)** Gross Domestic Product (GDP) is an estimate of the value of the output produced nationally over a given period of time. GDP increases when **economic growth** takes place during a period of recovery or boom, but falls during a recession or slump. An increase in GDP implies an increase in demand generally for the goods and services produced by an economy, although individual firms or sectors may not necessarily benefit.

- **Consumer needs and aspirations** These are at the heart of the willingness of consumers to want to buy goods and services. However, consumer needs, tastes and aspirations change over time. The demand for some products increases as needs grow or are created, while the demand for products that are no longer needed falls and eventually disappears completely. For example, the invention of new products, such as HD television and MP3 players, creates needs that did not exist previously. Changes in fashion are also significant in markets such as clothing and children's toys. Demand rises quickly for the latest 'must have' item, but can disappear just as quickly as goods go out of fashion.

In addition to the above, there are a number of other factors that can have an influence on the level of demand for a product. Promotional campaigns are designed to boost sales, although the extent to which they do this depends on the effectiveness of the actual techniques used. A change in the size or the structure of the population can also affect demand for certain products. A rise in the number of children being born, for instance, would increase the demand for baby products and, in the longer term, put pressure on services such as nursery care and education.

A change in any of the influences on demand, other than a change in price, results in a shift in the demand curve. For example, a significant rise in average incomes is likely to cause demand for foreign holidays to increase. This could be shown by drawing a new demand curve to the right of the original (shown by the move from D1 to D2 in Figure 1.10). Even though there has been no change in price, consumers have more money to spend. A fall in average incomes is likely to have the opposite effect on the level of demand (shown by the move from D1 to D3 in Figure 1.11).

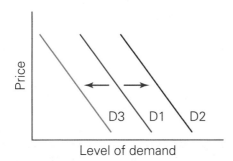

**Figure 1.11** Shift in demand

# Supply

This is concerned with the ability and willingness of firms to produce and sell the goods and services demanded by customers. The supply of a product can be illustrated using a supply curve. For most products, the supply curve slopes upwards from left to right, indicating that the level of supply increases as the price level increases.

Again, there are a number of factors that determine the amount of products that are supplied. The key influences include:

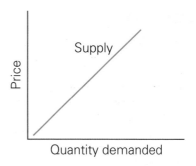

**Figure 1.12** Basic supply curve

- **The availability of raw materials and labour** All firms need materials and workers with appropriate skills in order to deliver the goods or services they set out to produce. The cost and availability of these resources have a direct impact on output levels. If the cost of these resources rises, then supply could fall, as the increased costs of production can potentially reduce the level of profits made.

- **Logistics** This refers to the distribution of goods (and other resources) between where they are produced and where they are likely to be consumed. Logistics involve a number of activities, including transportation and warehousing. The level of supply is likely to depend on how easily firms can get hold of the right quantity of materials to satisfy production. Many manufacturers operate just-in-time production systems that require flexibility from suppliers and rely heavily on the ability to receive orders at very short notice. Supply also depends on the speed and ease with which finished goods or services can be made available to customers.

- **The influence of profit** Profit is a key objective of most businesses in the private sector. The profit made on each item sold is simply the difference between the sales price and the cost of producing it. When the price of a product is very low, only the most efficient firms will be able to operate with low enough costs to make a profit. If the price of a product increases, however, then the supply of it is also likely to increase. This is not just because existing producers are able to make more profit, but also because less efficient firms can now enter the market successfully.

- **Government support** There are a number of ways in which government support is given to businesses, including grants, subsidies and low-rate or interest-free loans. For example, the New Deal, introduced in 1998 by the Labour government, pays subsidies to employers who hire long-term unemployed workers and also contributes to the cost of training them. These types of government support reduce firms' operating costs and the opportunity to make higher levels of profit leads to an increase in supply.

There are a number of other factors that can have an influence on the level of supply for a product. Changes in physical conditions, such as the weather or the quality of the soil, can have significant effects on agricultural production. Improvements in technology can also play a key role, leading to higher levels of productivity and lower unit costs.

Changes in any of the influences on supply, other than price, make the supply curve shift. A shift to the right would indicate that more products are being supplied at the same price as previously, perhaps as a result of a fall in the costs of raw materials or an increase in government subsidies (see the move from S1 to S2 in Figure 1.12). A shift to the left would mean that less is being supplied at the same price, as might be the case if the cost of raw materials were to increase or government subsidies were to fall (as shown by the move from S1 to S3 in Figure 1.13).

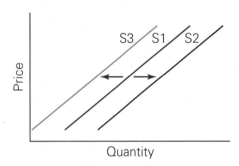

**Figure 1.13** Shift in supply

## Changes in supply and demand and their effect on the market price

We have seen that both the level of supply and the level of demand for a good or service is likely to change as the price level changes. Price increases stimulate greater output from firms but discourage demand from customers. At some point a price level is reached where the quantity demanded and the quantity supplied are the same – this is known as the market (or equilibrium) price. This price is not necessarily one that satisfies everyone on both sides. It may be too high for some customers, who are unable or unwilling to pay it. It may be too low for some firms to produce profitably. The market price is illustrated in Figure 1.14.

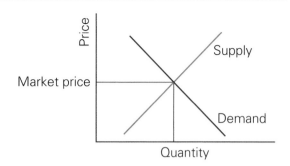

**Figure 1.14** Market price

A shift in either the supply curve or the demand curve can cause the market price to change. For example, assume that a children's toy based on a new television series becomes very popular, leading to a sudden and significant increase in demand in the period leading up to Christmas (shown in Figure 1.15 by a shift in the demand curve from D1 to D2). The manufacturers of the toy may have underestimated the level of sales and are unable to increase supply in the short term. As a result, the market price is pushed up (from P1 to P2) as at least some customers are prepared to pay more in order to obtain the product in time.

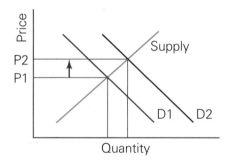

**Figure 1.15** Effect on market price of increased demand

If, however, the toy suddenly went out of fashion, manufacturers could be forced to sell at heavily discounted prices in order to get rid of unwanted stocks.

Improvements in technology, leading to lower operating costs, would cause the supply curve for a product to shift to the right. Assuming that demand remained unchanged, the price of the product would fall. As technology has become more advanced, computer manufacturers have been able to produce PCs and laptops at much lower costs and sell them at much lower prices.

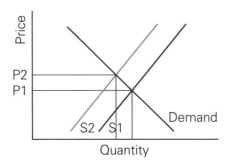

**Figure 1.16** Supply–demand–price relationship

A large increase in the cost of materials, fuel or labour is likely to have the opposite effect. The supply curve would move to the left and, assuming that demand remained unchanged, the price of the product in question would go up (Figure 1.16).

## Price sensitivity

The demand for most goods and services is sensitive to changes in price. Price rises tend to cause demand for a product to fall, whereas price cuts tend to have the opposite effect. Knowing this is of some use to businesses. However, it is even more useful to know the extent to which demand will change in response to a given change in price. Sales of some products are very sensitive to even small price changes, whereas other products are relatively unresponsive. The degree of price sensitivity is indicated by a product's **price elasticity of demand**. This can be calculated using the following formula:

$$\text{Price elasticity of demand} = \frac{\text{percentage change in quantity demanded}}{\text{percentage change in price}}$$

For instance, a business might reduce its prices by 10 per cent and find that sales increase by 20 per cent. The price elasticity of demand for its products would therefore be 2. Another business may also reduce its prices by 10 per cent but find that sales increase by only 2 per cent. In this case, the price elasticity of demand would be only 0.5. The higher the price elasticity of demand figure, the more sensitive demand is to price changes (known as being **price elastic**). If the figure is between 0 and 1, demand is said to be relatively unresponsive to price changes (known as being **price inelastic**).

Products that can be easily substituted for other similar, competing products are usually very sensitive to changes in price. This gives the firms that produce them little, if any, scope to charge higher prices in order to cover increased costs or raise profit margins. On the other hand, products with unique features that differentiate them from possible rivals are less sensitive to price changes. Firms have more freedom to increase prices, without any significant loss of sales. This is one of the main reasons why many businesses invest heavily in **branding**. This involves creating a unique identity, personality or image for a product. This image might focus on real features, such as design or safety. Alternatively, brand image could be built on psychological benefits, such as an aftershave or perfume that is perceived as making the wearer more desirable. Successful branding strengthens customer loyalty and makes demand less sensitive to price increases.

## Global interaction

Businesses that trade on an international scale are nothing new. However, in recent years there has been an increasing trend for business operations to be spread across the world. Markets in different countries share many of the same characteristics, with products being designed to appeal to global rather than local or national customer bases. The production systems of many businesses are integrated on a global scale, relying on supply chains that produce the cheapest or highest-quality materials and components sourced from around the world. This process is known as **globalisation**. It has allowed businesses to specialise in producing what they do best but still be able to sell in markets made up of hundreds of thousands, if not millions, of customers. Customers around the world have benefited in many cases from greater choice and lower prices, resulting from the ability of many businesses to produce and sell on such a vast scale. However, the competitive pressures created by these multinational corporations have made trading conditions much tougher for smaller businesses which, in many cases, have struggled to survive. The ability of national governments to regulate the activities of business organisations operating on a truly global scale is also limited, given the continuing disparities in areas such as health and safety and consumer protection.

# Key terms

**Branding** This involves creating an identity or personality for a product in order to differentiate it from competitors

**Business cycle** Regular patterns of fluctuating economic growth over a period of time within an economy

**Credit** This involves acquiring goods and services without paying for them immediately or, alternatively, borrowing money in order to pay

**Demand** This is customers' desire to have a product combined with willingness and ability to pay for it. The demand for a product can be shown using a diagram called a demand curve

**Economic growth** Where the value of income and output within an economy (as measured by Gross Domestic Product) increases over a period of time

**Fiscal policy** The actions taken by the government regarding public spending, taxation and borrowing in order to try and influence the level of economic activity

**Globalisation** The process by which national markets are becoming more similar and share the same characteristics due to the international operations of businesses

**Gross Domestic Product (GDP)** The total value of an economy's output over a given period of time

**Inflation** A rise in the average price level in an economy over a period of time

**Logistics** The distribution of goods (and other resources) between where they are produced and where they are likely to be consumed

**Monetary policy** This aims to influence the level of demand and output by attempting to influence the amount of money in the economy. This can involve controlling the money supply, the level of the exchange rate or the interest rate

**Price elasticity of demand** This indicates the level of sensitivity of a product's demand to changes in price. It can be calculated using the following formula:

$$\text{Price elasticity of demand} = \frac{\text{percentage change in quantity demanded}}{\text{percentage change in price}}$$

**Recession** A period of two consecutive quarters (i.e. six months) of negative economic growth when output on a national scale is falling (the term is also often used to describe an economic slowdown)

**Supply** The ability and willingness of firms to produce and sell the goods and services demanded by customers. The supply of a product can be illustrated using a supply curve

## Q Re-cap questions

1 Identify the four stages of the business cycle.
2 'Unemployment tends to rise when the level of national output is falling, and vice versa.' True or false? Justify your answer.
3 Explain what is meant by the multiplier effect.
4 Give two reasons why rising inflation can be damaging for UK businesses.
5 Analyse the effects of a fall in UK interest rates on a second-hand car dealer with a large overdraft.
6 Outline two ways in which the government can use fiscal policy to increase the level of economic activity.
7 Explain what is meant by monetary policy.
8 Identify and briefly explain two factors that could have an influence on the demand for rented property in the UK.
9 Describe two factors that could have an influence on the supply of oil internationally.
10 Briefly explain how the successful branding of a product could be used to reduce its price elasticity of demand.

# Grading tips

| | | |
|---|---|---|
| **P5** Describe the influence of two contrasting economic environments on business activities within a selected organisation.<br><br>This should include a description of a minimum of three economic topics, such as the impact of a recession, a change in the rate of inflation or a change in the cost and availability of credit. Note that this only needs to be done for one organisation, so use the business where most evidence can be gathered. | **M2** Compare the challenges to selected business activities within a selected organisation, in two different economic environments.<br><br>This requires you to develop the points made in P5 by explaining the effects of two different economic environments (such as recession and a booming economy) to activities such as production, human resources and marketing. | |

See page 37 for suggested Assignments for Unit 1.

# Part 4: The impact of political, legal and social factors

Economic factors are not the only influences on business that exist within the external environment.

## Political factors

One of the key roles played by successive governments in recent years has been to attempt to provide a healthy environment where businesses can grow and be successful. The activities and policies of local and national governments, as well as those of international bodies such as the European Union (EU), impact on business in a number of ways.

## Political stability

The UK has enjoyed over three decades of relative political stability. Frequent changes in government make it more difficult for businesses to plan ahead for the medium and long term. This is because political parties introduce their own policies and often reverse the actions taken by previous governments, in line with their election manifestos. These changes can quickly reduce the effectiveness of existing business strategies by altering the environment in which businesses operate.

## Fiscal policy

The purpose of fiscal policy is considered in some detail earlier in this unit (see page 25). It has already been noted that it involves a combination of public spending and taxation, aimed at influencing the level of activity in the economy. The main types of taxes used by the UK government are:

- **Income tax** This taxes the incomes of private individuals. Changes to this tax affect the level of disposable income available for individuals to spend and can have a significant impact on the level of demand within the economy. For example, a cut in the basic rate of income tax could lead to an increase in consumer expenditure.
- **National Insurance Contributions (NICs)** These are levied on the earnings of employees and the self-employed. They give the individuals concerned an entitlement to certain benefits, such as the State Pension. In the case of employees, NICs are paid by both the employee and their employer, so any changes could affect either or both parties. An increase in NICs reduces disposable income and could, therefore, lead to a fall in consumer spending. It could also mean that business costs increase, reducing profits and potentially discouraging firms from employing more workers.
- **Corporation tax** This is levied on company profits. Changing the level of corporation tax affects the amount companies have to reinvest. An increase in corporation tax could discourage investment, making it difficult for firms to remain competitive against foreign rivals.
- **Business rate** This is a tax that is levied on non-residential property. It is used to fund services provided by local government. The amount paid by a business depends on factors such as location, the size and the physical condition of the property. Business rates act as a fixed cost, so any increase in the amount charged would reduce the profits made.
- **Taxes on expenditure** Value Added Tax (VAT) is placed on most goods and services that are sold in the UK and is included in the price paid. In 2010, the standard rate of VAT in the UK was 17.5 per cent (due to rise to 20 per cent in January 2011). A limited number of goods, including food, books and young children's clothes, are zero rated, and some goods, such as domestic fuel and children's car seats, have a reduced rate of 5 per cent. Excise duty is another expenditure tax that is levied on a limited range of products, including petrol, alcohol and cigarettes. Unlike VAT, duty is not a percentage of the sales price but a set amount. In 2010, for example, the duty on a 75 cl bottle of wine was £1.69. An increase in expenditure taxes has the effect of increasing prices, which may cause sales to fall, depending on the sensitivity of demand for a product to a change in price.

## Providing infrastructure

The term infrastructure refers to the transport, communications and other basic utilities, such as sewerage, that are required to support the activities of business and the wider community. Traditionally, it has been the role of government to oversee the maintenance and improvement of the country's infrastructure. Public investment in the infrastructure can have a number of benefits:

- It can reduce business costs by speeding up transport and communication.
- It creates demand for businesses, such as construction companies, that are required to provide these facilities.

## Enhancing the skills of the working population

A highly skilled and flexible workforce is seen as being an important factor contributing to the productivity and competitiveness of an economy and the businesses within it. In recent years, both Labour and Conservative governments have highlighted the importance of improving the quality of education and training, putting in place a number of initiatives, and it remains a key political issue. For example, the Conservative Party's 2010 election manifesto promised to create 400,000 extra training places and 200,000 new apprenticeships if the party was elected.

## Organisations to support businesses

Over the years, the government has created a number of organisations to promote and support business activity. These organisations include:

- **Business Link** This provides free advice and guidance to businesses in England, via its website www.businesslink.gov.uk, which includes sections on starting up and growing a business, sales and marketing, finance and grants and employing people. Support is also given through advisers based at local level. Similar services are provided for businesses in Scotland by Business Gateway, for businesses in Northern Ireland by www.nibusinessinfo.co.uk and for businesses in Wales by Flexible Support for Business.
- **Regional Development Agencies (RDAs)** These were created by the Regional Development Agencies Act (1998). There are nine RDAs in England, all of which are funded by central government. Their purpose is to support economic development, employment and business competitiveness. Similar activities to those carried out by the RDAs are performed by the Welsh Assembly in Wales, by Scottish Enterprise and Highlands and Islands Enterprise in Scotland and the Department of Enterprise, Trade and Investment in Northern Ireland.

## Membership of international trading communities

The UK is a member of a number of organisations set up to promote trade between nations:

- **The European Union (EU)** This is a group of 27 countries that form a single market, permitting the free movement of goods, services, people and capital between members. UK membership of the EU removes any trade barriers with other member states, giving businesses access to a market made up of over 500 million people and creating significant sales opportunities. It also makes it easier for UK firms to recruit workers from and/or set up in other countries within the EU.

The UK is part of the European Union

- **The World Trade Organization (WTO)** This international organisation promotes free trade in goods and services by encouraging countries to abolish barriers to trade. It also deals with trade disputes that may arise between members, giving rulings and imposing sanctions if its decisions are ignored. By 2008, its membership had reached 153 countries.

## Legal factors

The introduction of new legislation (and changes made to existing laws) can also have a major impact on the business community in a number of ways. These laws have traditionally originated from the national government. However, as a member of the European Union, any legislation passed by the EU parliament has supremacy over national law.

## Providing a framework for business

The law has a direct impact on the way businesses are set up and operate. Businesses that wish to be set up as limited companies in the UK are required by law to be registered with the Registrar of Companies and provide a Memorandum of Association and Articles of Association. They are also required to provide Companies House with a great deal of information on their financial performance and have their annual accounts checked by an independent team of auditors. Meeting these requirements adds to business costs but also provides protection for company shareholders in the form of limited liability. Other more simple forms of business, such as sole traders and partnerships, are not required to provide detailed documentation. However, they are still required to pay tax on any profits made and produce evidence that the amounts paid are accurate. For this reason, such businesses still need to keep detailed records and produce accounts relating to their performance.

## Protection for consumers

Over the years, the government has also passed or amended legislation designed to prevent businesses from exploiting consumers and employees. Businesses are required by law to provide products that are safe, are accurately described and perform the functions that they claim to (see Unit 3.1 for a detailed description of the main consumer protection laws in the UK). As a member of the European Union, UK businesses are also subject to consumer protection legislation passed by the EU Parliament, such as the Consumer Protection (Distance Selling) Regulations of 2000 and 2005.

The existence of consumer protection legislation affects businesses in a number of ways. Businesses must comply with such legislation and keep up to date with any changes. Staff must also be trained to ensure that they understand and operate within the law. For example, sales staff must not behave aggressively or pressurise customers into buying goods or services. Complying with legislation takes time and adds to costs. However, it also means that firms can operate without the risk

of being prosecuted, the effects of which could also be significant, in terms of both the cost of fines and the damage to reputation.

## Protection for employees

Employees also receive a degree of protection under the law. In the UK, employees have a number of statutory employment rights, including the right to a written statement of employment particulars, an itemised pay statement and maternity, paternity and adoption leave. The **contract of employment** is a legal agreement setting out the terms under which an employee is employed by an employer, dealing with issues such as the duties to be carried out, the level of pay, entitlement to holiday and sick leave and periods of notice. A great deal of legislation exists regarding the recruitment and employment of workers in an attempt to ensure that individuals are treated equally and not discriminated against on the grounds of their gender, age or ethnic background (see Unit 13.2). The EU has also passed a number of directives affecting the employment of workers, including The Working Time Directive, introduced in 1993, which places limits on the length of the working week to 48 hours and sets out minimum requirements for rest periods and paid annual leave. Currently, the UK has an 'opt-out' clause that allows workers to have a longer working week by voluntarily deciding on their hours of work.

Making sure that a business meets the requirements of employment law increases costs. Most medium and large businesses have specialist human resources staff with the appropriate knowledge and skills. Employees who believe they are being treated or have been dismissed unfairly may decide to take action, perhaps by complaining to an employment tribunal. Dealing with such complaints can also involve significant costs and lead to negative publicity, damaging a firm's ability to attract and maintain employees in the future.

## Promoting competition

Creating an environment that promotes competition between businesses can result in a number of benefits for consumers and the economy as a whole. Competition puts pressure on firms to keep prices down. This means that costs have to be controlled, and reduced wherever possible, in order to continue to make profits. It can help to boost productivity, innovation and quality as firms fight for customers.

Recent UK governments have been committed to promoting competition. In 2003, The Enterprise Act was passed in order to create a more competitive environment within the UK. The Act gives the Office of Fair Trading the power to investigate markets that appear not to be operating in the interests of consumers. The Competition Commission is responsible for investigating business activities that are likely to lead to a loss of competition, such as the merger between two UK firms with a large share of the same market, creating a monopoly situation.

Competition policy in the UK is also heavily influenced by the European Union (EU). The creation of a single market is a central objective of the EU. EU law targets anti-competitive behaviour between firms affecting trade across national borders, whereas UK law is responsible for dealing with any activities that might reduce competition between firms within the UK.

## Social factors

Social changes can have a major impact on the performance of some businesses. Such changes may come about as a result of demographic changes, i.e. changes in the size or structure of the population, or more general changes in the attitudes and lifestyles of certain groups or society as a whole. In some cases, this may lead to the creation of brand new products; in other cases, the demand for long-established goods and services may go into irreversible decline.

## Demographic issues

Demography is the study of the population of a country, including changes in its size and structure. By 2008, the UK population had grown to 61,383,000, representing a rise of 0.7 per cent on the previous year. The rate of population growth in the UK has been increasing in recent years – the average annual figure since 2001 was 0.5 per cent, compared with 0.3 per cent between 1991 and 2001 and 0.2 per cent between 1981 and 1991. Until 2008, the main reason for this increase in the rate of population growth has been net migration (the difference between long-term migration into and out of the UK). The expansion of the European Union (EU) in 2004 led to a huge increase in the number of people moving to live and work in the UK from a number of new member countries, particularly Poland and the Czech Republic. This increase in **net migration** affected UK businesses in a number of ways. It provided a supply of labour that helped to fill vacancies and relieve skills shortages in a number of areas, including hospitality and catering. It also created opportunities to sell new product lines, such as foreign food and drink brands.

Since 2008, however, the main contributor to the increase in the size of the population

## Competition Commission intervenes in Safeway takeover

In August 2003, the Competition Commission (CC) published the findings of an investigation into the proposed acquisition of the Safeway supermarket chain by four of the UK's leading grocery retailers. The CC's report recommended that Tesco, Sainsbury's and Asda should be prevented from taking over any part of Safeway.

The investigation was triggered following concerns from the Secretary of State for Trade and Industry that, in the case of Tesco, Sainsbury's and Asda, any merger would lead to a substantial reduction in competition. In 2003, Safeway was the UK's fourth largest supermarket chain, with a 9.8 per cent market share, compared to 25.8 per cent for Tesco, 17.2 per cent for Sainsbury's and 16.6 per cent for Asda. At the time the Tesco bid was announced in January 2003, Sir Terry Leahy, Tesco's chief executive, promised to reduce Safeway's prices if Tesco's takeover bid was allowed to go ahead. He also claimed it would be 'perverse' to reject Tesco's bid simply because the retailer was more successful in competing for customers and gaining market share than its rivals.

**Source: Competition Commission, *Daily Telegraph***

### Activity

a) To what extent do you agree with the argument that a takeover of Safeway by another leading UK supermarket would lead to a reduction in competition in the UK grocery market?

has been the **natural change**, i.e. the difference between the number of births and deaths. The fastest population increase was among those aged 85 and over, the number more than doubling from 600,000 to 1.3 million between 1983 and 2008. The number of people aged 65 and over also rose, up by 1.5 million over the same period. The number of births has also increased in recent years, largely as a result of the increased number of migrant families. These changes in the structure of the population also affect the demand for certain products, such as nursing care for the elderly and nursery care for babies and toddlers.

## Other social factors

In recent years, a number of issues have attracted an increasing amount of attention from the media and the public in general. Concerns about the impact of business activity on the environment, for example, forced many firms to assess their operations and make improvements, for example to reduce pollution, the level of energy consumed and the amount of waste generated. Businesses have also faced pressure to adopt a more ethical approach in dealing with stakeholders, such as employees and suppliers, rather than focusing solely on meeting shareholder expectations.

## Key terms

**Business rate** A tax that is levied on business property – the revenue raised is used to fund services provided by local government, such as refuse collection

**Corporation tax** A tax levied on company profits

**Demographics** The study of the population, including the causes and effects of changes in its size and structure

**European Union (EU)** A single market of 27 countries and over 500 million people, permitting the free movement of goods, services, people and capital between members, and abolishing trade barriers between members

**Excise duty** A type of expenditure tax levied on certain goods, such as cigarettes and alcohol, where a set amount is added to the price charged

**Income tax** A tax on the income generated by private individuals

**Infrastructure** The systems of transport, communications and other basic utilities, such as sewerage, that are required to support the activities of business and the wider community

**National Insurance Contributions (NICs)** These are levied on the earnings of employees and the self-employed above a certain level. In the case of employees, both the employer and the employee are required to contribute. NICs give the individuals concerned an entitlement to certain state benefits

**Net migration** The difference between long-term migration into and out of the UK

**Value Added Tax (VAT)** This tax is placed on most goods and services that are sold in the UK and is included in the price paid. In 2010, the standard rate of VAT in the UK was 17.5 per cent

**World Trade Organization (WTO)** An international organisation that promotes free trade in goods and services by encouraging countries to abolish barriers to trade

## Q Re-cap questions

1 Briefly explain how political stability within a country is beneficial to businesses.

2 Identify two types of tax paid by businesses.

3 Examine the main benefits to UK businesses from government spending to increase the skills of the UK workforce.

4 Outline the role played by the following organisations:

   a Business Link

   b Regional Development Agencies.

5 Describe two ways in which the existence of consumer protection legislation affects a computer manufacturer such as Dell.

6 Describe two ways in which employees in the UK receive protection under the law.

7 Briefly explain why the government attempts to promote competition between UK firms.

8 Describe how the UK's membership of the European Union (EU) affects competition policy.

9 Explain two ways in which the size of a country's population can change over time.

10 Examine two possible consequences for businesses from the UK having an ageing population, i.e. a growing proportion of people over the retirement age.

## Grading tips

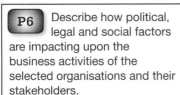

| **P6** Describe how political, legal and social factors are impacting upon the business activities of the selected organisations and their stakeholders. | **M3** Analyse how political, legal and social factors have impacted on the two contrasting organisations. | **D2** Evaluate how future changes in economic, political, legal and social factors may impact on the strategy of a specified organisation. |
|---|---|---|
| You need to describe the impact of two different political environments, as well as legal and social factors, identified in the unit specification. Some factors may have led to benefits, whereas others may have created extra challenges. It may be useful to look at two businesses operating in different countries with contrasting political, legal and social environments. | This requires a more in-depth examination of the effects of the factors identified in P6 and how the business has responded by making changes. Note that, although the organisations may be contrasting, the effects may be similar. | You are required to make judgements about how your chosen business will respond and change its strategy in response to future changes in the business environment. You may do this by looking at the possible benefits and drawbacks of any changes, and suggest alternatives that could be more successful, justifying your comments with appropriate evidence. |

## Assignments for Unit 1

### Assignment One

You are employed as a business analyst by your local Chamber of Commerce. You have been chosen to take part in a major project examining business activity in your region of the UK. You have been asked to research two contrasting businesses operating in your local area and produce a **written report** covering their purpose, ownership, organisational structure and strategic planning.

**Note** – read through the task, the relevant criteria and the assignment advice on pages 12 and 23 before choosing your two organisations, in order to ensure you are able to obtain all of the information needed. To ensure that your businesses are sufficiently contrasting, try and choose organisations operating in the profit and not-for-profit sectors. You should also choose businesses that vary significantly in size.

**Criteria covered** – P1 P2 P3 P4 M1 D1 (refer to assignment guidance at the end of each unit section)

## Tasks

1. For each of the two contrasting businesses chosen, write a description the type of business, its purpose and its ownership. This description must also indicate the extent of the liability of the owners to any debts that are built up. (P1)
2. Describe the stakeholder groups for each of your two businesses. This should include each business, customers, employees, suppliers, owners, trade unions and employer associations (where relevant), local and national communities and the Government. (P2)
3. Explain the views, needs and expectations of each of the different stakeholders that you have described in Task 2. Show how these stakeholder views affect the aims and objectives of each of your chosen businesses. (M1)
4. Following on from Tasks 2 and 3, write an evaluation discussing the different levels of influence of the stakeholders of one of your chosen businesses. You need to decide which stakeholders have most influence, providing evidence to justify your decisions. (D1)
5. For each of the two businesses chosen, produce a description of the following:
   a) The organisational structure, identifying and describing the main functional areas; and
   b) The process of strategic planning, showing how long-term planning takes place. (P3)
6. Following on from Task 4, explain how the organisational structure and the strategic planning of each business help them to achieve their aims and objectives. (P4)

## Assignment Two

Your employer, the local Chamber of Commerce, is also interested in finding out more about the impact of the wider environment on businesses operating in the local area. You have now, therefore, been asked to carry out research into the ways in which these businesses are influenced by economic, political, legal and social factors. You need to present your research findings in the form of a written report.

**Note** – in order to complete this assignment, you can continue with the two contrasting businesses used elsewhere in this unit. Read through the task, the relevant criteria and the assignment advice on pages 31 and 37 and decide whether you will be able to obtain all of the information needed. If not, you may choose one or more new businesses, but they must still be contrasting.

**Criteria covered** – P5 P6 M2 M3 D2

## Tasks

1. The first section of your report should describe how **one** of your selected organisations has been affected by **two** contrasting economic environments. This could look at the effects of operating during a period of economic growth and recession, or the impact of a change from low interest rates to high interest rates. (P5)
2. Following on from Task 1, you should produce a comparison of the challenges faced by your selected organisation as a result of operating in two different economic environments. This should involve looking at how key activities such as operations, human resources, finance and marketing are affected. (M2)
3. The next section of your report should identify and describe a number of political, legal and social factors that influence the activities of two selected business organisations and their stakeholders. (P6)
4. Produce an analysis of the political, legal and social factors described in Task 3. (M3)
5. The final section should be an evaluation of how future changes in economic, political, legal and social factors are likely to impact on the strategy of one of your business organisations. (D2)

# Part 1: How human resources are managed

## What are resources?

In this unit we are going to investigate the range of human, physical, technological and financial resources required in an organisation, and how the management of these resources can impact on business performance.

Before we start on this journey we need to spend some time considering what resources are.

Spend two to three minutes jotting down all the things that you have used today in order to get to and participate in college/school life – these would be your resources.

I would imagine your list would have included some of the following.

Bus fare/bus pass, food and drink – financial resources

Books, paper, pens to complete work set – physical resources

Calculator, computer, printer – technological resources

Your teachers, friends offering help and guidance – human resources

The simple exercise above has illustrated that you use the same kind of resources in your daily life as a business would. You are also probably aware you achieve the best results when you are able to coordinate these efficiently and effectively. This is exactly the same for businesses.

It is a well-known fact that the most important resource to any business is its employees. It is therefore imperative that staff are managed and looked after in order to ensure that they remain highly productive, delivering first-class customer service, ensuring that customers return time and time again. If a business is able to meet the needs and manage staff in the ways outlined below hopefully it becomes not only more efficient but more competitive.

## Staffing to meet changing business demands

Having the correct number of staff employed within a business can often be key to its financial security and success. Too many employees will

Employees are the human resources a business needs to function

make the cost of wages high and reduce profit but too few could damage customer relations.

There are a number of businesses which experience increases in demand at certain times of year – this is often referred to as seasonal demand. In order to cope, businesses may choose to employ temporary employees; for example at Christmas retail stores take on seasonal workers in order to meet increased demand. In the travel and tourism industry extra employees, such as holiday representatives, pool attendants, ride operators, are taken on by organisations that open for a summer season – for example Alton Towers. Alton Towers vary the number of extra people they employ throughout the season; for example their busiest time of year will be the six weeks' summer holiday from late July to early September.

So why do businesses increase employees as trade increases? After all if they did not they would actually make more profit – increased customers, wages remaining the same. The reason is to ensure that the same level of customer service is delivered throughout the busiest period. In order to do this a business will have to consider how many employees are needed to deal with the expected number of customers. This calculation is based on previous experience. A business like Alton Towers will review the visitor numbers for the same period last year and using this information calculate how many staff they need on the park to ensure maximum customer service and also ensuring the safety of all customers.

Our current economic situation has meant that businesses are now facing fluctuations in demand which will obviously have a large impact on the number of staff they employ. If orders reduce and sales slow down, a business is unlikely to be able to retain its current workforce. This was clearly illustrated when Honda had to lay off thousands of its workers based at its UK factory in Swindon at the end of January 2009.

## Honda lays off thousands of workers

Thousands of workers have left Honda's UK factory for a four-month sabbatical as the company stages one of the longest breaks in production during Britain's industrial history.

Production at the plant in Swindon was shut down until 1 June following a dramatic slump in sales.

The 4,200 workers involved will receive their full basic pay for the first two months, reducing to 60 per cent for the rest of the production shutdown.

Senior directors have stressed the firm's commitment to retaining its Swindon workforce as the new Jazz model is due to come into production in the summer.

**Source:** www.thisissouthdevon.co.uk/news/ Honda-plant-shut-months/article-656557-detail/ article.html.

## Honda staff return to work

The introduction of the Government's 'cash for bangers scheme' enabled the workforce to return. Thousands of staff headed back to work after having agreed a 3 per cent pay cut for the next ten months, while managers are having pay reduced by 5 per cent in the face of the big downturn in new-car sales. As many as 1,300 workers at Swindon have taken voluntary redundancy reducing the workforce to 3,400.

Although this was great news the plant will be still be producing fewer cars this year (2009–10) despite the popular Honda Jazz supermini starting production at Swindon this September. Honda had hoped to produce 228,000 vehicles but the figure has now been revised to 175,000. This reduced production figure reflects the drop in new-car sales figures that Honda have been experiencing – 34 per cent reduction in the first four months of 2009.

**Source: Adapted from** www.itv.com/ News/Articles/Honda-staff-return-to- work-293276191.html

## Coordination of team resources to meet targets

The overriding **aim** of the majority of businesses will be to make a profit. In order to achieve this, businesses set themselves aims and **objectives**. An aim is based on what the business wants to achieve with the objective explaining how this will be completed. In order to achieve objectives staff will need to be given targets to meet. In order to meet targets a business will have to organise its employees into teams. Individual teams will need to be aware of what is required of them and the timescales they have available to meet the target.

If we refer back to the Honda case studies above you will note that the total number of employees that returned to Honda had been reduced by 1,300 in order to meet the fall in predicted production levels. The company could not afford to employ so many people having suffered a 34 per cent reduction in sales. This illustrates that they had to coordinate their employees to meet the expected production level of 175,000 vehicles.

## Monitoring of team performance

Having placed the employees in teams and given them targets to meet it is important that progress is continually checked. If a team experiences problems meeting their targets this needs to be investigated and solutions found. One of the themes that runs through the case studies on Honda is the continual use of numbers and statistics. This illustrates that in order to run a business there has to be a means of measuring output, sales, and so on.

## Liaison with other departments

The majority of large businesses will be sub-divided into a number of different departments. One of the roles of the human resource department is to ensure there are sufficient staff employed. Let us consider a simple scenario in order to illustrate the point. If the marketing team has been really successful in establishing an increase in demand, the production department might need to increase production levels. In order to do this they require 20 **temporary staff** to be employed for a period of three months. This information would be communicated to the human resource department who would then need to discuss this with the finance department prior to starting the recruitment and selection process.

If you study the Honda case studies you will see that 1,300 employees took voluntary redundancy. The decision to reduce the workforce by this number would have been agreed with all of the departments that operate within Honda.

## Establishment of professional culture

It is the responsibility of the human resource department to outline and promote the **culture** and image the business wishes to display. Some businesses choose to work within a very informal relaxed culture whereas others promote a more rigid and formal atmosphere. Employees in the finance sector would expect to come to work either wearing a uniform or a suit. A car mechanic would expect to go to work in overalls and steel toe-capped boots.

While teams are often encouraged to 'get along' and participate in team-building exercises in order to improve motivation and productivity there must always be a dividing line between professional and private activities.

Team-building exercises can help to improve motivation and productivity

## Provision of appropriate incentives

If a business wants its employees to remain committed to the business they must be adequately rewarded. **Incentives** can be a method businesses use to recognise the achievements of employees and are considered to be motivational, providing a boost to performance as staff feel valued. They can also give teams a sense of achievement, encouraging open communication which in turn will allow them to perform to a higher standard with the aim of gaining further incentives.

Incentives can be broken down into financial or non-financial rewards which are additions to the employee's normal salary/pay. Financial incentives could include profit sharing, extra commission on sales, bonuses and share options. Non-financial rewards can include vouchers, prizes of gifts and holidays.

The John Lewis Partnership which includes Waitrose awards its staff a yearly bonus based on the last year's profit figures. Everyone receives the same percentage from the boardroom to the shop floor. In March 2009 all staff were awarded a bonus of 13 per cent of their annual salary.

Nike has elected to offer non-financial incentives as outlined in the case study on the next page.

## Creativity and initiative

In order for any business to remain competitive it is important that its employees work in a culture that actively encourages them to put forward ideas. It is the job of the human resource department to ensure the lines of communication throughout the business encourage and support employees who have excellent ideas. It is often those people who work on the 'cliff edge' that have the imagination and creativity to solve simple or complex problems. If this culture is not encouraged the business might not only lose good staff but fail to recognise and utilise excellent ideas.

## Outsourcing versus in-house decisions

In its efforts to employ the right number of staff the human resource department must still be mindful of the total wages bill.

## Non-financial incentives used in Nike

Nike uses retail vouchers to motivate staff in both the retail and wholesale arms of its business. Last year, it moved from offering Air Miles vouchers, which many staff felt were not relevant to them, to general retail vouchers. Elma O'Reilly, HR adviser, explains the vouchers are used in a variety of ways to motivate staff. 'We do things on a Saturday when we know that it is going to be really busy, like [saying] "today the first person that reaches a sale of £x amount will receive a voucher".' But she doesn't believe the monetary value of the reward is as important as the recognition factor and the fact it is so immediate. Being able to give the vouchers out at team meetings is also considered to be important and is one of the reasons why the company does not reward with cash. O'Reilly adds, 'When we give out vouchers for employee of the month or whatever, we do it in a group situation. It makes it a bit more special when they might not check their bank account every day and see the [money] going in.'

**Source:** www.employeebenefits.co.uk

Outsourcing allows another company to run part of your business. They will receive a set sum from the business for offering the service. The usual departments that are outsourced are outlined below:

- cleaning
- canteen
- payroll
- maintenance
- security.

It is also becoming popular for businesses to outsource some of their operations to other countries where labour rates are not so high. For example, some companies have relocated their call centres to India.

Some businesses save money by using hot-desking where employees share facilities rather than each having their own permanent space

## Maintenance of operation

As mentioned above the first part of managing human resources is to ensure that **staffing levels** are sufficient to meet demand but nobody is left standing around chatting to their friends. As you are probably aware there is nothing more frustrating than when you are unable to locate a shop assistant when you need one.

There are not many jobs available now that do not involve the use of equipment. This could be a computer, electronic till, or even complex machinery. The first step is for a business to ensure that there is sufficient equipment in place. Two employees 'hot desking' sharing one computer may not prove to be a very efficient way to work. Both may need the computer at the same time and arguments might ensue. Having established the correct level of equipment required, employees may need training on how to use this equipment in order to to work effectively and safely. Equipment is only labour saving and cost effective if it is used to its full capacity.

**Working capital** looks at the money that is immediately available to spend within the business. This area will be studied in greater depth in the section 'Be able to interpret financial statements' on page 64.

Often the human resource department will be responsible for overseeing the working conditions and facilities of employees. Facilities could include the toilets, canteen and staff room, access to a gym and prayer room. Many motivational studies have proved that employees' working conditions can greatly impact on levels of motivation. Although the Health and Safety at Work Act states the minimum requirements that a business must adhere to, it is usual for businesses to go beyond these requirements.

**Administration** is often an undervalued service. A lot of businesses would not be able meet and greet guests, take orders, give advice to customers, make and receive telephone calls, order goods, deal with incoming and outgoing mail if they were not supported by employees who carry out the role of administrators.

Businesses are most successful when they set themselves realistic targets. This gives owners, managers and employees something measurable to work towards. However, targets would be a total waste of time if they were not closely **monitored**. A business must have mechanisms in place which will identify if a target is likely to be met or not. If the reason the target has not been achieved is due to technological problems then the manager will need the skills necessary to **troubleshoot**. This term refers to the employee's ability to find and eliminate the problem. If the target was not met due to unforeseen circumstances the manager will need to have developed sufficient problem-solving skills to overcome the problem. Problem solving is a skill which involves four stages which are outlined below:

- Recognising and defining the problem
- Finding possible solutions – this will usually involve a range of different options
- Choosing the best solution
- Implementation and monitoring of the solution – has it been effective?

## Human resources

This section focuses on the processes used to recruit staff and what can be done to ensure they remain working for the company.

## Recruitment

This process starts with the initial decision that a new employee is required. Vacancies within a business can arise for a number of different reasons: staff may leave due to retirement or finding alternative employment, or perhaps the business has expanded and there is now too much work for the current staff to cope with. Having decided there is a need for a new employee, a number of different stages have to be gone through.

The first is to identify the type of work the new employee will be required to undertake. This is known as a job analysis. During the job analysis it will be decided exactly what the duties and responsibilities of the new employee will be. It is this document that will help formulate the **job description** and **contract of employment**.

Once the duties of the new employee have been established, a job description can be designed. The job description will inform potential applicants what their duties and responsibilities will be and can also act as a reference document should a dispute occur between the employer and employee. A job description should contain the following information:

- The job title
- Where the job will be located
- Who the job holder will be responsible for – if appropriate
- What the main duties of the job holder will be
- Who the job holder will be working with
- What the terms and conditions of the job are, including hours, overtime, shifts, and pay

As you can see from Figure 2.1 the job description provides the potential applicant with a basic outline of the kind of duties they would be expected to undertake. However, this is not the only document a business will use when trying to recruit new staff. Often they will want to inform a potential applicant of the qualifications, skills and attributes they will need to have in order to fulfil the role effectively and fit within the team. This document is known as the **personal specification**.

These two documents serve a number of purposes. From the potential applicant's point of view it allows them to see if they are suitable for the position. The applicant can consider if they have sufficient qualifications and skills to do the job and also if the roles outlined actually appeal to them. From the potential employer's point of view the documents will hopefully put off people who are not suitable for the job but not deter suitable candidates from applying. In addition, they must be factual – they must truly represent the job that is available.

All of the other processes that we have considered so far in this chapter will hopefully help retain current staff within the business, thus eliminating the expense of continually recruiting new staff. Keeping staff turnover rates low helps keep costs of recruitment down and also maintains the skills base within the company in order for it to run efficiently.

## Contract of employment

The Employment Rights Act 1996 outlines employees' rights at work, detailing what they can expect from their employer and outlining the way they should be treated. The Act is split into

---

# Safe Sale
## Job Description

**Post:** Administration Clerk

**Accountable to:** Office Manager

**Location:** Swindon Office

**Job summary:** Responsible for the processing of purchase orders received from the website. Communicating with customers via the telephone or emails.

**Hours of work:** 37.5 hours per week excluding lunch breaks

**Salary range:** £13,000 – £14,000 depending on age and experience

### Principal responsibilities

Responsible for the processing of purchase orders received from the website

Liaising with the warehouse staff to ensure speedy and efficient delivery of orders

Communicating with customers via email and on the telephone

Undertaking any other duties which may be allocated from time to time

---

**Figure 2.1** A job description for an administration clerk required for 'Safe Sale', a company that sells goods on the internet

a number of different sections. The statement of initial employment particulars outlines the terms and conditions of the employee's employment and must be supplied within two months of employment. This is often referred to as the contract of employment. This contract should contain the following information:

- The name of the employer and employee
- The date on which employment commenced
- For temporary contacts, the expected termination date
- The place of work and address of the employer – this could be different
- The job title and brief description of the position
- The rate of pay, frequency of payment, any bonuses, and methods of payments. This section is important as it guarantees payment even if the employer is unable to provide the employee with work
- The hours of work
- Holiday entitlement
- Maternity and paternity leave
- Terms relating to sickness including notification of sickness, pay and statutory sick pay

- Pension arrangements; if there is a company pension scheme, the contributions that will be taken out of the employee's gross pay and how much the employer will contribute
- Length of notice which the employee is entitled to receive or required to give to terminate employment
- Disciplinary and grievance procedures; procedures should be outlined and to whom the employee should speak
- Any other collective agreements affecting terms and conditions of work – for example links to trade unions.

## Employability skills

When you start seeking work you will need to consider whether you have the correct skills to apply for the jobs of your choice. The range of skills that 'Safe Sale' requires is outlined in Figures 2.1 and 2.2. These are examined in more detail below.

### Suitable qualifications

A lot of jobs require applicants to demonstrate a level of education. It is not always the type of qualification that is important but the proof that the candidate is able to learn at a specific level.

---

# Safe Sale
## Personal Specification

**Post:**                Administration Clerk

**Qualifications:**

Essential:          GCSE English and maths

                        Word-processing qualification

Desirable:         Level 3 ICT qualification

**Experience:**

Essential:          Experience of working with a range of ICT packages

                        Proven experience in clerical work, including data processing

Desirable:         Previous customer-service experience

**Skills/Ability/Knowledge:**

Essential:          The versatility to use a range of different ICT applications

                        Good communication skills

Desirable:         The ability to work within a team

**Other requirements:**

Must have a pleasant personality, good sense of humour, and the willingness to work in a fast-paced environment. The ability to work flexible hours during busy periods is essential. Willingness to assist in a variety of jobs is essential.

**Figure 2.2** An example of a personal specification for the job of administration clerk

Let us look back at the personal specification for 'Safe Sale'. The qualifications required are broken down into two sections – those that are felt to be essential and those that are considered desirable. Essential qualifications were GCSE maths and English, which would prove the applicant had a basic level of literacy and numeracy. The other requirement was a word-processing qualification. This qualification demonstrates the applicant's ability to use the keyboard effectively and lay out documents accurately. The desirable qualifications included a Level 3 ICT qualification. This provides evidence to the business that the applicant is confident using a range of ICT packages. It also indicates that the potential applicant would be easy to train on specialist ICT packages used within 'Safe Sale'.

## Experience in another role

The majority of jobs require potential employees to have worked in a similar environment. This often means they will need less training and will fully understand the demands and, in some cases, the limitations of the position they are applying for.

Within the personal specification the essential experience being sought was experience of working with a range of ICT packages and experience in clerical work including data processing. The desirable skill was previous customer service.

## Knowledge of products/services and experience of specific industry

When a business requests this level of knowledge and skills it is usually because it needs the new employee to start work immediately with limited, if any, training. The business might have a large order to fulfil and without someone who is already fully trained this would not be possible.

If a business needs to employ people who are already familiar with the product and have previous experience within the industry they would normally need to offer a good salary and working conditions in order to entice them away from their current employment. However, in the current economic climate of recession and increasing unemployment this might not be necessary. There may be a large pool of potential employees within the labour market who do have the skills and experience required as they have been made redundant from other businesses.

### Effectiveness in meeting personal and team/departmental targets

As discussed earlier in this unit, one of the ways that the effectiveness of employees is maximised is to set members of staff specific targets. It is therefore important all members of staff are not only able but willing to work towards these targets. If some employees are not prepared to do this the result is a disjointed, unmotivated and unhappy workforce.

If a team is set a target by management it might require individual members of the team to set themselves individual targets in order to complete the tasks they are required to do. The ability to pull together as part of a team and then take individual responsibility for tasks allocated is one that is vital if an employee is going to become successful in the workplace.

### Ability to observe and raise the professional standard of product/ service delivery

It is generally acknowledged that to keep a workforce fully motivated it is imperative to ensure everyone is involved in the decision-making process. If employees are involved in the decision-making process they will often see the need to raise professional standards, and be in a position to offer ideas and suggestions as to how this could be achieved.

## Personal skills

All positions will require employees to demonstrate a range of personal skills which help make them an excellent worker who is able to work in a team and deal with customers.

### Patience

Employees that are unable to deal calmly with others are not much use to a business. Impatient employees would have a negative impact on the image of the business and in the most extreme cases lose customers.

### Being hardworking

All employers want their employees to work to their maximum ability. A lazy employee will cost the business money in lost productivity. They could also demotivate other employees and therefore productivity is lost on more than one level.

### Be able to work as part of a team

Most jobs require applicants to demonstrate the ability to work well within a team. This skill illustrates to the potential employer that the applicant is able to communicate effectively, is flexible in their approach, has the ability to listen and consider other people's opinions and is able to get on with a variety of different people.

### Good interpersonal skills

These skills are quite subtle, but concern the way in which someone interacts with others. Respecting the views of others, being able to listen and empathise with others' views are all interpersonal skills that will help to enhance the effectiveness of an employee's performance.

Good interpersonal skills are important

## Cooperating with others

This skill will often be closely linked to team work. If you can work in a team you will have to cooperate with other team members. The opposite to cooperation is conflict which means an employee is unwilling to follow instructions or has the inability to work with other members of the team. Conflict has a very negative impact on a business and in extreme cases productivity and reputation might decrease.

## Negotiating skills

Negotiating skills concern someone's ability to discuss an issue with others and to reach a mutually agreeable conclusion. Negotiation may be a slow process that needs to be handled effectively. Negotiation can occur on many levels. Human resource managers may be required to negotiate with trade unions when changes to pay or working conditions are considered. Another form of negotiation might be internally when each department is bidding for a budget for the next financial year. For example, the marketing department might have to negotiate with the finance department regarding the amount of finance required to run a pre-planned advertising campaign. They might be asked to justify their anticipated increase in sales against the overall costs of the campaign. Earlier on in the chapter targets were discussed. Sometimes employees are asked to help set these targets and this might involve negotiation with senior management.

## Interviewing skills

Employees that have supervisor or management positions might be called upon to undertake yearly appraisals for the employees that they are responsible for. Appraisals involve reviewing an employee's performance over the past year and setting targets for the following year. This task will involve interviewing skills – the ability to impart information in a suitable manner coupled with the ability to listen effectively. Supervisory staff may have to interview employees regarding disciplinary or grievance procedures which will also have to be handled sensitively. The human resource department, which is generally responsible for the interviewing of potential employees, might ask specialist staff to form part of an interview panel.

## Key terms

**Aim** What a business hopes to achieve over a set period of time

**Contract of employment** Legal document that sets out the terms and conditions of employment

**Culture** Culture represents the expectations of behaviour within the business

**Incentives** Extra payments or rewards that are given to employees

**Job description** Identifies what the job entails – what tasks and responsibilities the job holder will be expected to fulfil

**Objectives** How a business will achieve its aims

**Personal specification** Outlines the qualifications and skills required in order to do the job

**Staffing levels** Number of staff required for the business to meet the targets set but not so many that employees are underutilised

**Temporary staff** Employees who are taken on for a set period of time in order to meet anticipated increases in demand

**Troubleshoot** The ability to deal with problems as and when they arise

**Working capital** The finance that is available to fund the day-to-day activities of a business. Working capital is calculated by deducting current liabilities from current assets

## Re-cap questions

1  Why is it important that businesses continually monitor their staffing needs to meet business demands?

2  What would the impact be on a business if it was unable to provide its staff with sufficient equipment to do their job?

3  How does effective recruitment and selection help a business remain competitive?

4  What information should be contained within the contract of employment?

5  Why are good communication skills and the ability to work in a team important in the majority of jobs?

6  Research a job description and personal specification from the internet and describe the employability and personal skills required.

## Assignment

| **P1** Describe the recruitment documentation in a selected organisation | **M2** Assess the importance of employability, and personal skills in the recruitment and retention of staff in a selected organisation | |
|---|---|---|
| P2 Describe the main employability, personal and communication skills required when applying for a specific job role | | |

### Assignment

The directors of a business would like to produce a report that summaries the organisation's current approach to staff recruitment and retention. As a respected member of the human resource department, you have been asked to write part of the report.

Your part of the report will be divided into three sections. In the first section, you will describe the recruitment documentation that the business uses (P1). In the second section you will describe the skills that the business requires for a specific key job role. You should describe all the employability, personal and communication skills that will be required (P2). The final part of your report be an assessment of the importance of these skills and how important they are in terms of the recruitment and retention of staff (M2).

# **Part 2:** Know the purpose of managing physical and technological resources

All businesses will need some level of physical and technological resources in order to produce their products or deliver a service. We now need to consider how the correct management of these can not only enhance productivity but company image. In order to illustrate the following theory it will be based on Jam Jars Production Ltd – JJP Ltd for short. JJP Ltd is a medium-sized production business that produces jam jars for jam and marmalade manufacturers. They do not sell directly to large jam producers but to smaller companies that make specialist or organic jams and preserves. The business employs 15 people on the production line which includes one of the directors. Six members of staff work in the office which deals with sales, administration, finance and marketing. The administration side of the business is run by the other director.

The production line at a jam factory

## Managing physical resources

JJP Ltd could not function without adequate buildings and facilities. The factory consists of a converted warehouse which houses all the machinery required for the production line with the offices taking over part of the second floor. The design of the production line ensures maximum efficiency. The business has also considered that to maintain a happy motivated workforce they will need to ensure that the business offers high-quality facilities. The toilet facilities have been modernised and regularly maintained; there are shower facilities, a kitchen with a kettle, fridge, microwave and comfortable chairs. JJP Ltd supply tea, coffee and milk for the staff. The overall atmosphere created by these pleasant surroundings makes the staff feel valued and appreciated. Hopefully this will help maintain loyalty to the business and sustain high levels of productivity.

Having established a good working environment for their staff it is important that JJP Ltd ensure that any maintenance required is carried out on a regular basis. This could include painting and decorating, updating equipment in the staff kitchen or re-painting the outside of the building. If regular maintenance is not carried out the building could fall into disrepair. A leak in the roof could cause major disruption to the production line as well as endangering the safety of the workforce. Offices that become gloomy and dismal can also make staff feel depressed and might also put off customers who visit the premises. An example of recent maintenance was the refurbishment of the staff toilets. Regular maintenance is imperative for a business if it wishes to maintain high levels of productivity and provide the right impression to customers.

Before JJP Ltd started manufacturing they had to invest in the right type of plant and machinery. Decisions had to be made concerning how much should be spent on the production line and how it should be laid out. If these decisions had been made incorrectly the end result would be lower productivity levels and reduced profits. Buying a piece of machinery that does not ultimately fulfil its role as anticipated is a very expensive mistake and one that must be avoided at all costs. Decisions over which piece of plant or machinery to buy can be extremely difficult. Machine A might cost £3,000 more but is capable of producing 1,000 items more than machine B. If the business cannot afford to buy machine A without borrowing money from external sources which one becomes the best buy? Obviously there is no right or wrong answer to this question.

While the production line uses machinery, the offices of JJP Ltd are heavily reliant on ICT equipment in the form of personal computers that are linked via a network, printer, photocopiers, scanners and a fax machine. However, computers also play a large part in monitoring and controlling the production process. The increasing use of information technology has enabled the company to turn the production line into a capital-, rather than a labour-, intensive business. The accuracy and reliability of the computer system has increased production levels and also the quality of the finished jam jars. Computers in the office have enabled the business to purchase and sell their products via the internet. The company website is proving a big success with their customers and the newly developed intranet has helped to keep workers informed of all the latest developments within the company. Although productivity and efficiency has increased, the initial capital expenditure required to purchase the equipment and subsequent staff training was expensive. It is going to be quite some time before this investment has been fully recouped.

The efficient production line at JJP Ltd needs to be supported with an effective stock-ordering system. Stock must be available as and when required by the production process. If too little stock is held the production line may come to a grinding halt losing the business money and possibly orders. Too much stock takes up valuable space, involves the investment of liquid funds and there is also the possibility it might become damaged, obsolete or disappear. It is therefore very important that both the production and administration director ensure that sufficient stock is always available.

Waste costs businesses money in two ways. If JJP Ltd uses their raw materials wastefully each jam jar will cost considerably more to produce, thus reducing profit. If waste can be minimised profit is likely to increase. All production processes create waste and increasingly businesses are expected to manage the disposal of this waste, rather than just put it in landfill sites and therefore recycling must be considered. See the article on Nissan's recycling success at www.initial.co.uk/news/news_194736.html.

All businesses have to consider what they would do should things start to go wrong. Emergency situations can arise on two levels. The first could be a crisis within the business. For example, the business is heavily reliant on the use of ICT so the two directors would need to devise a contingency plan in case the computer network fails. Instability within the economic climate might also raise serious problems. The business may suddenly find that one of its main customers has gone out of business owing them money and no longer requires jam jars. Correct planning will help ensure that JJP Ltd is able to deal with each of these scenarios. The second type of emergency is one which is caused by an accident, for example a fire

## Building site waste

The UK construction industry generates approximately 120 million tonnes of waste each year, of which about 25 million ends up as landfill. New measures being pushed through (see www.wrap.org.uk) will mean that contractors involved in large building projects will be encouraged to reduce and recycle waste. The Olympic Delivery Authority (see www.london-2012.co.uk/ODA) has been praised for setting a target to recycle or re-use 90 per cent of waste from the main construction site for the 2012 Olympics.

### Activity

The scheme is currently voluntary. If building firms are forced to comply, what impact will it have on them?

or flood. The main concern in this type of situation is to ensure there are sufficient systems in place to evacuate the premises quickly and safely. By law if a business employs more than five people it has to have a health and safety policy. This will identify and then try and reduce all hazards and risks found within the business. This is known as a risk assessment. The health and safety policy will outline the evacuation procedures that must be followed in an emergency situation.

All businesses need to insure against accidents. An **insurance** policy is designed to make a financial payment to compensate for an unwanted event occurring. For example, if a vehicle is insured for theft, if stolen the insurer will provide compensation, allowing the business owner to purchase another vehicle. The payment that a business has to make to the insurer in return for being insured or covered is known as a **premium**. The size of the premium will depend on the size of the risk faced.

A fire or flood would stop JJP Ltd producing jam jars alongside the cost of replacing damaged machinery. An insurance policy would cover the cost of replacement machinery should it become damaged due to an accident. This is not the only type of insurance that would be required – a business must take out insurance to cover accidents to their employees and customers who might visit the premises. An employee's liability policy would pay out should an employee have an accident at work. Public liability insurance would provide cover for customers and their property should an accident happen to them while on the premises. If a business fails to take out insurance they could be sued and ultimately the business might have insufficient funds to cover any damages awarded against them.

**Security** is very important as all businesses are at risk from accidents, intruders and fraud. Through the use of security systems, businesses may be able to reduce risks, for example through the use of fire alarms and the employment of security staff. CCTV cameras are increasingly used and can be very useful when trying to control unwanted visitors. They can also help provide evidence if crimes are committed against a business. Security is vital when using computers and all businesses will need to ensure they have sufficient virus protection and firewalls on their systems. JJP Ltd has started to sell via their website and as such has had to consider the security of their customers. The business decided to join PayPal in order to be able to offer a secure payment system to their customers.

## Vintage Choice

Vintage Choice provides chauffeur driven vintage vehicles for special events, such as weddings (see www.vintagechoice.co.uk). The business currently owns five vintage Austin cars, four of which are on the road, with the fifth in the process of being restored. Insurance for the vehicles is relatively low cost compared with that for modern vehicles. If a specialist limited mileage insurer is used, the annual premium can be as little as £60, even though some of the vehicles are extremely valuable. Within the FAQ section of the website the company has made the following comment – 'Please note our insurance policy precludes smoking in all of our vehicles'.

### Activities

a) Why do you think the premiums for these vehicles are so low when compared to car insurance for a 19-year-old? Consider the different risks involved for (i) a young person's car and (ii) these Vintage Choice vehicles.

b) Why has the company clearly stated that 'our insurance policy precludes smoking in all of our vehicles'?

# Managing technological resources

As well as their human and physical resources, a modern business may have valuable **intellectual property**. Put simply, good ideas have value! Intellectual property can consist of many different items such as:

- designs
- drawings, text
- music
- videos
- accumulated experience and skills
- software licences.

In order to stop other people copying ideas, photocopying large sections of text books or illegally copying videos and music, businesses take out **patents** and gain protection from **copyrights**. Without protection, intellectual property would be worthless as good ideas could be copied by rivals. However, technology has made it increasingly difficult to protect intellectual property. The legal use of software normally requires the use of a **software licence**.

## Patents

A patent protects new inventions and also covers how they actually work, what they do and how they do it, what they are made of and how they are made. It gives the inventor the right to stop others from making, using or selling the invention without prior permission. Further information concerning patents is available from the Patent Office – www.ipo.gov.uk.

## Copyright

A copyright protects the physical expression of ideas. Once an idea has been turned into a physical item – for example a piece of writing, a photograph, music, a web page, and so on, it is protected by copyright. This makes it illegal for anyone to copy the item. A copyright does not have to be applied for as registered protection is automatic. Copyright covers both published and unpublished works. The copyright is owned by the creator of the piece. Original work has copyright protection for the life of the creator plus 70 years after the year of their death. Copyright is regulated by the Copyright Designs and Patents Act 1988 (CDPA). This was amended in October 2003 by the Copyright and Related Rights Regulations 2003 which incorporated into UK law the changes required by EU Copyright Directive.

## Software licences

A software licence is a contract or agreement between the software publisher and end user. It can be a paper agreement but is usually part of the software itself and forms part of the installation process. All software whether published or not is automatically covered by copyright. Software licensing protects the copyright by placing restrictions on the end user in relation to how the product can be used.

## The Chocbox

The Chocbox is a safe and simple, innovative device designed to protect and insulate electrical connectors eliminating the use of electrical tape that no longer meets the current regulations (see www.chocbox.info for further information). Its inventor, Peter Moule, presented the product on the BBC Dragons' Den programme in 2007, and after winning the financial support of Dragons James Caan and Duncan Bannatyne, the Chocbox secured global sales contracts worth over £150 million. The success of the product is down to its effective simplicity and, no doubt, the financial support and expertise of the Dragons. However, when they were initially presented with the Chocbox there were concerns that while it was patented in the UK, at the time Moule had yet to apply for a worldwide patent.

### Activity

Why were the Dragons concerned about the lack of a worldwide patent for the Chocbox?

## Key terms

**Copyright** A form of legal protection designed to prevent the illegal copying of work produced by authors, artists and composers

**Insurance** A scheme whereby a business is compensated if an event, such as theft or fire, occurs

**Intellectual property** Ideas that have value, such as trademarks, logos and designs

**Patent** A form of legal protection designed to prevent the illegal copying of a product or production process

**Premium** The payment made in order to be covered by an insurance policy

**Security** Measures that a business uses to minimise unwanted threats such as fire or theft

**Software licence** A form of legal protection designed to prevent the illegal copying or use of computer software

##  Re-cap questions

1  Why is it important to maintain buildings and facilities on a regular basis?

2  Explain the impact poor facilities could have on employees.

3  What is the purpose of insurance? Identify and explain the purpose of the different types of insurance that JJP Ltd had taken out.

4  What is the difference between a copyright and a patent?

5  Investigate the different stages a business needs to go through in order to apply for a patent.

## Assignment

| | |
|---|---|
| **P3** Describe the main physical and technological resources required in the operation of a selected organisation | **M1** Explain how the management of human, physical and technological resources can improve the performance of a selected organisation |

**Assignment**

**Option A**

The business you work for has decided to carry out a 'resources audit', and you have been asked to do it. The audit involves producing a document for the management team that describes the physical resources and technological resources of the organisation (P3). The management team would also like a written explanation of how the management of resources (human, physical and technological) can improve the performance of the business (M1).

**Option B**

The management team of a business is interested in finding out more about the way in which it uses its resources. As a management consultant who is used to giving advice to businesses, you have been asked to carry out some research on resources used by the business and present your findings, using a PowerPoint presentation, to the management team of the organisation. The presentation will be divided into two parts. The first part will be a photographic summary of the physical and technological resources of the business. You will need to use these slides to help describe the resources the business currently has (P3). The second part of your presentation will explain how managing resources (human, physical and technological) can help to improve the performance of the business.

# **Part 3:** Know how to access sources of finance

Businesses need finance in order to start up but also to fund their day-to-day activities and longer-term plans. Knowing where they can access these funds is therefore vital. Sources of finance are classified as follows.

## Internal sources

These can be further broken down into being provided by the owner's savings, or retained profits.

When a business starts up it is the owner(s) who raise the initial money required. Sole traders and partnerships would invest a set amount into the business and this is known as the opening capital. If the business requires further injections of finance in order to survive the owners might be called upon again to make an investment out of their savings.

A limited company will raise its initial capital through the sale of shares. The people who purchase the shares become part owners of the business. If a limited company needs to raise further finance it might be able to sell additional shares either to current shareholders or new shareholders.

If a business is a sole trader all the profit belongs to the owner; in a partnership the profits would be shared between the owners in the agreed profit-sharing ratio. However rather than taking all the profit the owner(s) might decide to retain some of the profit in order to fund expansion and growth. In a limited company, profits are shared among the shareholders through the payment of dividends. It is up to the shareholders to decide how much of the profit they will receive and how much should be 'retained' within the business.

## External sources of finance

External sources of finance are those which are provided by organisations that are external to the business, such as banks or investors.

### Bank overdraft

This is where a business has permission from the bank to withdraw more money from their bank account than they have on deposit; it is a form of borrowing. Banks will normally grant an overdraft facility that allows businesses to overdraw up to a pre-arranged limit. Once a business draws on their **overdraft** they are charged interest on the amount they have borrowed for the number of days the debt is outstanding.

Advantages of a bank overdraft:

- Allows flexibility – a business can access funds immediately, as long as the overdraft has been approved by the bank
- Interest is charged on a daily basis

Disadvantages of a bank overdraft:

- Unsuitable when large sources of finance are required
- Rates of interest charged are usually higher than a bank loan
- The bank can change the interest rate at any time
- The bank can reduce or stop the overdraft facility without warning

---

### Harrogate Vegan Deli

Al Farquharson, owner and manager of Harrogate Vegan Deli, explains the value of the £2,000 overdraft limit that the business has been permitted by the bank:

'I don't use the overdraft every month, but sometimes it comes in very useful. If I need a little extra cash to pay suppliers I might dip into it, or if I need to pay the wages of my three staff, the overdraft may occasionally be used. In the busy summer months and in the build-up to Christmas I don't need to touch the overdraft, but it's reassuring to know that the money is available.'

#### Activity

What are the advantages to Al of having an overdraft facility on the business bank account?

# Business loan

A **business loan** is where a third party lends the business money. The loan will usually have an agreed repayment plan. Interest payable on the loan may also be required.

Businesses usually go to banks in order to secure finance. Loans can be either short or long term. A bank loan is usually secured against a fixed asset that the business owns. This is to ensure that if the business struggles to make repayments the bank is able to sell the fixed asset in order to recoup its investment. The funds will be borrowed over an agreed period of time and will be subject to interest charges.

There are two common types of loans from a bank. One has a fixed interest rate and the other a variable interest rate. A fixed-interest loan means that the amount of interest to be charged will be fixed and remain the same over the agreed time limit regardless of rises and falls in the Bank of England base rate. This allows a business to plan its repayments carefully. If a business takes out a variable-rate loan the interest charged on the loan could be subject to increases or decreases in line with the Bank of England base rate. A business that has a variable-rate loan might suddenly find their loan becomes more expensive if the interest rate increases.

# Commercial mortgage

This is a form of long-term loan used by businesses to purchase buildings or property. Mortgages are often repaid over a period of between twenty and thirty years. An enormous variety of mortgages are available including fixed and variable interest rates. Banks reduce the risk to themselves of lending such large sums of money by using the property being purchased as security. If a business cannot keep up its repayments, the bank has the right to repossess the property and sell it in an attempt to recoup the outstanding debt.

HSBC Bank (see www.hsbc.co.uk) offer **commercial mortgages** with a repayment term of between two and thirty years. They will lend up to 75 per cent of the purchase price of the commercial property and the interest rate can be fixed and paid either monthly or quarterly. The bank also offers a repayment holiday for all or part of the first two years of the mortgage.

# Venture capital

A **venture capitalist** is an investment business that tends to favour higher risk, but potentially higher return, enterprises. In return for providing finance and expertise, they will normally expect to become part-owners of the business. For businesses that need finance to grow, but have been judged to be too risky by high street banks, venture capital may be the solution.

The advantage of seeking venture capital is that the lender will often take an active role within the business. Often their incentive for investment is to see the business make substantial growth and then sell their shares. This type of finance is usually only suitable for limited company businesses as a proportion of shares will have to be exchanged for the investment being sought.

3i is a venture capital, or private equity, business that has now been operating for over 60 years (see www.3i.com). In this time 3i has invested over €29 billion to help with the growth of businesses throughout the world. 3i currently holds investments in almost 400 enterprises across thirteen countries. The investor's key sectors of interest include oil, technology, media, health care, and financial services. 3i emphasises to potential clients that it hopes to work in partnership with them, so that they might benefit not only from 3i's funding but from their business expertise.

# Hire purchase

**Hire purchase** is a contract between a lender (a bank or broker) and the business who wishes to purchase the product. The contract is often arranged by the seller. The arrangement allows the business to obtain a product they could not afford to purchase outright. The method of repayment is through regular instalments, often with interest being charged and as long as payments are regularly made it removes the uncertainty of the loan being repayable upon demand. However, if payments are not made and the contract is less than one-third of the way through the supplier can repossess the product. If the contract is more than one-third complete the supplier has to go to court to either gain the outstanding funds or reclaim the product. The main advantage of this type of finance is that the business has the use of the product over the period of the loan. The business will own the product once the last payment has been made with the payment of an option to purchase fee.

Hire purchase is often an expensive way of financing a purchase, but when retailers are struggling to sell hire-purchase agreements very attractive options may be provided such as interest being fixed at 0 per cent for a period of time.

## Leasing

This is the process of paying for the use of an asset, often without ever owning it. For very expensive items which might become out of date (obsolete) quickly, or where maintenance costs could be expensive, **leasing** may be a worthwhile option.

The biggest advantage of leasing equipment is the fact that there is no large initial payment; the cost is spread over a number of years. Repayment costs are often fixed which makes budgeting and control of cash flow much easier. There are also tax benefits as often lease rentals are considered operating expenses and as such can be offset against taxable profits.

The major disadvantages of leasing are the fact that the business never owns the product but is still responsible for its maintenance and repair. It remains the property of the leasing company during and after the lease. Although leasing allows a business to own the equipment immediately without a large lump sum payment it often works out considerably more expensive. Over the duration of a standard lease the business will pay for the cost of the equipment plus the leasing company's charges. After the lease expires the business will be required to carry on paying rental to use the product although these costs will reduce significantly.

### OMM

Photocopiers are expensive. High-quality, colour copiers can cost over £100,000 to purchase. As a result, many businesses opt to lease their copier. OMM offers a service where businesses can lease the latest copiers and take advantage of free training and support (see www.omm.co.uk). The option to include servicing arrangements in a leasing policy is also provided.

### Activity

What are the advantages and disadvantages of leasing a photocopier?

## Factoring

One of the major problems facing businesses is cash flow. This can be severely hampered when a business is unable to collect its debts from its customers, culminating with some businesses struggling with very high levels of outstanding debts. One way to raise this cash quickly is to sell the unpaid debt/invoice to a third party; the third party gives the businesses a percentage of the outstanding debt and it is then their responsibility to collect the debt. Some businesses allocate all their invoices to a factoring company. The advantage of this is that cash flow is instant and it reduces the need to run an efficient credit control system which will ultimately cut down on administrative tasks that have to be undertaken.

Barclay's Bank offers a debt **factoring** service to business customers. They offer to pay up to 95 per cent of the value of unpaid invoices within 24 hours. The service is aimed at businesses who regularly sell to a variety of customers on credit with expected sales of over £100,000 per annum.

## Share issue

When a limited company is first incorporated it will decide how many shares it wants to sell in total. This is known as its authorised **share capital**. The company will then decide how many of those shares it needs to sell in order to raise sufficient funds to begin trading. The number of shares which are offered for sale is known as the issued share capital. If the business does not sell all its authorised share capital when it is first incorporated it can sell the additional shares if it ever needs to raise further capital.

Private and public limited companies differ in the way that they can sell shares. Public limited companies can offer shares for sale to the general public, for example by advertising a **share issue** in a national newspaper. Private limited companies are not permitted to do this; if they wish to sell shares, they must do so privately, for example to colleagues, employees or by directly approaching investors.

One of the advantages of selling shares is that there are no repayments due to a third party and the finance raised does not carry interest charges. However, the business will have a range of different owners who might want to voice their opinions on the future direction of the venture. With large public limited companies this impact is very much limited as each individual owner will probably have too few shares to make a significant difference. A public limited company will also be run by a board of directors on behalf of the shareholders rather than directly by the shareholders. A further disadvantage is that shareholders will expect to receive a share of the profits – this is known as a dividend payment. Ordinary shareholders legally do not have to be paid a dividend but they are unlikely to want to retain their investment within the business if they do not receive any financial incentive to do so.

## Triframes

Triframes manufactures high-quality carbon fibre cycle frames for use by triathletes. Triathlon is currently the UK's fastest growing sport and demand for frames by cycle builders has grown rapidly over the last few years. The business was originally funded by the savings of the owner, Tim Spalding; however, with growth and the need for more equipment and bigger premises, finance requirements also increased. In June 2009, with the help of his accountant, Tim formed Triframes Ltd, a private limited company. The shares issued in the new business raised £120,000, with 40 per cent being owned by Tim, 30 per cent by his father-in-law, and 30 per cent by a venture capital company.

### Activity

What are the drawbacks to Tim of raising the finance for expansion in this way?

## Key terms

**Business loan** When a business borrows a sum of money and repays it with interest

**Commercial mortgage** A form of long-term borrowing used for the purchase of buildings or land

**Factoring** Sale of unpaid invoices to a third party in order to raise finance quickly

**Hire purchase** Purchasing something by making regular instalments rather than buying it outright

**Leasing** Making use of something, in return for a payment, without ever necessarily owning it

**Overdraft** A form of short-term borrowing whereby a bank allows a business to withdraw more money from their bank account than they have on deposit

**Share capital** The amount invested in a business by shareholders. They have purchased shares in the company

**Share issue** The process of selling shares, in a limited company, in order to raise finance

**Venture capitalist** An organisation that may be willing to provide financial support for a potentially more risky business investment

## Q Re-cap questions

1  Describe two different ways in which a business can raise finance internally.
2  Explain the difference between a bank overdraft and a bank loan.
3  Investigate the current interest rates available on a bank overdraft and loan. Which bank offers the best deals?
4  Analyse the differences between hire purchase and leasing if a business wanted to purchase a new car. Which type of finance would you recommend? Justify your answer.
5  Explain how factoring can help a business ease its cash-flow problems.

# Part 4: Interpreting financial statements

In order to manage financial resources effectively, owners/managers need to understand the cost structure of their organisations. If a business is to operate profitably, it needs to be able to cover its costs and recognise when it is making a profit or **loss**. Financial information will also allow a business to assess which products are most profitable and which should be withdrawn from sale.

## Definition of costs and break-even

In order to be able to manage costs effectively businesses will need to understand how to define costs and the impact they can have on profitability. Being able to control costs effectively could be the difference between making a profit or a loss, success or failure.

## Fixed costs

These are costs that do not change with the level of output. When output or production is zero, these costs must still be paid. For example, if factory premises are rented, the rent must still be paid regardless of the level of production. Other **fixed costs** may include loan repayments, business rates or the payment of salaries (which are normally unrelated to output).

## Variable costs

These are costs that change directly with the level of output. Technically, when output is zero, **variable costs** will also be zero. As production levels rise, variable costs will rise. Variable costs include raw materials, energy and the payment of wages to direct labour; with a higher output more hours are likely to be needed. Labour is only a variable cost if it can be directly related to the product being produced.

## Break-even analysis

**Break-even** is the point where no profit or loss has been made; all costs have been covered. If a business has a good understanding of its costs, it should be able to calculate what price it needs to charge and how much it needs to sell in order to achieve break-even. For some businesses, particularly new ones, a less ambitious target than making a profit is to break even: in other words, to just cover their costs with the revenue that they have generated in the hope that sales will increase over time allowing them to achieve a profit.

How do I work out if I have made a profit?

# Relapse T-Shirts

Relapse, run by Ruby McKenzie, produces T-shirts for less well-known UK bands to sell at their concerts and via their websites. She operates from a small factory unit on the outskirts of Manchester. The business has a relatively simple cost structure:

| | |
|---|---|
| **Factory unit rental** | **£1,200 per month** |
| **Business rates** | **£600 per month** |
| **Marketing** | **£200 per month** |
| **Ruby McKenzie's drawings** | **£550 per month** |
| **Other fixed costs** | **£450 per month** |
| **Material cost/T-shirt** | **£2.50 each** |

Ruby sells the T-shirts for £4.50 each. The maximum number she is a capable of producing per month (her **full capacity**) is 2,000 T-shirts. With the help of her bank's small business adviser, she recently carried out a break-even analysis. The results are shown in the table below.

It is often easier to look at this type of data in the form of a break-even chart. Here, the figures for fixed costs, total cost and **total revenue** can be plotted against output. This makes it easy to find the break-even point; this is simply where the line that represents total revenue crosses the line that represents total cost. The value of output on the horizontal axis is the break-even level of output. The value of sales on the vertical axis is the break-even level in sales revenue.

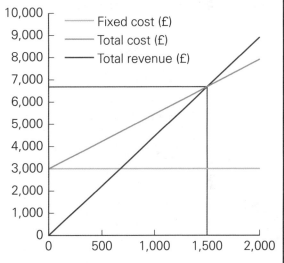

**Figure 2.3** Break-even graph for Relapse T-Shirt production on a monthly basis

Break-even analysis

| No. of shirts produced | 0 | 500 | 1,000 | 1,500 | 2,000 |
|---|---|---|---|---|---|
| **Fixed cost (£)** | 3,000 | 3,000 | 3,000 | 3,000 | 3,000 |
| **Variable cost (£)** | 0 | 1,250 | 2,500 | 3,750 | 5,000 |
| **Total cost (£)** | 3,000 | 4,250 | 5,500 | 6,750 | 8,000 |
| **Total revenue (£)** | 0 | 2,250 | 4,500 | 6,750 | 9,000 |
| **Profit or loss (£)** | 3,000 loss | 2,000 loss | 1,000 loss | Break-even | 1,000 profit |

For Ruby to break-even she needs to produce and sell 1,500 T-shirts per month. If she produces and sells more than this, she will make a profit; if she produces and sells less than this, she will make a loss. The difference between the 2,000 T-shirts she produces on a monthly basis and the break-even point of 1,500 T-shirts is known as the **margin of safety**. This is the amount that production could fall without sustaining a loss. This information is extremely useful as it could help Ruby plan her output and create sales targets. The analysis could also be used to show the impact of a change in a cost, or in price.

Break-even can also be calculated numerically. The formula is as follows

$$\frac{\text{Fixed costs}}{\text{Contribution}} = \text{Break-even point in units}$$

Contribution = sales price – variable costs.

If we use the figures supplied for Relapse T-Shirts the calculation is as follows

$$\frac{3,000}{4.50-2.50} = 1,500 \text{ T-shirts}$$

## Jane's Burgers

Midlands fast-food take-away 'Jane's' produces the famous Jane's Burger. The business has provided the following cost breakdown of their prize-winning cheeseburger. Fixed costs are per burger based on estimated annual sales of 5,000 burgers. The sales price for each burger is £1.99.

Bread bun = 7p  Burger = 20p  Salad = 6p
Cheese = 10p    Pickle = 3p   Sauce = 3p
Wages = 10p     Rent of premises = 20p

Using the figures above, complete the following questions:

1. Classify the above costs into fixed and variable. Justify your choice.
2. Calculate the break-even point using the formula supplied above.
3. Draw the break-even graph for Jane's Burgers.

## Limitations of break-even

While break-even is a useful tool which indicates whether it would be financially viable to produce a product its calculations are based on some assumptions and therefore as a tool it does have limitations which are outlined below:

- It assumes that all fixed costs will remain constant regardless of the levels of output or circumstances. This will not necessarily be the case – the landlord might put up the rent.

- The sales price remains constant. Again this is rarely true as businesses tend to offer discounts to regular customers or reduce prices to remove old stock.
- It also assumes that the only factor affecting costs and sales revenues is increases in production which again is unlikely – the price of raw materials could fluctuate especially if being imported and affected by fluctuating exchange rates.
- It also assumes that all goods are sold.

Do I have sufficient budget to buy this?

# Budgets and variance

Budgeting is the process of making financial plans. A **budget** will normally be set by a business at the start of a financial year and may include financial targets for various costs and for revenue. Accurate budgeting is the most effective way for a business to control cash flow allowing it to grow and invest in new opportunities as and when they arise.

There are a number of benefits of drawing up a business budget, including being able to:

- Manage cash flow in and out of the business more effectively
- Allocate appropriate resources to projects
- Monitor the overall performance of the business
- Meet the overall objectives of the business
- Improve decision making within the business
- Identify problems before they occur – falling sales of a particular product might lead to a new marketing campaign to improve sales
- Make plans for the future
- Increase staff motivation and morale.

As stated above budgets are normally reviewed, or monitored, on a regular basis in order to establish whether the business is on track to achieve its financial targets. The **monitoring** process will allow **variances** to be calculated; this is simply the difference between the forecast (or target) value and the actual value. There are two types of variance:

- A **favourable variance** occurs when sales revenue is higher than expected, or costs are lower than expected. For example, if sales were expected to be £4 million, but turned out to be £7 million, then there would be a favourable variance of £3 million. If expenses were expected to be £750,000 and were in fact only £700,000 this give the business a £50,000 favourable variance. If these two favourable variances are considered together the overall profit of the business would have been increased by £3,050,000 – another favourable variance.

- An **adverse variance** occurs when sales revenue is lower than expected, or costs are higher than expected. If sales had been budgeted at £4 million, but turned out to be £3.5 million the adverse variance would have been £500,000. If total costs were expected to be £800,000, but turned out to be £950,000, then there would be an adverse variance of £150,000. Adding these two variances together the impact on profit would have been a reduction of £650,000 – another adverse variance.

## General reasons for variances

| | |
|---|---|
| Sales variance – favourable | This is when the sales figure is higher than budgeted. The reason might be due to an increase in sales price which has not affected the number of items sold. The second could be an increase in sales volume either due to promotional offers or a promotional campaign used to stimulate demand. |
| Sales variance – adverse | This is when the final sales figure is lower than originally budgeted. The sales price might have been reduced and this has not triggered an increase in demand. The sales volume has decreased – sales have been falling. |
| Expenses – favourable | This is where the cost of expenses is lower than originally budgeted for. This could be due to the fact that less was used than anticipated or the cost of the expense has reduced. The business may have been able to secure discounts for large orders or early payments. |
| Expenses – adverse | This is where the cost of expenses was higher than budgeted. This could be because the cost of the product/service has increased and this was not considered when the budget was formulated. Usage of the product/service was higher than originally budgeted for. |

## Bridlington Pizzas

| | Budget (£) | Actual value (£) |
|---|---|---|
| Sales revenue | 80,000 | 65,000 |
| Rent | 10,000 | 12,000 |
| Materials | 28,000 | 22,000 |
| Advertising | 2,000 | 500 |
| Wages | 14,000 | 18,000 |
| Loan repayments | 1,500 | 1,500 |

On the advice of their Business Link agent, Bridlington Pizzas produced a six-month budget for the period beginning 1 July 2009. A summary of the details of the budget are shown opposite, along with the actual figures recorded by the owners on 31 December 2009.

### Questions

a) Using the data provided, calculate the variances for the six-month period.

   If the variance is favourable record it either as +£700 or £700F

   If the variance is adverse record it either as −£700 or £700A

b) Why do you think the Business Link agent advised the business to produce this budget?

c) Having monitored the budget, what actions might Bridlington Pizzas decide to take?

## Working capital

Having set budgets and calculated when income and expenses are expected a business must now consider if its calculations leave it sufficient liquid funds to survive. These funds are known as working capital. Working capital is the money that is available in the short term for the business to spend. It is calculated by taking current assets away from **current liabilities**.

If it is to survive, a business needs to ensure that its current assets are more than its current liabilities in order to pay for its day-to-day expenses. When considering budgets a business also needs to consider if it has sufficient funds to cover emergency situations that might occur. These are known as reserves. An example of an unforeseen event could take the form of a downturn in sales, or a rise in energy costs. Further information on this is found in section on the balance sheet on page 66.

## Financial statements

The owners of a business, whether they are shareholders, partners or simply a sole trader, will need to know how well the business is performing and its financial position. Other stakeholders such as investors and employees may also be interested in the financial successes and failures, strengths and weaknesses of an organisation.

The two key financial statements are:

- The **profit and loss account**, which shows how much profit (or loss) a business has generated at the end of a given time period, usually one year.
- The **balance sheet**, which states the value of the **assets** and **liabilities** of a business at a particular point in time.

These two documents, known as the final accounts of a business, are normally produced annually. It is important that they are produced accurately as the contents will be used to determine how much tax a business is liable to pay. Public limited companies (plcs) must, by law, produce these statements and publish them so that all their shareholders can see how well they are performing.

## The profit and loss account

Below are the Trading Profit and Loss and Appropriation Account for Hardbodies Gym Ltd for the financial year ending on 31 December 2009.

| Hardbodies Gym Ltd<br>Trading Profit and Loss Account for year ended<br>31 December 2009 | | |
|---|---|---|
| | £000 | £000 |
| Sales | | 182 |
| Less cost of sales | | |
| Opening stock | 4 | |
| Plus purchases | 28 | |
| Less closing stock | (3) | |
| Cost of goods sold | | (29) |
| **Gross profit** | | 153 |
| **Less expenses** | | |
| Wages | 35 | |
| Rent and rates | 27 | |
| Energy | 12 | |
| Advertising/publicity | 3 | |
| Maintenance/repairs | 2 | |
| General expenses | 10 | (89) |
| **Net profit before interest and tax** | | 64 |
| Interest charges | | (3) |
| Corporation tax* | | (6) |
| **Net profit** | | 55 |
| Add retained profit | | 5 |
| General reserve | | (5) |
| Proposed ordinary share dividends ** | | (10) |
| **Retained profit** | | 45 |

*Corporation tax has been set at approximately 10 per cent

**Dividend payment was agreed as 50p for every share held

The account is arranged in two columns to make it easier to calculate sub sums. For example all the expenses are listed in the first column so that the total can be carried over to the second column to allow the total of £89,000 to be taken away from the gross profit. Figures in ( ) indicate the figure must be deducted.

The following are the key points

- For the year that ended 31 December 2009 the gym generated sales revenue of £182,000. This will have been from memberships, entrance fees and selling food, drink and supplements.
- The value of the stock held by the gym on 1 January 2009 (the first day of the year) was £4,000. This is known as the **opening stock**.
- During the year, the gym bought stock valued at £28,000. This value is known as **purchases**.
- At the end of the year (on 31 December 2009) the gym was holding stock valued at £3,000. This is known as the **closing stock**.
- The value of the stock that was actually used during the year (known as the **cost of sales**) is calculated using the following formula:

Cost of sales = opening stock + purchases – closing stock

So in the case of the gym, the value of cost of sales was calculated as follows:

Cost of sales = £4,000 + £28,000 – £3,000 = £29,000

- The **gross profit** for the year is the difference between the values of sales and the cost of sales. This does not take into account the other costs of the business. Gross profit is calculated using the following formula:

Gross profit = sales – cost of sales

So for the gym, gross profit was calculated as follows:

Gross profit = £182,000 – £29,000 = £153,000

- **Net profit before tax and interest** is calculated by deducting all the other expenses from gross profit. So, net profit is calculated using the following formula:

Net profit before interest and tax = gross profit – expenses

For the gym, net profit before interest and tax was calculated as follows:

Net profit before interest and tax = £153,000 – £89,000 = £64,000

- The final net profit figure is calculated after interest payments and corporation tax have been deducted.

> Net Profit = net profit before interest and tax – interest charged and tax

For the gym, net profit was calculated as follows:

> Net profit
> £64,000 – £3,000 – £6,000 = £55,000

- A limited company has to pay its shareholders dividends. This is a reward for the shareholders' investment in the business. It is quite common for some businesses to retain some of their profits in order to expand in the future. A business might also move some of its profits into a reserve account. This final part of the account is known as the Appropriation Account – this illustrates how the profits of the business have been distributed.

The Gym had £5,000 of retained profit from last year and this has been added to the profit of £55,000 made this financial year. The Gym decided to move £5,000 into the general reserve and pay its shareholders a dividend of £10,000. This means that every £1 share receives a divided of 50p. Having made these deductions the Gym has a retained profit to be carried forward of £45,000.

## The balance sheet

Below is the balance sheet for Hardbodies Gym Ltd on 31 December 2009. This provides a snapshot of the financial position of the business on this date.

| Hardbodies Gym Ltd<br>Balance Sheet as at 31 December 2009 | | |
|---|---|---|
| | £000 | £000 |
| **Fixed assets** | | |
| Equipment | | 70 |
| Fixtures and fittings | | 16 |
| | | 86 |
| **Current assets** | | |
| Stock | 3 | |
| Debtors | 12 | |
| Deposits and cash | 11 | |
| | 26 | |
| **Liabilities due in less than one year (current liabilities)** | | |
| Creditors | (2) | |
| Proposed ordinary dividend | (10) | |
| Working capital | | 14 |
| Net current assets | | 100 |
| **Liabilities due in more than one year (long-term liabilities)** | | |
| Bank loan | | (25) |
| | | 75 |
| | | |
| **Financed by:** | | |
| 20,000 £1 ordinary shares | | 20 |
| General reserve | | 10 |
| Profit and loss account | | 45 |
| | | 75 |

The key features are explained below:

- The **fixed assets** are the long-term items of value that are owned by the gym. They are likely to be held by the business for at least a year. In this balance sheet they are divided into 'equipment' (gym equipment) and 'fixtures and fittings'. The latter is likely to include such items as carpets and furniture. Because the premises are rented (see 'rent' in the profit and loss account) an entry for buildings does not appear on the gym's balance sheet. On 31 December 2009 the fixed assets of the gym were valued at £86,000.

- The **current assets** are the short-term items of value that are held by the gym. These are likely to be held for less than a year and will change quite frequently. The value for 'stock' in the balance sheet was the value of stock on 31 December 2009; this is the same value as the 'closing stock' found in the profit and loss account. **Debtors** are classed as a current asset because they owe the business money; as such, they are valuable to the business. Cash and deposits represent the money the gym has immediately available to spend. The deposits would include money held within bank accounts.

- The **liabilities due in less than one year** are the short-term debts that the gym has. For some businesses, an overdraft would be included in the current liabilities. However, for the gym there were just two items. **Creditors** are individuals, or other businesses, that the gym owed money to. Proposed ordinary share dividends appear here as the business has not yet paid this amount to their shareholders; it is only proposed. Liabilities due in less than one year thus had a value of £12,000.

- Working capital is often referred to as money for day-to-day expenses. However, a value for working capital is often included in a balance sheet. Working capital is calculated by Current assets – current liabilities. The gym's, working capital is as follows:

  £26,000 – £12,000 = £14,000

This is the difference between the short-term assets of the business (money and items that will become worth money in the near future) and the short-term liabilities (what the business owes that will need to be paid back in the near future).

- Liabilities due in more than one year include any long-term loans or debts that the business has. The gym has a bank loan for £25,000 which will be due for repayment sometime in the future.

When all the assets (fixed and current) are added together, and all the liabilities are deducted a value of £75,000 is obtained.

How the business has been funded is illustrated in the 'Financed by' section of the balance sheet. In the case of limited companies the initial capital would have been raised through the sale of shares.

For the gym, the 'Financed by' section contained three items:

- Hardbodies Gym Ltd raised an initial sum of £20,000 through the sale of 20,000 ordinary shares with a face value of £1.

- **Reserves** are the gym's accumulated profit from previous years that had been retained within the business. This profit has been ploughed back into the business. The gym had already created a general reserve. £5,000 extra funding was moved into this account from the profit made at the end of 2009. The account now has a total value of £10,000.

- Profit and loss account shows the entry of £45,000. £40,000 of this was the net profit that the gym generated in the year ended 31 December 2009 and £5,000 retained profit from previous trading years. At a later date some, or all, of this money could be distributed to the shareholders.

- The bottom line of the balance sheet had a value of £75,000. This shows, down to the last pound, where the finance for the gym had come from. The balance sheet balanced!

- The total of the items in the 'Financed by' section are sometimes referred to as the **capital employed**; this is the total amount invested in a business, in this case in the form of shares issued, the general reserve and profit and loss account.

> Using the accounts for Hardbodies Gym, list the financial strengths and weaknesses of the business for the year ended 31 December 2009.

# Ratio analysis

Making an assessment about how well a business has performed and how strong its financial position is, simply by looking at the accounts is not always that straightforward. Let us consider the information in the case study below.

> Spend a few minutes considering which business you now think has performed better.

## Web designers

Consider the following data that is drawn from the year end accounts for 2009 for two web design businesses:

|  | Net profit (£) |
|---|---|
| **Grohl Webs Ltd (GWL)** | 26,000 |
| **Cobain Web Design Ltd (CWDL)** | 185,000 |

Which businesses performed better? At first glance it would appear that CWDL is much more successful as they have achieved £159,000 more profit than (GWL). However, when we consider the next paragraph below look a little different.

|  | **Grohl Webs Ltd** | **Cobain Web Design Ltd** |
|---|---|---|
| **Employees** | 1 | 38 |
| **Long-term liabilities** | 0 | £120,000 |
| **Shareholders** | 2 | 15 |

If we take GWL the profit only has to be shared between two shareholders potentially giving them £13,000 each. On the other hand CWDL has to share its £185,000 profit between 15 shareholders which could potentially given them £12,333 each. CWDL also has a long-term debt of £120,000.

The financial performance and position of a business can be measured in three basic ways:

- By measuring the solvency of a business. If a business is solvent it is able to settle its debts when they are due to be paid. If a business is insolvent then it is not capable of doing this. Clearly, being solvent will help a business to maintain the confidence and support of creditors. If, for example, a supplier is not paid on time they may refrain from supplying further stock and the business may be forced to close.

- By measuring the profitability of a business, rather than simply measuring the **profit** of a business, it may be more informative. It may also be useful to establish how much value has been added to inputs; how much gross profit has been generated as a result of a sale.

- By measuring the general performance of the business. For example, how long stock is being held for, and how long debtors are taking to pay their invoices.

The ratios that can be used to measure solvency, profitability and performance are summarised in the table below:

| Ratio | What it measures | How it is calculated | What it means |
|---|---|---|---|
| **Measures of solvency** | | | |
| Current ratio | A firm's ability to meet its short-term debts. It is a measure of solvency. | $$\frac{\text{Current assets}}{\text{Current liabilities}}$$ | The figure should not normally fall below 1.5. If it reaches a value of 1 then there may be concern that short-term debts may not be able to be met. A value higher than 2 may indicate that too much finance is tied up in short-term assets rather than being actively used within the organisation. |
| Acid test | As above | $$\frac{\text{Current assets} - \text{stock}}{\text{Current liabilities}}$$ | As above, but a more stringent test of ability to settle short-term debts. Removes the uncertain variable of stock, which may not be as valuable as believed, or may be difficult to dispose of. The calculation thus includes what are generally regarded as the most liquid assets (the ones closest to cash). A minimum value of 1 is normally recommended. |
| **Measures of profitability** | | | |
| Gross profit margin | The percentage of sales revenue which is gross profit | $$\frac{\text{Gross profit}}{\text{Sales}} \times 100$$ | Can be used to compare how much value is added to an item in between being bought in as stock or materials and being sold by the firm. A low gross profit margin might indicate high stock costs, or retail price being too low. Comparisons can be made with other firms (if possible) or previous years. |
| Net profit margin | The percentage of sales revenue which is net profit | $$\frac{\text{Net profit}}{\text{Sales}} \times 100$$ | Can be used to decide which of a range of products are worth continuing with. A low net profit margin might indicate that costs are too high. Comparisons can also be made with other firms (if possible) or previous years. |
| Return on capital employed (ROCE) | The percentage return the firm is able to generate on long-term capital employed | $$\frac{\text{Net profit}}{\text{Capital employed}} \times 100$$ | Can be used to show how efficiently a firm is using its capital. Comparisons can be made with other firms (if possible) or previous years. The percentage can also be compared with the prevailing rate of interest. |

| Measures of performance | | | |
|---|---|---|---|
| Stock turnover | How long stock is, on average, being held for before it is replaced | $\dfrac{\text{Average stock}}{\text{Cost of sales}}$ x 365 days | If stock is perishable (if it goes out of date, such as fresh food) stock should be held for a very short period of time. Holding high levels of stock can be expensive in other ways; stock can deteriorate in value and may be vulnerable to theft. A high turnover of stock is often seen as an indicator of a healthy business. |
| Debtor collection period | How long, on average, debtors take to pay | $\dfrac{\text{Debtors}}{\text{Sales}}$ x 365 | A business should be aware that this is only an average. Many businesses allow up to 90 days for debtors to pay. However, a high debtor collection period could indicate that a business is struggling to get its invoices paid on time and could be facing a potential cash shortage. |
| Asset turnover | How high the level of sales are in relation to the assets of the business | $\dfrac{\text{Sales}}{\text{Assets}}$ | The higher this value is, the better the business may be judged to be performing. A high value may indicate that assets, such as machinery and equipment, are being used effectively to generate sales. |

## Ratios for Hardbodies Gym

Following the production of the 2009 accounts, the accountants for Hardbodies Gym provided the owners with an analysis of the financial performance of the business for the year, and of its financial position on 31 December 2009. A summary of the report is shown below:

### Solvency

Current assets were valued at £26,000, while current liabilities were valued at £12,000. The current ratio was calculated as follows:

Current ratio = 26,000/12,000 = 2.17

This means that the gym had £2.17 available to cover every £1 of immediate debt. This shows a position of solvency.

The acid test was calculated as follows

Acid test = 26,000 – 3,000/12,000 = 1.92

This means the gym had £1.92 of liquid current assets to pay its immediate debts. This also shows a position of solvency, even after the often uncertain variable of stock has been removed.

## Profitability

The gross profit margin for the year was calculated as follows:

Gross profit margin = 153,000/182,000 × 100 = 84.07%

This shows that for every £100 of sales, the gym generated £84.07 of gross profit. For a service-sector business, we would expect a high figure. However, this figure shows healthy profitability.

The net profit margin for the year was calculated as follows:

Net profit after deduction of interest and tax = 55,000/182,000 × 100 = 30.22%

This shows that for every £100 of sales, the gym generated £30.22 of net profit. This again shows a healthy profitability. It seems that the costs of the gym are under control.

The return on capital employed (ROCE) was calculated as follows:

ROCE = 55,000/75,000 × 100 = 73.33%

This shows a healthy return on the capital invested in the business. At the time of writing, bank deposits were yielding returns of no more than approximately 5 per cent. A return of 73.34 per cent thus compares extremely well.

## Performance

Stock turnover was calculated as follows:

Average stock = (4,000 + 3,000)/2 = 3,500

Stock turnover = 3,500/29,000 × 365 = 44 days

This shows that stock is turned over approximately every 44 days. As most of the stock is long-life supplements, such as vitamin-enriched supplements, 44 days is a reasonable amount of time as the stock is not particularly perishable.

The debtor collection period was calculated as follows:

Debtor collection period = 12,000/182,000 × 365 = 24 days

This shows that the gym had to wait an average of 24 days for debtors to pay. This seems a reasonable amount of time for a business of this type; it seems to be collecting debts quickly.

The asset turnover was calculated as follows:

Asset turnover = 182,000/(86,000 + 16,000) = 1.78

This shows that the gym earns approximately £1.78 in sales for every £1 it has invested in assets.

## Key terms

**Adverse variance** Where actual sales are lower than expected or actual costs are higher than expected

**Assets** Items of value that are owned by a business

**Balance sheet** A statement of the assets and liabilities of a business at a particular point in time

**Break-even** The point where neither a loss nor profit has been made

**Budget** A financial plan or target

**Capital employed** The total of all the long-term finance of a business. Capital employed will normally include share capital and reserves

**Closing stock** The value of stock held at the end of a trading year

**Cost of sales** Calculated by adding together opening stock and purchases, then deducting closing stock

**Creditors** Individuals and businesses that are owed money by an organisation. Creditors are classed as a current liability in the balance sheet

**Current assets** Short-term items of value that are held by a business. Examples include cash, stock and debtors

**Current liabilities/liabilities due in less than one year** Short-term debt that a business has. Examples include an overdraft and money owed to creditors

**Debtors** Individuals and businesses that owe money to an organisation. Debtors are classed as a current asset in the balance sheet

**Favourable variance** Where actual sales values are higher than expected, or actual cost values are lower than expected

**Fixed assets** Long-term items of value that are owned by a business. Such assets will normally be held for more than one year. Examples include buildings, vehicles, machinery and fixtures and fittings

**Fixed cost** A cost that is not linked to productivity

**Full capacity** When a business is producing its maximum level of output

**Gross profit** Calculated by deducting cost of sales from the value of sales

**Liabilities** What a business owes

**Liquidity** A firm's ability to access money

**Loss** A situation where total cost exceeds total revenue

**Margin of safety** The difference between the current levels of production and break-even point

**Monitoring** The process of comparing forecast or target values against outcomes

**Net profit** Calculated by deducting expenses or overheads from gross profit

**Opening stock** The value of stock at the beginning of a trading year

**Profit and loss account** Shows how net profit, sometimes after tax, has been calculated

**Profit** The amount by which total revenue exceeds total cost

**Purchases** Stock or materials that have been bought during a financial year

**Reserves** The retained profit of an organisation. The value of reserves will be stated in the firm's balance sheet

**Total revenue** The money that a business generates from selling its goods and services

**Variable cost** A cost that is directly linked to productivity

**Variance** The difference between a forecast value and an actual value

## Q Re-cap questions

1 Identify three fixed and variable costs.

2 Describe the limitations of break-even.

3 Identify the formula to calculate break-even. Make up some figures to illustrate how the formula works.

4 Explain how gross and net profit are calculated – use figures to illustrate your answer.

5 What are the benefits and limitations of using ratio analysis to interpret the final accounts of a business?

## Assignment

|  **P4** Describe the sources of internal and external finance for a selected business | | |
|---|---|---|

### Assignment

**Option A**

You have started work for Business Link. Your manager has asked you to produce a booklet that explains the internal and external sources of finance that are available to businesses. Included in the booklet will be a short case study of a business, explaining what sources of finance they have used.

**Option B**

You have started work as an adviser for Business Link. Your manager has asked you to attend a local business enterprise exhibition on behalf of Business Link. Your role will be to create a display for the show that summarises the sources of internal and external sources of finance that businesses can use. While at the exhibition, you will be on hand to explain to delegates, mainly people who have recently started or are planning to start a business, what the various sources of finance available are. Delegates will also ask you which sources of finance might be appropriate for their business situations.

## Grading tips

| | | |
|---|---|---|
| **P6** Illustrate the use of budgets as a means of exercising financial control of a selected company | **M4** Analyse the reasons why costs and budgets need to be controlled, explaining the problems which can arise if they are left unmonitored | **D1** Evaluate how managing resources and controlling budgets can improve the performance of a business |

### Assignment

You work for a business in the finance department, where your activities involve managing budgets. The business has recently been bought out by a business tycoon renowned for his relaxed attitude towards financial controls. The new owner is cynical about the use of budgets and is also unsure as to whether a strict approach is needed with regard to the management of other resources. You and a colleague in the finance department have been asked to make a presentation to the new owner and the board of directors. The presentation will show how budgets can be used, explain why they are useful and will explain to what extent controlling budgets and managing other resources effectively can help improve the performance of the business.

## Grading tips

| | | |
|---|---|---|
| **P5** Interpret the contents of a trading and profit and loss account and balance sheet of a selected company | **M3** Interpret the contents of a trading and profit and loss account and balance sheet of a selected company explaining how accounting ratios can be used to monitor the financial performance of the organisation | **D2** Evaluate the adequacy of accounting ratios as a means of monitoring the state of the business in a selected organisation, using examples |
| **P7** Illustrate the financial state of a given business by showing examples of accounting ratios | | |

### Assignment

In order to complete this assignment you will have been given a set of accounts for a selected business. This should include a profit and loss account and a balance sheet.

Explain the contents of the profit and loss and balance sheet supplied. Within your explanations consider how ratio analysis could be used to monitor the performance of the selected business.

Use a range of ratios to illustrate the financial position of the selected business. Start by describing the ratio and then applying it to the selected business. Next, analyse and evaluate the advantages and disadvantages of only using ratio analysis to make decisions when monitoring the financial performance of the selected business.

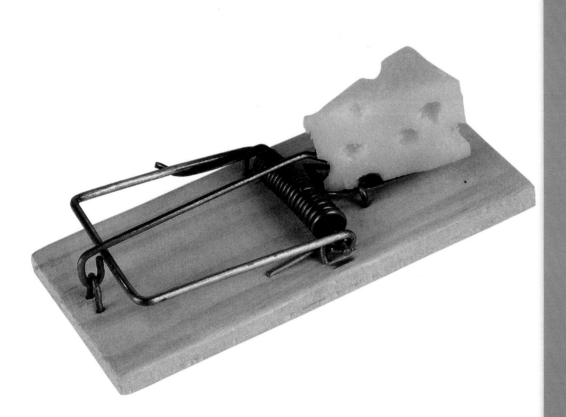

## The importance of marketing

Stop for a moment and think of all of the products available for you to buy at any time, night or day, should you have the desire (and the money!) to do so. The choice of goods and services on sale to us is enormous and is becoming greater on a daily basis. Over the years, the flow of new products being launched onto the high street has got faster and faster. New technologies have allowed firms to produce brand new products, as well as improving the quality and performance of many established brands. Blu-ray DVD and high-definition television offer consumers a new experience in home entertainment, while mobile phones now perform a wide range of functions beyond simply allowing users to make calls.

A mobile phone is no longer just used for making calls, it can perform many other functions

These goods and services are developed and produced by thousands of businesses around the world competing against each other for consumers' incomes. Some of these businesses are large national, or even multi-national, companies, supplying products that have become household names. Others may operate on a much smaller scale, targeting a much smaller number of customers located in a particular city or town. Whatever the case, all businesses need to offer goods and services that customers want to buy. To do this they need to gather a great deal of information about their customers – including who they are, what they need and want and how much they are prepared to pay. Finding out the answers to these questions is not as easy as it sounds, especially given the fact that different customers may have very different needs, and these needs are likely to change over time. Those firms that are able to maintain an in-depth understanding of their customers are much more likely to be successful, benefiting from growing sales, increasing **market share** and rising profits.

**Marketing** is the business function that is concerned with understanding the customer and attempting to ensure that products match customer needs as closely as possible. It is a term that is often misunderstood and inaccurately used. Many people believe that marketing is simply another term for selling and promotion when, in reality, it is a much more complex process. Clearly, the term is connected to the concept of the **market**, where customers and suppliers come together to trade goods or services. However, the marketing process begins well before the point at which products are exchanged between firms and their customers. According to the Chartered Institute of Marketing (CIM), marketing is 'the management process responsible for identifying, anticipating and satisfying customer requirements profitably'. This suggests that customers and their needs are not only the starting point for marketing but are central to everything that the process involves. Not only do firms need to identify and respond to the present needs of their customers, but they must also attempt to predict and, wherever possible, influence future demand.

Marketing has become a key function for all businesses, regardless of their size or the sector in which they operate. Some firms see the customer as being central to the achievement of their overall, **corporate objectives**. In such cases, identifying and responding effectively to customer needs is at the heart of all business planning and decision making. These firms are said to have a **market orientation**. Adopting such an approach requires the firm and its managers to be constantly alert to any changes in the marketplace, and able to respond quickly to both opportunities and threats as they arise. However, not all businesses choose to adopt this approach. Other types of business orientation include:

- **Product orientation** – this approach is taken by firms who believe that, by producing the best product available, they will automatically attract more customers than their rivals. If a business is able to do this, market success is likely to be limited to the short term as, sooner or later, competitors respond with their own versions. Constant research and development (R&D) is, therefore, required to update the product, in order to stay ahead. A key drawback of this approach is that the decision as to what represents the 'best' product is usually based on the views of managers or engineers within the business, rather than what the customer actually wants or needs.
- **Production orientation** – firms adopting this approach focus on finding the most cost-effective means of producing goods or services, so that any savings can be passed on in the form of lower prices. This is based on the belief that customers always choose the lowest priced products available. This may be the case in some markets – for example, for car insurance where there may be little, if any, differentiation between the policies provided by insurance companies. However, in other markets, factors such as design, image and durability may have just as much, if not more, influence on purchasing decisions.
- **Sales orientation** – this approach concentrates on informing as many people as possible about the existence of a firm's products and using various selling and promotional tactics in order to persuade them to buy. In such cases, the focus is on what the business can produce, rather than what the consumer might actually want. Sales staff may contact potential customers on the telephone, offering special offers and free gifts that are 'too good to refuse', in order to secure sales on the spot. In recent years, there has been increasing concern about the 'hard-sell' tactics used by banks and insurance companies to sell additional financial services products to customers taking out loans and credit cards.

## Setting objectives

The use of marketing by firms to generate customer satisfaction is designed to achieve their overall goals, known as **corporate objectives**. These objectives interpret the overall aims of the business – often referred to as its **mission** – into specific targets affecting the organisation as a whole and providing it with direction. Setting clear objectives is a key part of the decision-making process. For example, students with a good idea of what they want to achieve by the time they leave school or college – entering, perhaps, into a specific career or following a particular degree, are likely to find it easier to put together a suitable course of study. Although simply knowing what you want to achieve cannot guarantee success on its own, it should make the task of picking appropriate subjects more straightforward. The same thing applies to businesses – knowing what they want to achieve makes it easier to choose actions and activities that should hopefully improve the chances of success.

A common mistake is to assume that all businesses are set up and driven forward by the desire to make a profit. Although this is undoubtedly the case for some, there are many other reasons why businesses are set up, creating a range of possible objectives that may also change over time.

## Private sector aims and objectives

The private sector is the part of the economy that is made up by firms that are owned by private individuals or other businesses. In the case of limited companies, these owners are referred to as shareholders. A common objective of private sector firms is to make a profit in order to provide a return on the investment made by these owners and the risks they have taken in doing so. Some firms may choose **profit maximisation** as their main objective, where they attempt to make as much profit as possible, in the shortest possible time. However, firms that charge excessive prices or attempt to sell poor-quality products in order to maximise revenues or keep costs down are unlikely to benefit from repeat custom and may struggle to attract new customers as their reputation deteriorates. Most firms, therefore, tend to work towards the objective of achieving an optimum level of profit in the long term, which provides a sufficient return to shareholders but also considers the interests of other stakeholders, such as employees, customers and suppliers.

In the short term, however, it may not be possible to make any profit. Ensuring **business survival** may be an immediate objective for newly-established firms, or for those suffering from adverse economic conditions, such as recession or rising interest rates. Losses can be supported temporarily by borrowing or cash injections from investors. However, securing the finance required to ensure survival depends on being able to demonstrate that sales will grow in the future, allowing the business to **break even** and eventually become profitable. Even when economic conditions are more positive, a newly-established business may be more interested in pursuing growth, rather than profit, as a key objective, in order to secure a bigger – or even a dominant – market share. This is likely to involve heavy spending on advertising and sales promotion, or charging prices that undercut competitors, both of which will require the firm to sacrifice short-term profits (see Unit 1.2 for more detailed coverage of private sector aims and objectives).

## Public and voluntary sector aims and objectives

The public sector is made up of organisations that are controlled and funded by either national or local government, including public corporations such as the BBC and public services like the National Health Service. The voluntary sector consists of non-profit-making enterprises, such as charities. For organisations based in either sector, the key objective is to provide a high standard of service to the public. For public sector organisations in particular, the quality of service may be measured both in terms of the range of provision and the ability to meet the standards set out in the service level agreements made between the organisation providing the service and the body responsible for setting it up and funding it. Because organisations in the public and voluntary sectors do not set out to generate profits, goods and services are, in many cases, provided either at cost. Many public services, such as nursery places for pre-school children and nursing care for the elderly, are provided either at cost or at below cost in order that even those on low incomes can benefit. However, in such cases there is likely to still be a great emphasis on efficiency, i.e. using resources effectively and cutting out waste

wherever possible, in order to generate the maximum benefit from the funds available.

## From corporate to marketing objectives

**Marketing objectives** are the specific targets set by an organisation put in place to help it achieve its corporate, or overall, goals. They provide direction for whoever has responsibility for carrying out the marketing function within a business, in order to support the achievement of its corporate goals. Marketing objectives are an essential starting point for the marketing planning process for any organisation, regardless of size or sector. Without them, choosing appropriate marketing activities and putting together effective marketing strategies becomes incredibly difficult. However detailed the planning process has been, managers cannot assume that their plans will be effective once they are implemented. Unforeseen changes, either within the business or the external environment, can reduce the effectiveness of a firm's strategies. However, unless managers have clearly set targets against which to compare actual performance, they will struggle to measure and evaluate the success achieved so far. This will make it hard to decide what, if any, corrective action needs to be taken.

Common marketing objectives include:

- **Sales or revenue targets** – most firms will set specific targets for generating sales and revenue – either in overall terms or relating to individual products or areas of the business. Sales can be measured in terms of volume, i.e. the number of items that it aims to sell or the number of customers it wants to attract. Alternatively, the value of sales refers to the revenue or income generated by selling goods or services – this is calculated by multiplying the quantity of items sold by the price charged. Sales growth is often seen as particularly important to newly established and expanding firms. Increasing the number of items sold implies that the business is succeeding in either attracting new customers or establishing brand loyalty with existing customers – and, preferably, both! It should also mean that revenues are increasing, unless the sales increase has resulted from a reduction in price. In the short term, a firm may need to sacrifice profit in order to expand its customer base, because of heavy promotional expenditure or the need to keep prices at or below the level charged by competitors. However, opportunities to increase profitability may appear in the long term as brands become well-known and customer loyalty is established, reducing the need for constant promotion and creating scope for increasing prices. Increased production and sales may also result in economies of scale, where unit costs fall as the level of output rises.

- **Market share** – firms often set sales targets in terms of the overall share they wish to capture of the market in which they are operating. Market share is calculated using the following formula:

$$\text{Market share (\%)} = \left( \frac{\text{sales of an individual firm or product}}{\text{total sales in the market}} \right) \times 100$$

Increasing market share requires a business to perform better than its competitors. In expanding markets where the overall level of sales is growing, it implies that the firm is winning a greater proportion of new sales. However, in stable or declining markets where overall sales are unchanged or actually falling, the only way to increase market share is to take existing customers away from competitors. This will require aggressive marketing tactics, including price cuts and heavy advertising, and is almost certain to provoke retaliation from rival firms. The main problem with pursuing this objective is that continual price cuts, sales promotions and expensive advertising campaigns can significantly reduce profits without any guarantees of success in the long run.

- **Market leadership** – a business may decide to pursue the objective of increased market share until it becomes the market leader. This means that the percentage of sales generated by its products is greater than any other firm operating in the market. A firm that is responsible for over 25 per cent of market sales is said to be in a monopoly position, particularly if the market share of other firms is insignificant. Market leadership creates a number of marketing and other advantages. Achieving such a position implies that a firm is meeting customer needs more effectively than rivals, generating promotional benefits and possibly leading to an even greater market share. Being market leader may also give a business more control over the prices it charges its customers, rather than having to follow other firms, as well as giving the firm greater bargaining power to negotiate lower prices with suppliers. Remaining market leader is, however, likely to be a difficult task, as competitors attempt to attract customers away in order to improve their own market share.

- **Brand or product awareness** – the term 'brand' refers to a product, a range of products or a business that has a clear identity, distinguishing it from other competitors within the market. Establishing a strong brand identity can lead to customer loyalty and a greater willingness to pay prices above the market average. However, customers cannot buy products if they do not know they exist in the first place! Firms attempt to increase brand awareness for new products by using a range of promotional techniques, such as advertising, direct mail, free samples and public relations. Simply being aware that a product exists does not automatically lead to its purchase, so any promotion used needs to be persuasive as well as informative. There is always a risk that the expenditure needed to provide this promotional support will not be recouped, if customers are not sufficiently satisfied with the product to make repeat purchases in the future. Nevertheless, creating awareness is an essential first step in generating sales, leading to increased market share in the future.

- **Changing perceptions** – a business may wish to change its public image, or that of its products, for a number of reasons, perhaps as a result of negative publicity, changing social attitudes or the introduction of new legislation.

McDonald's introduced a healthier food range to improve their image

Growing concern about healthy eating and child obesity in the last decade led the world's largest fast food chain, McDonald's, to begin to introduce, in 2004, a range of healthier items to its menus, such as salads, yoghurts and fruit, alongside more traditional burgers, fries and milkshakes. The company has continued to take steps to change public perceptions, printing nutritional information on food packaging and securing a deal with Innocent Drinks in 2007 to sell its fruit-based smoothies in a number of the retailer's UK restaurants.

- **Innovation** – no matter how successful a firm's products are, eventually sales are likely to start to decline as customers' tastes change and competitors produce better alternatives. Ideally, businesses should be developing new products ready for launch onto the market before this happens, giving them time to build up customer awareness before existing products are removed. However, some firms, such as Sony and Apple, focus on developing a reputation for continuous innovation, turning newly invented ideas into commercially successful products ahead of the competition. This is a high-risk strategy, as it requires a long-term commitment and investment, which may not deliver any rewards. Being the first to get to market does not necessarily mean getting it right, leading to customer disappointment giving competitors the opportunity to learn from mistakes and launch their own superior versions. However, sole suppliers of successful new brands are able to charge premium prices, allowing them to generate as much revenue as possible before rivals enter the market.

**Figure 3.1** Possible marketing objectives

## Influences on marketing objectives

Marketing objectives need to be formulated alongside the objectives for the other functional areas of the business, such as operations, finance and human resources. These functional objectives need to complement each other, in order to reflect and support the achievement of the overall mission of the firm. The marketing objectives set by an individual business depend, therefore, on the nature of the business and what it is trying to achieve, given the circumstances faced at any given time.

## Innovation at Dyson

Fifteen years and 15,000 prototypes were required before inventor James Dyson succeeded in putting his first 'bag-less' vacuum on sale in the UK in 1993. Within two years, it had become the number-one seller in the UK and, by 1997, was generating more sales than rivals Hoover and Electrolux combined. By the mid 2000s, Dyson vacuums were being sold worldwide in over 40 countries and were market leaders in the US and Australia, as well as Western Europe. By 2009, the total number of units sold stood at 31 million.

The company, still privately owned by James Dyson, made an operating profit of £89 million

in 2007, up 7 per cent on the previous year. In addition to vacuums, the company has produced a number of other innovative products, including a two-drum washing machine and the award-winning Airblade hand drier. In October 2009, the company revealed its latest invention, the Dyson Air Multiplier Fan, a no-blade desk-top cooling device.

**Source: Reuters, dyson.com**

### Activity

Discuss the main benefits that have resulted from Dyson's innovative approach.

As well as the overall objectives of the firm, typical influences on the choice of marketing objectives include:

- **Resources available to the firm** – marketing activities place demands on a firm's financial and human resources. For example, while rapid sales growth and market leadership may be seen as desirable, smaller businesses may lack the funds or the management expertise required to plan, coordinate and finance the marketing campaigns required for this.
- **Changes in consumer tastes** – given that satisfying consumer requirements lies at the heart of marketing, it makes sense that any changes will have a significant impact on what a firm should realistically set out to achieve. In many cases, this presents opportunities for new products, growth in sales and improving market share. However, those firms who have failed to anticipate and adapt to change will struggle to survive (see case study: Falling popularity of pubs).
- **Competitors' actions** – the presence of competitors in a market can have a significant impact on firms' behaviour. The greater the number of firms, the more fierce the competition is likely to be, making it more difficult to increase market share and placing downward pressure on prices, limiting the scope for increased revenue.
- **Economic conditions** – fluctuations in the level of economic activity – including changes in unemployment, income levels and interest rates – have a huge impact on the level of consumer demand. The onset of recession may well mean that years of steady market growth is brought to a sudden halt, making trading conditions much tougher for the firms within it. In November 2009, after nearly a decade of rapidly rising sales and profits, soft drinks producer, Innocent, announced a pre-tax loss of £11.2 million for 2008. A 20 per cent fall in the value of the company's sales in the first six months of the year was blamed on a decline in consumer spending resulting from the rising cost of fuel bills and food basics, along with the economic downturn.

## Key marketing techniques

Once a business has a clear idea of its objectives, it can begin to put together a strategy in order to attempt to achieve them. A strategy is a plan of the medium-term and long-term activities required to achieve the objectives that have been set. The strategy chosen must also take into account the resources available to the firm and the conditions in the wider market – both opportunities and threats – in order to be realistic. This means that market strategies need to be 'firm-specific'. Even within the same industry, businesses will be pursuing strategies that reflect their individual goals and circumstances. For example, within the hotel industry, the UK's largest chain, Premier Inn, might choose to protect its position as market leader by charging cheaper prices than its main rivals, while up-market hotel chain, Malmaison, may be pursuing further sales growth by improving the quality of its room and restaurant facilities.

---

## Falling popularity of pubs

The effects of the credit crunch, rising utility prices and cheap supermarket alcohol are just a few of the reasons given for the falling popularity of UK public houses. It has been estimated that one in eight pubs across the country will have closed down by 2012. Pub beer sales fell to an all-time low in the summer of 2009, with around 161,000 fewer pints sold between July and September than over the same time during the previous year. Other possible causes of the decline include the ban on smoking in public places, an 8 per cent increase in excise duty on alcohol and poor summer weather.

However, some pub owners are refusing to go down without a fight. The Old Crown at Hesket Newmarket in Cumbria is run as a cooperative – 148 local residents paid £1,500 each for a share in the pub. The Black Swan, forty miles away in Ravenstonedale, has succeeded in increasing trade by opening a shop within the pub, selling gifts and essential goods. Lucy Townsend and Andy Clark own pubs in prime country sport locations in the south of England. A large proportion of their revenue is generated from food sales and operating as a bed and breakfast.

**Source: BBC online**

### Questions

a) Suggest how the marketing objectives of pubs in the UK may have changed in recent years.

b) Identify the main influences that have led to these changes.

Another point to consider is that because strategies are, by nature, long term, managers are required to make decisions based on forecasts and predictions of market conditions in a number of years' time. This means that they should be able to adapt to any future changes – both within and outside the business – that might occur.

## Growth strategies

Growth is a key objective of most new and many established businesses. Not only do larger firms have the potential to generate greater profits, they are also likely to be more secure and able to survive when trading conditions become more difficult. There are a number of possible strategies that a firm can adopt in an attempt to achieve and maintain growth. A useful apporach was of examining these growth strategies is to use an approach developed by Igor Ansoff and known as **Ansoff's Matrix**.

**Figure 3.2** Ansoff's Matrix

Ansoff's Matrix identifies four possible strategies that a firm could adopt. It also indicates the likely level of risk involved with each option, based on the firm's level of market understanding, including the reactions of customers and competitors.

### Market penetration

This involves increasing sales of existing products in existing markets. The risk involved in doing this is usually relatively low, as the business has experience of producing and selling the product already. It should also have established a good understanding of customer needs and market conditions.

There are a number of possible ways of further penetrating the market, including:

- Encouraging existing customers to increase their usage and buy more frequently
- Attracting brand new customers to the market, perhaps by reducing prices to make products more affordable
- Taking existing customers away from competing firms

The third option may be the only one possible in markets that have become saturated, i.e. the scope for further growth is very limited. However, this is likely to require expensive promotional campaigns to persuade customers to change their minds. It is also likely to provoke retaliation from competitors, as they attempt to hold on to their market share.

### Market development

This involves taking existing products and finding new markets in which to sell them. The level of risk involved here is greater than is the case with market penetration, as it involves entering into unfamiliar territory. Nevertheless, a firm might still choose to do this if sales in its existing market have become saturated or the level of competition is eroding profit margins in existing markets. Market development could mean:

- Repositioning products in order to target new market segments or groups of customers
- Selling products in overseas markets

The success of this strategy depends on the extent to which a firm's existing products are able to satisfy the needs of customers in other markets and market segments. Extensive market research can be used to identify differences in customer characteristics and requirements, but even this is not completely reliable as customer needs are complex and subject to change.

### Product development

This involves launching a new product into a market in which a firm already operates. The business can use its knowledge of the market to either adapt existing products or develop new products, in order to meet customer requirements more effectively. Stagnating chocolate sales during the 1990s encouraged a number of confectionery manufacturers to develop new products, closely related to their existing brands. For example, Mars produced ice-cream versions of its Mars, Snickers, Bounty, Twix and Galaxy/Dove brands. It also joined forces with United Biscuits in the UK to develop Galaxy and Milky Way individually-wrapped cakes. Nestlé, on the other hand, developed a

## Growth of Firefly Tonics

Firefly Tonics is a small, London-based company that produces and sells a range of healthy soft drinks made from fruit and herbs. Originally, the company's owners set out to attract busy, 20-something professionals in need of a health fix. However, on the basis of market-research results into product usage, the company now targets a much wider range of customers, including teenagers and people in their 40s and 50s. The company has also expanded into a number of overseas markets, including Germany, Japan, The Middle East and Scandinavia.

**Source: Firefly Tonics**

### Questions

a) Describe the growth strategies deployed by Firefly Tonics.

b) Examine one alternative strategy that the company could employ to continue growth in the future.

range of chocolate desserts, based on its Milkybar, Rolo and Smarties brands.

Despite these notable successes, research suggests that the failure rate associated with new products is incredibly high, at around 80 per cent. The substantial costs of research and development, market research and advertising involved, and the slim chances of success makes this strategy as risky, if not more so, than that of market development.

### Diversification

Involves taking a new product into a new market. This strategy carries the greatest degree of risk – the firm has no experience of the market and little hard evidence that any customers will be sufficiently interested in buying newly developed products. Despite this, firms may be tempted by the chance to generate significant profits, if successful. Finnish company Nokia started out as a tyre manufacturer before moving into mobile phones. By the end of 2007, it held a 40 per cent share of the global mobile handset market, generating sales of €51 billion and profits of €8 billion.

## Survival strategies

Although most firms aim to do much better than simply survive in the long term, there are likely to be points when managers are forced to draw up strategies to avoid business closure. New firms need to build up customer awareness quickly and convert this interest into sales in order to begin providing revenue before start-up finance runs out. However, even long-established businesses are not immune to the threat of failure. During periods of recession, many firms in both the secondary and tertiary sectors of the economy are forced into closure, as unemployment rises and demand begins to fall. After nearly 100 years of trading, Woolworth's was forced into administration at the start of the 2008–9 recession. The company was one of many well-known high-street retailers, including MFI, Whittards of Chelsea and Zavvi, who failed to survive. Other retailers, including Marks and Spencer and Debenhams, were forced to use short-term tactics, such as pre-Christmas sales, in an attempt to attract customers back into their stores. However, the impact of the economic downturn was not spread evenly across all retailers and some actually continued to grow, despite the tough trading conditions. The marketing strategies of discount retailers, Aldi and Lidl, allowed both companies to continue to expand. The key features of these strategies are:

- Selling products, including premium food ranges, at prices that are significantly lower than competitors.
- Selling a limited range of products, in comparison to competitors, in order to benefit from the discounts generated from buying in bulk – both stores have a product range consisting of around 1,000 items, in comparison to an average of 30,000 items stocked by the larger supermarket chains.
- Selling products of a comparable quality to those of competitors, so that they are not seen as cheap but inferior substitutes.

Attracting customers from a range of incomes and combining high quality and low prices to offer maximum value for money, both companies are aiming to establish a strong degree of customer loyalty, increasing their chances of both short-term survival and growth in the long term.

## Branding

**Branding** is a technique used by firms to differentiate themselves and/or their products and make them stand out from those produced by competitors. It is usually done by using a combination of names, slogans, logos, signs and symbols. This makes it easier to identify and remember the brand, and is usually linked to certain aspects of the product, emphasising its key features. In some cases, a number of different products may be sold under one 'family brand', covering a number of different products, such as the Dove range of soaps, bath and shower creams, deodorants and hair-care products produced by Unilever.

Successful brands become instantly recognisable, household names

Building a brand is a key marketing activity, particularly for firms producing products that perform similar, if not identical, functions to many others on the market. Successful branding acts as a major influence on customer-buying behaviour by creating a **brand image**. This highlights features that customers are actively seeking and helps to reduce the amount of time that they need to spend looking for the 'right' product. It also attempts to embody a particular set of beliefs within the brand and convey these to customers.

According to Professor David Jobber, there are seven key aspects to building a successful brand:

- **Quality** – consistent delivery of the 'core benefits' customers expect is essential. Although customers tend to associate a certain level of quality with different brands, they need to be confident that this quality will be delivered whenever the brand is purchased.

- **Positioning** – this refers to how customers view a particular product in relation to others in the market. For example, Sainsbury's food ranges might be perceived by customers as being more up-market than Lidl's, but less up-market than those sold by Marks and Spencer. It is difficult, if not impossible, to produce one brand that satisfies the needs of all of the customers within a market. Effective positioning can help firms to identify a core segment within the market on which to focus. On the other hand, a firm may produce a number of different brands in order to target various market segments and meet customer needs more effectively. Conducting a **brand-mapping** exercise can be useful in helping firms decide which areas of the market to target. This involves choosing key variables, such as price and image, that differentiate brands within a market, and then plotting the position of each product (see Figure 3.3). Mapping identifies areas of the market that are already crowded and others where gaps may exist.

**Figure 3.3** A brand map of UK supermarkets

- **Repositioning** – a firm may decide to change brand positioning to reflect changes in consumer needs or competitors' behaviour. For example, a new, rival product may be positioned next to an existing brand, damaging its market share and reducing its profitability.

- **Communications** – the success of a brand depends heavily – if not wholly – on customer perceptions. Promotional techniques need to be used not just to increase customer awareness, but also to convey and reinforce the brand's image.
- **Credibility** – customers must believe in a brand's ability to deliver its promises, in order to purchase it. If a firm is the first to supply a market it may enjoy what is known as 'first mover advantage', i.e. the chance to win customers and build up their loyalty before the competition arrives. For firms entering an existing market, the credibility that their brands can offer more has to be sufficiently high to tempt customers to change their usual buying behaviour.
- **Long-term perspective** – successful brands seldom appear overnight but result from a great deal of investment – both in terms of effort and finance. Products may need to be repositioned a number of times before the correct place within the market is found. Even once the brand is established, its success can never be taken for granted, as market conditions are certain to change over time.
- **Internal marketing** – successful brands do not only depend on customer credibility – those responsible for managing the brand within the firm need to believe in it too, if they are to convince others to buy it.

Creating a successful brand can lead to a number of potential benefits:

- **Sales growth** – the most popular brands, or brand leaders, are those with the highest share of a market, or a segment within it. This makes it easier for firms to persuade retailers to give up shelf space and stock their products, as well as helping to support the launch of new products in the future.
- **Customer, or brand, loyalty** – this should mean a relatively high rate of repeat purchases, allowing managers to concentrate promotional activity on maintaining brand image, rather than constant price discounts and sales promotions.
- **Greater scope to increase prices** – the ability of customers to associate easily with the qualities of a particular brand is likely to make them less sensitive to price increases, resulting in higher profit margins.

Successful brands have the potential to become global in nature, instantly recognised and sold in markets across the world, and become highly

| 2009 Rank | 2008 Rank | Brand | Country of Origin | Sector | 2009 Brand Value ($m) |
|---|---|---|---|---|---|
| 1 | 1 | Coca Cola | United States | Beverages | 68,734 |
| 2 | 2 | IBM | United States | Computer services | 60,211 |
| 3 | 3 | Microsoft | United States | Computer software | 56,647 |
| 4 | 4 | GE | United States | Diversified | 47,777 |
| 5 | 5 | Nokia | Finland | Consumer electronics | 34,864 |
| 6 | 8 | McDonald's | United States | Restaurants | 32,275 |
| 7 | 10 | Google | United States | Internet services | 31,980 |
| 8 | 6 | Toyota | Japan | Automotive | 31,330 |
| 9 | 7 | Intel | United States | Computer hardware | 30,636 |
| 10 | 9 | Disney | United States | Media | 28,447 |

**Figure 3.4** Interbrand/Businessweek's Top 10 Global brands 2008

valuable to the companies that own them. In September 2009, multinational corporation, Unilever, paid $1.88 billion (around £1.14 billion) for the Sara Lee personal care brands, including Radox, Sanex and Brylcreem, in order to increase its presence in western Europe. The value or power of a brand – known as its **brand equity** – comes from the degree of name recognition and customer loyalty it enjoys, and the extent to which this translates into higher sales volumes and profit margins, relative to rival brands.

## Brand extension

**Brand extension** is a marketing strategy that involves using a name of an existing successful brand to launch new products, or new versions of existing products. For example, a number of fashion designers, such as Gucci and Armani, have used their luxury image to launch a number of up-market product lines, including perfumes, watches and children's clothes. The process is sometimes referred to as brand stretching if the new product is being launched into an unrelated market, such as the extension of the easyJet brand into the cinema and online movie rental market. One of the key benefits of using brand extension successfully is that it reduces the resources required to generate new product awareness. New product launches are expensive and high risk but, if customers already recognise and trust the existing brand, they are more likely to be willing to try any products associated with it. However, brand extension also involves risks. If new products are unsuccessful, this may dilute the image and value of the original brand, damaging sales and profits.

## Relationship marketing

Traditionally, the focus of marketing activities has tended to be narrow and short term, concerned with attracting as many new customers as possible, in order to win sales in the present, with little or no consideration of the future. This approach is often referred to as **transactional marketing**. An alternative approach, known as **relationship marketing**, acknowledges the importance of retaining customers in the long term. Regular contact with customers is used to establish and build a lasting one-to-one relationship, whether or not a sale is generated on every occasion. Over time, the firm can build up an in-depth understanding of customers's tastes and preferences, and the ongoing nature of the relationship means that it is better able to recognise when these needs change. This information can be stored on databases and used to build up detailed customer profiles, which can be used to identify the most likely purchasers of different products. Customers can also be kept informed of any special offers or promotions that may be of particular interest to them.

## Limitations and constraints on marketing

The pressure to succeed, often in the face of fierce competition from other firms, could tempt marketing managers to behave irresponsibly, exaggerating or even making false claims about their products in order to achieve their objectives. This has led to the Government passing a number of laws over the years, in order to provide protection for the consumer. Government legislation is one of a number of constraints on business activity, all of which are designed to encourage them to behave responsibly.

## Legal constraints

### Sale of Goods Act (1979)

This requires traders to sell goods as they are described and of a satisfactory quality. Quality is considered to be satisfactory if, at the time of purchase, goods are fit for purpose, free of any minor defects (including appearance), durable and safe to use. Under this law, it is the seller of the goods, not the manufacturer, who is responsible for the condition of the goods, although the onus is on the purchaser to prove that the goods were faulty at the time of purchase. Consumers can request a refund, repair or replacement within a 'reasonable time', which is not defined and depends on the nature of the goods in question. The Sale of Goods Act was amended by the Sale and Supply of Goods Act 1994 and the Sale and Supply of Goods to Consumers Regulations in 2002.

### The Consumer Protection from Unfair Trading Regulations (CPRs)

These regulations came into force in the UK in May 2008, in order to bring UK law in line with the European Union's Unfair Commercial Practices Directive (UCPD). The purpose of the UCPD is to harmonise consumer protection legislation across all EU member states, making it more straightforward for businesses based in one country to market their products to consumers across the EU. Under the CPRs, a trader may face action against it if it misleads, behaves aggressively or otherwise acts unfairly to consumers before, during or after a purchase is made. Misleading or aggressive practices are defined as any behaviour that is likely to cause the average consumer to take a decision different to that which was originally intended. Examples of this include:

- Falsely stating that a product will only be available for a limited amount of time, in order to pressurise customers into making an immediate purchase.
- Offering prizes as part of promotional competitions that are not made available, so that the participants have no chance of winning them.
- Advertising free gifts and then telling consumers they need to pay an additional fee in order to obtain them.

In order to avoid duplication, the CPRs replace a number of older UK laws, including most of the Trades Descriptions Act (1968) and parts of the Consumer Protection Act (1987).

### Consumer Credit Acts (1974 and 2006)

This legislation is designed to regulate credit agreements and offer protection to consumers who use credit to purchase products. It requires most businesses that sell goods or services on credit to be licensed by the Office of Fair Trading (OFT). Under the law, it is a criminal offence, punishable by fine or imprisonment, to trade without a licence. Firms must ensure that consumers have a full understanding of any agreements that they enter into, providing them with a clear statement of any terms and conditions, including the procedure to be adopted in the event of termination, early settlement or default. Customers must also be provided with information relating to any interest or other charges, an explanation of how the Annual Percentage Rate (APR) is calculated and annual statements relating to the credit agreements.

## Consumer Protection (Distance Selling) Regulations

The Distance Selling Regulations (DSRs) came into force in October 2000 and were further amended in April 2005. They were implemented in response to an EU directive aimed at providing additional rights to consumers buying at a distance and encouraging greater confidence in buying products via this method. Distance selling includes situations where products are sold to consumers without face-to-face contact via telephone, mail order, the internet, interactive TV, fax or text messaging. The purpose of the regulations is to ensure that any traders who engage in distance selling as part of the normal course of their business meet certain basic requirements. Consumers must be given clear information in writing about products before they buy, including:

- a detailed description of the goods and services on offer
- methods of payment
- delivery arrangements
- sources of supply
- rights to cancellation.

Consumers are also entitled to a cooling-off period of seven working days to cancel any agreements made.

## Data Protection Act (1998)

The purpose of this law is to regulate how personal information held by businesses on individuals – including actual and potential customers – is used. Under the Act, businesses must ensure that any personal information they are storing is:

- processed fairly and lawfully
- processed in line with the individual's rights
- processed for one or more purposes specified at the time of collection
- accurate and, where necessary, kept up-to-date
- adequate, relevant and not excessive
- securely protected against unauthorised use
- kept no longer than is necessary
- not transferred outside the European Economic Area (EEA) unless adequate protection is provided.

The Act also gives individuals a number of rights, including the right of access to any data being held on them by firms, the right to have any inaccuracies corrected and the right to refuse information being used for the purposes of direct marketing. The 1998 Act replaced the earlier 1984 Data Protection Act and was designed to bring the UK in line with EU directives on data protection.

## Voluntary constraints

A number of organisations and rules have been created over the years to supplement the law and encourage a greater degree of self-regulation of individuals and firms responsible involved in advertising and promotion. The Advertising Standards Authority (ASA) is an independent body

---

# Fines for banks who mis-sell

In October 2008, the Alliance and Leicester Bank was fined a record £7 million by the Financial Services Authority (FSA) for mis-selling Payment Protection Insurance (PPI). PPI is often sold when people take out mortgages, loans and credit cards to cover repayments if the policyholder is made redundant or unable to work. According to the FSA, during a two-year period between 2005 and 2007, the bank's sales staff had repeatedly failed to explain clearly that the inclusion of PPI was optional when loans had been taken out, despite the fact that many customer groups, including the self-employed and people over 65 years old, are often not covered by the insurance. They also uncovered evidence suggesting that staff had been trained to pressurise any customers who questioned it.

**Source: Which?**

## Activity

a) Explain why the behaviour of the Alliance and Leicester Bank resulted in it being fined.

b) Discuss one other potential consequence for the bank resulting from the publicity generated by the FSA action.

which acts as the watchdog of the advertising industry in the UK. Its purpose is to ensure that all marketing communications are 'legal, decent, honest and truthful', encouraging them to compete fairly and behave in a socially responsible manner. Rules designed to encourage this responsible behaviour are set out in two main **Codes of Practice**, which are endorsed and administered by the ASA:

- **The British Code of Advertising, Sales Promotion and Direct Marketing** – written by the Committee of Advertising Practice, and referred to as the CAP, these rules relate to non-broadcast advertisements, such as those appearing in newspapers and magazines, brochures and leaflets, cinema and video commercials.
- **BCAP** – drawn up by the Broadcast Committee of Advertising Practice and covers TV and radio advertising.

The ASA helps firms, advertising agencies and other bodies to produce promotional materials that comply with the standards outlined by the Codes. It is also responsible for investigating complaints and, although it does not have the power to fine those in breach of the standards, it can refer cases to the Office of Fair Trading. In addition, the negative publicity generated by ASA rulings can do a great deal of damage to firms who refuse to comply, possibly leading to a loss of customers, suppliers and distribution.

## Pressure groups and consumerism

The term **consumerism** refers to the growing importance and power of consumers in recent decades. This trend has led to the formation of a number of pressure groups and other organisations set up to protect and promote consumer interests A pressure group is an organisation made up of people with a common interest who come together to pursue that interest. Pressure groups can have a significant impact on business behaviour, persuading – or, in many cases, forcing – them to adapt product ranges, change suppliers or adopt more sustainable sources of materials, by generating publicity and lobbying politicians. Which? is the largest consumer body in the UK, with over 650,000 members. It is a registered charity that has campaigned for over 50 years to influence the marketing activities of various businesses. However, the extent to which any pressure groups can influence business activity depends on customers' reactions to any campaigns that are launched.

## Acceptable language

The language used in promotional material has the power to engage and persuade customers, attracting sales and creating household brand names, but also the potential to cause offence and create negative publicity. Whether language is acceptable or not depends to a large extent on the product and the target market. For example, the controversy caused by fashion clothing chain, French Connection, when it launched its notorious FCUK logo in 1999, helped it to capture a large slice of the youth market and transform the fortunes of the business. By 2004, however, the logo had lost its notoriety, had ceased to shock and was dropped from the company's advertising campaigns.

## Key terms

**Ansoff's Matrix** An approach that identifies four possible growth strategies that a firm could adopt – market penetration, product development, market development and diversification. It also indicates the likely level of risk involved with each option.

**Brand equity** The value or power of a brand, relative to rival brands, coming from the degree of name recognition and customer loyalty it enjoys, and the extent to which this translates into higher sales volumes and profit margins.

**Brand extension** Involves using a name of an existing successful brand to launch new products, or new versions of existing products.

**Branding** A technique used by firms to differentiate products using a combination of names, slogans, logos, signs and symbols, in order to make them stand out from competitors.

**Codes of Practice** Rules designed to encourage firms to adopt and maintain responsible behaviour when advertising goods and services.

**Consumerism** A term referring to the growing importance and power of consumers in recent decades.

**Innovation** The process of turning newly invented ideas into commercially successful products.

**Market** Any situation where buyers and sellers come together to trade goods or services, either at a specific location, such as a shop on the high street, or via a form of communication, such as the internet.

**Market leadership** A business, or product, with the highest percentage of sales within a given market.

**Market share** The percentage of total sales in a market accounted for by one product or firm.

**Marketing** The business function that is concerned with understanding the customer and attempting to ensure that a firm's products match customer needs as closely as possible in order to satisfy them.

**Marketing objectives** The targets or goals set by a firm relating to its overall corporate objectives and acting as a basis for marketing strategies.

**Profit maximisation** The objective of attempting to make as much profit as possible, in the shortest possible time.

## Q Re-cap questions

1  What is the purpose of marketing?
2  Explain what is meant by the term 'marketing orientated'.
3  Outline two likely objectives of a) a private sector business and b) a public sector organisation.
4  Explain the link between a corporate objective and a marketing objective.
5  Identify three possible marketing objectives for discount supermarket chain, Aldi.
6  Explain, using examples, the difference between market penetration and market development.
7  Outline two other possible growth strategies that a business could adopt.
8  Identify two points in time when a business might be more concerned with survival than making a profit.
9  Briefly explain the purpose of branding.
10 Examine two benefits of creating a successful brand for a manufacturer of organic cereals.
11 Explain what is meant by the term 'brand extension'.
12 Analyse two benefits for internet and telephone bank, First Direct, from using relationship marketing.
13 Identify three legal constraints on the marketing activities of UK firms.
14 Briefly describe the role of the Advertising Standards Agency (ASA).
15 Explain what is meant by the term consumerism.

# Grading tips

**P1** Describe how marketing techniques are used to market products in two organisations

You only need to choose one product from each organisation (although you can do more if you wish), so think carefully before you choose. You need to be able to clearly identify the marketing techniques used, e.g. branding, writing about the technique in context by giving examples that relate to each organisation's products.

**M1** Compare marketing techniques used in marketing products in two organisations

Comparing requires you to find both similarities and differences in the marketing techniques used by your chosen organisation. For example, the name of each company may be important to the product's brand, or products may have individual identities. You may find it helpful to produce a summary of these similarities and differences in a table.

**D1** Evaluate the effectiveness of the use of techniques in marketing products in one organisation

Demonstrating evaluation involves 'weighing up the evidence' but remember that you only need to do this for one organisation! You could do this by prioritising the main benefits and drawbacks of the techniques used by the organisation – some benefits/ drawbacks will be more significant than others. Carry out research and produce data as evidence for your arguments. You must give a clear judgement about which techniques were most effective, based on this evidence.

**P2** Describe the limitations and constraints of marketing

Write about both legal and voluntary limitations, giving examples to highlight exactly how the organisations' marketing activities have been constrained.

See page 118 for suggestions for Assignments for Unit 3.

# Part 2: Using market research and marketing planning

## Introduction to market research

Effective marketing requires accurate, up-to-date and comprehensive information. Managers need information on customer requirements, the level of market demand, the activities of competitors and the state of the economy. This information has to be updated on a regular basis as markets are subject to change, which can be sudden and unexpected. **Market research** is the process of gathering and analysing data on the market. By finding out more about customers' opinions, a firm can build up a more detailed understanding of customer needs. The customer satisfaction generated by existing products can be measured and monitored over time, so that any problems can be recognised and the necessary changes can be made. Not only can market research provide data relating to the current state of the market, it can also be used to forecast trends and anticipate customer needs in the future. This allows firms to adjust their product range appropriately, in order to continue to meet customer demand and compete effectively against rivals within the market. Although market research cannot eliminate the risk of business failure, it can improve the quality of decision-making and, therefore, increase a firm's chances of success.

## Primary and secondary information

The information required by businesses can be collected by using two types of research – primary research and secondary research:

### Primary research

**Primary**, or field, **research** involves gathering data for the first time and for a specific purpose. It is collected in a way that is appropriate to the firm in question, its products and its customers. Primary research can be time consuming and expensive to conduct, but is necessary if the firm requires up-to-date information that relates directly to its needs.

Some of the most commonly used methods for gathering primary data are as follows:

- **Observation** – this involves watching and recording people's behaviour, e.g., counting the number of shoppers that stop and look at a point-of-sale display in a supermarket on a particular day.
- **Experiments** – can be used by researchers to measure the reaction of customers to changes in certain aspects of a product. For example, a new flavour of breakfast cereal might be put on sale in a particular region of the UK by its manufacturer in order to test customer responses, before going ahead with a national launch.
- **Focus groups** – consist of a small number of people who have been invited to discuss their opinions and attitudes on a given product or topic. A trained group leader or moderator is responsible for managing the discussion, encouraging all participants to contribute and preventing any individual from dominating the discussion.
- **Surveys** – are used to obtain market research from large numbers of people, known as respondents. There are a number of different ways of doing this, including face-to-face or telephone interviews, postal or internet surveys. The method chosen depends on the type and amount of data required, as well as the cost, speed and ease of obtaining it.

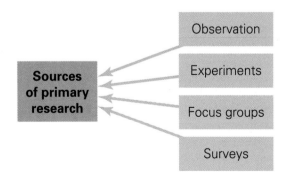

**Figure 3.5** Sources of primary research

## Primary research at Innocent Drinks

Innocent Drinks has possibly been the UK's most talked about business success story of the twenty-first century thus far. Set up in the late 1990s by university friends Richard Reed, Adam Balon and

Jon Wright, the company's sales have grown at a phenomenal rate. By 2007, it had captured more than a 70 per cent share of the UK smoothie market, generating sales of over £130 million.

However, the original business plan was based on rather quirky primary research carried out by the company's co-owners at a London music festival in 1998. Richard, Adam and Jon invested £500 of their own money in the ingredients needed to produce smoothies to sell at the festival. A big sign was erected saying, 'Do you think we should give up our day jobs to make these smoothies?'. Two bins were place underneath the signs, one labelled 'Yes' and the other labelled 'No' and customers were encouraged to vote by placing empty smoothie bottles in the appropriate bin. By the end of the weekend, the result was overwhelmingly encouraging.

**Source: Innocent website**

### Activities

a) Explain why the data gathering carried out by Innocent was an example of primary research.

b) Suggest two other possible ways that Innocent could carry out primary research in the UK soft drinks market.

## Secondary research

**Secondary**, or desk, **research** collects data that already exists. It has been collected by someone else for a different purpose. The sources of such data may come from within the firm itself, such as sales invoices or the results of past customer satisfaction surveys, which is known as **internal secondary data**. This source of data is cheap and quick to access, and may be particularly valuable as it cannot be easily accessed by rival firms. However, it may be out of date and of little relevance for new projects. In such cases, the results of research carried out by other organisations, such as other companies, specialist market research agencies and the

Government, could be used. This is known as **external secondary data**.

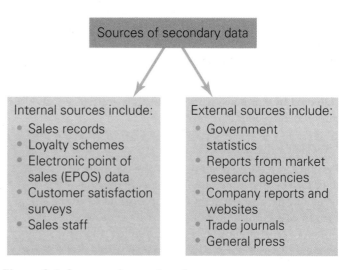

**Figure 3.6** Sources of secondary data

The advantages and disadvantages of secondary data vary from source to source. For instance, a great deal of economic data contained in government documents and websites is free to access and is updated regularly but, as it is available to everyone, is unlikely to give a business an edge over its competitors. Reports compiled by market researchers, such as Mintel, contain up-to-date and detailed analysis of markets and sectors, but can be expensive to obtain.

## Primary or secondary research?

The decision as to whether to use primary or secondary research depends on the firm concerned and the decisions it needs to make. Any firm planning to conduct market research should certainly consider using secondary data, as there is little point in spending time and money carrying out primary data if suitable data already exists and can be accessed more quickly and cheaply. Generally, only larger businesses have the expertise and finance to carry out large scale primary research that gives accurate and unbiased results. A firm can also waste valuable time updating information which does not significantly improve the quality of decisions, but the resulting delay may mean that market opportunities are missed. However, data from secondary research needs to be treated with caution. As it will have been collected for another purpose, it may not be relevant to a firm's specific needs. In addition, the market in which a firm operates may be affected by sudden or frequent change. In such cases, a firm should be able to justify committing resources, in order to carry out primary research. Collecting primary data does not have to be expensive and is more likely to produce up-to-date information on customers and the market.

## Quantitative and qualitative information

Before carrying out either primary or secondary market research, a firm needs to consider the nature of the information it wishes to collect. Quantitative research involves gathering large quantities of numerical data that can be subjected to statistical analysis. It is concerned with finding 'hard', factual data, such as market size and growth, a firm's individual market share and customer preferences, rather than what may have caused this to happen. Quantitative data is usually collected via the use of techniques such as observation or surveys and is based on a carefully chosen sample.

Qualitative data, on the other hand, is concerned with finding out 'soft' information, such as customer attitudes, beliefs and opinions. Its purpose is to understand consumer behaviour by identifying possible reasons or causes. The techniques used to gather qualitative data are those more likely to encourage more detailed responses from those being interviewed, such as interviews and focus groups.

## Limitations of market research

Market research has the potential to dramatically improve the quality of a firm's decision-making, allowing it to achieve or maintain a competitive edge over rivals. However, it may not, in fact, be possible to realise these benefits for a number of reasons:

- **Validity of the data collected** – the value of any data collected by market research depends on its accuracy. Market conditions can change very quickly, meaning that even recently gathered data becomes out-of-date and irrelevant. The methods used to collect data can also

| Quantitative research might ask … | Qualitative research might ask … |
| --- | --- |
| • How many new cars were sold in the UK during 2009?<br>• What has been the percentage growth in sales of organic food in the last ten years?<br>• What were the top ten tourist destinations within the European Union during 2008?<br>• How many times have you been to watch a film at the cinema in the last three months?<br>• Have you ever ordered books, CDs or DVDs online from Amazon? | • What is the main reason you would buy a new, rather than a second-hand, car?<br>• Why do you buy more organic food products than you did ten years ago?<br>• Why do you prefer to go abroad for your holidays, rather than spending them in the UK?<br>• In what ways could your local cinema improve its customer service?<br>• Why do you prefer to order goods online, rather than buying them in-store? |

**Table 3.1** The differences between qualitative and quantitative research

compromise its quality. For example, research may be based on unrepresentative samples or interviewers and questionnaires may be biased, pushing respondents towards certain answers.

- **Cost effectiveness** – gathering and analysing data can be a very expensive process. Smaller businesses are unlikely to have the financial resources required to conduct extensive primary research themselves or to pay others to do so on their behalf, regardless of the potential benefits. In all situations, the costs of market research must be considered in relation to the benefits, even by organisations with large marketing budgets. If the benefits of constantly updating market intelligence are negligible, then to do so would not be seen as cost effective.

- **Time constraints** – in an ideal world, firms would have the time to build up a detailed profile of their customers and their needs. However, in reality, managers are often forced to make decisions based on incomplete information, in order to seize opportunities ahead of rival firms. Being the first to market can create a significant competitive edge, justifying the risk of acting now, rather than later.

- **Legal and ethical constraints** – the existence of laws such as the Data Protection Act (1988) places restrictions on the way that any data collected or held by market researchers can be used. For example, it must be made clear to research participants why the data is being collected and their consent must be obtained (see Unit 3.1). In addition, organisations such as the Market Research Society set out guidelines to encourage firms to behave in an ethical manner when gathering data from members of the public.

## Marketing planning

The purpose of marketing planning is to identify a firm's objectives and the strategy required to achieve them. Once the business is clear as to the direction in which it wants to go, it needs to decide exactly how it intends to get there. It also needs to put in place an alternative course of action, should its original strategies fail to deliver.

Firms can benefit from the marketing planning process in a number of ways:

- **It encourages firms to think ahead** – any current success enjoyed in the present has a better chance of continuing in the future if managers consider what could change within the market and how to respond.

- **It provides direction** – setting out the firm's objectives and strategies in a clear and well-communicated plan should help to coordinate the different areas of the business and ensure that everyone is working towards the same goals.

- **It makes it easier to monitor and evaluate performance** – progress can be measured by comparing actual performance to targets, allowing for adjustments to strategies if necessary.

## The marketing planning process

There are a number of key stages that must be carried out in order to create an effective marketing plan:

1. **Conduct a marketing audit**

   Change is a constant feature of business environment. It is, therefore, essential, that a firm attempts to establish a detailed picture of the state of the market before deciding on any targets or goals. An **external audit** involves an analysis of market conditions. It examines a number of different factors, including:

- Total market size, growth and trends over time
- Key competitors, their market share, product range and prices
- Consumer opinions and buying habits
- Image/reputation of different firms within the market
- Promotional activities used by different firms within the market
- The range of distribution channels available
- The state of the economy and key influences on demand.

A useful tool to use when analysing the environment is the **PESTLE** framework. This encourages managers to use market research to identify any possible **political, economic, social, technological, legal** and **environmental** influences on business performance. These may present opportunities that the firm can build upon, or threats that could damage it if it fails to respond (see Table 3.2).

| External influence | Explanation | Examples |
|---|---|---|
| Political | The impact on businesses of the activities and policies of local and national governments, as well as that of international organisations such as the Economic Union. | • The decision to nationalise privately owned companies, e.g. the Northern Rock Bank in February 2008.<br>• Possible relaxing or tightening controls on immigration from non-EU countries.<br>• The effects of the continuing conflict and presence of British troops in Afghanistan. |
| Economic | The impact on businesses of changes in the level of economic activity or in key economic variables. | • Changes in the level of consumer spending.<br>• Changes in interest rates or exchange rates.<br>• Changes in the level of inflation or unemployment. |
| Social | The impact on businesss of changing attitudes and the size and structure of the population. | • Increasing numbers of people over retirement age within the population.<br>• Increasing numbers of people from different ethnic groups within the UK.<br>• Growing concerns about the effects of smoking, alcohol and drug abuse. |
| Technological | The impact on businesses of newly invented products and processes. | • The development of new markets and the decline of existing ones – e.g. video replaced by DVD.<br>• Improvements in the speed and quality of global communications.<br>• Reduction in production costs leading to cheaper goods and services. |
| Legal | The impact on businesses caused by the introduction of new laws or changes to existing legislation. | • The introduction of the National Minimum Wage in the UK in 1999.<br>• The possible introduction of minimum prices for alcohol.<br>• The introduction of the Consumer Protection Distance Selling Regulations in 2000 and 2005. |
| Environmental | The impact of concerns about effects of business activity, such as pollution and congestion, on the wider environment. | • The impact of climate change on the farming industry.<br>• Falling levels of fossil fuels, such as oil and gas, forcing up the price of power.<br>• Consumer pressure on firms to reduce waste and switch to more energy-efficient methods of production. |

**Table 3.2** The PESTLE framework

Managers also need to have a clear picture of the firm's recent performance and the resources that are likely to be available to it, in order to make the planning process effective. An **internal audit** seeks to establish:

- The level of sales, costs and profits generated (in total and/or by product, branch or area)
- The effectiveness of marketing resources, including staff expertise and the quality of communications – within the marketing department, with other departments within the business and with the wider environment
- The appropriateness of the current marketing mix in terms of meeting marketing objectives and satisfying the needs of the customer groups being targeted.

Once managers have examined the market using the PESTLE framework, they may then carry out a **SWOT analysis**. This is a technique that evaluates an individual product or proposition, a part of the business or an entire firm in terms of its internal **strengths** and **weaknesses**, as well as its external **opportunities** and **threats**.

Like PESTLE, SWOT analysis encourages managers to think about both the firm's present situation but also what might happen in the future. For example, if managers are aware of possible opportunities in the future, they can develop and implement plans that fully exploit these opportunities, as and when they arise. Similarly, action can be taken to deal with weaknesses and threats, before they become a serious danger to the firm's success. Within the external environment, factors may act as an opportunity for some firms, but a threat to others. For example, growing fears about the effects of high-fat foods on childhood obesity could act as a threat to a crisps manufacturer, such as Walkers, but an opportunity for a manufacturer of healthy snacks.

2. **Establish objectives**

Once managers have a clear picture of the current position of the business and the nature of the environment in which it operates, they can begin to set specific targets or objectives for the marketing function. Marketing objectives are designed to achieve a firm's overall, corporate objectives by setting particular goals for marketing activities. This helps to provide the marketing team with a clear direction and a benchmark against which to measure actual performance.

Setting vague or open-ended objectives, such as improving performance, is, however, of little help. In order to be effective, marketing objectives should be **SMART**, i.e., specific, measurable, achievable, resourced and timed. They need, for example, to concentrate on a specific

| **Strengths** (internal) | **Weaknesses** (internal) |
|---|---|
| • Strong brands and unique selling points (USPs)<br>• Competitive prices<br>• Consistently high quality<br>• Reputation for innovation<br>• Effective distribution network<br>• High levels of staff expertise and motivation<br>• High levels of profitability and/or liquidity<br>• Prime location | • Weak brands and undifferentiated products<br>• Uncompetitive prices<br>• Quality problems<br>• Lack of new product development<br>• Ineffective distribution<br>• Lack of staff expertise or poor motivation<br>• Low profitability and/or cash-flow problems<br>• Poor location |
| **Opportunities** (external) | **Threats** (external) |
| • Market growth<br>• Access to new markets<br>• Growth in the domestic economy<br>• Favourable exchange rate<br>• Competitor weaknesses<br>• Technological developments<br>• Demographic changes<br>• Social and environmental issues | • Declining markets<br>• Increasing levels of trade protection<br>• Economic downturn/recession<br>• Unfavourable exchange rate<br>• Increasing competition<br>• Technological developments<br>• Demographic changes<br>• Social and environmental issues |

**Table 3.3** SWOT analysis

area of performance, such as sales volume, revenue or market share. Alternatively, they may focus on increasing brand awareness, changing customer perceptions or developing new products. It also makes it easier to measure and compare progress if objectives are expressed in numerical terms, such as a given level or percentage increase, and are given a deadline. Although objectives need to be challenging in order to drive the business forward, they need to be achievable and appropriately resourced, to give the firm a realistic chance of success.

|  | Explanation/example |
|---|---|
| Specific | Worded precisely and relating to a clear area of performance, e.g. sales growth, market share. |
| Measurable | Expressed quantitatively, e.g. increase sales of Product X by 10 per cent. |
| Achievable | Although they should be challenging, they should also be realistic, given the time scale, the firm's resources and the conditions within the market. |
| Resourced | This includes providing sufficient finance and staff with appropriate skills and experience to devise and implement marketing activities. |
| Timed | Providing a deadline, e.g. to increase sales of Product X by 10 per cent within 2 years. |

**Table 3.4** The SMART approach to setting objectives

3. **Devise a strategy**

A marketing **strategy** is a plan of the medium-term and long-term activities required to achieve the marketing objectives that have been set and fill the gap between where the business is now and where it wants to be. Marketing strategies vary from business to business, reflecting their differing aims and the conditions that they face. Typically, however, the strategy will include details for the intended product mix, sales support, advertising and sales promotion.

The strategy chosen must also take into account the resources, including financial resources available to the firm. The marketing budget outlines the finance available to achieve marketing objectives. The size of the marketing budget depends on the overall resources available within the business and the ability of marketing managers to justify their planned expenditure. However, if the budget is too small, this may well reduce the effectiveness of the strategy, damaging the performance of the business.

4. **Implement strategy**

Once a marketing strategy has been developed, it needs to be carefully put into action. Marketing **tactics** are the short-term activities that are used to keep the strategy on course, assuming the objectives set are realistic. They might include using special introductory offers, mid- or end-of-season sales, or advertising campaigns. Progress needs to be reviewed on a regular basis to ensure that targets are achieved within the set budget and deadlines. Regular monitoring allows the business to take corrective action quickly if problems occur internally or if the external environment changes. Sticking rigidly to a plan that is no longer relevant is likely to be just as damaging to the firm in the long term as not bothering to plan at all, so managers have to be prepared to be flexible.

5. **Evaluation**

The final stage in the **marketing plan** involves reviewing its impact by actual performance against the objectives that were set at the beginning of the process. Market research is used to gather the data needed to complete an analysis of actual sales, costs and profits,

**Figure 3.7** A model of marketing planning

in relation to the budgeted figures. This is a vital part of the marketing plan as it not only identifies differences – or variances – between budget and actual figures, it also attempts to identify why these differences occurred. The results of this analysis can then be used to inform future marketing planning.

## Key terms

**Experiments** A method of primary research involving attempting to recreate market conditions in order to test the reaction of customers

**Focus groups** A method of primary research, involving a small number of people who have been invited to discuss their opinions and attitudes on a given product or topic, under the guidance of a trained mediator

**Market research** The collection, processing and analysis of data relating to a firm's market

**Marketing audit** An investigation into the marketing resources controlled by a firm, its relationship with customers and competitors and the general state of the market

**Marketing plan** A report containing details of a firm's marketing objectives and strategy

**Observation** A primary research technique involving watching and recording the behaviour of customers

**PESTLE** A framework for analysing a firm's external environment, identifying possible political, economic, social, technological, legal and environmental influences

**Primary research** Research involving the collection of new data for the first time and for a specific purpose

**Qualitative research** Is concerned with finding out 'soft' information, such as customer attitudes, beliefs and opinions, using techniques such as focus groups

**Quantitative research** Involves gathering large quantities of numerical data that can be subjected to statistical analysis, using techniques such as large-scale surveys

**Secondary research** Research that involves collecting data that already exists and was collected by someone else for a different purpose. It can include internal data from within the firm or external data from sources outside the firm

**SMART objectives** Targets that are specific, measurable, achievable, resourced and timed in order to improve their effectiveness

**Strategy** A medium- to long-term plan, designed to achieve a firm's objectives

**SWOT analysis** A technique that evaluates an individual product or proposition, a part of the business or an entire firm in terms of its internal strengths and weaknesses, as well as its external opportunities and threats

**Surveys** Primary research carried out on a large sample of people, usually based around a questionnaire

**Tactics** Short-term activities designed to support the achievement of a firm's long-term strategy

## Re-cap questions

1  Briefly explain why firms carry out market research.
2  Explain two benefits of carrying out regular market research for a firm designing computer games software.
3  Using examples, explain the difference between quantitative and qualitative data.
4  Describe the difference between primary research and secondary research.
5  Compare the benefits of using a survey and a focus group to collect primary data.
6  Describe the difference between internal secondary research and external secondary research.
7  Describe two limitations of market research.

8 Briefly explain the purpose of marketing planning.

9 Outline two benefits of carrying out marketing planning for a new business.

10 Identify the main stages in the marketing planning process.

11 Explain what a marketing audit sets out to do.

12 How is the PESTLE framework used by businesses?

13 What is the purpose of a SWOT analysis?

14 Explain the difference between a marketing strategy and a marketing tactic.

15 Explain why evaluation is an important stage of the marketing planning process.

## Grading tips

| **P3** Describe how a selected organisation uses marketing research to contribute to the development of its marketing plans | **M2** Explain the limitations of marketing research used to contribute to the development of a selected organisation's marketing plans | **D2** Make justified recommendations for improving the validity of the marketing research used to contribute to the development of a selected organisation's marketing plans |
|---|---|---|
| This can be any organisation, including your school or college, commercial business or a not-for-profit enterprise, but you need to be able to also obtain information on its marketing planning process, so choose carefully. | This requires you to expand in some detail on the limitations you identify, not just saying what they were but how they affected the development of the marketing plan. Giving relevant examples will help you to do this. | Don't just make a list of possible ways of improving the quality of marketing research carried out by your organisation. You need to give reasons why your recommendations would lead to improvements and also consider why other ways might not be suitable. For example, commissioning a MINTEL report may produce better-quality data, but the cost prohibits smaller organisations from doing so. |
| **P4** Use marketing research for marketing planning | | |
| Try to use a range of marketing research data. This does not have to be data collected yourself but you must show how it is used in the planning process. | | |

See page 118 for suggestions for Assignments for Unit 3.

# Part 3: Targeting customer groups

## Consumer markets

The terms **customer** and **consumer** are often used interchangeably, but they do not mean the same thing. A customer is the individual (or business) who buys a product. The consumer is the individual (or business) who actually uses it. Kellogg's customers include supermarket chain Sainsbury's, which buys the cereals it manufactures to sell to its own customers – the people who shop in its stores. Even these shoppers may not be the final consumers of the products they buy – for example, parents may buy items, such as children's cereals, shampoos and soft drinks, for younger members of the family that they do not intend to use themselves. Understanding and influencing both customers and consumers is, therefore, important for businesses, as both groups determine whether or not products are bought. Manufacturers must be aware of supermarket requirements, in terms of packaging and storage, delivery items and price. Both manufacturers and retailers need to be aware of the needs of the people who buy products and those that actually use them. Children may prefer cereals that are chocolate flavoured and contain lots of sugar, whereas parents are more likely to be interested in those containing healthier ingredients. Somehow, the often contrasting needs of both customers and consumers need to be addressed, if products are to be successful.

In industrial markets, firms are likely to deal with professional **buyers** when attempting to sell their goods and services. These are people who are employed by firms to purchase products on their behalf. Unlike most consumers, they have a great deal of expertise and market knowledge. It is their responsibility to obtain the best deal for their employer, in terms of price, quality, or dependability of supplies, in order to support the firm's operations.

## Market segmentation in consumer markets

**Consumer markets** are made up of individuals and households buying goods and services for personal consumption, either by themselves or by others. Businesses who sell products directly to consumers, rather than other businesses, are often referred to as **B2C** firms. The range of goods and services produced for these markets is huge, ranging from baked beans to sports cars, chocolate bars to holidays homes. Individual consumer needs can vary considerably, increasing the challenges faced by businesses in trying to satisfy them effectively.

However, in many cases it is possible to identify groups of consumers who share certain characteristics that lead to similar wants and needs. These groups, or **segments**, within the market allow firms to develop goods and services that aim to meet customer needs more effectively than would be the case with the 'one size fits all' approach of standardised products. Firms can develop a range of products appealing to customers of different ages, earning different incomes or pursuing different lifestyles. Alternatively, they can concentrate on specific segments within the overall market.

Satisfying customer needs more effectively helps to create brand loyalty and gives greater scope for charging premium prices, increasing market share and generating higher levels of profits. Segmentation also allows businesses to deploy market communications more effectively. Spreading advertising and other promotional activities across too wide an audience is costly and runs the risk of missing key customers. Dividing up the market means that specific consumer groups can be reached more frequently and at a lower cost.

## Types of market segmentation

Firms divide markets into different segments on the basis of specific customer characteristics that influence purchasing behaviour. The main types of segmentation include:

- **Geographic segmentation** – this involves splitting up a market into groups based on customer location. Firms need to be aware of regional differences in consumer tastes, particularly those that trade on an international scale, so the key product features can be adjusted accordingly.
- **Demographic segmentation** – this involves dividing the market into groups based on factors such as gender, age, occupation, income,

## Research findings identify new retiree types

Research from consumer research agency Experian has signaled a dramatic change in the holiday destination choices of the UK's growing pensioner population. The growing life expectancy of people within this demographic segment has increased dramatically between 1945 to 2009 – from 63 to 78 for men and from 68 to 82 for women. This means that, by 2019, there will be 2.4 million more people over 65 than is the case today. Changes in Experian's Mosaic database shows that more and more older people are choosing to retire to inland market towns, historic cities and major cultural destinations, rather than the coastal destinations that were traditionally popular.

As a result of its research, Experian identified the following new groups of retiree:

- **Beachcombers** – middle-class retirees opting for smaller riverside or coastal communities, rather than the major coastal resorts.
- **Balcony downsizers** – well-off but frail people in their 70s and 80s, living in privately owned, purpose-built apartments requiring minimal maintenance.
- **Golden retirement** – wealthy pensioners choosing to live busy lives and inhabit prestigious retirement communities.
- **Bungalow quietude** – retirees on relatively low incomes, often living in bungalows in areas that are unattractive to younger families.
- **Country-loving elders** – wealthy pensioners living in former farms or older properties in quiet villages and market towns.

**Source: The Daily Telegraph**

### Questions

a) On what criteria is the latest Experian segmentation based?

b) Explain how UK businesses could use this information to satisfy customer needs more effectively.

## Choosing the correct target groups

Once the criteria for market segmentation have been chosen and applied, a firm must choose which ones to target. In order to do so, it might consider:

- **Accessibility** – although the potential market may be large, the cost of generating sales may be very high if customers are spread over too wide an area. There may be trade barriers erected by governments to restrict the level of international trade. There may also be legal constraints on firms entering certain markets; for example, mobile phone operators, such as Orange, O2 and T-Mobile, have to hold licences in order to be able to provide services in the UK.

- **Profitability** – the market segment chosen has to be sustainable. This means that it must contain enough customers to generate profit levels that are in line with company objectives.

- **Prospects for future growth** – although a segment may be too small to be profitable, there may be sufficient evidence of growth in the future to justify targeting it now. An early presence in a market can give a firm a head start over rivals in building up brand awareness and consumer loyalty, which may prove invaluable as the market grows and more competitors are drawn in.

- **Ability to serve the customer group** – once customer needs have been identified, a firm must be able to produce goods or services to satisfy these needs but also make a profit in the long run.

- **Corporate objectives** – the segments targeted must also fit in with the overall targets of the business. For example, a small business may be able to profitably exploit a market segment containing a small number of customers. However, a large or expanding firm may not be interested in the low levels of sales involved.

There are a number of targeting strategies that a firm can adopt:

- **Niche/concentration marketing** – involves concentrating on targeting one, well-defined group of customers within the overall market. Small firms often choose to target market niches as their relatively low overheads mean that they can make profits without producing in large volumes. However, the potential for significant growth in sales is unlikely, restricting the possibility of benefiting from economies of scale.
- **Mass/undifferentiated marketing** – involves producing and selling a single product to the whole market. This strategy depends on customer needs being similar, if not identical. Producers can reduce unit costs by producing in large volumes, and pass these cost savings on to customers in the form of lower prices.
- **Differentiated marketing** – involves producing a range of products that are tailored to meet the needs of the customers in different segments, creating greater levels of customer satisfaction across the market as a whole.

## Operating in business or industrial markets

A large number of businesses do not deal directly with consumers. Instead they sell goods or services to other businesses, either directly or online. This type of firm is often referred to as **B2B** (business to business). Examples could include a producer selling goods on to a wholesaler, or to a retailer. Alternatively, it could involve supplying industrial equipment or providing legal, accountancy or IT services. There are likely to be a number of stages in the supply chain, as raw materials are transformed into finished goods before being distributed to the final consumer. This means that the volume of B2B transactions is much higher than B2C transactions within the economy.

In business, the process of acquiring the right quantity of goods or services, at the best possible price and quality, is known as procurement.

The group of employees within a firm who have an influence, either directly or indirectly, on purchasing decisions is referred to as the **Decision Making Unit (DMU)**. The DMU is not only likely to include the firm's buyers, but also other employees with an interest in the goods or services being purchased. Major purchases will involve input from production managers and technical staff, the finance department and senior management.

## Market segmentation in business or industrial markets

Like consumer markets, **business markets** can be segmented by firms in order to identify and satisfy customer needs more effectively. The segmentation criteria used by an individual business depends, to a large extent, on the products being supplied and the nature of the markets within which it operates. Nevertheless, the following are commonly used:

- **Company size** – the size of a business can affect the way it purchases goods and services. Large companies are likely to have specialist purchasing or procurement departments, made up of staff with skills in assessing the benefits of different supply sources, as well as clear policies regarding the way in which supplies should be purchased. They are more likely to deal directly with the manufacturer, due to the large volumes involved, and force different suppliers to bid for contracts, in order to push prices down. Small suppliers are likely to be less informed and obtain supplies from distributors or even retailers.
- **Value of contracts** – some large manufacturers may find it more cost effective to deal with customers placing contracts over a certain value. Large orders shift stocks more quickly, generate economies of scale and can reduce the costs of distribution.
- **Product** – in many cases, a firm's customers will be dictated by the products that they produce. For example, a car components producer may concentrate on producing supplies for the car manufacturing industry, but adjust its products to meet the different needs of customers.
- **Industry** – the needs of business customers in different sectors, such as agriculture, manufacturing, retail and finance, may also vary significantly. For example, a law firm may specialise in dealing with one particular sector, or set up different divisions that focus on a particular area.

- **Region** – significant variations in the needs of businesses in different locations – within a country or across the world – may make it beneficial for a firm to segment the market on a geographical basis. It could decide to focus on one particular segment or, alternatively, produce a range of products to match different customer needs.

- **Public/private sector** – the Government is a major employer and provider of services, such as health, defence and education. Firms that supply goods or services to the Government are known as B2G businesses (business to Government). Some firms may choose to sell exclusively to government bodies. Others may adopt a different approach when dealing with the public and private sectors.

## Key terms

**ACORN** Stands for A Classification of Residential Neighbourhoods – a system of household classification that is commonly used in geo-demographic segmentation

**B2B** Stands for business to business, that is, a firm that sells to other firms, rather than directly to consumers

**B2C** Stands for business to consumer, that is, a firm that sells directly to consumers

**Buyer** An employee responsible for carrying out the purchase of supplies and services on behalf of a business

**Business market** A market consisting of firms that trade with each other, rather than selling to consumers

**Consumer** The final user of a product

**Consumer market** A market made up of individuals and households buying goods and services for personal consumption, either by themselves or by others

**Customer** The individual or firm purchasing a good or service from another firm

**Decision Making Unit (DMU)** A group of employees within a firm who have an influence, either directly or indirectly, on purchasing decisions

**Demographic segmentation** A method of market segmentation which involves dividing the market into groups based on factors such as gender, age, occupation, income, education, religion or ethnic background

**Differentiated marketing** A strategy which involves producing a range of products that are tailored to meet the needs of the customers in different segments

**Geo-demographic segmentation** A combination of geographic and demographic segmentation, based on the belief that similar households in certain locations have similar attitudes and lifestyles leading to the same (or similar) buying habits

**Geographic segmentation** A method of market segmentation based on splitting a market into groups based on customer location

**Market segmentation** The process of dividing a market into different groups or segments of consumers who share certain characteristics that lead to similar wants and needs

**Mass marketing** A strategy which depends on customer needs being similar, if not identical, so that one standardised product can be produced and sold to the whole market

**MOSAIC** Another household classification system used in geo-demographic segmentation

**Niche marketing** A strategy which involves concentrating on targeting one, well-defined group of customers within the overall market

**Psychographic segmentation** A method of market segmentation which involves dividing customers into groups based on opinions, interests and lifestyle

## Re-cap questions

1  Using examples, explain the difference between a customer and a consumer.

2  What is the difference between a B2B firm and a B2C firm?

3  Explain what is meant by a market segment.

4  Describe one benefit of market segmentation for the consumer and the producer of a product.

5  Outline what is involved in the following types of segmentation: a) geographic segmentation; b) demographic segmentation; c) psychographic segmentation.

6  Explain why geo-demographic segmentation is seen as a more sophisticated approach to market segmentation.

7  What is ACORN and how is it used?

8  Give two reasons why a large market segment may prove to be inaccessible.

9  Explain why a business might continue to target a segment of a market, even though it is currently unprofitable.

10  Outline three other criteria that a business might consider when deciding how to segment a market.

11  Explain what is meant by niche or concentration marketing.

12  Outline the main differences between an undifferentiated and a differentiated marketing strategy.

13  Explain the difference between a consumer and a buyer.

14  Within a business, what is the purpose of a Decision Making Unit (DMU) and who does it consist of?

15  State four possible ways of segmenting a business or industrial market.

## Grading tips

|  **Explain how and why groups of customers are targeted for selected products** This requires you to look at a minimum of six different target groups and look at products in both consumer and business markets. | | |
|---|---|---|

See page 118 for suggestions for Assignments for Unit 3.

# Part 4: Developing a coherent marketing mix

## Introduction to the marketing mix

A product's marketing mix refers to the key elements that influence the customer's decision to purchase it. The decision as to whether to choose one product over another – or even to go ahead and buy anything at all – can be a complex process. Do the perceived benefits on offer justify paying the price charged? Can the customer afford to pay the price? To what extent is the decision to buy based on **advertising** or other promotional activities? How easy is it to obtain the product once the choice has been made? The answers to these questions will differ considerably from customer to customer. Nevertheless, all of these possible influences can be brought together under four main areas, known as the four 'Ps' – product, price, place and promotion:

**Figure 3.8** The marketing mix

- **Product** – not just features and functions, but also a number of other aspects such as design, appearance, quality, reliability and durability. The right combination of these factors makes the product appeal to customers and stand out from the competition.
- **Price** – choosing the right price is not necessarily about charging as little as possible. Although value for money is an important influence on the buying decision, price is often seen as an indicator of quality, making customers suspicious of prices that are significantly below those of competitors.
- **Place** – involves ensuring that customers are able to access goods or services as easily as possible. Well-designed and carefully priced products may still fail to sell if they are not available when and where customers wish to buy them.
- **Promotion** – is concerned with informing customers, both actual and potential, about the various aspects of a product and/or the firm responsible for it, in an attempt to persuade them to buy it. A wide range of promotional methods exist – the challenge is to choose the most effective combination that creates the right image for the product and reaches the customer groups being targeted.

The elements chosen to make up the marketing mix for a product depend, to a large extent, on what the marketing department is trying to achieve. As a general objective, the marketing mix is chosen to satisfy the needs, requirements and aspirations of customers within the groups or segments being targeted. More specific objectives will lead to greater emphasis being placed on certain elements within the mix. For example:

- **Developing new goods or services** – the focus here is most likely to be on product design and features, attempting to differentiate new products from those that already exist.
- **Supporting brand building** – greater emphasis may well be placed on promotion, in order to influence customer perceptions and develop a specific brand image, supported by a careful choice of distribution channels.
- **Increasing market share** – this may rely on a pricing strategy that undercuts competitors and/or aggressive advertising and sales promotion to tempt customers away from rivals.

Whatever a business is attempting to achieve, it must create a marketing mix that is coherent and integrated. This means that the various elements chosen must complement and support each other in order to be effective. It could be argued that product is the most important element of the mix because, without a viable product, success in the long term is highly unlikely. However, many seemingly good product ideas, resulting from extensive market research, still fail because of insufficient or inappropriate support from the other elements

## The marketing mix of Jimmy Choo

Jimmy Choo is an upmarket brand of women's shoes, handbags and accessories. The exclusive product designs are manufactured in Italy. The brand's upmarket image is reflected in the premium prices charged, typically ranging from £400 for a pair of shoes to over £1,000 for a handbag. Promotional methods have been carefully chosen to build the 'luxury, lifestyle brand'. Jimmy Choo shoes became internationally famous after featuring on popular television series, *Sex in the City*. The brand has subsequently been supported by regular endorsements from famous public figures such as actress Jennifer Anniston, singer Kylie Minogue and even US First Lady Michelle Obama. The designer collections are sold through a limited number of prestigious retailers, as well as the brand's own boutiques.

The decision, therefore, to team up with high-street clothes chain, H&M, came as a surprise to many in the fashion retail industry. The collaboration resulted in a range of Jimmy Choo-designed footwear, ranging in price from £30 to £170, as well as a limited collection of women's wear and handbags. The products went on sale in 200 H&M stores across the world in November 2009. Although the move was a big hit with H&M shoppers, it raised concerns that the position of the Jimmy Choo brand at the luxury end of the fashion market could be seriously damaged.

**Source: www.thisismoney.co.uk**

### Activity

a) Describe the key features of the marketing mix for Jimmy Choo.

b) Do you think that selling a limited collection of Jimmy Choo designs was a good idea for i) the Jimmy Choo brand; ii) H&M? Give reasons for your answers.

of the marketing mix. For instance, the manufacturer of a new, exclusive brand of perfume is more likely to succeed in generating revenue by selling it at a premium price in a limited number of upmarket **retailers**, than by attempting to reach as many customers as possible through a national chain of discount stores.

## Product

The features of a product – either a good or a service – will vary considerably, depending on the type of market in which it is located and the customer needs that it is attempting to satisfy. For example, within the car market, major manufacturers such as Toyota, VW and Renault-Nissan produce a range of cars, some of which focus on affordability and fuel economy, others of which concentrate on style and speed. Individual models within the product range are designed to satisfy the specific needs of different customer segments.

The basic model design can be further adapted with additional features to generate even higher levels of customer satisfaction.

Despite these differences, there are a number of key features that combine to produce a successful product design:

- **Core benefits** – these are the basic functions that the product is designed to perform. Most goods and services provide physical benefits – a car provides transport; a restaurant provides meals. However, psychological benefits may also be provided by the product's brand image; for example, a meal at Heston Blumenthal's innovative restaurant, The Fat Duck, is designed to do much more than satisfy customers' hunger!

- **Convenience** – not only do products need to provide the functions they promise, they also need to be user-friendly, in terms of being easy to operate, store and transport.

- **Safety** – firms must ensure that product designs conform to safety legislation. Product recalls as a result of safety concerns can be a costly exercise in terms of lost sales and compensation. A reputation for high standards of safety can become part of a product's USP (unique selling point), helping to differentiate it from the competition. For example, low-cost airline, Ryanair, makes frequent use of its excellent safety record in its marketing literature.
- **Reliability** – customers need to be confident that the products they buy will perform consistently over a reasonable period of time. Consistent reliability can help to give products a competitive edge over cheaper rivals.
- **Durability** – this is likely to vary from product to product; for example, it would be unreasonable to expect a cheap, disposable Biro to last as long as a Mont Blanc fountain pen, costing £300. Nevertheless, products need to meet or, preferably, exceed customer expectations in order to avoid customer dissatisfaction.
- **Aesthetics** – this refers to the extent to which product styling appeals to customers. The popularity of Apple products, such as the iPod or MacBook, comes from their slick appearance as well as the functions they perform.

## The product life cycle

The product life cycle is a technique that firms can use to analyse the position of existing products, in order to discover how well they are performing. It illustrates how the sales of a product change over time and implies that all products pass through similar stages from their development to the point at which they are eventually withdrawn from the market. These stages are development, introduction, growth, maturity and decline. Just like the human life cycle, however, the length of the product life cycle – and the various stages within it – can vary considerably. Some products enjoy rapid initial growth before sales then fall just as quickly; others grow at a steadier pace, and seemingly remain on sale forever.

- **The development stage** – new ideas are generated, developed and tested with the help of extensive market research. The majority of new product ideas do not make it beyond this initial stage. Those that do may be subject to years of research and development before they are released into the market. Product prototypes may be created and field trials carried out to test potential customer reactions and make final adjustments (or take the decision to abandon the project). This is a particularly expensive, and therefore risky, time for a firm. The product has not yet gone on sale so is generating no revenue, but large sums of money have to be invested to cover development costs and also begin to build up customer awareness as the launch date approaches. This means that the firm is incurring high costs, with no guarantees that the new product will be successful or that it will ever become profitable.
- **The introduction stage** – this stage begins with the launch of the new product into its market. Although the firm may have already taken steps to create customer awareness, there is still likely to be a great deal of promotional activity, aimed at increasing this awareness further and persuading customers to change their spending habits. Retailers may also need to be persuaded to stock the brand, which may be difficult to do if this involves using up space currently occupied by successful products. Sales are likely to be relatively low but growing, if the response from the market is favourable. However, the revenues generated are unlikely to exceed costs at this stage, especially given that low production volumes are likely to result in relatively high unit costs. The firm will also need to carry out market research to test customers' reactions, modify the product if necessary and possibly take the decision to withdraw it.

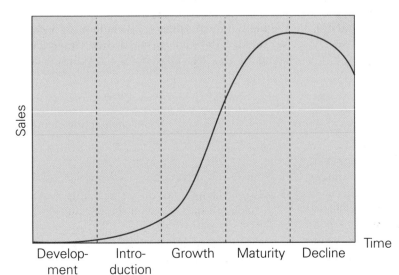

**Figure 3.9** The product life cycle

- **The growth stage** – this stage is characterised by an increasingly rapid rate of sales growth as customer awareness becomes more widespread. More and more new customers join those who have already tried the product in the past and have started to make repeat purchases. Growing sales makes it easier to persuade retailers to make more room on their shelves and the producer will need to concentrate on ensuring that supply keeps up with demand. Competing products may have already started to enter the market, so pricing and promotional strategies may need adjusting to ensure continuing growth in market share.

- **The maturity stage** – the product has now been established in the market for some time. The rate of sales increase begins to slow down, as all those customers who are likely to buy the product are already doing so, and some may even be attracted away by similar products launched by competitors. Although the product may reach saturation point, with little chance of further growth in its present format, it is likely to still be profitable. High production volumes generate economies of scale, reducing unit costs, and widespread product awareness reduces the need for heavy advertising.

- **The decline stage** – eventually, sales will begin to decline as competition becomes too intense and customers are attracted to rival products. Firms may decide to withdraw any marketing support but continue to supply the product, in order to 'milk' any remaining profits and satisfy remaining customers until replacements are ready to be launched.

Firms often attempt to prevent their products from going into terminal decline by using a number of possible **extension strategies**. Minor

## Brompton Bikes

Folding bikes may not seem like an obvious 'must have' fashion accessory. However, sales at Brompton Bikes have grown by 25 per cent, thanks to attempts by the company to offer customers more choice and style. Although the basic design remains the same, there are now over 140 different frame and handlebar colours to choose from, including flamingo pink, cornflower blue and apple green. The inclusion of different parts means that there are up to 4 million possible design permutations. The starting price for the bikes is £600. The nature of demand for the bikes, once the preserve of middle-aged eccentric men, has changed significantly in recent years – between 35–40 per cent of customers are women and the average age of riders has now dropped below 40.

The company uses skilled employees to produce around 100 bikes a day at its factory in Kew, West London. Each finished bike carries 16 stamps to identify it with the craftsmen responsible for building it. The factory is working at full capacity but there is still a ten-week delivery waiting time, although further investment is planned. Annual sales of £10 million in a market worth £450 million, means that Brompton's share of the UK bike market remains small. However, production rose from 7,000 in 2002 to 25,000 in 2009 – a figure which is expected to double in the next few years.

**Source: guardian.co.uk**

### Activity

a) Describe the key features of Brompton Bikes.

b) What evidence is there to suggest that Brompton Bikes are still in the growth stage of the product life cycle? How could the company make use of this information in their marketing strategies?

adjustments can be made to the product to create a 'new and improved' design; its price may be reduced; or new promotional offers can be introduced. These tactics may revive sales and encourage further growth or simply slow down sales decline and postpone a product's eventual withdrawal from the market. Either way, by prolonging the length of the product life cycle, they can generate the profits required to fund investment in further new product development.

The product life cycle cannot be used to forecast the length of time any product will remain on the market or even when it will pass from one stage to another. Often, it is only possible to recognise the different stages of the product life cycle once the product has passed through them, particularly as a slowdown or fall in sales may prove to be temporary. However, it highlights the fact that the **marketing mix** will need to be adjusted as the product passes through the cycle, in order to prolong its life for as long as possible.

## Price

Price is a key determinant of demand. For most consumers, it has an important influence on the decision to purchase. If the price of a product is set relatively high, many customers who would like to buy a product may not be able to afford to do so. Affordability is likely to become even more significant during periods of recession, when unemployment – or the threat of it – forces people to cut back on spending. Alternatively, customers may decide that the price does not represent value for money, having considered the benefits that the product has to offer. However, price sensitivity appears to vary considerably between different customers and products. A number of price comparison websites, such as confused.com and uswitch.com, have been set up in recent years to help consumers find the cheapest deals for insurance, personal loans and other financial services products where the degree of differentiation is relatively low. Customers are usually much more willing to pay premium prices for goods and services with a strong brand image, such as designer clothes and accessories, top hotels and restaurants, because of the psychological benefits derived from their exclusive nature. The extent to which customer demand responds to changes in price is measured by **price elasticity**. If demand is relatively **price elastic**, customers tend to be relatively sensitive to changes in price: if customers are relatively insensitive to price changes, demand is described as being **price inelastic**.

## Pricing strategies

A firm's pricing strategy outlines the level of prices it plans to charge for its products over the medium to long term. The strategy chosen is determined by a number of factors, including the firm's objectives, the other elements within the product's marketing mix and the stage it has reached in the product life cycle. The main pricing strategies include:

- **Premium pricing** – involves charging a price well above the market average for products with unique features, differentiating it from rivals. The price is used as part of an integrated marketing mix indicating high quality, luxury and exclusivity.
- **Economy pricing** – involves charging prices well below the market average for basic, no-frills products aimed at price-sensitive customers. Budget airlines, including Ryanair and easyJet, and supermarket own-brands, such as value ranges produced by Tesco's and Morrison's, are good examples of this type of strategy.
- **Price skimming** – this strategy also involves the launch of new products but uses a high price to enter the market. Its success depends on the product's appeal to early adopters, i.e. consumers who are willing to pay in order to be among the first to try a product, and is often

**Figure 3.10** Pricing strategies

used for the launch of new games consoles and other groundbreaking electronic goods. Supply is likely to be limited initially in order to re-inforce the 'exclusive' image of the product, but the high profit margins generated help to cover product development costs. Initially high prices can also be reduced as initial customer segments are exhausted, or as competitors launch rival products.

- **Penetration pricing** – this is a new prod-uct strategy using low prices initially to enter the market and increase market share. Rapid growth in sales can help to generate the revenue required to recover the product's development costs. There may be scope to in-crease prices in the longer term, once the product has become established and a degree of brand loyalty has developed.

- **Psychological pricing** – the purpose of this strategy is to appeal to customers' emotional reactions, rather than their rational decision-making. For example, pricing a product at £9.99, rather than £10.00, can create the ini-tial impression of being much better value for money than a saving of 1p. Another aspect of this approach is that raising prices can actually increase demand, as consumers often see price as a reflection of quality.

- **Captive product pricing** – this strategy is often used when the main product being sold is accompanied by one or more complemen-tary products. For example, when deciding to buy a new printer, customers tend to focus on its cost, rather than that of the ink cartridges it requires. The price of the main product can, therefore, be set relatively low, in order to en-courage sales, in the knowledge that revenue can be recouped over the long term by charg-ing a relatively high price for complements.

- **Product line pricing** – where a firm produces a range of products that are sold at different prices to reflect their features or benefits, from the lowest to the highest prices, for example, the prices of Apple's range of iPods reflect the features and storage available.

## Place

This element of the marketing mix is concerned with the distribution of products. The ways in which goods and services are distributed to cus-tomers can have a significant impact on their success in the marketplace. The **channel of dis-tribution** describes how a product passes from its original producer to the end user, the consumer. This can be a simple transfer from producer to consumer, as is the case with many service pro-viders, some manufacturers of consumer goods, such as Dell Computers, and producers of indus-trial goods. Alternatively, the chain of distribution can comprise a number of stages, involving inter-mediaries such as **wholesalers** and **retailers** (see Figure 3.11 below):

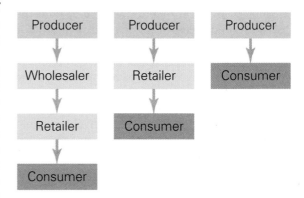

**Figure 3.11** Stages in the chain of distribution

## Vertu mobiles

Vertu is a producer of mobile phones – with a dif-ference. Handsets made by the company, a sub-sidiary of Nokia, are produced from a variety of precious metals, with sapphire faces and leather sides. The internal mechanisms used are of the highest quality and can be upgraded so that own-ers can make use of the latest technology. Prices start at £3,700 for a stainless steel model and rise to £15,000 for the top-of-the-range platinum version. The phones are aimed at the luxury and business segments of the mobile market and the company has repeatedly denied any intention to introduce any other, more affordable models.

### Activities

a) What pricing strategy is used by Vertu (justify your answer)?

b) Explain why customers would be willing to pay £15,000 for a mobile phone when a wide range of cheaper models are available on the market.

In recent years, increasing ownership of personal computers and developments such as faster broadband speeds has led to a steady increase in online sales. Dealing directly online can offer a number of benefits, creating access to a global customer base at a relatively low cost and eliminating the price mark-ups added on by intermediaries. In many cases, however, consumers still prefer the option of a physical presence to examine a choice of different brands before making their purchases, so manufacturers will supply their goods to appropriate intermediaries. They may choose to sell direct to the retailers that best suit the product's image. In 2002, entrepreneur Will Chase launched gourmet snack range Tyrrells Potato Chips through a range of carefully chosen retailers, including a network of hotels, gastropubs and independent retailers, supermarket chain Waitrose, and up-market department stores Fortnum & Mason, Harvey Nicholls and Selfridges, all of which were carefully chosen to support the brand's gourmet image. Chase was even prepared to sue supermarket giant, Tesco, when, in 2006, it began to sell bags of its potato chips at reduced prices without permission in some of its stores, threatening to damage the image of the brand.

Manufacturers may also sell their goods on to wholesalers in order to maximise their market exposure. Although the UK grocery market is dominated by supermarket giants such as Tesco, Asda and Sainsbury, a large number of tiny independent retailers continue to operate on a local basis. While it may only be cost effective for grocery manufacturers to supply directly to the large supermarket chains, they can also sell in bulk to wholesalers who, in turn, can supply in smaller quantities to independent stores, maximising market coverage.

There are a number of factors that can affect the choice of distribution channel, including:

- **Cost** – the shorter the chain of distribution, the greater the scope for charging low prices. At each stage in the chain of distribution, a mark-up will be added by the intermediary involved, increasing the final price paid by the consumer, without adding anything to the revenues generated by the producer. Ultimately, however, it may be cheaper for the producer to pass on the distribution of products to intermediaries, rather than take on the responsibility and the expense of getting goods to consumers directly.
- **Control over the product** – as soon as a manufacturer passes on goods to a wholesaler or retailer, it risks losing control over the prices that are charged or the way it is promoted. The producer may, therefore, choose to sell directly to the public, either online or by setting up its own chain of retail outlets, in order to avoid any damage to the brand's image.
- **Market exposure** – mass-produced goods, including well-known brands such as Walker's crisps and Cadbury's, need access to mass markets. In such cases, the producer is likely to use a number of different distribution channels, in order to reach as many customers as possible. It would simply not be cost effective for the producers of such goods to deliver to every retailer in the country. Therefore, goods are delivered directly to the depots of large supermarket chains, such as Sainsbury's and Asda, while wholesalers are used to pass goods on to smaller retailers, such as newsagents and independent convenience stores.

## Promotion

The purpose of promotion is to communicate with the customer. This communication is designed to:

- Inform customers – about product features, availability, special offers, and so on
- Persuade customers – to try brand new products, to switch from competitors, and so on.

There are a number of ways in which a business can communicate with its customers and it is unlikely to rely on using one method. The combination of methods chosen is referred to as the **promotional mix**.

The main elements that a firm can use to make up its promotional mix include **advertising**, **personal selling**, **public relations** and **sales promotion**.

**Figure 3.12** Components of the promotional mix

## Moonpig

**moonpig.com**

Moonpig is a fast-growing online greeting cards service. For £2.99 plus postage, customers choose from a range of more than 10,000 designs, licensed from other designers, and personalise them by adding their own captions or downloading pictures. Orders placed before 2 p.m. weekends are dispatched the same day. The company also delivers bouquets of flowers. The popularity of the concept has increased rapidly since the Moonpig website was first launched in 2000.

Although the company now advertises on daytime TV and on street hoardings, most of its new business is generated by word-of-mouth recommendations, or by card recipients placing orders. In the first year of trading, the company distributed 40,000 cards. By the summer of 2009, Moonpig had over 2.5 million customers, generating sales worth £20.9 million and profits of £6.7 million. The company's busiest day to date was in February 2009, when a record 99,000 orders were dispatched. Originally, the cards were produced at Moonpig's main offices in London and delivered to the post office by company founder and owner, Nick Jenkins. Production now takes place at the company factory in Guernsey and cards are shipped using trucks that are specially designed to cope with the island's narrow lanes.

**Source: times online, www.moonpig.com**

### Activities

a) Describe the chain of distribution used by Moonpig.

b) Discuss the importance of distribution for a greeting cards business such as Moonpig.

## Advertising

This is a paid for method of communication which can take many forms. Advertising media include television, radio, cinema, newspapers, magazines, billboards and the internet. Marketing managers need to decide which media are likely to be most effective in reaching the target audience. For example, magazines are usually aimed at particular segments, in terms of gender, age, interests and lifestyle. The growth in popularity of satellite television has, to some extent, reduced the effectiveness of TV advertising in reaching huge audiences, although it remains a popular method for promoting mass-marketed products. The creation of a number of channels aimed specifically at children, such as Nickelodeon and Disney, has also allowed the producers of children's goods and services to target younger audiences very effectively. The continuing growth in use of the internet has made it an increasingly important advertising medium. The relatively cheap cost of setting up and maintaining a website has allowed even the smallest of businesses to reach global markets. Search engines, such as Google and Yahoo, set up to help people navigate the internet more effectively, finance their operations via paid advertising. The popularity of social networking sites has also turned them into an important channel for marketing communications, with the two leading sites, Facebook and MySpace, attracting well over 100 million visitors each month.

## Personal selling

This involves sales teams making direct contact with customers, either face-to-face, via the telephone or the internet. It can be used where the customer base is relatively small, making it cost effective for direct contact with individuals to take place. It is also more likely in situations where customer needs are complex and differ from one to the other, or where technical aspects of the good or service require explanation from trained sales staff. Personal selling is a common promotional activity in industrial goods markets and in the sale of some services. For example, companies selling double glazing or solar heating will need to discuss individual customers' needs. The sale of financial services to both individual consumers and businesses also tends to involve a great deal of personal contact to avoid the risk of mis-selling and the possibility of fines for the company involved.

## Public relations

This involves attempting to send out a particular message or generate an overall image, without having to pay for advertising. It includes activities such as issuing press releases or the sponsorship of events and sports teams, in order to raise its profile and, hopefully, generate favourable publicity.

## Sales promotion

This involves using a range of techniques, such as price cuts, competitions and special offers such as 'Buy One, Get One Free' (BOGOF). These are short-term tactics designed to boost demand and shift stocks more quickly. In particular, they aim to attract new customers by tempting them with special offers in the hope that they continue to buy in the longer term.

The promotional mix not only varies from firm to firm but from product to product. It has to be designed to fit in with the firm's overall marketing strategy, in order to be effective. The main objective for Pepsi when launching a new soft drinks range on to the market will be increasing customer awareness by using TV, magazine and billboard advertising. Alternatively, cereals manufacturer, Kelloggs, frequently uses sales promotion techniques, such as competitions and money-off coupons to revitalise demand and extend the life of its long-established brands.

| Promotional method | Advantages | Disadvantages |
|---|---|---|
| Advertising | • Potential to reach mass audiences<br>• Can be tailored to some extent to reach certain customer groups | • Can be very expensive<br>• One-way communication, so difficult to tell if the message has reached the right people |
| Personal selling | • Allows specific customers to be targeted directly<br>• Interaction means that individual customer needs can be assessed and appropriate information given | • Can be expensive if the customer base is large<br>• Potentially high annoyance factor from cold-calling |
| Sales promotion | • Can lead to sudden and significant increases in sales<br>• Effects can be identified easily | • Effects may be short-term, lasting only as long as the promotion<br>• Customers may stock up on goods while the promotion lasts, causing sales to fall when the promotion ends |
| Public relations | • Can raise the profile of a product or business relatively cheaply | • The message passed on to the public is out of the control of the firm concerned |

**Table 3.7** Methods of promotion – advantages and disadvantages

## A new generation of BOGOFs

In late 2009, two of the UK's leading supermarket chains, Tesco and Sainsbury, announced plans to launch variations of the traditional 'Buy One, Get One Free' or BOGOF sales promotion. The moves have been made in response to criticisms about the levels of waste generated by such offers. For years, grocery shoppers have been frustrated by BOGOF promotions that give away food and other perishable products, which are then wasted because they go off before they can be used. Tesco's 'Buy One, Get One Free Later' (BOGOFL) initiative on perishable items involves customers receiving a voucher so that free goods can be reclaimed at a later date. Under the Sainsbury's promotion, known as 'Buy Now, Free Next Time' customers receive a coupon giving them two weeks to claim a second item. Both initiatives were seen as a response to a government report, published in August 2009, which criticised retailers for using marketing initiatives to encourage consumers into buying goods they do not need.

**Source: Telegraph, Marketing Week**

## Questions

a) Explain two benefits of using sales promotions, such as BOGOFs, for retailers.

b) Do you think that supermarket customers will prefer the new BOGOFL promotions (justify your answers).

---

The main influences on the mix of activities chosen to promote a product include:

- **The nature of the product** – as already noted, huge markets need to be created and maintained to absorb goods that are produced on a large scale. The manufacturers of consumer durables, food and drinks products use a combination of TV, newspaper and other advertising to build up brands and increase public awareness. Specialist sales teams will deal with intermediaries, such as wholesalers and retailers, to ensure that they give sufficient exposure to their brands in store. A producer of industrial goods is unlikely, however, to require mass-marketing techniques, and employ expert sales staff to manage clients on a one-to-one basis.

- **The cost of the promotion** – some companies, such as Dell and Apple, have the resources to spend millions each year on advertising. Others, such as small or new firms, may be limited to adverts in Yellow Pages or leafleting houses in the local area. Marketing budgets act as a constraint on the marketing activities of all firms, regardless of size. Marketing activities also need to be cost effective. Advertising on television at peak, mid-evening weekday slots may appear expensive, but can allow a firm to convey its message to an audience of millions of people.

- **The size of the market** – firms attempting to communicate with large numbers of customers require mass media, such as TV, newspapers and the internet. Firms with smaller numbers of customers, or those targeting particular niches, may find mass-media methods costly and ineffective. They may prefer to use a more direct approach, perhaps advertising in specialist magazines or journals, or using personal selling to attract customers.

# Key terms

**Advertising** A paid-for method of communication which can take many forms, including television, radio, cinema, newspaper, magazine, billboard and internet

**Captive product pricing** A strategy used when the main product being sold is accompanied by one or more complementary products, so that setting a low price for the main product can be counter-balanced by charging high prices for complements

**Channel of distribution** The route showing how a product passes from its original producer to the end user, the consumer

**Economy pricing** A pricing strategy involving charging prices well below the market average for basic, no-frills products aimed at price sensitive customers

**Extension strategy** Making relatively minor adjustments to the product to prevent it from entering the decline stage of the product life cycle, for example creating a 'new and improved' design, reducing the price or introducing new promotional offers

**Marketing mix** The key elements that influence the customer's decision to purchase it, which comprise product, price, promotion and place

**Penetration pricing** This is a new product strategy using low prices initially to enter the market and increase market share

**Personal selling** Involves sales teams making direct contact with customers, either face-to-face, via the telephone or the internet

**Price elasticity** The extent to which customer demand responds to changes in price. Relatively sensitive demand is described as being price elastic, whereas relatively insensitive demand is known as being price inelastic

**Price skimming** A pricing strategy involving the launch of new products using a high price to enter the market

**Product line pricing** A pricing strategy where a firm produces a range of products that are sold at different prices to reflect their features or benefits, from the lowest to the highest prices

**Product life cycle** A technique that illustrates how the sales of a product change over time, implying that all products pass through similar stages from their development and to the point at which they are eventually withdrawn from the market. These stages are development, introduction, growth, maturity and decline

**Promotional mix** The combination of methods chosen to promote a product

**Psychological pricing** The purpose of this pricing strategy is to appeal to customers' emotional reactions, rather than their rational decision making

**Public relations** A method of promotion which involves attempting to send out a particular message or generate an overall image, without having to pay for advertising

**Retailer** Businesses that buy consumer goods from manufacturers and/or retailers to sell on to the final consumer

**Sales promotion** A form of short-term promotion involving using a range of techniques, such as price cuts, competitions and special offers such as 'Buy One, Get One Free' (BOGOF)

**Wholesaler** Intermediaries in the distribution chain who buy from producers in bulk and sell to retailers in smaller quantities

## Re-cap questions

1　State the four elements of the marketing mix.
2　Explain why it is important for a firm to have a coherent marketing mix.
3　Identify five key features of a successful product.
4　Briefly explain what the product life cycle is used for.
5　State the key stages of the product life cycle. For each stage, describe what is happening to the rate of sales growth.
6　Outline two limitations of using the product life cycle.
7　Identify three factors that might influence a firm's choice of pricing strategy.
8　Give two examples of products that use an economy pricing strategy.
9　Explain the difference between price skimming and price penetration.
10　Identify two possible intermediaries that confectionery manufacturer, Cadbury, might use to get its products to consumers.
11　Describe two factors that might influence a firm's choice of distribution channel.
12　Outline the two main functions of promotion.
13　List five different advertising media.
14　State one advantage and one disadvantage for Barclay's Bank of using a) personal selling; b) public relations to promote its products.
15　Using examples, describe the purpose of sales promotion.

## Grading tips

**P6** Develop a coherent marketing mix for a new product or service

The mix can relate to a brand new product or an existing product being launched into a new market. As well as describing the main elements of the mix – product, price, promotion and place – you must show how they link together and complement each other.

**M3** Develop a coherent marketing mix that is targeted at a defined group of customers

In addition to P6, you need to describe the key characteristics of your chosen customer group and explain how the marketing mix you have developed satisfies the needs of these customers.

## Assignments for Unit 3

### Assignment One

You have just been recruited as a junior journalist by the magazine, Marketing Week. The magazine is planning to run a series of articles looking at the marketing activities of a number of well-known businesses. As part of the project, you have been asked to carry out research and produce a written report that compares and evaluates the marketing activities of two companies in relation to a specified product. The report must also contain details about the limitations and constraints affecting the marketing activities of each organisation.

**Note** – read through the task, the relevant criteria and the assignment advice on page 90 before choosing your two organisations. This will help to ensure that you are able to obtain all of the information needed.

**Criteria covered** – P1 P2 M1 D1

**Tasks**

1. Select one product (or product range) from each of your chosen businesses and describe the marketing techniques used. (P1)
2. Describe the main constraints and limitations on the marketing techniques used by each business. This should include a discussion of any legal constraints and adherence to voluntary codes. Illustrate the points made by using examples. (P2)
3. Produce a comparison by highlighting the differences and similarities between the marketing techniques used by the two businesses. (M1)
4. Choose one of your businesses and evaluate the effectiveness of its marketing activities. Use relevant data as evidence to support your judgements. (D1)

**Assignment Two**

**Scenario** – your editor at Marketing Week now wants you to conduct an investigation into the marketing research carried out by a business of your choice. You are required to produce a presentation based on your findings. This must show how market research contributes to the development of the organisation's marketing plans. It must also explain the limitations of the market research and make justified recommendations as to how it could be improved.

**Note** – read through the task, the relevant criteria and the assignment advice on page 99 before choosing your organisation. You may choose one of the businesses used previously in this unit, or find another where you are able to more easily obtain all of the information needed. For example, you could choose to use marketing research from your own school or college.

**Criteria covered** – P3 P4 M2 D2

**Tasks**

1. Select an organisation and describe the market research that has been carried out. Using examples, show how the research has been used to develop the organisation's marketing plans. (P3)
2. Explain the key limitations of the market research used by your selected organisation to develop its marketing plans. (M2)
3. Suggest a number of recommendations for improving the validity of the market research

that has been used by your selected organisation. You must justify any recommendations made, showing clearly how they would improve the marketing planning process within the organisation. (D2)

4. Use the market research obtained from your organisation by suggesting ways in which its marketing planning can be adapted. For example, the research results may provide evidence for launching new products, withdrawing existing products or targeting new markets or segments (P4).

**Assignment Three**

Your next project for Marketing Week is to write a series of articles looking at market segmentation and explaining how and why groups of customers are targeted for different products.

**Note** – read through the task, the relevant criteria and the assignment advice on page 106. You need to produce six articles in total, covering both the consumer and business to business market and showing different methods of segmenting a market.

**Criteria covered** – P5

**Tasks**

1. Produce a series of factsheets for six different products. Each factsheet should identify the product and describe the customer segment being targeted. It should also contain an explanation of how and why the customers are targeted. (P5)

**Assignment Four**

All of your research into other businesses has started you thinking seriously about setting up one of your own. You have been advised by your bank manager that you will need to develop a coherent marketing mix for your product before they will consider giving you any financial support.

**Note** – read through the task, the relevant criteria and the assignment advice contained on page 118. The two tasks below do not need to be carried out separately. Criteria P6 and M3 can be achieved simultaneously by developing a coherent marketing mix that is aimed at a defined group of customers

**Criteria covered** – P6 M3

**Tasks**

a) Develop a coherent marketing mix for a new product – either a good or a service. It can be based on a completely new idea or involve launching an established product into a new market. Your marketing mix should include at least the 4 Ps of product, price, promotion and place. (P6)

**OR**

b) Develop and describe in detail a coherent marketing mix that targets a defined group of potential customers. You must clearly define the needs and aspirations of this group of customers. You must also show how aspects of the product, price, promotion and place have been chosen to appeal to these needs and aspirations. (P6 M3)

# Part 1: Different types of business communication

## What is communication?

Communication is about the sending and receiving of information. For communication to be effective, it must be understood in the way intended by the sender. The only way of assessing the extent to which the process has been effective is to have two-way communication by generating feedback.

Figure 4.1 illustrates the process of two-way communication.

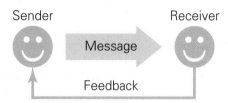

**Figure 4.1** The process of two-way communication

Businesses generate a huge flow of communication, sending and receiving regular messages to and from owners, employees, customers, suppliers, the government and other organisations. This unit looks at some of the key issues concerned with business communication.

# Types of information

Businesses require a great deal of information to function effectively. This information may relate to employees, operations, customers, suppliers or competitors. Businesses also generate a great deal of information that they send to these and other groups, including the government. In many cases, this information is not required immediately, so it needs to be stored safely and securely.

Information can come in many forms:

- **Verbal** – e.g. the comments made by staff at a meeting, or a telephone enquiry from a customer
- **Written** – e.g. completed application forms received from job applicants, or an invoice from a supplier
- **Onscreen** – e.g. a meeting using teleconferencing facilities between managers in different business locations
- **Multimedia** – e.g. interactive resources used to train employees
- **Web based** – a company website used to promote its products and to recruit new employees.

# Purposes of information

Accurate and up-to-date information is essential for effective decision making. This information is needed by businesses for a number of different purposes:

- **Updating knowledge** – Businesses are likely to experience internal change over time. New employees are recruited; others leave; and organisational structure may be adjusted to improve efficiency. The environment in which businesses operate is also subject to regular change. Economic conditions may become more favourable, creating opportunities that a business may miss unless its managers are fully informed. Political, social, technological, legal or environmental changes can also have major effects on the way a business operates. In many cases, the rate of change may be sudden or rapid. Existing knowledge needs to be updated regularly, therefore, to improve the chances of making decisions that are appropriate to the firm's current circumstances.
- **Informing future developments** – Continuing business success requires careful planning. For example, workforce requirements change over time. Unless the correct steps are taken, a firm can either be faced with skills shortages disrupting operations, or employees that are surplus to requirements adding to costs. Product portfolios need to be adjusted to continue to match customer demands but new product development takes time. Decisions about future developments need to be based on accurate information about market conditions.
- **Strategic direction** – A strategy is a medium- to long-term plan, designed to achieve the overall objectives of a business. For example, a business that wishes to increase sales and profits may decide to increase its share of the existing market, launch new products or enter into new markets. Information needs to be gathered so that market conditions can be assessed, trends can be identified and future requirements can be forecast accurately.
- **SWOT analysis** – This is a technique that can be used to examine an individual product or an entire business. It involves identifying key internal strengths and weaknesses, as well as external influences that are likely to create opportunities or act as threats. Obviously the effectiveness of the technique depends on the ability to gather detailed information, both from within the business and from the environment in which it operates. Once this has been done, managers can decide what action to take in order to build on strengths, take advantage of opportunities and deal with any weaknesses or threats.
- **Offering competitive insight** – A great deal of market-research activity involves gathering information on the behaviour of competitors. This includes information on their products, their prices, their promotional activities and the methods that they use to distribute their products to customers. Competitive insight is likely to have a significant impact on the marketing mix chosen by a business for its own products. Any changes in competitors' behaviour also need to be noted and the implications considered.
- **Communicating sales promotions** – Promotional activity involves communicating messages to customers to inform them and persuade them to buy a firm's products. Market research can be used to provide information on consumer behaviour, helping a business to choose appropriate promotional techniques. The promotional message sent out to the customer also needs to be carefully considered to ensure that it achieves the objectives set.

- **Inviting support for activities** – Information is also required when a firm uses the services of another to support its operations. Small businesses are unlikely to have the expertise to carry out all business functions in-house and so pay accountants, solicitors and other professionals to provide the services required. Even larger firms may find it more cost effective to outsource certain functions, such as personnel or IT. The information needs to be passed between the businesses and stored securely.

## Sources of information

Business information may come from a wide variety of sources. The actual sources used depend to a large extent on the nature of the information required. It is often advisable to use a number of different sources to check the validity of the information obtained (see below).

## Internal

This refers to any information that is generated from inside a business. The main sources of internal information are:

- **Financial** – The accounting function within a business records information on the business's financial performance. This includes figures on sales, profits and costs. This information is needed to analyse performance, highlighting areas where the business may be doing particularly well and identifying any problems that require corrective action.
- **Human resources** – Firms store a great deal of information on their employees, including personal details, pay levels, qualifications, previous training and existing skills levels. Changes in the size of the workforce and levels of staff turnover are also calculated on a regular basis. The human resources department of a business will also need to hold details of applicants for job vacancies while the recruitment process is taking place. This information is needed for effective workforce planning. Much of it is also required for legal reasons and to monitor equal opportunities.
- **Marketing** – Firms store a great deal of information relating to their products. This may include the results of recent market research or details of previous promotional campaigns. This can be used to inform the decision-making process and the planning of future campaigns or changes to the marketing mix.
- **Purchasing** – This covers information on the suppliers of materials and services that support a firm's operations. It will consist of details of past and current suppliers, as well as the goods or services supplied, delivery and payment details, including the availability of discounts. An up-to-date knowledge of the different suppliers in a market – including those that have not been used in the past – can help to ensure that the business is using the right supplier to meet its needs.
- **Sales** – Details of past and current sales levels are required to measure the current performance of individual products and sales staff. These figures may form the basis of performance-related pay and staff bonuses. They may also be used to identify sales trends, so that production can be adjusted appropriately.
- **Operations** – Records of production levels (in the case of a manufacturer) or the number of customers served (in the case of a service provider) are also needed to measure and monitor performance. Information regarding stock and quality levels can help a business to run more efficiently.

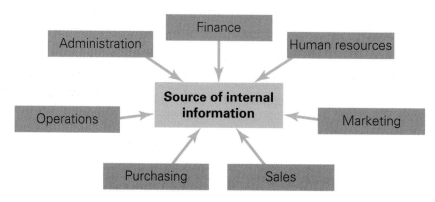

**Figure 4.2** Sources of internal information

- **Administration** – This involves keeping records of communications with external groups, such as customers and suppliers, as well as communications taking place within the organisation. These records may be required, for example, if there is a dispute with a supplier over payment terms.

## External

This concerns information that comes from groups or individuals outside an organisation. Key sources of external information include:

- **Government** – The Office of National Statistics produces data on economic and social trends, which can help in producing forecasts for future demand or generate ideas for new products. Much of this data is available free online. Other government-related websites, such as www.directgov.co.uk and www.businesslink.gov.uk, also provide a great deal of information on a variety of useful areas for businesses.
- **Trade groups** – Businesses operating in the same industry often come together to form groups to carry out research and provide support to their members. For example, the British Plastics Federation is a leading trade association within the UK plastics industry. It has its own business support network, organises events and provides a number of services, including free downloadable guides, advice on exporting and help in finding product suppliers.
- **Commercially provided** – There are a number of commercial organisations that have been set up to generate information for business use. Mintel is a well-known market-research agency that produces reports on different market sectors and sells them to interested businesses.

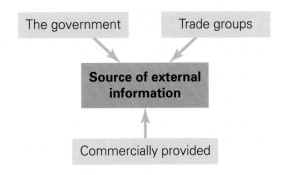

**Figure 4.3** Sources of external information

Other businesses, such as Dun & Bradstreet and OneSource, offer their clients access to a database containing the profiles of millions of private and public sector organisations. Firms can also subscribe to a number of commercial journals and magazines that provide information for certain trades or professions.

## Reliability of data sources

Information fuels the decision-making process. However, unless this information is accurate, up to date and relevant, the quality of decision making is likely to be poor. Existing information can become out of date very quickly, so it is important to check exactly when it was first collected. Information that was gathered for another project may not be entirely relevant and fail to meet the current needs of the business. Data are also a key issue but may be difficult to clarify, particularly those obtained from external sources. Nevertheless, it is important not to simply assume that all published information is valid, but to try and establish whether the information obtained is factual, based on the opinions of the author or simply false.

## Key terms

**Communication** The process of sending messages between individuals, groups and organisations

**Competitive insight** Gathering information on rival firms and analysing their behaviour

**Out-sourcing** Handing over part of a firm's operations to another

**Strategy** A medium- to long-term plan drawn up to achieve a firm's aims and objectives

**SWOT analysis** An analytical tool used to identify and examine a firm's internal strengths and weaknesses, as well as any external opportunities and threats

## Re-cap questions

1  Give two examples of the following information used by a business: a) verbal, b) written and c) web based.

2  Explain why it would be particularly important for a business operating in a very competitive market to update its knowledge regularly.

3  Describe how a business can benefit from carrying out a SWOT analysis. Identify two pieces of information it might request for each of the SWOT categories.

4  Briefly explain what is meant by competitive insight.

5  Identify two sources of internal information within a business.

6  Suggest two sources of external information that a small, newly established business could use to carry out market research.

7  Outline two reasons why information from external sources may be unreliable.

## Grading tips

|  **P1** Explain different types of business information, their sources and purposes.<br><br>You must look at and explain a range of different types of information for a business, explain where the information has come from and how it is has been or is being used. | | |
|---|---|---|

See page 147 for suggestions for Assignments for Unit 4

# Part 2: Presenting business information effectively

Communicating information effectively means that the message received has to be understood in the way intended by the sender. The way that information is presented affects the way in which people understand it, so the presentation methods chosen need to be carefully considered.

## Presentation methods to meet the needs of the user

- **Documents** – These come in a variety of forms, including reports, letters, minutes of meetings and invoices. The key benefit of producing documents is that they provide a record, acting as evidence of the information that has been communicated, and allowing it to be reread and referred to at points in the future.
- **Use of style** – The style of a presentation is used to convey a particular atmosphere or mood. This could be light-hearted and humorous or sober and serious and created via the use of images, font, voice tone and/or music. It is used to reinforce the message being conveyed.
- **Verbal presentations** – These provide opportunities to deliver information in a more engaging way, allowing two-way communication by giving the audience the chance to ask questions so that key points can be clarified.
- **Role plays** – These involve acting out a situation in a controlled but realistic manner. They are often used to train existing staff to deal with potentially difficult situations, or to assess the abilities of job applicants. Although they take time to set up, role plays provide an environment in which to practise skills before they are properly introduced.
- **On-screen multimedia presentations** – These involve a variety of different media, with the possible use of slides, sound, pictures and video. This variety, if used correctly, can help to engage the audience and maintain their interest by illustrating different types of information in the most suitable format.
- **The use of images** – Pictures or images can be very effective in seizing the attention of the receiver and conveying and reinforcing a message clearly and instantly. Images are also often used to communicate a basic message across a number of languages.

An internationally recognisable symbol

- **Web-based presentations** – Modern web-based presentations are able to incorporate all of the multimedia functions outlined above, which can be received by viewers across the world via the internet.
- **Multilingual support** – The increasing globalisation of business operations has highlighted the need for businesses to be able to communicate in a number of languages with employees, customers and suppliers. For example, product descriptions and information often appear on packaging in several languages. Careful thought is also needed when choosing brand names, to avoid embarrassment or offence to customers in foreign markets.

## Output requirement

A presentation needs to sustain the interest of the audience throughout if the message it contains is to be communicated effectively. It needs to be eye-catching, contain variety and be easy for the audience to understand. There are a number of techniques that can be used to achieve these objectives. In particular, the following points should be considered.

### Page layout

The way that information is set out on a page or slide makes a significant initial impact. It can help to give text a more interesting appearance, to convey a particular style and to make it easier to read. The temptation to crowd a page or slide with large amounts of information should also be resisted – generally speaking, less is better! It is important to take a consistent approach, i.e. the font style and sizes used for titles, subtitles and the main text should be the same throughout the presentation. Large amounts of text should be arranged into sections and paragraphs and these can be broken down further by using bullet points. Tables, diagrams and other images can also be used to introduce variety, but only if they are relevant and help to enhance understanding.

## Text formatting

Text can be presented in a number of formats, including letter style, size, bold and italic. Different formats can be used to make a presentation look more attractive or to draw attention to key words, points or sections. Word-processing software gives presenters a huge range of choice, making it easy to try out a number of different formats in order to choose the most appropriate. The appearance of text can also be changed by justifying it. This means lining text up against the left-hand margin (left justifying), the right-hand margin (right justifying), both margins (fully justifying) or putting it in the middle (centring). Careful thought needs to be given to the size, colour and font style used, particularly with visual presentations. Small print or font styles that may look good close up may be difficult to read further away, and most lighter colours become practically invisible when enlarged.

---

### International Change Manager

**SAVE THE CHILDREN INTERNATIONAL**

Location: Hammersmith, London

Contract: Permanent

Hours: Full time

Salary: up to £50,000 pa

**For further information and application details, visit www.savethechildren.net/alliance/get_involved/work**

---

Job advertisements often use a variety of text formats

## Use of tables

These are used to summarise and present large quantities of data by grouping them into columns and rows. This gives the data a more attractive appearance and makes them easier for readers to understand.

## Working with tables

Table 4.1  UK consumer expenditure on tobacco products

| Year | Cigarettes | Other tobacco products £ billion | Total |
|------|-----------|----------------------------------|-------|
| 2000 | 10.8 | 0.9 | 11.7 |
| 2001 | 11.1 | 1.0 | 12.1 |
| 2002 | 11.5 | 1.0 | 12.5 |
| 2003 | 11.3 | 1.0 | 12.3 |
| 2004 | 11.3 | 1.0 | 12.3 |
| 2005 | 11.4 | 1.0 | 12.4 |
| 2006 | 11.4 | 1.1 | 12.5 |
| 2007 | 11.5 | 1.1 | 12.6 |
| 2008 (p) | 11.7 | 1.4 | 13.1 |

Source: TMA

### Questions

a) Looking at the table of figures above, examine one advantage and one disadvantage of presenting data in the form of a table.

b) Suggest two other ways in which the data could be presented.

## Information from a range of applications

The presenter may wish to include information from a range of sources and applications. Written text, tables and graphs taken from a spreadsheet, video clips and articles and images taken from the internet can all be easily and quickly inserted into the final written document or visual presentation by using the 'copy and paste' function on a computer or via the use of a scanner. Hyperlinks can also be included, allowing the presenter instant access to relevant web pages.

## Use of specialist software and hardware

The wide range of software packages available makes it relatively easy to put together a professional-looking presentation, even for those with a limited knowledge of IT. Microsoft's Word, Excel and PowerPoint all produce good results, while a number of desktop-publishing packages exist for use by the more adventurous.

Visual presentations can be supported by a range of hardware, including projectors, screens, overhead projectors (OHPs) and flip charts. The size of the audience is a key consideration in deciding which hardware to use. Large numbers of people gathered together in a hall or theatre will require a screen linked to a computer, and a microphone for the presenter, so that the presentation can be seen and heard correctly. Smaller venues, such as seminar rooms, may mean that an OHP can be used. This involves placing a series of pre-written slides on the glass of the projector, which are then reflected onto a smooth surface, such as a wall or screen. The presenter has to be careful to place the slides the right way up and in the right order. Flip charts can also be used effectively for presentations to small groups of people. This can be either as the focus of the presentation by writing down information beforehand or by using them to note down points raised by the audience during the presentation. Using software or hardware effectively requires a certain level of knowledge and skill, so it makes sense to practise beforehand.

## Presenting corporate communications

The term 'corporate communication' refers to any messages sent by a business to external groups or organisations. These messages could be aimed at a number of groups, including potential recruits, customers, suppliers and the general public. Examples of the kinds of communications that could be issued include:

- **Mission statements** Many businesses wish to communicate their values and overall objectives to interested groups, such as employees and customers. This can help to explain why the business was set up and what it is attempting to achieve. A mission statement is a published summary of these values and objectives. It is usually short, consisting of a couple of sentences, in order to get the message across and provide a clear focus.
- **Advertising** This is one of many possible methods of promotion that a business can use. It is a paid-for method of communication using media such as television, radio and cinema, newspapers, magazines and billboards. Advertising is particularly suitable for use in markets consisting of large numbers of customers, on a regional, national or even international scale. Communication can be very sophisticated, using sound, text and images to convey information about a product and persuade customers to buy it.
- **Packaging** As well as helping to store and protect a product, packaging can play a key role in promoting the goods inside it. Product

Virgin's use of colour and lettering makes its aircraft and trains more distinctive

names, key descriptive words, logos and colour are used to attract customers' attention and develop a distinctive brand image. Some information may also be required by law, such as the weight, ingredients and nutritional details of food products.

- **Logos** These are words or images that represent a product. Their purpose is to trigger memory, instantly reminding customers of product features and benefits. Logos can act as powerful promotional tools, sending the same message out across different markets, regardless of the language used. Successful logos are simple and distinctive, making them easy to recognise and remember.

- **Livery** This can refer to the uniform worn by an employee or the design used on vehicles or aircraft. Distinctive livery can help to support a brand by creating an instantly recognisable corporate image.

- **Strap lines** A strap line is a slogan or catchphrase that is used in the promotion of a product or a business. Famous examples include Nike's 'Just do it' and Microsoft's 'Where do you want to go today?' They can also perform a powerful promotional function, attracting customer interest and promising the benefits of using a product.

- **Endorsements** Product endorsements involve actors, pop stars, sports personalities and other celebrities giving their approval for a good or a service. This is a commonly used form of promotion, but its effectiveness depends to a large extent on the image of the celebrity used.

- **Sponsorship** This is a very basic form of communication that can nevertheless be very effective in promoting a business and its products. It involves providing financial or other support for an event, such as a sporting competition or an arts festival, or for another organisation, such as a local football team or youth centre. In return, the event or organisation acknowledges the sponsorship by displaying the name of the sponsor on hoardings or sports kits. The purpose of sponsorship is to keep the name of a business or its products in the public eye. Sponsorship can provide businesses with national or international exposure when, for example, a game or event is televised.

## Logos

Look at the three logos below and answer the questions that follow.

a) Identify three features of a logo.

b) In your opinion, which of the logos above is the most effective? Justify your answer.

# Key terms

**Corporate communications** Messages that are sent out about a business, either internally or to external groups such as customers and suppliers

**Justifying text** A way of presenting printed text so that it is either centred or lined up against the left-hand or right-hand margin (or both) on a page

**Livery** This refers to distinctive uniforms worn by employees or to the design used on buildings, vehicles and other business assets to convey a specific corporate identity or image

**Logo** A word or image that is used to represent a product

**Mission statement** A short, published summary of a firm's values and objectives

**Role play** Acting out a situation in a controlled but realistic manner

**Strap line** A slogan or catchphrase that is used in the promotion of a product or a business

**Text formatting** The way that written words are presented, including letter style and size, the use of bold and italic

# Re-cap questions

1   Identify and briefly describe three different methods that a business might use to present information a) to employees and b) to customers.

2   Outline two points that should be kept in mind regarding the page layout of written documents, such as letters and reports.

3   Briefly explain three other output requirements when presenting business information.

4   State three pieces of information that might be contained on a product's packaging.

5   Using examples, explain how logos are used to communicate a particular message about a product or business.

6   Describe what is meant by a strap line and show, using examples, how they are used by businesses.

7   Explain how a) sponsorship and b) endorsements are used by businesses for promotion.

# Grading tips

| **P2** Present complex internal business information using three different methods appropriate to the user's needs. | **M1** Analyse different types of business information and their sources. | **D1** Evaluate the appropriateness of business information used to make strategic decisions. |
|---|---|---|
| You must present information on your business in three different ways, e.g. a verbal presentation on health and safety, a leaflet outlining the company's policy on ICT use, or a web page highlighting the company's internal structure. You must also provide an explanation of the purpose of the information and who the materials are intended for. | This builds on P1 by providing a detailed account of the information and its sources, giving reasons for their choice and the benefits and drawbacks of using them. | You must reach a clear conclusion as to whether the information used by the business is the most appropriate for important strategic decisions that needed to be made. Your evaluation must be based on at least two sets of information, e.g. marketing, human resources or financial information. You must justify your comments by looking at alternative information and sources that could be used, comparing the advantages and disadvantages of doing so. |

| | | **D2** Evaluate the effectiveness of business information and its communication as key contributors to the success of an organisation, using examples to illustrate your points. |
|---|---|---|
| | | You could investigate one or more other organisations with a track record of excellent communication and information systems and compare them to your own business, highlighting what it does well and how it could improve. |
| **P3** Produce corporate communications. | | |
| You must produce materials that could be used for external communications about your chosen business. This could be an advertising poster or brochure on the company's products or a press release for a forthcoming product launch or competition. You may use the same or a different organisation from that chosen in P1. | | |
| **P4** Evaluate the external corporate communications of an existing product or service. | | |
| You must make basic judgements about the methods of external communication used by a business. | | |

See page 147 for suggestions for Assignments for Unit 4

# Part 3: The issues and constraints relating to the use of business information in organisations

## Legal issues

There are a number of laws relating to data protection that influence, and in many cases constrain, the way information is used by businesses.

## Data Protection Act (1998)

This law was designed to regulate the use of any personal information held by businesses on individuals – including actual and potential customers and employees. Under the Act, businesses must ensure that any personal information they are storing is:

- processed fairly and lawfully
- processed in line with the individual's rights
- processed for one or more purposes specified at the time of collection
- accurate and, where necessary, kept up to date
- adequate, relevant and not excessive
- securely protected against unauthorised use
- kept no longer than is necessary
- not transferred outside the European Economic Area (EEA) unless adequate protection is provided.

The Act also gives individuals a number of rights. These include the right to access any data held on them by firms, the right to have any inaccuracies corrected and the right to prevent information being used for marketing purposes.

The Data Protection Act has a number of implications for businesses. Databases are often used to keep records of customer details. These may be used to analyse customer spending patterns or to contact customers with details of forthcoming promotions. Some businesses also keep details of unsuccessful job applicants in case suitable vacancies arise in the future. In such cases, businesses must ensure that they adhere to the requirements of this law.

## Freedom of Information Act (2000)

This piece of legislation, which came into force in 2005, gives everyone in the UK the right to request information held about them by public sector organisations. Such organisations include:

- government departments and local authorities
- schools, colleges and universities
- the police
- hospitals and doctors' surgeries.

Requests for any other kind of information can be made, other than requests by people concerning information about themselves, which are dealt with under the Data Protection Act (see above). In some cases, information can be withheld but, in such cases, an explanation has to be provided by the public organisation as to why the request is being denied.

## Computer Misuse Act (1990)

This law makes it illegal to access, copy or use software or data stored on a computer without obtaining permission from the owner. Any individual or organisation found guilty of doing so can be fined and/or sent to prison for up to five years. In particular, the law turned three activities into illegal offences:

- Accessing material stored on computers without permission
- Accessing computer material without permission, with the intention to commit further offences (a process known as **hacking**) by overcoming passwords and other security systems
- Altering data stored on a computer without permission – this includes planting **viruses**, which are computer programs designed to create a nuisance or cause damage to other computers and the files contained within them.

Computer misuse within a business context could involve an employee accessing confidential information on the research and development of new products, without permission and with the intention of selling the information to a rival firm. It could also involve passing on customer details to competitors.

In addition to the laws outlined above, businesses must ensure that none of their communications breaks equal opportunities legislation, such as the Sex Discrimination Act and the Race Relations Act. For example, advertisements and recruitment documents, such as job application forms, must not discriminate against any groups on the grounds of sex, race or ethnicity. More recent legislation, such as the

Disability Discrimination Act (1995/2005) and the Employment Equality (Age) Regulations 2006, also make it illegal to discriminate against anyone on the grounds of disability or age.

## Ethical issues

Ethical behaviour involves doing what is morally right, rather than simply operating within the law. A great deal of external communication carried out by businesses involves advertising and other forms of promotion. A key function of promotion is to influence customers' behaviour and persuade them to buy one particular brand over another. Sophisticated psychological techniques are used to give products a particular emotional appeal. For example, advertisements for BMW and Mercedes cars imply status; many food products aimed at babies and young children focus on parents' health concerns; and toiletries such as Lynx suggest a clear connection between usage and sex appeal. Pressure on managers and advertising agencies to produce successful results may make it tempting to exaggerate claims about product features and performance. The Advertising Standards Authority, or ASA, often receives complaints from the general public about advertisements that are thought to be unethical or misleading. If its resulting investigation upholds these complaints, the ASA can refer the firm concerned to the Office of Fair Trading, which can impose heavy fines.

## Codes of practice

A number of organisations and rules have been created over the years to regulate business activities, including communication. The codes of practice they include are designed to supplement the law by encouraging firms and their employees to take a greater degree of responsibility, known as **self-regulation**. The ASA acts as the watchdog of the advertising industry in the UK, set up to ensure that all marketing communications are 'legal, decent, honest and truthful'.

## Cheryl Cole advert receives complaints

The Advertising Standards Authority (ASA) received over 40 complaints in May 2010 over an advertisement for L'Oréal haircare products featuring top celebrity Cheryl Cole. During the advert, the singer and X Factor judge claimed that using the company's Elvive Full Restore 5 range of shampoos and conditioners had helped to get her 'mojo' back, giving her hair 'a healthy shine', and making it 'feel stronger' and 'full of life'. The complaints focused on the fact that Ms Cole wears hair extensions, meaning that the product's effects were exaggerated and that the same look could not be achieved by simply using the product.

However, the complaints were rejected by the ASA. According to the advertising watchdog, L'Oréal's product testing had provided evidence that similar results were achievable without the use of hair extensions. It explained, 'We consider that most consumers would interpret the ads to mean the product would have an effect on the look and feel of hair that was weak, limp, lifeless, dull or straw-like … they are also likely to understand that individual results would vary according to their own hair type.' The ASA also pointed to the fact that the adverts did contain a statement saying that Ms Cole's hair was 'styled with some natural hair extensions'.

**Source: BBC News**

### Questions

a) Was L'Oréal's Elvive advertisement against the law? Justify your answer.

b) In your opinion, was L'Oréal acting ethically by producing such an advert? Discuss your views with someone who holds the opposite view to yours.

Rules designed to encourage firms to behave in a socially responsible manner are set out in two main codes of practice:

- **The British Code of Advertising, Sales Promotion and Direct Marketing** This covers non-broadcast advertisements, such as those appearing in newspapers and magazines, brochures and leaflets, cinema and video commercials.
- **BCAP** This covers TV and radio advertising.

The ASA administers these codes of practice and helps firms and advertising agencies to comply with the standards outlined in them.

## Organisational policies

Firms are also likely to draw up their own policies regarding the procedures that should be followed by employees in terms of internal and external communications. These policies are designed to achieve a number of objectives. Employees are trained to follow certain guidelines when communicating with customers or suppliers in order to ensure consistency and present a particular corporate image. These guidelines may also be needed to ensure confidentiality and prevent important information falling into the hands of competitors. Many firms also have specific IT policies in order to reduce the threat posed by hacking and viruses. These policies may forbid staff from using computers at work for logging on to personal email accounts, sending personal emails or accessing social networking sites such as Facebook, and from using memory sticks, cards and other devices. An increasing number of firms are also adopting environmental policies that include cutting down on the amount of paper and energy wasted as a result of the communication process.

The term **whistle blowing** refers to the act of informing on someone within an organisation who is carrying out activities that are either illegal or against the interests of the business. It may also involve informing on the whole organisation if it is behaving in a way that is damaging to the interests of stakeholders such as shareholders, employees or customers. In such cases the whistle blower may be forced to go to the media with this information. Individuals are protected from any retaliation by employers by the Public Interest Disclosure Act (1998), as long as they have raised the concern and attempted to resolve it internally first. Many larger organisations have whistle-blowing policies, setting out the procedures that employees should take in such situations.

## Information ownership

It is important to find out about the ownership of information before using it, in order to confirm whether or not it can be used and, if so, to ensure that the correct procedures are followed. The term **intellectual property** refers to the ownership of inventions, designs, composed music or other written materials. In many cases, this material may be protected under the law by the creation of **patents**, **trademarks** and **copyrights**. In such cases, permission must be obtained – often at a significant cost – before this material can be used or copied. Using product names, logos or other communication materials in a way that is found to be in breach of the law can result in expensive fines for those concerned.

Businesses carrying out market research using published sources, including the internet, must also ensure that proper credit is given to the authors of such materials if they are used in presentations, reports or other documents. Note that this also applies to students when writing assignments, so make sure you refer to any guidelines produced by your school or college before you begin your research.

## Operational issues

### Security of information

Larger businesses in particular generate a huge amount of communication on a daily basis. It is therefore important to be clear both about the purpose of this communication and also who it is intended for. A great deal of information generated and held by businesses is sensitive and confidential: i.e. it should only be accessible to certain individuals or groups and not be available to the whole organisation or the general public.

This email is intended solely for the above mentioned recipient and may contain confidential or privileged information. If you have received this email in error you are on notice of its status and please notify us immediately and delete the email. You must not copy, distribute, disclose or take any action in reliance on it: to do so may be a breach of confidence. Any views expressed in this email and any attachment are those of the individual sender and are not necessarily agreed or authorised by Hodder Education. While every reasonable precaution is taken to minimize the risk of viruses contained within this email, we cannot accept liability for any damage which you sustain as a result of software viruses. It is advised that you carry out your own virus check before opening any attachments.

An email disclaimer

This could involve personal information on employees, the bank details of suppliers or plans for new products. Approved users need to gain access to confidential information reasonably quickly and easily, in order to be able to do their jobs effectively. Management Information Systems (MIS) can be used to control communications and maintain security. Approved usernames and passwords provide access to information stored in computer files, as well as ensuring that emails are sent to restricted groups of staff within an organisation. These usernames and passwords are often changed regularly in an attempt to keep information secure.

## Backups

Backing up computer data basically involves saving it on a disc, memory stick, another hard drive, or even by keeping paper files. Modern computers have many features to protect data from accidental or deliberate damage, including hermetically sealed hard drives to protect them from dust, and firewalls to stop viruses and other unauthorised access via the internet. However, computer data is still very vulnerable, so making regular backups is an essential part of managing information within an organisation. On an individual level, modern software packages such as Windows 7 and Mac OS X v10.5 include backup facilities, but it is advisable to keep at least one copy of data in a separate physical location in case the computer is seriously damaged and the data cannot be recovered. Copies made using discs, memory sticks or paper are an easy and cheap solution but obviously need to be kept in a safe place. In addition, they may not be suitable for storing large amounts of information. The MIS function within large firms is likely to be responsible for backing up information regularly. There are also a number of software companies who offer backup services. This may be useful for firms without the facilities to do this in-house but can also be expensive.

## Health and safety

Prolonged or repeated use of IT equipment as part of the communication process can lead to a variety of health problems in the workplace, including neck- and backache or hand, wrist or arm strain. These kinds of problems usually result from poorly designed workstations, lack of or inappropriate use of equipment or a failure to take regular breaks. In the UK, health and safety protection in the workplace is provided by the Health and Safety at Work Act (1974). The Act requires employers to carry out a number of actions, including:

- Assessing visual display units (VDUs) for problems and taking steps to reduce any risks
- Ensuring that workstations meet health and safety requirements
- Providing health and safety training and information
- Planning work to include regular breaks or changes in the kind of work being carried out.

All of the above regulations also affect employees who work from home. There is no legal limit on how long staff can work without a break from computer-based work, or the minimum number of breaks that should be given over a period of time. However, guidance from the Health and Safety Executive suggests that taking frequent short breaks – for instance, ten minutes after every hour of IT work – is more effective than taking long breaks less frequently.

## Organisational policies

It is good practice for businesses to draw up their own policies regarding information and communication, in order to reflect their own organisational needs and ensure effective operations.

## Business continuance plans

Business continuance planning involves taking steps to help a firm cope with unexpected events that could damage its performance and even force it to close down. Also known as business continuity planning, it outlines the procedures that should be put into place immediately after a crisis or disaster has occurred, to allow the firm to continue to function. Potential crises could include:

- IT system failure
- Power cuts
- Theft or vandalism
- Loss of key customers or suppliers
- Loss or illness of key staff.

Key sections of a business continuance plan should cover the following:

- Identifying potential crises that could arise
- Outlining actions that could prevent these crises from occurring in the first place
- Highlighting essential functions that must continue if the business is to survive, so that limited resources can be allocated appropriately
- Setting out the steps that should be taken to deal with the crisis.

The plan should be tested and updated regularly to maximise its effectiveness in the event of a crisis occurring.

## Costs and impact of increasing sophistication of systems

Many recent technological developments have been aimed at improving the speed and effectiveness with which individuals and businesses can communicate with each other. Firms have a wide range of options to choose from, involving sophisticated computer software and hardware, laptops, smartphones such as the BlackBerry, and teleconferencing, all of which provide their employees with almost instant access to information, to their customers and to each other. This is in addition to more traditional methods such as letters and faxes. However, these modern systems come at a cost, using up limited business resources. The rate at which software and equipment become out of date (known as **technical obsolescence**) is also increasing. Businesses are often forced to consider carefully whether the cost of regular updates to information and communication technology can be justified by the performance and efficiency gains achieved.

## Key terms

**Business continuance plans** The process of identifying any unexpected events that could damage a business's performance, and identifying the action that would need to be taken to help it cope

**Codes of practice** Rules and guidelines that are drawn up to influence the behaviour of businesses in a certain area, such as advertising

**Computer virus** Computer program that is designed to create a nuisance or cause damage to other computers and the files contained within them

**Copyright** Legal protection given to written materials, such as books, articles, plays, music and song lyrics, to prevent them from being used or copied without permission

**Ethical behaviour** Behaving in a manner that is considered to be morally correct, rather than just within the law

**Hacking** Accessing computer material without permission with the intention to commit further offences

**Intellectual property** The ownership of inventions, designs, composed music or other written materials

**Patents** Legal protection for new inventions, such as products or processes, preventing them from being used or copied without the permission of the owner

**Self-regulation** An agreement among firms operating in a particular sector or area to behave according to a set of rules and standards, without the need for laws to be passed

**Technical obsolescence** Where a new, technologically superior product is launched, making older versions out of date

**Trademark** A name, logo or symbol that is used by a business to support a brand and distinguish itself or its products from others on the market. Registering a trademark with the Patent Office gives the owner exclusive use

**Whistle blowing** Where an individual or group of workers within a business exposes activities taking place that may be illegal or damaging to the organisation or to groups connected to it

**Re-cap questions**

1 Identify three key pieces of legislation that affect business communications.

2 Explain how business communications could be affected by a decision by a firm to adopt a social responsibility policy.

3 Identify and briefly describe two codes of practice that affect the way in which businesses advertise their products.

4 Suggest two reasons why a business would wish to include rules on the use of emails in the IT policy issued to staff.

5 Explain, using examples, what is meant by whistle blowing.

6 Identify two methods used for protecting intellectual property.

7 Briefly explain how management information systems can be used to keep information confidential within a business.

8 Briefly examine two methods that a small business could use to back up computer information.

9 Describe the main employer responsibilities towards workers using computers, under the Health and Safety at Work Act.

10 Outline the key steps involved in drawing up a business continuance plan.

## Grading tips

|  **P5** Explain the legal and ethical issues in relation to the use of business information.<br><br>You may use the same organisation for this as for previous criteria, or a different business if the information is easier to obtain from another source. You need to obtain and describe the organisation's ethical policy in relation to business information and also show, using examples, how it complies with relevant legislation. | **M2** Analyse the legal, ethical and operational issues in relation to the use of business information, using appropriate examples.<br><br>This builds on P5 and P6, requiring a detailed examination of the legal, ethical and operational issues faced, the reasons behind the procedures and systems in place and key benefits and drawbacks. | |
|  **P6** Explain the operational issues in relation to the use of business information.<br><br>You can use the same or a different organisation to those used previously. You must look at a range of operational issues, showing how the business keeps information confidential, the health and safety issues involved, the systems developed to manage information, including the software and training required. | | |

See page 147 for suggestions for Unit 4 Assignments.

# Part 4: Communicating business information using appropriate methods

A business's choice of communication method or methods plays an important role in ensuring that the message reaches the intended audience and is understood in the manner intended. Often the basic message has to be adapted, and a variety of methods has to be used to deal with different audiences. For example, a manufacturer is likely to communicate information regarding the launch of a new product differently to intermediaries, such as wholesalers and retailers, using sales teams and advertising in trade journals such as *The Grocer*. On the other hand, it may use methods such as television advertising or direct marketing to send out product information to consumers. A detailed understanding of the nature of the audience is therefore required to maximise the effectiveness of the communication methods used.

## Audience requirements

The basic structure of the audience can have a significant impact on the way a message is received and understood. In particular, the following possible influences should be considered.

## Demographic characteristics – e.g. age, gender and ethnicity

There is a variety of techniques that can be used to attract and maintain audience interest. The use of photographs, video clips and other images can help to illustrate the key points made in presentations. Case studies and anecdotes can also be used for this purpose. Careful choice of such techniques can also help to create a more personal experience for the listener or reader. However, for this to happen, the examples used need to be relevant and reflect the experiences of those in the target group. For example, using actors from Channel 4 soap opera *Hollyoaks* for product endorsements may be effective in appealing to young people but fail to have any impact on older audiences. Firms employing staff or dealing with customers whose first language is not English may need to translate presentations and other key communications documents.

## Special needs and accessibility

The Disability Discrimination Act (1995/2005) makes it unlawful for a firm to give unfavourable treatment to anyone, including employees and customers, as a result of their disability. In the context of communication, this means that all reasonable steps must be taken to ensure that people with disabilities are not disadvantaged. Creating accessibility could include:

- Providing documents in large text, using coloured backgrounds or providing paper copies of slide presentations for those with visual impairments
- Providing special equipment and a supportive environment for those with hearing impairments, such as induction loop systems or employees who are trained to use sign language
- Considering the layout of rooms and buildings for those with mobility problems, including the use of ground-floor seminar rooms.

## Readability and legibility

The nature and presentation of the language used in written documents can also have a significant impact on the effectiveness of communication. Word tone and style of the words can be chosen to appeal to specific audiences. For example, a catalogue or brochure produced by a building materials supplier for use with retailers and construction firms is likely to contain detailed descriptions and explanations using technical language, whereas the same products may be promoted quite differently to personal customers, focusing on stylish looks or easy-to-use features.

Written documents also need to be presented in a way that makes them easy to read. Page layout and text formatting have already been discussed in this unit (see Part 2). Document pages should not contain so much information that it becomes too difficult or boring to read; font colours need to contrast boldly with the backgrounds on which they appear; and font size should be big enough for the audience to see, taking special account of those with visual impairments or those who will be

Catalogues must use appropriate language for the subject

reading it at a distance, e.g. people driving past an advertising hoarding.

## Interest and attention span

Information on the level of interest and the attention span of the intended audience should also be taken into account. For example, delivering a presentation on pension arrangements for retired workers may generate more interest among sales consultants and managers within the industry than among young factory workers required to attend meetings at the end of their shifts. Age can also have an impact on the attention span of the listener, viewer or reader. Young children, for example, find it difficult to concentrate for more than a few minutes at a time. This means that a succession of short clips of video or text tends to be more effective in holding interest.

## Distraction avoidance

Noise is the term used in communications to refer to anything that prevents a message being transmitted effectively from the sender to the receiver. This could include distractions such as people talking or arriving late, traffic noise, mobile phone ring tones or text alerts. It is therefore important to try and create an environment where people can read or listen to presentations without such disturbances. It is common for presenters to ask people to behave in a suitable manner by arriving on time and switching mobiles off before the presentation begins.

## Business- or industry-related experience and knowledge

In general, people with existing knowledge of a business or the industry in general are likely to require less detail, in the form of information and explanation, than those who are encountering a firm for the first time. This may mean that a new customer requires much more information about products, prices and payment details than an existing customer. By the same token, a new employee, recruited straight from school, college or university will need much more training than someone who has worked for a number of years for a different company in the same industry or sector.

## Methods of written communication

The key benefit of written communication over other forms is that it creates evidence that the communication took place and what was said. This may prove invaluable should disputes arise in the future. It is advisable, therefore, to keep copies of any written communications that are sent or received. It may also be a good idea to follow up non-written communications, such as a telephone conversation, with a letter or email summarising its content. Any form of written communication, and particularly those being used in a business context, should be carefully checked for spelling and grammar mistakes. The level of formality used depends on the relationship between the sender and the receiver, as well as the topic under discussion, but the tone should always be polite and professional.

The most commonly used forms of written communication are:

- **Letter** Business letters are relatively flexible and can be used for a variety of purposes and with many different groups, including employees, suppliers and customers. They have a relatively formal and traditional image but are still an important and frequently used form of communication. For example, candidates for a job vacancy – both successful and unsuccessful – are usually informed by letter. The layout and style of business letters vary from business

---

**Key features of a good business letter**

A letter heading featuring the business's name and/or logo

The date the letter was written

The address of the person to whom the letter is directed

A suitable salutation – e.g. 'Dear Mr or Mrs XXX' (if the person's name is known) or 'Dear Sir or Madam' (if not)

The subject heading

The body of the letter, set out neatly in paragraphs and using relatively short, uncomplicated sentences

The complimentary close (e.g. 'Yours sincerely').

---

to business but should be in keeping with the firm's overall corporate image and should create a good impression. The tone is usually formal, courteous and objective, rather than casual, overly familiar or aggressive. Any letters that lack a logical structure, use an inappropriate tone or contain spelling or grammar errors are likely to create a poor overall impression.

- **Memorandum** A memorandum (or memo) is a form of communication used within an organisation. There is a standard format for heading a memo, but the content and length are decided by the sender.
- **Fax** This is used to communicate externally with other businesses or between departments in different locations. A document containing written or typed text or images is sent via a telephone line by feeding it into a facsimile machine at one end; a copy of the document then appears via another machine at the receiver's end. Despite the widespread use of computers and scanning devices, faxes are still commonly used to send documents quickly from one destination to another.
- **Invoice** This is a document that is used to request payment for goods and services that are sold by businesses on credit. It confirms a number of details, including a description of the goods sold, quantity, unit price, any discounts given, the overall amount to be paid and the date by which payment should be made. Invoices that are sent to customers and also received from suppliers are kept as part of the accounting process and used to draw up a firm's final accounts. They are usually kept on file for a number of years as evidence in the case of any tax enquiries or disputes over payment.

- **Flow chart** This provides an illustration involved in a particular process. It may be used to highlight the steps that need to be taken to produce a product, complete a programme of training, deal with a customer complaint or create an advertising campaign.
- **Publicity materials** These can take a number of formats, including TV and newspaper advertisements, billboards, leaflets, brochures, catalogues and point-of-sale materials. The two key functions of publicity materials are to provide information about products and to persuade customers to buy them. They need to communicate a clear message to their target audience in order to achieve this.
- **Email and screen based** The impact of email as a communications method has grown dramatically in the last decade or so. It has become the most commonly used form of written communication within business organisations, used principally for sending instantaneous and relatively informal messages. However, as is the case with many forms of written communication, their effectiveness depends on how quickly they are read and acted on by the recipient. Screen-based communications include the use of TV screens in airports, railway stations and other businesses to convey information to customers, including details about changes to travel arrangements, general news updates and various forms of publicity.
- **Short message service (SMS)** For many years, SMS (or text messaging, as it is more commonly known in the UK) has been used as a method of social, rather than business, communication, by mobile phone users. However, an increasing number of firms are beginning to see the

benefits of SMS as a method of direct marketing to specific segments within markets.

- **The worldwide web** The discovery of the many possible business applications of the internet has led to an explosion in its use in recent years. Firms of every size have recognised the benefits to be gained from setting up websites in order to do some, if not all, of the following:

o communicate with markets around the world, increasing sales opportunities

o gather market-research data from primary sources by encouraging customer feedback, as well as allowing access to published secondary sources

o source the most appropriate suppliers, leading to lower prices and/or better quality.

A billboard advertisement

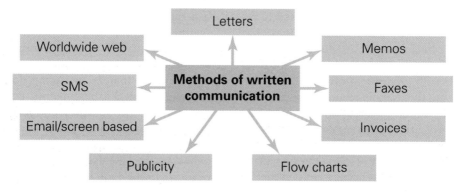

**Figure 4.5** Methods of written communication

# Methods of non-written communication

These methods of communication offer the chance to interact and provide instant feedback between the parties involved. The most common methods used include:

- **Telephone calls** These remain a very popular method of one-to-one communication, both within an organisation and between it and other businesses. Modern telephone systems allow callers to access destinations around the world quickly and cheaply, to switch from one line to another and to hold conversations with a number of different speakers at the same time. However, long conversations can be expensive, especially if dealing with a large number of recipients.
- **Video conferencing** This involves holding meetings by using screens and telephone lines between people in two or more different locations. The purpose is to attempt to create face-to-face communications when it is inconvenient or too costly to bring the people involved together in the same venue.

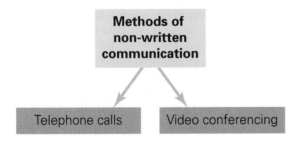

**Figure 4.6** Methods of non-written communication

# Technologies

Recent advances in technology have impacted on business communications in a number of ways, including:

- **Computers** Modern business communications rely heavily on the use of computer systems to generate, store and retrieve information. The ability to set up internal communications within an organisation means that information can be shared quickly and easily between key business functions, such as marketing, operations and human resources, allowing a business to coordinate its activities more effectively.

- **Touch screens** These facilitate interaction by allowing the user to communicate by making direct contact with a screen. A commonly used method is self-service supermarket checkout tills where customers scan their purchases, then check out and press payment options.
- **Digital broadcasting** The increasingly widespread use of digital television is allowing more and more businesses to have two-way communications with their customers. Digital television has a number of advantages over traditional television broadcasting. For example, it allows viewers to make choices and express opinions by clicking buttons on their remote controls.
- **DVD (digital versatile/video disc)** This is now a very common form of storing information, replacing previous methods such as VHS tapes and CDs. Improved storage capacity has meant a significant improvement in the quality of data that can be stored.
- **Mobile phones** The pace of technological change regarding the power and facilities available via mobile phones has continued to accelerate since the first phones were introduced a couple of decades ago. Modern mobiles now allow fast access to the internet, so that users can log on to websites and their email, regardless of location. Mobile phone technology continues to accelerate, permitting any number of new communications functions in the future.
- **WAP (wireless application protocol)** This is the technology used by devices such as smartphones to access the internet to check email, send texts and access websites. Continuing developments in technology are likely to further improve the range and quality of services on offer.

# Communication skills

There are a number of situations in which both internal and external communications can take place. **Formal communications** take place through recognised channels, such as official meetings between managers, employees, suppliers or key customers. **Informal communications** are the unscheduled meetings, usually between employees, that occur on a daily basis. Both formal and informal communications are needed within a business. The former are used to send out official messages and to keep management informed. The latter are used to interpret what happens on a day-to-day basis. The main potential problem with informal communication is that it is out of the control of management and may lead to the spread of mis-information, i.e. the spread of distorted or false messages throughout an organisation.

- **Verbal/non-verbal** It may also be useful to categorise communication in terms of verbal and non-verbal methods. **Verbal communications** rely on the spoken word and include methods such as telephone calls, visual presentations and video conferencing. **Non-verbal communication** methods include traditional forms of communication, including the sending of letters, memos and faxes, as well as more modern forms of communication such as email and text messaging.

- **Listening** This is a vital skill that is often overlooked in the communication process. Many people believe that they are listening but, in fact, they are not actively concentrating on what is being said. Listening requires effort, so that the messages being sent out are registered, understood and made sense of. It may also be necessary to seek clarification or further information (see below).

- **Understanding** Wherever possible, the communication process should be designed to allow for feedback. This is necessary in order to ensure that the message has been understood by the receiver in the way intended by the sender. For example, someone delivering a presentation to a group of people should pause regularly to take questions from them, or build in activities requiring the audience to act upon the information that has been given to them.

- **Seeking clarification** This involves the receiver of a message putting questions to the sender in order to achieve a full understanding by clarifying any areas of doubt. Many people are reluctant to seek clarification, as they believe this may suggest that they lack intelligence. However, seeking clarification should be encouraged, to avoid confusion and ensure that everyone has a clear understanding.

- **Responsiveness** Communication is an ongoing process. Presenters need to be able to respond appropriately to the needs of the audience by answering questions and dealing with any points raised. Even where information is not immediately available, every effort should be made to provide answers as soon as possible. Full concentration is required from an audience if the message is to be communicated effectively to everyone. Presenters should, therefore, be looking out for signs that people are not listening and take action to deal with this.

- **Eye contact, facial expressiveness and body language** Effective presentations are not just about what a person says but also about how they say it. Making regular eye contact is important, as it suggests confidence and a good understanding of the topics being delivered. Refusing to do so sends out a message that the presenter is nervous and badly prepared. Facial expressions can also reinforce the message being delivered. These need to reflect the tone of the message being sent – for example, adopting an overly cheerful manner while making an announcement about staff redundancies would be considered inappropriate. Both of these are examples of body language, which is a term used to describe any non-verbal communication. Many of the signals sent out by people occur subconsciously but still have a significant effect on the message being communicated. For example, a job candidate who slouches in a chair and fiddles constantly with her hair is likely to give the impression of not being interested, regardless of the verbal responses given.

- **Use of appropriate professional language** The language used in business communication must be professional at all times. This means adopting a tone that is polite and relatively formal; being overly friendly or too casual should be avoided in the workplace, as it can be misinterpreted and may undermine authority.

- **Ability to adapt communication techniques to audience requirements** The same message may need to be adapted so that it can be understood by different audience groups. For example, a team delivering the findings of a primary research survey to colleagues in the marketing department may include a number of technical terms. However, they may choose to communicate in a more general way when delivering the same findings to non-marketing managers elsewhere in the business.

- **Presentational skills** Oral presentations can be a daunting prospect. Standing up before an audience, remembering points, responding to questions and, at the same time, dealing with equipment such as computers or OHPs are not skills that come naturally. Part 4 of Unit 10 contains some useful advice on delivering oral presentations effectively. Key advice includes:

o Practise beforehand with any equipment or slides, so that they can be used correctly.

o Ensure that you have a good understanding of the topic, allowing you to speak confidently to the audience, rather than having to refer constantly to notes.

o Keep the pace slow enough for the audience to understand but fast enough to maintain interest.

o Remember to make regular eye contact and use positive body language.

- **Ability to invite commitment to shared goals** This involves winning people over and securing the support of an audience. It is much easier to communicate a message if this can be done than if the audience is bored or hostile. Experienced writers and speakers are skilled at interacting with people, persuading them of the benefits to be enjoyed from pursuing a particular course of action.

## Key terms

**Accessibility** The extent to which people with disabilities are able to receive the same messages as able-bodied people, both as a result of changes to the physical environment and the communication methods used

**Body language** Facial expressions, body posture and other gestures, many of which are made subconsciously, that have a significant effect on the message being communicated

**Fax** Where a document is sent via a telephone line by feeding it into a facsimile machine at one end; a copy of the document then appears via another machine at the receiver's end

**Formal communication** This takes place through recognised channels, such as official meetings between managers, employees, suppliers or key customers

**Informal communication** Unscheduled meetings, usually between employees, that occur on a daily basis

**Invoice** A document used to request payment for goods and services that are sold by businesses on credit

**Legibility** The extent to which written text can be easily read as a result of the layout, font size and style used

**Memorandum** A relatively informal type of written communication used within an organisation

**Non-verbal communication** Methods that rely on the use of the written word, including letters, memos, faxes, email and text messaging

**Short Message Service (SMS)** Known in the UK as text messaging, and increasingly being used by firms as a method of direct marketing to specific segments within markets

**Verbal communication** Methods that rely on the use of the spoken word, including telephone calls, visual presentation and video conferencing

**Video conferencing** Holding meetings by using screens and telephone lines between people in two or more different locations

**Wireless application protocol (WAP)** The technology uses by devices such as smartphones, to access the internet, in order to check email, send texts and access websites

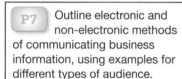

## Re-cap questions

1 Explain why a business should think carefully about the age, gender and ethnicity of the people in the target market before designing an advertising campaign for a new product.

2 Outline two ways in which a manager delivering a presentation to the workforce of a large company could make it accessible to disabled employees.

3 Explain what is meant by distraction avoidance.

4 Describe one key benefit of written communication over verbal communication.

5 Identify three forms of written communication that could be used to send information from one business to another.

6 Identify two forms of non-written communication used by businesses.

7 Explain why listening is an important part of the communication process.

8 Explain why many people are reluctant to seek clarification about information given to them.

9 Using examples, explain how body language is part of the communication process.

10 Suggest three measures that a person should take before delivering a presentation.

## Grading tips

| P7 Outline electronic and non-electronic methods of communicating business information, using examples for different types of audience. | | |
|---|---|---|
| Make sure you describe a range of electronic and non-electronic methods, backed up with examples showing how they were appropriate for the intended audience. | | |

### Assignments for Unit 4

#### Assignment One

You work in the human resources department of a business. You have been asked by your manager to produce a series of resources related to business information and communications, which will be used as a basis for staff training. The resources will investigate where business information comes from and how it is used to make strategic decisions. They will also contain examples of corporate communications.

**Note** – read through the tasks below, the relevant criteria and the assignment advice on pages 126 and 132 before choosing your organisation.

**Criteria covered** – P1 P2 P3 P4 M1 D1 D2

### Tasks

1. Produce a factsheet outlining the different types of business information, their sources and purposes. (P1)

2. Produce a presentation on complex internal business information used within your selected business, giving three different methods that are appropriate to the user's needs. (P2)

3. Produce a piece of corporate communications for your selected business. (P3)

4. Write a report evaluating a piece of corporate communications for an existing product or service produced by your selected business. (P4)

5. Write a written report that analyses the different types of business information and their sources. (M1)

6. Develop Task 5 further by evaluating the appropriateness of business information used to make strategic decisions. (D1)

7. Develop Tasks 5 and 6 further by evaluating the effectiveness of business information and communications. This must consider how business information and communications contribute to the success of your business. Use examples to support the points made. (D2)

## Assignment Two

You have now been asked to produce a written report on the legal, ethical and operational issues faced by the company that you work for.

**Note** – read through the tasks below, the relevant criteria and the assignment advice on pages 138 and 147 before choosing your organisation. You may continue with a business used previously in this unit, or find another where you are able to more easily obtain all of the information needed. You may also use different businesses in order to cover criteria P5 and P6 satisfactorily.

**Criteria covered** – P5 P6 M2

### Tasks

1. Write an explanation of the legal and ethical issues faced by your selected business in relation to the use of business information (P5). This must include:

2. A description of the organisation's ethical policy with examples of how it affects business information.

3. An explanation of how the organisation complies with legislation relating to business information.

4. Explain the operational issues in relation to the use of business information in a selected organisation. You should look at a range of issues, such as health and safety and confidentiality. You must also describe the systems developed to manage information, including the software and training required. (P6)

5. Produce an analysis of the legal, ethical and operational issues faced by your selected organisation or organisations. This should examine in detail the reasons for the policies and procedures relating to the use of business information, as well as their benefits and drawbacks.

## Assignment Three

Your final task in this project is to produce a leaflet outlining the main electronic and non-electronic methods used for communicating business information to different types of audience.

**Note** – read through the task, the relevant criteria and the assignment advice on page 146. Make sure that you cover all of the communication methods identified by the specification.

**Criteria covered** – P7

### Tasks

1. Produce a factsheet outlining the electronic and non-electronic methods used for communicating business information. Use examples to show the most appropriate methods for different audiences.

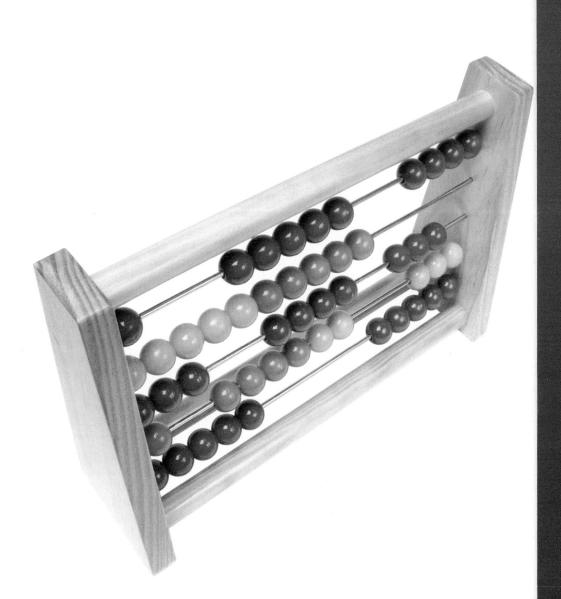

# Part 1: The purpose of accounting

In 2007, Innocent Drinks – the UK's number one smoothie producer – generated sales worth £112 million and made a pre-tax profit of £12.1 million. Twelve months later, despite annual sales of over two million smoothies, control of two-thirds of the UK market and sales growth of 82 per cent in Europe during 2008, the company's sales revenue had fallen to £99 million and the previous year's profit had been turned into a pre-tax loss of £11.2 million. Although the news of this dramatic change in performance was greeted with surprise by many analysts, it is unlikely that the results were unexpected by Innocent's senior management. The company's **accounting** systems would have alerted management about the deterioration in performance long before the figures were actually published.

The purpose of accounting is to collect, prepare and analyse financial data relating to a firm's performance. Access to such data is vital for the effective management of a business. Accounting information not only allows managers, such as those at Innocent Drinks, to measure the extent of a company's progress and the effectiveness of past decisions, it also informs current decision making, allowing them to plan for the future.

There are a number of reasons why accounting is required by businesses, including:

- **To record transactions and report performance** – limited companies are required by law to publish financial accounts on a yearly basis. All the transactions undertaken over the course of the financial year have to be recorded in order to produce a summary of the company's performance for shareholders and other stakeholders at the end of the year. Recording transactions also provides managers with the information needed to ensure that the business is run smoothly on a day-to-day basis.
- **To monitor activity** – information on the performance of the business needs to be produced on a constant basis, so that it can be compared regularly to the targets set out by managers. This should reveal if sufficient progress has been made towards achieving business objectives within the timescale required.
- **To control activity** – constant monitoring of performance allows corrective action to be taken quickly, before problems begin to seriously damage business performance. For example, unless details of all credit purchases are recorded, payment to one or more suppliers may be missed, resulting in damaged relationships, possible interest charges and even a refusal to supply in the future. Similarly, failure to keep a record of all sales could mean that a lack of payment from customers goes unnoticed, causing cash flow problems and reducing profits.
- **To manage the business** – managers are not just concerned with monitoring and controlling current activities. They also need to draw up strategies to guide future performance, in order to ensure that corporate objectives continue to be met. Decisions about the future are inevitably based on a certain degree of uncertainty, but having a detailed and accurate picture of current performance should help to improve the effectiveness of any strategies that are devised.

## Financial accounting and management accounting

It can be useful to distinguish between two types of accounting – **financial accounting** and **management accounting**. Financial accounting is concerned with providing information for external users, such as potential investors, suppliers or the Government, by compiling the final accounts. Management accounting focuses on providing information that can be used by managers to improve decisions regarding the control of current business activity and the planning of future actions.

## Measuring financial performance

Profit is a key indicator of business success. It provides a measure of how well a business can turn inputs into outputs, creating the widest gap possible between revenues and costs. Accurate accounting records are needed in order to measure and monitor levels of profit. Accounting data will also provide evidence as to how profit has been made, why any changes to profit – either increases or decreases – have occurred, and how any improvements to profit can be made.

The key profit figures that managers will be keen to find out include:

- **Gross profit** – this is the difference between the sales revenue generated from selling products and the direct costs incurred in manufacturing goods, buying in goods produced elsewhere for resale, or the materials required to provide services. Although it does not take into account all of the costs incurred, gross profit provides a basic measure of a firm's ability to turn inputs into outputs successfully.
- **Net profit** – this takes into account all of a firm's costs by taking gross profit and subtracting any other expenses incurred. This is a key indicator of how well a business can control overheads, such as managers' salaries, advertising and administration costs.

- **Value owed to and by the business** – value owed to a business refers to the money a firm expects to receive in the near future from debtors, i.e. customers who have bought goods or services and have yet to pay. Although the cash has yet to be received, it is included in a firm's sales revenue, boosting profit. Value owed by the business refers to the money owed to suppliers as a result of purchasing goods or services on credit. Although the business has not yet made payment, it is treated as a cost, reducing profits.

## Capital income

**Capital income** is the money that is raised to set up a new business or expand an existing one. One of the most important sources of capital income is the finance generated by the business owners from their own savings. A business with only one owner – known as a **sole trader** – may struggle to raise sufficient finance from this particular source. In many cases, the only way that sole traders can raise the finance necessary to expand is by turning

## Sainsbury's financial performance boosted by strong sales

In November 2009, supermarket group J Sainsbury announced an increase in profits of nearly 33 per cent over the previous six months. Despite difficult trading conditions resulting from the economic recession, the company succeeded in generating pre-tax profits of £342 million in the six months

to 3 October 2009, up from £258 million on the same period for the previous year. Excluding fuel sales, the retailer's like-for-like sales – which take out any impact resulting from opening any new stores – rose by 5.7 per cent.

Following the announcement, the company confirmed its decision to press ahead with plans to create 10,000 new jobs by March 2011 and to increase its retail space by 15 per cent, through a combination of expanding existing supermarket branches and the opening of new outlets.

**Source: www.bbc.co.uk/news**

### Questions

a) Briefly describe Sainsbury's financial performance in the six months to October 2009.

b) Explain how senior managers within Sainsbury's are likely to use accounting data to manage the company more effectively.

c) Using the internet, carry out research and compare the financial performance of other leading UK supermarkets, such as Tesco, Asda and Morrisons, to that of Sainsbury's over the same period of time.

the business into a partnership. Additional owners or **partners** will invest their own savings into the business, increasing the capital available. However, all sole traders and most partners have unlimited liability. **Unlimited liability** means that owners are personally responsible for any debts that their business might incur, discouraging many people from investing in them. Many businesses are set up as **limited companies** in order to overcome this. Owners of limited companies are given shares, in exchange for their investment in the business, and are, therefore, known as shareholders. Shareholders also enjoy **limited liability**, where the extent of their financial responsibility is limited to their investment in the business, rather than the total business debt. Shareholders are entitled to receive a **dividend**, or a proportion of the profits that have been generated. The size of the dividend received by each shareholder depends on the number of shares held, the total level of profit made over a given period of time and the amount of this profit that the company's directors decide to distribute, rather than reinvest back into the business.

Firms can also raise capital income by borrowing. **Bank loans** are often used by businesses to finance the purchase of capital equipment. The size of the loan and the length of time that the money is borrowed can be varied to reflect the needs of the business. The loan has to be repaid with interest, making borrowing more expensive than using personal finance. However, the terms for repaying the loan are agreed beforehand, allowing the business to include the repayment schedule in its budgets. The rate of interest on the loan can be fixed or variable. The figure charged depends on a number of factors, including the amount borrowed and the perceived risk of default, which may mean that small or newly-established businesses are forced to pay higher rates. In addition, banks usually expect businesses to provide a form of security, such as property, which may place a limit on the amount that small businesses are able to borrow.

A **mortgage** is a large, long-term loan used by businesses (as well as individuals) to purchase property. The length of a mortgage is typically between 20 and 25 years. A mortgage can also be raised against property that the business already owns outright, so that the funds can be used for another purpose, for example to purchase machinery.

## Revenue income

**Revenue income** is the money generated by a business as a result of its day-to-day operations. The main source of revenue income for most businesses comes from the sale of goods or services. This could be in the form of **cash sales**, where customers pay immediately, or **credit sales**, where customers pay for the goods or services they have received at some point in the future. Firms often agree to credit sales with other businesses as a means of winning sales, especially if the customers concerned can provide evidence of a positive bank balance and a record of prompt payment to suppliers.

Some businesses have other sources of revenue income, in addition to sales. Some firms own property that is unused and can, therefore, be rented out to other firms. The **rent received** provides funds that can be used within the business. A firm might also generate income by selling goods on behalf of another business, known as **commission received**.

## Capital expenditure

**Capital expenditure** is the money that a business spends in order to acquire **tangible fixed assets**, that is, any physical items of value brought into the firm and used over time to produce goods and services. Fixed assets include land and buildings, such as offices, shops or factories, machinery and equipment, vehicles and fixtures and fittings. There are also a number of **intangible assets** that can be valuable to a business. For example, taking out a **patent** on a newly invented product or production process (or buying an existing patent from another business) gives a firm the right to be the only one to produce or use it for up to a maximum of twenty years. **Trademarks** are names, symbols or logos that can also be used exclusively by firms if they are registered with the Patent Office. Their value to firms comes from the fact that they can make products instantly recognisable and distinctive from competing brands. **Goodwill** is another potentially valuable intangible asset that is gradually built up by a business through a positive business image, the skills and loyalty of its workforce and its excellent relations with customers and suppliers. The value of goodwill is recognised in the sales price of a business when it is sold to another organisation.

An office building is an example of a tangible fixed asset

## Revenue expenditure

**Revenue expenditure** refers to any expenses incurred by a business as a result of its day-to-day operations. It does not include any spending required to purchase fixed assets, such as machinery, but does include the cost of the power needed to make it work. Other common types of revenue expenditure include:

- **The cost of premises** – a firm may not have the resources to buy its premises outright, or may simply wish to avoid getting into too much debt by taking on a mortgage. In either case, it could choose instead to rent premises, which will involve regular – usually monthly – payments to whoever owns the property. Business premises generate a number of additional costs, such as heating, lighting and insurance. Business rates also need to be paid on most commercial properties, including shops, offices, warehouses and factories.

- **The cost of administration** – the term 'administration' refers to all of the various activities carried out in order to support business activity. Such expenses include telephone bills and stationery costs.

- **Staffing costs** – the costs of employing people extend beyond paying their **wages** or **salaries**. Many businesses offer extra perks to their employees, such as company cars, contributions to pension schemes and private medical insurance. Employers also need to pay National Insurance Contributions and Employers' Liability Insurance to provide protection against staff making claims for injuries that may have occurred in the workplace. Firms may also choose to pay to train their employees, in order to give them the skills required to perform effectively.

- **Selling and distribution costs** – these include the cost of paying the salaries of sales staff and covering any expenses incurred by them, as well as the costs of transporting goods to wholesalers, retailers or even directly to the final consumer.

- **Finance costs** – there are a number of expenses resulting from having to deal with banks and other financial institutions. Firms would struggle to function without a bank account allowing them to make payments to suppliers and receive payments from customers. The charges made by banks for managing day-to-day financial transactions, such as paying in cheques, can be substantial. In addition, the interest paid on overdrafts, bank loans and mortgages is treated as a revenue expense.

- **The cost of purchasing stock** – the kind of stock purchased by a business depends on the nature of its activities. For example, a car mechanic will buy in stocks of spare parts in order to repair customers' vehicles, a restaurant will purchase food ingredients for the meals contained on its menus, wine and other drinks.

# Capital and revenue: income and expenditure

In April 2009, Vanessa James set up her own business, A Cut Above, offering mobile hairdressing services and beauty treatments to customers in her local area. She decided to operate as a sole trader initially, in order to keep the start-up as simple as possible. She rents an office on the high street of the village where she lives and employs two staff, on a part-time basis, to help carry out the work. Vanessa used some of her savings to buy equipment, such as hairdryers, scissors and other equipment, as well as staff uniforms, in order to give the business a more professional image. She obtained a personal loan from her bank to buy a new van, which is used by the staff to get to clients' houses. Vanessa also uses it every week to buy stocks of hair-care products and other supplies from a local producer. She sells a range of these products to customers on behalf of the manufacturer, and is paid 15 per cent of the sales price as a commission for any sales she makes.

a) Identify at least two examples of the following, based on Vanessa's business: capital income, capital expenditure, revenue income, revenue expenditure. Present your findings in the form of a table.

# Key terms

**Accounting** The business function responsible for collecting, preparing and analysing financial data about a firm's performance

**Capital expenditure** The money spent by a business in order to acquire fixed assets, such as buildings and machinery

**Capital income** This is the finance used to set up a new business or to expand an existing one. The main sources are owners' capital, loans and mortgages

**Commission received** An example of revenue income generated when a firm sells goods on behalf of another business

**Goodwill** When the price that a business is sold for reflects the value of it having a well-known name, established reputation and degree of consumer loyalty

**Gross profit** The difference between a firm's sales revenue and the cost of the goods sold

**Intangible fixed asset** Assets that belong to a business but that do not have a physical presence. They include goodwill, patents and trademarks

**Mortgage** A long-term loan used to buy land or property

**Net profit** Profit left over once all expenses incurred by a business have been deducted from its sales revenue and any other income generated over a given period of time. It is calculated by taking gross profit and deducting expenses

**Patent** Gives an individual or firm the exclusive right to produce or use a newly invented product or process for up to 20 years

**Revenue expenditure** Any expenses incurred by a business as a result of its day-to-day operations. It includes rent, insurance, staff wages and the cost of stocks

**Revenue income** The money generated by a business as a result of its day-to-day operations. It is made up of revenue – either from cash or credit sales – but may also come from rental income or commission received from selling the products of other firms

**Tangible fixed asset** These are physical assets, such as buildings, machinery and vehicles, that are kept within a business for a number of years and are used to produce goods or services

**Trademark** A name, logo or symbol used to differentiate a firm or its products from its rivals

## Q Re-cap questions

1 Briefly outline the purpose of accounting.
2 State two reasons why accounting data is recorded by firms.
3 Explain why managers need to monitor accounting data on a regular basis.
4 Outline the role played by accounting data in managing a business successfully.
5 Explain why profit is seen as a key indicator of business performance.
6 Outline the difference between gross profit and net profit.
7 Using examples, briefly explain what is meant by capital income.
8 Explain why the sources of capital income of a sole trader are likely to be more limited than those of a partnership or a limited company.
9 Suggest two reasons why small businesses may struggle to raise loan capital.
10 Explain what is meant by a mortgage.
11 Outline what is meant by revenue income.
12 Identify and briefly describe three sources of revenue income.
13 Explain what is meant by capital expenditure.
14 Give three examples of intangible fixed assets.
15 Using examples, explain what is meant by revenue expenditure.

## Grading tips

 **P1** Describe the purpose of accounting for an organisation

Although your description can be brief, it must contain sufficient detail to describe clearly the main purpose of accounting. Make sure that you choose an organisation where it is possible to obtain relevant examples of historical accounting data which has been used to record, monitor, control and manage the business, allowing financial performance to be measured.

| P2 Explain the difference between capital and revenue items of expenditure and income | | |
|---|---|---|
| You need to include an accurate definition of what each category means and then choose suitable examples from a specific type of organisation to support your explanations. These examples should be relevant to the nature of the business. For example, 'the cost of supplies' could refer to most businesses, whereas 'the cost of food ingredients, soft drinks, wine and other alcohol' would be relevant to a restaurant or hotel. Make sure you are clear as to whether you are dealing with a sole trader, a partnership or a limited company. | | |

See page 180 for suggestions for Assignments for Unit 5.

# Part 2: Cash flow forecasting

The ability to make an acceptable level of **profit** is an important long-term objective of most businesses. Profit is the amount of revenue left over once all costs have been accounted for. It is an indicator of a firm's success and also provides an important source of funds for future investment. However, in the short term, maintaining a positive cash flow may be even more important than making a profit. **Cash flow** refers to all of the money flowing in and out of a business on a day-to-day basis. Cash flows into a business from a number of sources, including payments from customers, investments by owners, bank loans and **overdrafts**. Cash flows out of a business in order to cover all of the expenses incurred, such as the cost of supplies, wages, rent and electricity. Business owners or managers must ensure that there is sufficient cash within the business to meet any payments, as and when they are due.

## Cash flow forecasts

Attempting to predict the size and timing of future cash inflows and outflows can help a business to manage cash flow effectively. This information can be used by managers to compile a **cash flow forecast**. This is a statement of all the expected cash flows into and out of a business over a future period of time. Although future cash flows cannot be predicted with 100 per cent accuracy, cash flow forecasts can highlight any points in the future where cash flow is likely to become negative, that is, more money is expected to flow out of the business than to flow into it. If managers are aware of such a situation in advance, they can attempt to secure the finance needed to continue to pay any debts that fall due. A common way of dealing with negative cash flow in the short term is to use the overdraft facility set up on the firm's business account (or to increase its size if necessary), repaying the funds when cash flow becomes positive again. If, however, cash flow is expected to remain negative for longer periods of time, managers will need to take more drastic action to improve the firm's performance.

Cash flow forecasts are usually compiled on a month by month basis, for up to twelve months ahead. Figures are updated regularly, as information becomes available, in order to make forecasts as accurate as possible. The exact contents of an individual firm's cash flow forecasts will depend on the nature of its cash receipts and expenditure. However, the basic structure for a cash flow forecast shows the following:

- **Opening balance** – the balance of cash from the previous period (also known as the balance brought forward)
- **Total receipts** – the sum of all of the individual sources of cash inflow for the period
- **Total expenses** – the sum of all the individual items of expenditure for the period

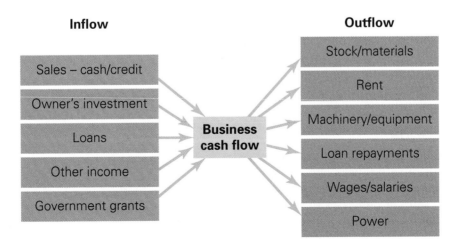

**Figure 5.1** Key sources of cash inflow and outflow

| | January £ | February £ | March £ | April £ | May £ | June £ |
|---|---|---|---|---|---|---|
| Opening balance | 1,000 | 3,800 | 4,000 | (400) | 200 | 3,500 |
| Total receipts | 15,200 | 12,700 | 11,300 | 12,500 | 14,300 | 15,500 |
| Total expenses | 12,400 | 12,500 | 15,700 | 11,900 | 11,000 | 11,800 |
| Net cash flow | 2,800 | 200 | (4,400) | 600 | 3,300 | 3,700 |
| Closing balance | 3,800 | 4,000 | (400) | 200 | 3,500 | 7,200 |

**Figure 5.2** The basic structure of a cash flow forecast

- **Net cash flow** – the difference between total receipts and total payments
- **Closing balance** – the sum of the opening balance and the net cash flow, representing the cash balance at the end of the period (also known as the balance carried forward).

The basic layout of a six-month cash flow forecast is shown above.

January's opening balance of £1,000 refers to any cash left over at the end of December in the firm's bank account. The net cash figure of £2,800 for January is calculated by taking the total value of cash inflows (total receipts) of £15,200 and subtracting the total value of the cash outflows (total expenses) of £12,400. January's closing balance of £3,800 is found by adding together the figures for the opening balance and net cash flow. Note that the closing balance for each month becomes the opening balance for the following month – the cash that remains in the bank account on the last day of January is the same amount as that at the start of February, and so on.

Note also that the figures for March's net cash flow and closing balance are in brackets, indicating a negative amount. As a result, the opening balance for April is also negative. By drawing up the forecast, managers are able to spot that the business will have insufficient cash to meet its outgoings in March, unless action is taken.

## Credit periods

Managers need to take account of the timing, as well as the size, of cash inflows and outflows, in order to control cash flow effectively. Some firms insist on **cash sales** or purchases with their customers or suppliers. This means that payment has to be made at the same time that goods or services

are supplied. For example, it is highly unlikely for a supermarket or other retailer to hand over goods to customers unless they have some way of paying for them at the point of sale. However, it is common for business between firms to take place on the basis of credit sales or purchases. Although goods or services are supplied, payment is not received or made immediately, but requested by invoice to take place at an agreed point in the future, typically in 30 to 90 days' time. Therefore, if, for example, a business is given a 30-day **credit period** by its suppliers, any purchase invoices received in January do not have to be paid until February, and so the amount owing would appear on the cash flow forecast to be paid in this month. If, on the other hand, the business allows its customers to have a 60-day credit period, receipts from sales expected to be made in January would not appear on the cash flow forecast until March.

The period of time between having to pay for supplies and receiving cash for goods or services sold to customers is known as the cash cycle (see Figure 5.3). The longer this period is, the greater the risk that a firm will suffer from cash flow problems.

**Figure 5.3** The cash cycle

# Cash flow forecasts – receipts

A firm's cash flow forecast provides a breakdown of the cash it expects to receive in the near future, usually on a month-by-month basis. The main sources of cash inflow include:

- **Cash sales** – these are sales made by a firm where the customer pays immediately for the goods or services supplied. There is no difference between when the sale is made and when payment is received, and the value of the sale will appear on the cash flow forecast in the month it is expected to occur. Insisting on cash sales removes any uncertainty that customers may actually fail to pay at the time agreed in the future, which could result in cash flow problems. However, if business customers prefer to pay on credit, sales are likely to be lost to competitors who are willing to offer credit terms.
- **Credit sales** – these are sales where the business supplies goods or services at a certain point in time, then sends an invoice requesting payment at an agreed point in the future. Customers with outstanding payments are referred to as **debtors** in the firm's accounts. The credit sale appears on the cash flow forecast in the month when payment is expected to be received, rather than when the sale is agreed. Offering credit terms to business customers is often used to win sales, especially if the firm concerned is established and can provide evidence of being creditworthy.
- **Owners' capital** – this is the money put into the business by the owner or owners and may come from savings or redundancy. This is usually the main source of finance for a business when it is first set up, but may also be required once the business is established to fund expansion or to resolve cash flow crises.
- **Loans** – funds may be borrowed from a number of sources, including the friends and family of the owners of the business. Alternatively, funds can be raised by taking out a loan with a bank. Loans provide a significant injection of finance into a business and are often used to finance capital expenditure on premises, machinery and other fixed assets. However, loans have to be repaid – usually with interest – at some point in the future and the repayments will recreate a cash outflow.
- **Other income** – some firms may own assets that generate cash inflows, such as rental income from property or dividends from owning shares in other businesses. In addition, commission may be earned from selling products produced by other businesses.
- **Government grants** – this is a sum of money that may be provided by one of a number of organisations, including Business Link and the Regional Development Agencies, for a specific purpose, such as to help cover the costs of start-up.

# Cash flow forecasts – payments

This section of the cash flow forecast provides details on all of the payments the business expects to have to make in future months. The major sources of cash outflow include:

- **Cash purchases** – businesses will need to buy in stocks of the materials used to produce the goods or services it sells to its customers. In some cases, it will pay its suppliers immediately. This may be because it is unable to obtain trade credit, or it may be reluctant to take on any debt. In such cases, the estimated cost of the supplies will appear on the cash flow forecast in the month that they are expected to be ordered and delivered.
- **Credit purchases** – securing credit on the purchase of supplies of stock or materials can be of significant benefit to a business, giving it time, in theory, to sell to customers and receive payment before it needs to pay suppliers itself. These suppliers are regarded as **creditors** for accounting purposes, until any outstanding debts have been settled. However, offering or receiving credit can make it more difficult to manage cash flow effectively. However long the credit period offered by suppliers, a firm must have sufficient cash to settle its debts, when required to do so.
- **Revenue expenditure** – this refers to any cash outflows to cover regular expenses incurred in the day-to-day running of the business, such as wages, rent, insurance, heating and lighting. It will also include bank charges and any interest incurred on loans or overdrafts. These payments may be required every month, or less frequently, such as on a quarterly or even yearly basis. Payments may be made in arrears (relating to a past period) or in advance (relating to a forthcoming period). However, for the purposes of a cash flow forecast, payments will appear in the month that they fall due.

- **Capital expenditure** – this refers to less frequent payments required when a business needs to acquire fixed assets, such as machinery and premises. This is most likely to occur when the business is first set up, but it may also be necessary to replace worn-out equipment, update technology or expand operations. It may also be required to register patents or acquire trademarks. Figures for this will appear on the cash flow forecast when the capital expenditure is expected to take place.

| | April £ | May £ | June £ | July £ | Totals £ |
|---|---|---|---|---|---|
| (A) Opening balance | 0 | 800 | 620 | 2,040 | |
| | | | | | |
| Receipts | | | | | |
| Owner's capital | 10,000 | 0 | 0 | 0 | 10,000 |
| Bank loan | 10,000 | 0 | 0 | 0 | 10,000 |
| Cash sales | 0 | 8,000 | 8,000 | 8,000 | 24,000 |
| Credit sales | 0 | 0 | 4,000 | 4,000 | 8,000 |
| Rent received | 0 | 250 | 250 | 250 | 750 |
| Commission received | 0 | 0 | 1,500 | 0 | 1,500 |
| (B) Total receipts | 20,000 | 8,250 | 13,750 | 12,250 | 54,250 |
| | | | | | |
| Expenses | | | | | |
| Equipment | 7,700 | 0 | 3,000 | 0 | 10,700 |
| Fixtures & fittings | 3,500 | 0 | 0 | 0 | 3,500 |
| Stock purchases (cash) | 4,500 | 2,500 | 2,500 | 2,500 | 12,000 |
| Stock purchases (credit) | 0 | 2,500 | 3,000 | 3,000 | 8,500 |
| Wages | 1,000 | 1,000 | 1,000 | 1,000 | 4,000 |
| Advertising | 500 | 400 | 300 | 300 | 1,500 |
| Telephone | 40 | 40 | 40 | 40 | 160 |
| Rent and rates | 650 | 650 | 650 | 650 | 2,600 |
| Insurance | 60 | 60 | 60 | 60 | 240 |
| Loan repayments | 200 | 200 | 200 | 200 | 800 |
| Bank charges | 50 | 80 | 80 | 80 | 290 |
| Drawings | 1,000 | 1,000 | 1,500 | 1,000 | 4,500 |
| (C) Total expenses | 19,200 | 8,430 | 12,330 | 8,830 | 48,790 |
| | | | | | |
| (D) Net cash flow (B – C) | 800 | (180) | 1,420 | 3,420 | 5,460 |
| (E) Closing balance | 800 | 620 | 2,040 | 5,460 | 5,460 |

**Figure 5.4** A detailed cash flow forecast for a new business

## Value added tax

**Value added tax (VAT)** is an expenditure tax levied on most goods and services sold in the UK. Any business that has a sales turnover of more than £68,000 per year (figures for 2009) is required by law to register for VAT. This means that it must charge VAT on top of the sales price for the goods or services that it sells. The standard rate of VAT in the UK has been 17.5 per cent for some years, although this was reduced temporarily to 15 per cent from the end of November 2008 to the beginning of January 2010. In theory, the VAT charged to customers should be passed on to HM Customs and Excise. However, VAT registered businesses can also claim back any VAT they pay on any goods and services purchased on which the tax is levied, such as stock, equipment and stationery (note that VAT is not charged on expenses such as rent, wages and insurance). If the amount received in VAT is greater than the amount paid, the surplus must be passed on, usually on a quarterly basis. If, however, the reverse is true and the amount paid in VAT is greater than the amount received, the difference can be claimed back.

A firm that is registered for VAT needs to adjust its cash flow forecasts to take this into account. Any VAT collected on sales needs to be shown as a separate entry under the 'receipts' or 'cash inflow' section, while any VAT paid on purchases should be entered separately in the 'expenses' or 'cash outflow' section (see Figure 5.5 below):

Note that in the diagram below:

- The VAT on sales figure is calculated as 17.5 per cent of the value of sales receipts
- The VAT on purchases figures is based on payments for equipment and materials
- The VAT payable to Customs and Excise is calculated every quarter and is the surplus of VAT on sales and VAT on purchases
- The VAT figure paid to Customs and Excise for the quarter April to June comprises
  o VAT on sales (£1,750 × 3) – VAT on payments (£875 + £700 + £700) = £2,975
- The VAT figure paid to Customs and Excise for the quarter July to September comprises:
  o VAT on sales (£1,750 × 3) – VAT on payments (£700 × 3) = £3,150

## Cash flow management

Failure to manage cash flow successfully will affect a firm's ability to trade effectively and generate profits. Businesses with large positive cash balances at the end of every month are not necessarily profitable ones. Although sufficient cash needs to be kept back to pay for expenses, any surplus should be put to work, buying machinery and stock that can be turned into products and sold at a profit, rather than sitting in bank accounts earning no income. However, the problems caused by negative net cash balances tend to be even more serious. Cash flow problems may mean that suppliers cannot be paid on the

| | April £ | May £ | June £ | July £ | Aug £ | Sept £ |
|---|---|---|---|---|---|---|
| **Receipts** | | | | | | |
| Sales | 10,000 | 10,000 | 10,000 | 10,000 | 10,000 | 10,000 |
| VAT | 1,750 | 1,750 | 1,750 | 1,750 | 1,750 | 1,750 |
| | | | | | | |
| **Payments** | | | | | | |
| Equipment | 1,000 | 0 | 0 | 0 | 0 | 0 |
| Purchases | 4,000 | 4,000 | 4,000 | 4,000 | 4,000 | 4,000 |
| VAT on purchases | 875 | 700 | 700 | 700 | 700 | 700 |
| VAT paid to Customs & Excise | | | 2,975 | | | 3,150 |

**Figure 5.5** VAT entry on the cash flow forecast

dates agreed, damaging relationships and leading to the withdrawal of credit or even a refusal to supply at all. This, in turn, could mean that the firm struggles to meet its orders on time, creating customer dissatisfaction and a loss of sales. If the business is unable to pay its debts, it may be taken to court by its creditors, which could result, in some cases, in it being forced to close down.

Although it may not always be possible to avoid cash flow problems, being able to pinpoint what is causing the problems is essential if an effective solution is to be found.

## Causes of cash flow problems

- **Giving customers too much credit** – offering trade credit can help to win sales and retain customers. Credit sales do not necessarily create cash flow problems, as long as managers plan for the delay in payment for sales. However, the longer the credit period offered to customers, the longer it will be before cash flows into the business. The wider the gap between having to pay expenses involved in meeting orders and receiving money from sales, the greater the risk of cash flow turning negative. Firms selling on credit may also struggle if customers fail to pay by the date agreed, or go out of business without paying at all.
- **Overtrading** – rapid expansion without securing sufficient finance can also lead to cash flow problems. The costs of materials and labour will be increasing and will usually need to be covered well in advance of payment being received from customers, especially if they have been granted generous credit terms. The wider the gap between cash outflows and cash inflows, the greater the risk of experiencing cash flow problems.
- **Investing too much in fixed assets** – capital investment is usually required when a business is first set up or chooses to expand. However, acquiring premises, machinery and equipment can involve a significant amount of finance, leaving insufficient finance to cover the expenses incurred in running the business on a day-to-day basis.
- **An unexpected fall in sales** – the actual level of sales can differ dramatically from those expected for a number of reasons. Initial estimates may have been based on inaccurate market research, over-exaggerating the strength of demand. However, even accurately researched sales

figures can fail to materialise due to an unexpected increase in competition or a sudden and sharp downturn in the economy. A firm may have already purchased stock, machinery and hired labour, in anticipation of much higher sales. These will still need to be paid for, even if they are unlikely to generate the cash inflow required to prevent a cash flow crisis.

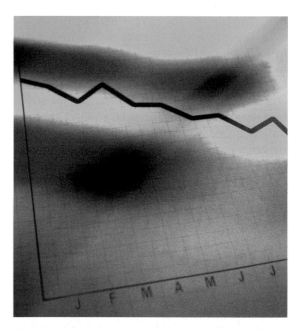

There a number of causes of cash flow problems

## Cash flow solutions

In the long term, the most effective solution to cash flow problems – and the best way of avoiding them in the first place – is to generate enough cash inflow from sales to cover any outgoing expenses. Increasing the rate of stock turnover (how quickly stock is sold) should lead to an increase in cash inflow, particularly if the transactions involve cash, rather than credit, sales.

However, it may not always be possible to do this, particularly in the short term. For example, it may take a while for a new firm to make the market aware of its products and for sales to start to grow. Changes in the business environment, such as the arrival of a new competitor, worsening economic conditions or a change in consumer tastes can damage the cash flow situation of a previously successful firm. It may take some time before managers can formulate a strategy that can respond effectively to these changes.

Being able to forecast periods of negative cash flow will allow managers to take preventative action before problems actually arise. However, unexpected events make it impossible to forecast future cash flow with 100 per cent accuracy. Managers must, therefore, monitor cash flow continuously so that action to deal with any problems can be taken as soon as it is required.

Common methods of preventing or resolving cash flow difficulties include arranging an overdraft, effective credit control, (re)negotiating terms with creditors and reviewing and rescheduling capital expenditure.

## Arranging an overdraft

An overdraft is a facility on a bank account to withdraw beyond the funds paid in, up to an agreed amount. Overdrafts are a very flexible way of borrowing and can be an effective short-term means of filling the shortfall between cash inflows and outflows. The amount actually borrowed varies from month to month, depending on the firm's needs. The interest charged is based on the size of the overdraft and length of time it is borrowed for. An overdraft can, therefore, be a cheaper means of borrowing in the short term than a bank loan. However, the interest rate charged is much higher than a loan, making them more expensive in the long term. The bank can also demand that any money borrowed is repaid immediately, although this is unlikely to happen unless the business is considered to be high-risk.

## Effective credit control

Some businesses, especially those that are small or newly-established, spend insufficient time monitoring **debtors** and pursuing late payments as and when they occur. Compiling a list of outstanding debts in chronological order (known as an **aged debtors analysis**) can help to prioritise those customers who should be dealt with most urgently. Often, a telephone call or letter can be enough to prompt payment. Firms also have the right to charge interest on late payments, withdraw credit arrangements on future sales to late payers, or take legal action to recover money owed to them, but may choose not to do so to avoid damaging valuable customer relationships.

## (Re)Negotiating terms with creditors

Once a business is established and has built up a record as a reliable payer, it is likely to be offered credit terms by its suppliers. Delaying payment for one, two or even three months could help avoid a negative **cash flow** situation. Suppliers may be willing to extend existing credit periods in order to maintain a good relationship with their customers and continue to receive orders in the future. However, even if credit terms are extended, this is only likely to be a short-term solution to cash flow difficulties, and the funds for making payments will need to be found eventually.

## Reviewing and rescheduling capital expenditure

Owning fixed assets, such as factories, offices, machinery and other equipment, adds to the value of the business and gives managers complete control over how they are used. However, capital expenditure is a major drain on business finance. As a result, many firms choose to rent premises, such as offices, shops or factory units, and lease vehicles, photocopiers, computers and other equipment instead. The cost of renting and leasing can be even more expensive than purchasing assets in the long term. However, in the short term, it can help to postpone a significant outflow of cash until the firm becomes more financially secure. It also gives owners or managers of newly-established businesses time to see if the assets are needed often enough to justify their ownership.

## Firms encouraged to pay their bills on time

Local authorities in the north east of the UK have been the first to sign up to a Prompt Payment Code, introduced by the Government, which guarantees businesses that their invoices are paid within days. The Code was introduced in an attempt to prevent small firms from suffering from cash flow problems while waiting for bills to be paid. According to Government statistics, around 4,000 UK companies closed during 2008 due to bills not being paid promptly.

**Source: The Northern Echo**

a) Make a list of possible ways in which a small business could ensure that its customers pay their bills on time.

b) Identify at least one potential benefit and one potential drawback for each suggestion made.

# Key terms

**Aged debtors analysis** A list of all customers' overdue accounts in order, beginning with the most outstanding

**Cash flow** The cash that flows into and out of a business over a period of time

**Cash flow forecast** A detailed estimate of a firm's future cash inflows and outflows on a month-by-month basis

**Cash sale** Where customers pay for goods or services as soon as they are received

**Credit sale** Where goods or services are provided to customers who pay for them at a later date

**Credit period** The amount of time given by firms to their customers to pay for credit sales, typically between 30 and 90 days

**Closing balance** The amount of cash held by a firm (either on the premises or in its bank account) at the end of each month

**Creditor** A supplier from whom a firm has bought goods or services on credit

**Debtor** A customer who has bought goods or services on credit from a firm

**Net cash flow** The difference between a firm's total cash receipts and total cash payments

**Opening balance** A firm's cash balance at the start of a month

**Overdraft** A facility on a bank account that allows an individual or business customer to withdraw money beyond the funds that have been paid in

**Overtrading** Where a firm experiences cash flow problems as a result of expanding too quickly without sufficient finance

**Profit** The difference between the revenue earned by a firm and the costs incurred by it over a given period of time

**Value added tax (VAT)** An expenditure tax levied on most goods and services purchased in the UK

# Q Re-cap questions

1 Briefly explain the difference between profit and cash flow.

2 State two sources of cash inflow and two sources of cash outflow for a business.

3 Briefly explain the purpose of a cash flow forecast.

4 Why is it difficult to predict future cash flows with 100 per cent accuracy?

5 Explain the difference between a cash sale and a credit sale.

6 What does the opening balance on a cash flow forecast represent?

7 Explain how the following are calculated a) net cash flow; b) closing balance.

8 What is the link between the opening balance and the closing balance on a cash flow forecast?

9 How is value added tax (VAT) dealt with on a cash flow forecast?

10 Describe two possible causes of cash flow problems for a business.

11 Briefly examine two possible consequences for a business from failing to manage cash flow effectively.

12 Briefly explain what is meant by an overdraft.

13 Examine one advantage and one disadvantage for a firm of using an overdraft to deal with cash flow problems.

14 Suggest two methods that a business could use to encourage customers to pay on time.

15 Describe one benefit and one drawback for a firm of leasing equipment, rather than purchasing it.

# Grading tips

**P3** Prepare a 12-month cash flow forecast to enable an organisation to manage its cash

Make sure that your cash flow forecast is accurate by reading the details of your firm's cash flow carefully, including the timings of inflows and outflows

**M1** Analyse the cash flow problems that a business might experience

Begin your analysis by describing what is happening to the net cash flow and the closing balance in your prepared cash flow forecast by looking for patterns or trends. For example, what are the figures at the start of the cash flow forecast, does either figure become negative, when does this occur, does the figure get worse, when does it begin to improve/ become positive, what are the figures at the end of the 12-month period? The next step is to identify the main causes of the trend in the cash flow by looking at individual items of receipts and expenditure. For example, are sales very low or certain expenses very high at certain times?

**D1** Justify actions a business might take when experiencing cash flow problems

You need to identify and describe more than one possible action your business could take to resolve its cash flow problems, examining the advantages and disadvantages of each. Based on this, you could then recommend the solution(s) that are most appropriate for dealing with the cash flow problems.

See page 180 for suggestions for Assignments for Unit 5.

# Part 3: Profit and loss accounts and balance sheets

The financial data relating to performance over the course of a year forms the basis of a firm's final accounts. Limited companies are legally required to publish a set of final accounts every year. This means that, in addition to being used internally by managers, they may also be used by a number of external users, such as suppliers, customers, competitors and potential investors. A firm's published accounts are made up of a profit and loss account and a balance sheet. They are also accompanied by notes and directors' reports that provide more detailed explanations of the contents of the accounts.

## The purpose of the profit and loss account

Profit is a key indicator of business performance. Determining the level of profit generated by a business over a period of time is therefore necessary in order to measure its success. In simple terms, profit is the difference between revenue and costs. However, accountants refer to a number of different measures of profit, each of which relates to a different aspect of a firm's performance. The document used to illustrate the income generated, the various costs incurred and the different levels of profit produced is known as the **profit and loss account** (or the **income statement**, in the case of limited companies).

## Calculating gross profit in the trading account

The starting point for calculating profit is the revenue and the costs associated with a firm's trading activities. The **trading account** is the section of the profit and loss account where **gross profit** is calculated. It ignores any sources of income or expense other than those produced as a direct result of making sales. For example, a high street fashion retailer buys in stocks of clothes, shoes and accessories from manufacturers and generates income or revenue from selling them to customers. It may have other sources of income and will certainly incur other costs, but these are not included in the trading account.

Gross profit is the difference between the sales revenue generated and the cost of the goods sold. In order to calculate gross profit, the following figures must be identified:

- **Sales turnover** (or **revenue**) – this refers to the receipts from selling goods or services during the last year. It is calculated by multiplying the selling price by the quantity of goods sold. Any amounts paid back to customers in relation to **sales returns** (sometimes referred to as **returns inward**) is likely to be shown separately. So:

- **Cost of goods sold** – this reflects the expenses that have been incurred in buying in or producing the goods that have been sold by the business during the last year. It is sometimes simply referred to as cost of sales. The starting point for this is the value of any stock left over from the previous trading period (known as **opening stock**). To this needs to be added the value of any stocks purchased during the current period (**purchases**), minus any **purchase returns** (sometimes referred to as returns outward). Purchasing goods from other businesses may mean that transport costs are also incurred. These costs are referred to as **carriage inwards** and are added to the cost of purchases. From this subtotal, the value of any stock left over at the end of the period (known as **closing stock**) must be deducted.

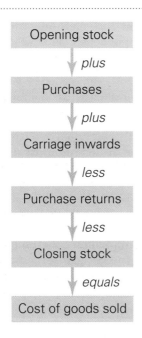

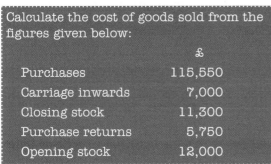

## Calculating net profit

Gross profit only takes into account the direct income and costs generated by sales. **Net profit**, on the other hand, is what a business is left with once all operating costs have been deducted and any non-operating income has been added in. This is calculated in the profit and loss section, which follows on from the trading account. The starting point for the profit and loss account is, therefore, gross profit.

A business may have sources of income, in addition to sales turnover, that must be taken into consideration when calculating net profit. Examples include:

- **Discounts received** – a firm may agree to a percentage discount on credit purchases with suppliers for prompt or early payment. Any discount received is treated as 'other income', increasing the level of net profit made.
- **Commission received** – a firm may sell goods on behalf of another business and be paid a percentage of any revenue generated. This is also treated as 'other income', adding to the net profit made.
- **Rent received** – a firm may own property that it does not use as part of its own operations and choose, therefore, to rent it out to private individuals or other businesses. Any rental income generated increases the level of net profit made.

| Trading Account of<br>N J Simmons Building Supplies<br>For the year ending 31 March 2010 | | | |
|---|---|---|---|
| | £s | £s | £s |
| Sales turnover | | | 95,000 |
| Less Sales returns | | | 2,000 |
| Net sales | | | 93,000 |
| Less Cost of goods sold: | | | |
| Opening stock (as at 01/04/09) | | 15,000 | |
| Plus Purchases | 48,000 | | |
| Plus Carriage inwards | 650 | | |
| | 48,650 | | |
| Minus Purchase returns | 1,500 | | |
| Equals Net purchases | | 47,150 | |
| | | 52,150 | |
| Minus Closing stock (as at 31/03/10) | | 14,500 | |
| Cost of goods sold | | | 37,650 |
| **Gross profit** | | | **55,350** |

**Figure 5.6** The trading account for a sole trader

There are also a number of indirect expenses or overheads that may be incurred as a result of running a business over the course of the year. These overheads are determined to a large extent by the nature of the business, and are identified individually on the profit and loss account. They are likely to include:

- Staff wages and salaries
- Rent
- Advertising
- Heating and lighting
- Telephone
- Stationery
- Delivery (sometimes known as **carriage outwards**)
- Discounts allowed to customers
- Insurance
- Business rates
- Interest on loans

### Depreciation

Firms also recognise that the value of some fixed assets, such as vehicles and machinery, falls over time by charging an annual **depreciation** expense to the profit and loss account. Although this does not involve any movement of cash, this spreads the cost of buying such assets over the time they remain within the business, rather than deducting their full cost from profit in the year they are actually purchased. The two most common methods of calculating depreciation are:

- **The straight line method** – this produces a fixed amount of depreciation which remains the same each year over the life of the asset. The formula used for calculating this is:

$$\frac{\text{Cost of the asset} - \text{residual value}}{\text{Number of years of useful life}}$$

The residual value of an asset refers to its expected value at the end of its useful life, that is, when the business intends to dispose of it. For example, a business that buys an asset costing £20,000 and plans to keep it for four years before selling it for £4,000 would allow for a depreciation charge of £4,000 each year.

- **The declining balance method** – this applies a fixed percentage against the book or current value of a fixed asset. It means that the annual amount charged for depreciation falls over time. For example, depreciating an asset costing £20,000 by 25 per cent each year would allow a depreciation charge of £5,000 in the first year, £3,750 in the second year, and so on.

The various expenses incurred by a firm over the year are added together and deducted from gross profit, reducing the net profit figure. Additional sources of income are added together, increasing net profit. If the expenses incurred by the business are greater than its gross profit and any other income, a net loss will be recorded. The final net profit (or loss) figure is then transferred to the firm's balance sheet, increasing (or decreasing) the value of the business.

## Calculating depreciation

Phil Jones runs his own taxi firm and has just bought five new cars, each costing £12,000, to use within the business. In the past, he has always calculated depreciation using the straight-line method. However, he has been advised to switch to the declining balance method, so that a greater proportion of the cars' value will be accounted for in the first few years' of ownership. He plans to replace the cars in four years' time, when he believes they will be worth around £4,000 each.

### Questions

a) Using the straight-line method of depreciation, calculate the annual depreciation charge and the net book value of the five cars over a four-year period.

b) Using a rate of 25 per cent, use the declining balance method to calculate the annual depreciation charge and the net book value of the five cars over a four-year period.

c) Compare your results.

```
           Profit and Loss Account of
            N J Simmons Building Supplies
           For the year ending 31 March 2010
                              £          £
Gross profit                          55,350
Add other income:
Discount received                      2,000
                                      57,350
Less overheads:
Wages                     15,000
Lighting and heating       1,260
Advertising                1,000
Business rates             5,450
Insurance                  2,500
Depreciation               5,000
Stationery                 1,640
Interest on loans          2,500
Total expenses                        34,350
Net profit                            23,000
```

**Figure 5.7** Calculating net profit for a sole trader

## The purpose of the balance sheet

The profit and loss account gives details of income, expenses and any resulting profit for one particular year. Any profit made can be added to the existing wealth of the business – if a loss has been made, this wealth will be reduced. It may also be useful to have a more detailed picture of the wealth accumulated by a business over time, giving an idea of the level and sources of finance raised by the business and how this has been spent. The purpose of a **balance sheet** is to show the financial position of a business at a particular point in time. It can be used to find out information about any items of value owned by the business (its **assets**), any debts owed by the business (its **liabilities**) and the finance invested in the business since it was set up.

You have been provided with the following information:

|                       | £      |
|-----------------------|--------|
| Net sales             | 47,000 |
| Cost of sales         | 16,500 |
| Rent                  | 6,000  |
| Wages and salaries    | 12,000 |
| Rent received         | 3,000  |
| Heating and lighting  | 600    |
| Telephone             | 360    |
| Advertising           | 600    |
| Stationery            | 500    |

a) Calculate the net profit for the business, based on the figures given.

## Presentation of the balance sheet

The most common way of presenting a balance sheet is by using the **vertical format**. This means that the various sections of the balance sheet are arranged in a particular way to reflect their **order of permanence**. This means, for example, that the first items to be listed are fixed assets, beginning with land and buildings and followed by machinery, equipment and vehicles, which are more likely to deteriorate over time. Fixed assets are likely to remain within the business for a long time and would be difficult to dispose of quickly. Fixed assets are followed on the balance sheet by current assets: stock, debtors and cash, which are more liquid and likely to be used up or disposed of more quickly. The presentation of a relatively simple balance sheet for a sole trader is given opposite.

The balance sheet of a limited company may be presented in a slightly different way to the simple format given above. Details relating to reinvested profits and owners' capital are usually given under the heading 'shareholders' funds', which is made up of share capital (finance raised by selling shares in the company) and reserves (including retained profit).

| | Fixed assets – tangible (premises, machinery) and intangible (patents, trademarks, goodwill) |
|---|---|
| *(plus)* | Current assets – such as stocks and cash |
| *(less)* | Current liabilities – such as creditors and overdrafts |
| *(equals)* | Total assets minus current liabilities |
| *(minus)* | Long-term liabilities – such as loans and mortgages |
| *(equals)* | Net assets |
| **Financed by:** | |
| | Opening capital – the amount invested at start-up |
| *(plus)* | Net profits – the profit transferred from the profit and loss account |
| *(less)* | Drawings – money taken out of the business by the owner(s) |

**Figure 5.8** The structure of a simple balance sheet in vertical format

## Key components of the balance sheet

### Fixed assets

**Fixed assets** are any items of value that are kept within the business over the long term, that is, more than one year, rather than being purchased for resale in the near future. They are used repeatedly as part of the firm's operations, for example to produce goods and services. **Tangible fixed assets** are physical items such as land, buildings, machinery and vehicles. **Intangible fixed assets** include **patents**, which give a firm the exclusive right to use or produce a product or process for up to 20 years, and **trademarks**, that is, the names, logos and symbols that differentiate products from rivals. **Goodwill** refers to the specific value brought to a business by factors such as customer loyalty, good relationships with suppliers or the skills and qualities of the workforce. This figure is sometimes included under intangible fixed assets if a firm is about to be sold in order to reflect the true value of the business to the purchaser. The value of certain fixed assets, such as machinery and vehicles, has to be adjusted each year to take depreciation into account. Therefore, balance sheets often give the **net book value** of these assets, which is the difference between their original value and any **accumulated depreciation** (the annual depreciation charge x number of years of ownership).

### Current assets

**Current assets** are items of value owned by the business that are likely to be turned into cash within twelve months of the date of the balance sheet on which they appear. They include:

- **stocks** – supplies of raw materials, components, part-finished or finished goods, depending on whether the business is a manufacturer, retailer or service provider
- **debtors** – customers who have bought goods or services on credit and have not yet paid
- **cash** – any cash that is kept on the business premises as well as the money in the business's bank account.

### Current liabilities

**Current liabilities** are any debts owed by the business that will need to be repaid in less than one year's time (sometimes referred to as 'amounts falling due within one year'). Current liabilities include **trade creditors**, who are suppliers from whom the business has received goods or services but has not yet paid. **Overdrafts** are also treated as a current liability because the bank is entitled to demand immediate repayment of any amounts outstanding, although this is unlikely in practice.

### Working capital

**Working capital** is the difference between the value of a firm's current assets and current liabilities. It is sometimes referred to as net current assets. In either case, it appears on the balance sheet as a subtotal before the entry 'net assets minus current liabilities'. Working capital shows the **liquidity** of the business: the extent to which it is able to deal with its short-term debts. A positive figure indicates that a business should be able to pay off these debts when they fall due – a negative figure would, therefore, suggest that the business could be experiencing financial difficulties. However, too high a figure could suggest that the business is holding too much of its wealth in the form of current assets and could be run more efficiently.

> Produce a figure for working capital from the figures given below:
>
> |  | £ |
> | --- | --- |
> | Stocks | 27,500 |
> | Overdraft | 10,000 |
> | Creditors | 8,750 |
> | Debtors | 12,250 |
> | Tax due | 10,500 |
> | Cash on the premises | 500 |
> | Bank account | 6,500 |

## Long-term liabilities

**Long-term liabilities** include any borrowings that need to be repaid in more than one year's time (sometimes referred to as 'amounts falling due after one year'). The main items in this section are medium- or long-term **bank loans** and **mortgages**, which may have been used to finance the purchase of property.

## Net assets

This figure represents the **value of total assets** (fixed and current) **minus total liabilities** (current and long-term). It should always be the same as the total of **opening capital plus net profits less drawings**, given in the 'financed by' section. This is because the balance sheet shows how all of the finance raised by a business has been used to buy assets. Finance can either be raised by borrowing (shown by current or long-term liabilities), investment by the owners or profit transferred from the profit and loss account. This means that, once total liabilities have been deducted from total assets, what remains has to represent the owners' capital and/or profits made by the business.

## Transfer of net profit from the profit and loss account

The net profit generated over the year acts as a source of capital to finance business activity. It is, therefore, included in the 'financed by' section, showing an increase in the wealth of the business. In the case of a limited company, the balance sheet would show an increase in 'reserves' to reflect any profit retained by the business and not distributed to shareholders.

## Capital employed

This figure represents the long-term finance that has been used by the business since it began. For example, the capital employed of a sole trader would include the funds invested by the owner at start-up (known as **opening capital**) and any net profits transferred from the profit and loss account. From this figure is deducted any money taken out of the business by the owner for his/her own personal use (referred to as **drawings**). This needs to be done to account for the funds and to show that, by doing this, the finance available to the business has been reduced. Many businesses rely heavily on long-term borrowings as a source of finance. This section of the balance sheet may, therefore, also contain long-term liabilities in order to recognise this, rather than deducting the figure to calculate net assets. Note that, for the purposes of calculating the return on capital employed (ROCE) ratio, long-term liabilities are included in the figure used for capital employed (see page 175).

| N J Simmons Building Supplies Balance Sheet as at 31 March 2010 | | | |
| --- | --- | --- | --- |
| | £ | £ | £ |
| *Fixed assets* | | | |
| Land and buildings | | | 100,000 |
| Machinery | | | 20,000 |
| Vehicles | | | 10,000 |
| | | | 130,000 |
| *Current assets* | | | |
| Stocks | | 14,500 | |
| Debtors | | 10,000 | |
| Cash | | 7,000 | |
| | | 21,500 | |
| *Less: Current liabilities* | | | |
| Creditors | 5,500 | | |
| Overdraft | 10,000 | 15,500 | |
| *Working capital* | | 6,000 | |
| *Total assets minus current liabilities* | | | 136,000 |
| *Less: Long-term liabilities* | | | |
| Bank loan | 15,000 | | |
| Mortgage | 50,000 | 65,000 | |
| **Net assets** | | | **71,000** |
| *Financed by*: | | | |
| Owner's capital | | | 25,000 |
| *Add*: Net profit | | | 23,000 |
| *Less*: Drawings | | | 23,000 |
| | | | **71,000** |

**Figure 5.9** A balance sheet for a sole trader

# Key terms

**Balance sheet** Shows the financial position of a business at a particular time, giving details of the value of its assets, its liabilities and the amount invested by the owners

**Capital employed** The long-term finance of a business, made up of owners' equity, retained profits and long-term loans

**Carriage inwards** The costs incurred by a firm transporting materials from suppliers

**Carriage outwards** The costs incurred by a firm transporting finished goods to customers

**Closing stock** The value of stock remaining in a business at the end of the financial year

**Cost of goods sold** The cost of the sales made by a business over the course of the financial year. It is calculated by taking the value of a firm's opening stock and adding in purchases and then deducting the value of its closing stock

**Current assets** Items of value owned by a business that are likely to be turned into cash within twelve months of the date of the balance sheet on which they appear

**Current liabilities** Debts owed by a business that need to be repaid less than one year from the date of the balance sheet on which they appear

**Depreciation** The process of spreading the cost of a fixed asset over the number of years of its useful life

**Drawings** The money taken out of a firm with unlimited liability by its owner(s)

**Fixed assets** Items of value owned by a business and kept over the long term in order to produce goods or services. Tangible fixed assets are physical items, such as buildings and machinery, whereas intangible fixed assets are non-physical items, including patents, trademarks and goodwill

**Gross profit** The difference between the sales revenue earned by a business and its cost of goods sold over a certain period of time

**Net profit** The difference between gross profit and indirect expenses such as overheads. In other words, it is the profit made by a business once all operating expenses have been deducted from sales revenue

**Opening stock** The value of stock held by a business at the start of the financial year

**Profit and loss account** A document making up the final accounts of a firm detailing its revenues and costs over a given period of time and the resulting profit or loss made

**Sales turnover** The value of sales made by a business over a given period of time. It can be calculated using the formula: sales price x quantity sold. It is also referred to as sales revenue

**Trading account** The section of the profit and loss account that shows how gross profit is calculated, giving details of a firm's sales revenue and the cost of goods sold

**Working capital** This is the day-to-day finance used to run a business. It is also known as net current assets. The size of a firm's working capital can be calculated by subtracting current liabilities from current assets

# Q Re-cap questions

1   What is the purpose of a profit and loss account?
2   What information is shown on the trading account section of the profit and loss account?
3   State the formula for calculating gross profit.
4   Explain how the cost of goods sold for a firm is calculated.
5   What is net profit and how is it calculated?
6   Briefly explain what is meant by the annual depreciation charge.
7   Outline two ways in which a firm's annual depreciation charge can be calculated.
8   Describe two sources of income, other than sales revenue, that a business might receive.
9   Briefly outline the purpose of a balance sheet.

10 Balance sheets are often presented in a vertical format – briefly explain what this means.

11 Assets are listed on a balance sheet in order of preference – briefly explain what this means.

12 State three current assets that are likely to appear on a firm's balance sheet.

13 Using examples, briefly explain the difference between a current liability and a long-term liability.

14 What does working capital represent and how is it calculated?

15 What are drawings and how do they affect the balance sheet?

## Grading tips

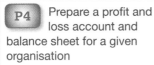 **P4** Prepare a profit and loss account and balance sheet for a given organisation

You must make sure that you include all items of income and expenditure and clearly label cost of goods sold, gross profit, overheads and net profit on your profit and loss account. You must also use a vertical format for your balance sheet, listing items in the correct sections and showing the necessary subtotals.

See page 180 for suggestions for Assignments for Unit 5.

# Part 4: Reviewing business performance using ratio analysis

Once financial data has been gathered and turned into a set of accounts, managers need to examine them in order to draw conclusions about the business's recent performance. For example, is the business generating more sales with existing resources? Is this resulting in greater levels of profit or is it struggling to keep its costs under control? **Ratio analysis** is a technique that is commonly used to make better sense of financial data and help to inform the decision-making process. Although the technique cannot make the decisions itself, it can alert managers to possible areas of concern, so that appropriate action can be taken.

Rather than looking at figures such as **sales revenue** or profit in isolation, ratios put these figures into the context of the individual business concerned by comparing them to other relevant data. So, for example, instead of simply looking at the total profit generated by a business over a year, ratio analysis might compare this figure to the amount of capital that is available to the business. A small business with relatively little capital available would not be expected to generate the same levels of profit as a major, multinational corporation with much greater resources. However, ratio analysis could help to reveal which business is the most effective at generating profit, given the resources available.

Ratio analysis is based mainly on figures taken from a firm's profit and loss account and the balance sheet. In the case of limited companies, these accounts are published, meaning that other groups, in addition to managers, can access and analyse the data contained in them. These groups may include:

- **Suppliers** – who will want to know if the firm has enough cash to pay its bills on time, before offering or extending trade credit
- **Lenders** – who will want to see evidence that the firm is operating profitably and has the resources to pay back the money borrowed
- **Customers** – who will be interested in how much time they can expect before they have to pay for credit sales
- **Employees** – who will be interested in the level of profit generated by the firm before

demanding better terms and conditions, such as pay increases
- **Competitors** – who will be interested in finding out any possible weaknesses in performance that they can use to their advantage.

There are a number of ratios that can be used to measure different areas of business performance, including **profitability**, **liquidity** and **efficiency**.

## Measures of profitability

Profit and profitability are connected terms, but do not mean the same thing. Profit is simply the difference between revenue and costs. Profitability, on the other hand, looks at how successful a firm is at generating profit, relative to its overall size. A supermarket chain operating on a national scale across the UK would be expected to have a much higher level of capital, sales and profits than a small, single grocery store. However, whether or not it also operates more profitably depends on how well it converts its capital and sales into profits by controlling costs.

There are three key profitability or performance ratios – the **gross profit** percentage of sales (gross profit margin), the **net profit** percentage of sales (net profit margin) and the **return on capital employed (ROCE)**:

- **Gross profit percentage of sales (gross profit margin)** – this ratio expresses the gross profit produced by a firm over a period of time as a percentage of the sales revenue made in the same period. Remember that gross profit is the difference between the revenue from sales and the cost of making them. The formula for calculating this ratio is as follows:

$$\frac{\text{Gross profit}}{\text{Sales revenue}} \times 100$$

For example, a figure of 30 per cent would mean that the firm would earn 30p in gross profit for every £1 in sales revenue generated. In general terms, therefore, a business will want this figure to be as high as possible, although it is likely to vary, depending on the industry and the nature of the goods sold. For example, firms operating in the budget sector of the market may have low margins, because they charge low prices, but are still able to make high levels of profit due to the volumes sold.

Gross profit is a very crude measure, however, as it does not take into account any of the indirect costs incurred by the business as a result of its operations. Calculating the figure for one year also tells us relatively little. However, comparing this ratio over time (or between firms) can be more useful to managers. For example, if the ratio decreases between two years, this would mean that sales revenue is falling at a faster rate (or increasing at a slower rate) than the cost of sales. This may be because additional competition has forced a firm to reduce its prices in order to maintain the same volume of sales.

- **Net profit percentage of sales (net profit margin)** – this ratio expresses net profit produced by a firm over a period of time as a percentage of the sales revenue made in the same period. Net profit takes into account the overheads incurred by a business, as well as the cost of sales, and is, therefore, seen as a more comprehensive measure of profit. The formula for calculating this ratio is as follows:

$$\frac{\text{Net profit (before tax and interest)}}{\text{Sales revenue}} \times 100$$

For example, a figure of 10 per cent would mean that the firm concerned would be generating 10p of net profit from every £1 of sales revenue. Again, in most situations, a firm would wish this figure to be as high as possible and increasing over time.

Comparing this ratio with the gross profit percentage of sales can reveal a great deal about the business. A significant difference between the two figures suggests a high level of overheads. If the net profit ratio is declining over time but the gross profit figure remains stable, this suggests that the firm is struggling to control overhead costs, such as the salaries of managers or sales staff, advertising or administrative costs.

- **Return on capital employed (ROCE)** – this ratio measures how well the funds that have been invested in the business are used to generate profit. It is seen by many accountants as one of the most important ratios that can be used to indicate performance, and is sometimes referred to as the primary ratio. The formula used to calculate this figure is as follows:

$$\frac{\text{Net profit before tax and interest}}{\text{Capital employed}} \times 100$$

Capital employed refers to any sources of long term finance that have been put into the business and can be calculated by referring to a firm's balance sheet. For a relatively simple business, this would include the capital invested by the owners and any profit retained by the business (minus any drawings taken out by the owners), in addition to any long-term loans that may have been taken out. In a limited company, capital employed is the total of any long-term borrowing added to the shareholders' funds.

Although this ratio is likely to vary between different industries, generally speaking, a high or increasing figure suggests that managers are using resources more effectively.

| Ratio | Action to improve it |
|---|---|
| Gross profit percentage of sales | • Increase prices without reducing the volume of sales, for example, if demand is relatively insensitive to price changes<br>• Reduce the cost of sales without a corresponding reduction in sales price, for example, by cutting wastage or switching to a cheaper supplier |
| Net profit percentage of sales | Reduce overheads by:<br>• Delayering and reducing the level of management salaries<br>• Encouraging staff to waste less power in order to reduce heating and lighting bills |
| Return on capital employed (ROCE) | • Find ways of generating more net profit from the same level of capital employed<br>• Maintain the same level of net profit by reducing the lower level of capital employed, for example, once long-term loans have been paid off |

Table 5.1 Improving profitability ratios

The following figures are taken from the accounts of a limited company:

|                  | 2009 (£000) | 2008 (£000) |
|------------------|-------------|-------------|
| Sales turnover   | 4,200       | 3,780       |
| Cost of sales    | 3,300       | 3,000       |
| Overheads        | 570         | 540         |
| Fixed assets     | 1,505       | 1,414       |
| Working capital  | 273         | 182         |
| Long-term loans  | 560         | 455         |
| Share capital    | 140         | 140         |
| Reserves         | 1,078       | 931         |

a) Calculate the following profitability ratios for 2009 and 2008

i. gross profit margin

ii. net profit margin

iii. return on capital employed

b) Comment on the company's profitability over the period.

## Measures of liquidity

Although the level of profit made is important, the short-term financial health of a business can also have a significant impact on its ongoing success. Liquidity is concerned with the management of a firm's working capital, that is, the balance between **current assets** and **current liabilities**. Current assets are those that can be converted relatively easily into cash, as well as cash itself. These include **debtors**, who are customers that have bought goods or services on credit and should, therefore, soon pay what they owe. **Stocks** are also seen as being relatively liquid because, although they have not been bought by customers (or, in some cases, even turned into goods) yet, they should generate cash in the near future. Too much working capital can indicate that a business is not making the most efficient use of its resources. Firms will want to avoid very high levels of stocks, for example, as they can be expensive to store and may quickly go out of date. They may also avoid large cash balances, which are unlikely to generate any income, or high levels of debtors who may take time to pay. However, holding insufficient levels of liquid assets means that the business is running the risk of not being able to pay **creditors**, or meet any other current liabilities when it needs to.

There are two ratios that are commonly used to measure liquidity:

- **Current ratio** – this ratio compares the level of current assets to current liabilities. It is calculated using the following formula:

$$\frac{\text{Current assets}}{\text{Current liabilities}}$$

It is expressed as a ratio – for example, a current ratio of 2:1 would mean that the value of a firm's current assets is twice that of its current liabilities. Accountants would normally recommend that the value of the current ratio should be between 1.5 or 2:1. This would mean that the business has £1.50 of current assets for every £1.00 of current liabilities and should, in theory, be able to pay off any short-term debts when they fall due without tying up too many resources in working capital.

- **Acid test ratio (liquidity ratio)** – at first glance, a current ratio of 1:1.5 suggests that a business is in a comfortable financial position. However, this figure could give a misleading view about a firm's liquidity if a large proportion of its current assets is made up of stocks of raw materials or finished goods. Stocks are less liquid than debtors or cash. This means that it is harder to turn stocks into cash quickly without losing any of their value. For example, it may be necessary to reduce the sales price of goods that have been in stock for relatively long periods of time below their original costs, in order to encourage customers to buy them.

The acid test ratio is a much stricter measure of liquidity because it does not include stock. Instead, the combined value of debtors and cash balances (**liquid assets**) is compared to the value of current liabilities. The formula for this ratio is, therefore, as follows:

$$\frac{\text{Current assets} - \text{stock}}{\text{Current liabilities}}$$

The recommended value of the acid test ratio is normally around 1:1, that is, £1 of liquid assets for every £1 of current liabilities. A value below this should be investigated, as it may well mean that the business concerned will experience problems in meeting its short-term debts. However, apparently healthy figures for the acid test ratio can hide liquidity problems if, for example, the firm has a high level of debtors who are given long credit periods, are late payers or at risk of going out of business. It is particularly useful, therefore, to use this ratio alongside the debtors' payment period ratio (see page 177).

Low levels of liquidity can be improved by increasing the level of cash within the business, in order to ensure any bills can be paid. This can be done in a number of ways, such as increasing owners' investments or selling off unused assets owned by the business. However, some businesses are able to survive indefinitely with what would appear to be very low levels of liquidity. Large firms in particular are able to pressurise smaller suppliers into accepting late payments when cash flow becomes tight. An established firm with a good record of profitability is also likely to find it relatively easy to persuade the bank to extend its overdraft facility temporarily.

> The following figures are taken from the accounts of a limited company:
>
> |  | 2009 | 2008 |
> |---|---|---|
> | Stocks | 39,000 | 30,000 |
> | Debtors | 32,000 | 27,000 |
> | Cash | 5,000 | 4,000 |
> | Current liabilities | 38,000 | 32,000 |
>
> a) Calculate the company's current ratio and acid test ratio.
>
> b) Comment on your results.

## Measures of efficiency

It is useful to have an indication of how well a firm manages its resources, in terms of its debtors, its creditors and the level of stock held by it. Failing to control these aspects of performance and deal with any problems that arise could well affect the future profitability and even the survival of a business.

Three of the key ratios used to measure efficiency are:

- **Debtors' payment period** – this ratio shows how long it takes customers to pay on average. Many firms sell to other firms on credit, offering credit periods of 30, 60 or even 90 days, whereas other businesses, such as retailers and restaurants, deal largely in cash sales. It is important for firms dealing in credit sales to monitor the actual amount of time taken to recover any debts from customers, in order to avoid problems with cash flow. The formula used to calculate this ratio is as follows:

$$\frac{\text{Debtors}}{\text{Annual sales turnover}} \times 365$$

Ideally, most firms would want this figure to be as low as possible, signifying that payment for credit sales is recovered as quickly as possible. In practice, what represents an acceptable level will depend on the circumstances of the individual firm. However, concerns should be raised if the debtors' payment period increases significantly over time, and action taken to improve the efficiency of the firm's credit control systems.

- **Creditors' payment period** – many businesses also buy from their suppliers on credit in order to ease pressure on their cash flow. This ratio shows how long, on average, a firm is taking to settle debts owed to its creditors. Negotiating long credit periods gives firms more time to generate the money required to pay for purchases. The formula for calculating this figure is as follows:

$$\frac{\text{Creditors}}{\text{Annual purchases}} \times 365$$

If a firm's creditors' collection period is longer than its debtors' collection period, this means that its customers are paying for sales before it has to pay for its suppliers. Such a situation should improve cash flow. However, a situation where the creditors' collection period is much shorter than the debtors' collection period could help maintain good relations with suppliers and allow the firm to benefit from discounts for prompt payment. However, it could also lead to cash flow difficulties.

- **Rate of stock turnover** – this ratio is used to indicate how quickly a business uses or sells its stock. The formula used for calculating this is as follows:

$$\frac{\text{Average level of stock}^*}{\text{Cost of sales}} \times 365$$

*where average stock = (opening stock + closing stock)/2.

The amount of time that stock stays within a business can vary dramatically. Supermarkets selling a high percentage of perishable food items would expect to hold stock for very short periods of time, whereas the stock held by a car dealer at the luxury end of the market may take much longer to sell. However, holding stock runs the risk that the cash used to buy supplies may not be recovered if these supplies cannot be sold on to customers. Therefore, most businesses would prefer to move

| Ratio | Action to improve it |
|---|---|
| Debtors' payment period | • Reduce or withdraw future credit to late-paying customers<br>• Offer incentives, such as discounts, for customers who pay on time or for cash sales |
| Creditors' payment period | • Attempt to negotiate longer credit periods with suppliers in order to create more time to pay |
| Rate of stock turnover | • Consider reducing prices or using other promotional methods to boost sales<br>• Reduce the average level of stock or eliminate it completely by introducing just-in-time methods of production |

Table 5.2  Improving efficiency ratios

or shift stock as quickly as possible. Managers should be concerned if the number of days that stock is held begins to increase over time, or if the ratio for their business compares unfavourably with other similar firms.

## Measuring efficiency

James Grainger owns and runs a nursery, growing and selling a number of plants and shrubs

to garden centres in Worcestershire and Warwickshire. The following information was taken from the accounts of the business:

|  | Year 1 | Year 2 |
|---|---|---|
| Sales turnover | 250,000 | 240,000 |
| Purchases | 125,000 | 150,000 |
| Opening stock | 10,000 | 15,000 |
| Closing stock | 15,000 | 22,000 |
| Debtors | 25,000 | 37,000 |
| Creditors | 22,000 | 20,000 |

### Questions

a) Calculate the following ratios for James' business for both years:

   i.  debtors' payment period

   ii.  creditors' payment period

   iii.  rate of stock turnover

b) On the basis of your results, what action, if any, would you recommend James takes (justify your recommendations).

## Key terms

**Capital employed** The long-term finance of a business, made up of owners' equity, retained profits and long-term loans

**Creditors** Suppliers from whom a business has bought goods or services on credit but has yet to pay

**Current assets** Items of value owned by a business that are likely to be turned into cash within twelve months of the date of the balance sheet on which they appear

**Current liabilities** Debts owed by a business that need to be repaid in less than one year from the date of the balance sheet on which they appear

**Debtors** Customers who have bought goods or services from a firm on credit but have yet to pay

**Efficiency** Is concerned with how well a firm manages or controls its resources, including debtors, creditors and stock

**Gross profit** The difference between the sales revenue earned by a business and its cost of goods sold over a certain period of time

**Liquidity** Is concerned with the short-term financial health of a firm and its ability to meet any debts that will fall due in the near future. It can be measured by using accounting ratios such as the current ratio or the acid test ratio

**Net profit** The difference between gross profit and indirect expenses such as overheads. In other words, it is the profit made by a business once all operating expenses have been deducted from sales revenue

**Profitability** Is concerned with how successful a firm is at generating profit in relation to the resources and revenue it makes. It can be measured using accounting ratios such as return on capital employed

**Ratio analysis** A technique used to examine a firm's financial accounts in order to gain an understanding of how well it has performed. It makes it easier to compare a firm's performance over time, or with that of other firms

**Sales revenue** The value of sales made by a business over a given period of time. It can be calculated using the formula: sales price × quantity sold. It is also referred to as sales turnover

**Stock** Supplies of raw materials, components, part-finished and finished goods held by a business that are used up as part of its operations

## Q Re-cap questions

1 Briefly explain the purpose of ratio analysis.

2 Identify three groups, other than managers, who might be interested in information on a firm's financial performance.

3 Explain, using examples, what is meant by profitability.

4 What is the difference between the gross profit margin of sales and the net profit margin of sales?

5 What does the return on capital employed show?

6 Explain what is meant by the term liquidity.

7 Explain why managers should be concerned if liquidity levels fall too low within a business.

8 Can liquidity levels become too high? Explain your answer.

9 Outline two ratios that can be used to calculate a firm's level of liquidity.

10 Examine two steps that could be taken to improve a firm's liquidity position.

11 Why is it important for managers to be aware of the debtors' payment period for a business?

12 Suggest two ways in which a firm can improve its debtors' payment period.

13 A business has a debtors' payment period of 60 days and a creditors' payment period of 30 days – explain one possible consequence of this for the business.

14 Explain how a firm's rate of stock turnover can be calculated.

15 Examine one method that a business could use to improve its rate of stock turnover.

# Grading tips

| **P5** Perform ratio analysis to measure the profitability, liquidity and efficiency of a given organisation | **M2** Analyse the performance of a business using suitable ratios | **D2** Evaluate the financial performance and position of a business using ratio analysis |
|---|---|---|
| You must explain clearly what is meant by the terms profitability, liquidity and efficiency, as well as explaining the meaning and use of individual ratios. You must also demonstrate that you can carry out ratio analysis to measure the profitability, liquidity and efficiency of a given organisation. | Having chosen and calculated a range of ratios to measure profitability, liquidity and efficiency, you will be given ratios for the same organisation from the previous year and asked to compare your results to them. You must be able to identify any changes and their significance: that is, do they show an improvement or deterioration in performance? | Working in groups, you must produce a detailed and fully justified assessment of the performance of your business, based on your ratio analysis. This could include an investigation into the possible reasons for either an improvement or decline in performance, based on evidence contained in the accounts, for instance a large increase in certain expenses causing a fall in profitability. |

## Assignments for Unit 5

### Assignment One

A friend of yours has just started his own business – a smoothie and snack bar based in rented premises in the town where you live. He has been successful in negotiating one month's credit with his main supplier, but he has been warned that this will be cancelled if invoices are not paid on time. He has some money of his own to invest in the business and has also managed to obtain a low interest rate loan with help from a local Business Link adviser. Cash flow is likely to be very tight in the initial months, until the business becomes better known and starts to attract more customers. In a recent conversation about the business, you were alarmed by your friend's claim that he did not have the time or resources to keep detailed accounts and you are determined to convince him of the importance of doing so.

**Note** – read through the tasks below, the relevant criteria and the assignment advice on pages 155 and 156.

### Tasks

1. Describe the purpose of accounting for an organisation. Using examples that are relevant to your friend's business, explain the main reasons why keeping accounting records is important. (P1)
2. Using examples based on your friend's business, produce a factsheet explaining the difference between capital and revenue items of income and expenditure. (P2)

### Assignment Two

Karl Roberts and his wife Lynda are planning to set up a children's clothes shop and have spent the last few months carrying out research into their business proposal. They have produced a forecast of expected sales and cost of supplies for the first year (see below):

| | Sales | Cost of Supplies |
|---|---|---|
| January | 0 | 6,000 |
| February | 10,000 | 9,900 |
| March | 16,500 | 10,800 |
| April | 18,000 | 12,000 |
| May | 20,000 | 13,200 |
| June | 22,000 | 13,200 |
| July | 22,000 | 11,400 |
| August | 18,000 | 12,000 |
| September | 20,000 | 11,400 |
| October | 19,000 | 11,400 |
| November | 19,000 | 11,400 |
| December | 20,000 | 11,400 |

Lynda has contacted a number of suppliers and is keen to use two of them in particular, even though neither is willing to let them buy goods on credit. She has also found a shop that is currently available for rent on the high street of the town where they live. The rent is £1,500 per month and the business rates are £550 per month, but she believes that the cost will be justified by the amount of sales generated by the prime location. At the start of January, the couple plan to spend £15,000 on equipment, fixtures and fittings for the shop and begin trading in February. They also want to spend £10,000 on a new van, which will be used to pick up supplies each month. They intend to spend £500 per month on advertising initially, in order to raise awareness, reducing the amount to £250 from May onwards. Karl and Lynda have identified a number of other expenses, including heating and lighting costs of £100 per month, paid quarterly, telephone charges of £50 per month and insurance of £1,800, which they plan to pay in full at the beginning of January. They also intend to take £3,000 in drawings every month.

Karl and Lynda plan to invest £20,000 of their own savings in the business but realise this will not be enough to get the business up and running. They have decided to apply for a £15,000 bank loan which they hope will be paid into their business bank account by the beginning of January. The monthly repayments of £500 will begin in February. In order to obtain the loan, they need to produce a business plan containing a number of financial documents, including a cash flow forecast.

**Note** – read through the tasks below, the relevant criteria and the assignment advice on page 165.

**Criteria covered** – P3 M1 D1

**Tasks**

1. Produce a 12-month cash flow forecast to enable Karl and Lynda to manage their business' cash. You may find it useful to do this using a spreadsheet. (P3)
2. Analyse the cash flow problems that are likely to arise for Karl and Lynda's business, based on the cash flow forecast produced in Task 1. (M1)
3. Justify at least two possible actions that Karl and Lynda could take to deal with the problems you have identified in Task 2. Analyse the main advantages and disadvantages of each suggested action. Based on your analysis, recommend which action or actions you think should be taken. (D1)

**Assignment Three**

In January 2009, Ania Borkowska set up a wholesale business importing food, drinks and other products from her native Poland and selling them to small retailers in the north west of England. The business, known as Polish Fine Foods, was initially set up as a sole tradership, using Ania's own savings and a loan from her parents. However, the business was so successful in its first few years that Ania decided to expand and is thinking of turning it into a private limited company. She wants to produce a set of accounts to show how well the business is currently performing in order to attract investors but does not know how to do this. She has, therefore, approached your firm of accountants to do this on her behalf. She has been careful to keep detailed records of all of the firm's financial transactions and provides you with the following information:

Financial data on Polish Fine Foods for the year ending 31/12/10

| | £ | £ |
|---|---|---|
| Owner's investment | 20,000 | |
| Sales turnover | 144,000 | |
| Value of stock at 31/12/09 | 5,250 | |
| Value of stock left at 31/12/10 | 8,500 | |
| Stock purchased during the year | | 102,750 |
| Warehouse rent & rates | | 10,800 |
| Wages for part-time staff | | 9,000 |
| Advertising | 4,200 | |
| Insurance | 980 | |
| Depreciation | 1,500 | |
| Loan interest | 1,720 | |
| Electricity | 1,200 | |
| Telephone | | 600 |
| Motoring costs | 1,400 | |
| Drawings during the year | | 10,000 |
| Equipment | | 15,000 |
| Van | 8,000 | |
| Customers yet to pay | 18,000 | |
| Cash in bank account | 2,000 | |
| Outstanding trade credit | | 17,000 |
| Loan from parents | | 10,000 |

**Note** – read through the tasks below, the relevant criteria and the assignment advice on page 173.

**Criteria covered** – P4

**Tasks**

1. Use the information provided to produce a profit and loss account and balance sheet for Ania's business. When compiling the balance sheet, make sure that you use the vertical format and calculate the subtotals required. When compiling the profit and loss account, make sure that you label the 'cost of goods' and the 'overheads' sections and calculate gross profit and net profit. (P4)

## Assignment Four

Refer to Assignment Three. You have decided to use the accounting data supplied by Ania on her business to draw up a table of accounting ratios. Ania's father has very kindly supplied you with accounting details on a similar business that he set up in Essex three years ago, in order to draw a comparison:

| Ratio | Borkowska Wholesale Ltd | Polish Fine Foods Ltd | Comments |
|---|---|---|---|
| Gross profit percentage of sales | 25.4% | | |
| Net profit percentage of sales | 14.2% | | |
| Return on capital employed (ROCE) | 35% | | |
| Current ratio | 2.0:1.0 | | |
| Acid test ratio | 1.5:1.0 | | |
| Debtors' payment period | 32 days | | |
| Creditors' payment period | 30 days | | |
| Rate of stock turnover | 37 days | | |

**Note** – read through the tasks below, the relevant criteria and the assignment advice on page 180.
   **Criteria covered** – P5 M2 D2

### Tasks

1. Perform ratio analysis to measure the profitability, liquidity and efficiency of Ania's business, Polish Fine Foods. Copy out the above table and complete the third column. Use the information contained in the profit and loss account and balance sheet produced for Assignment Three. (P5)
2. Analyse the financial performance of Polish Fine Foods using suitable ratios. (M2)
3. Evaluate the financial performance of Polish Fine Foods using ratio analysis. (D2)

# Part 1: Constituents of the promotional mix

Aleksandr Orlov is no ordinary insurance salesman. The computer-generated Russian meerkat leads the award-winning advertising campaign of insurance comparison website, comparethemarket.com. A number of TV adverts have featured the furry creature, wearing a smoking jacket and cravat, complaining about the number of people accidentally logging on to his website, comparethemeerkat.com, rather than comparethemarket.com, when looking for cheap insurance. Aleksandr goes on to explain the difference between the two, signing off with his now famous catchphrase, 'seemples'. VCCP, the agency responsible for the series of advertising campaigns, has also made clever use of the internet to raise the company's profile with younger consumers. The TV adverts released to date, the latest of which also feature fellow meerkat and IT assistant, Sergei, can all be found on YouTube. Aleksandr has his own page on Facebook, which claims over half a million fans. One advert featuring Aleksandr in a jacuzzi, which was launched on the social networking site rather than TV, received over 1,500 'thumbs up' hits within 90 minutes of going live in October 2009.

Product promotion is a vital element of any firm's marketing mix. It involves communicating information about the goods or services that a business has to offer, highlighting their key features and the benefits of using them. Promotion is also about persuading customers to buy products by influencing their attitudes and behaviour. Creative promotion can help to generate a strong **brand image** for a product, differentiating it from rivals and giving it a competitive edge within the market. The comparethemarket.com campaign has been a huge marketing success. Brand awareness increased from 20 per cent to 59 per cent within nine weeks of the start of the meerkat adverts, with usage of the site rising by 80 per cent.

# The purpose and objectives of the promotional mix

'The **promotional mix**' is the term that describes the different methods used to promote a good or service. The purpose of these methods is to communicate with the target audience. Existing customers need to be reminded of the benefits of using the product and be reassured that their purchasing decision has been the right one. The attention of potential customers needs to be attracted, their existing views need to be challenged in order to persuade them to change their current buying patterns and try the product for the first time. A successful promotional mix can help to achieve a firm's marketing objectives, such as sales growth or increased market share.

Most firms tend to use a combination of promotional tools rather than relying on one particular method. This is in order to ensure that the promotional message is communicated effectively, i.e. that it is received by as many people in the target audience as possible, while attempting to keep costs as low as possible.

# Elements of the promotional mix

A wide number of promotional tools can be chosen as the elements of a product's promotional mix. The elements that are actually chosen depend on a number of factors, including cost, the nature of the product and the size of the audience.

Methods commonly used by firms to create a promotional mix for their products are discussed below.

## Advertising

Advertising is a paid-for method of communication using mass media. This includes broadcast media such as television, radio and cinema, and printed media such as newspapers, magazines and billboards. This type of promotion is usually used for goods and services that require large audiences on a regional, national or even international scale. One of the key factors influencing the choice of media is cost. Advertising rates vary considerably, even within the same media type. Some of the main influences on cost include audience size and timing. For example, TV advertising at peak time on a major channel is likely to cost much more than off-peak advertising on less popular channels as the campaign will be seen by a much bigger audience.

The choice of media also depends on the target market. An advertising campaign will not be effective, no matter how much money is spent, if it fails to reach the intended audience. Marketing managers must therefore use appropriate media, in order to increase the chances of success. Trade journals are an obvious example, as they are aimed at particular sectors or professions. The magazine market is heavily segmented in terms of age, gender and lifestyle. For instance, *GQ* magazine is aimed at 'sophisticated men aged between 25 and 39 with a desire for style'. The growth of satellite

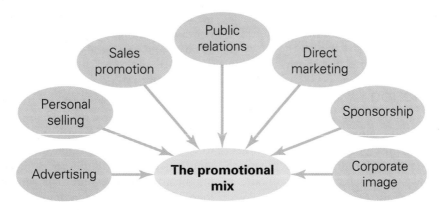

**Figure 9.1** Components of the promotional mix

TV has led to the creation of a number of music, sports and children's channels, and has also allowed businesses and advertising agencies to target products more specifically.

In recent years, there has been a significant increase in the use of so-called new or electronic media. Setting up a simple website is relatively cheap and easy, meaning that even the smallest business can have access to customers around the world. Search engines such as Google and Yahoo not only carry advertisements but also allow customers to carry out sophisticated searches to uncover suitable suppliers. Email and mobile phones can provide very accurate channels of communication. For example, firms can buy lists of the email addresses of customers within a particular target group. These customers can then be sent advertisements for products that are likely to be of interest to them. As technology develops, the use of advertising via text messaging is also likely to become more popular.

## Personal selling

Personal selling involves sales staff making direct contact with customers. This may be done via the telephone, particularly when dealing with a large number of customers that are spread out on a national scale. Sales staff may also approach customers face to face, particularly when the customer base is relatively small. In some situations, a meeting may be required to explain the technical features of the product or to assess customer needs. For example, a business providing conservatories or new windows may use trained sales staff to assess a property and make appropriate recommendations. Employing and training a large sales team are likely to be expensive but may be effective in building good customer relationships.

## Sales promotion

Sales promotion covers the use of a range of techniques, including money-off coupons, competitions, free samples, product demonstrations, loyalty cards and special offers such as 'buy one, get one free' (BOGOF). Their purpose is to have a direct influence on customers' buying behaviour by offering some kind of financial incentive. In particular, they are used to encourage customers to choose one product over a number of similar competing goods or services. The introduction of a sales promotion can have a sudden and dramatic effect on demand. However, customers who would have bought in any case also get to enjoy the benefits of sales promotions. Giving discounts to these customers results in a loss of revenue. Customers may also respond by stocking up on products during the sales promotion, leading to a sharp fall in demand once the period is over.

## Public relations

Public relations (PR) consist of any activities that are used to send out a particular message about a business. The aim of PR is to generate positive publicity and raise the profile of a business, without having to pay for advertising. Individuals such as pop stars, film actors and other celebrities rely on PR to stay in the public eye by appearing at events such as film premieres and TV awards. A business may organise a press conference or issue a press release to announce an event. It may also cooperate with a newspaper or TV channel to produce a news article. In such a situation, however, the business loses control of how the message is passed on to the public, which could lead to it being portrayed in a less than flattering way.

## Direct marketing

This involves communicating on a one-to-one basis, sending materials such as advertisements, catalogues, samples and vouchers through the post to members of the target audience. Increasingly, promotional materials are also now directed at customers via email and mobile phone text. Direct marketing can be a very effective way of targeting promotional material at key groups of customers. However, this relies on a business having access to accurate and up-to-date mailing lists containing the necessary customer details, such as home and email addresses.

## Sponsorship

Sponsorship involves a business providing support for an event or another organisation. This may take the form of making a financial donation to cover costs, or it could mean providing equipment or resources. Publicity is generated by the organisation in question displaying the name or logo of the sponsor. Top sports teams, national sporting and artistic events and even television programmes receive significant funding from sponsorship by well-known companies (see Table 9.1). However, sponsorship is also used by smaller businesses to generate publicity by supporting local teams and events.

| Organisation/event | Sponsor(s) |
|---|---|
| 2012 London Olympics | Adidas, BMW, BP, British Airways, BT, EDF, Lloyds TSB (official partners) |
| Chelsea FC | Samsung |
| Altrincham FC | Go Goodwins Coaches, Carole Nash Insurance, Dunne & Gray Solicitors |
| Andy Murray (tennis player) | Royal Bank of Scotland, HEAD, Highland Spring |
| Coronation Street (TV soap opera) | Cadbury's (1996–2007) |
| V Festival 2010 | Virgin Media (main sponsor) |
| RHS Chelsea Flower Show 2010 | M&G Investments |
| Leeds Year of Volunteering 2010 | First Direct bank |

Table 9.1 Examples of companies involved in sponsorship

## Corporate image

Promotional activities are also used to maintain or change public perceptions about business organisations in general. These activities may not refer to specific products but are designed to present the company in a certain light, perhaps as being highly innovative, exclusive or passionate about the environment. Marks and Spencer, Waitrose and many other companies make regular press releases and have dedicated pages on their websites explaining their support for suppliers and their actions to protect the environment. This corporate image helps to generate sales by creating a corporate personality that appeals to the target audience.

## Deciding on an appropriate promotional mix

The elements used to make up the promotional mix vary from product to product. An individual product's promotional mix may also change over time. Marketing managers must therefore consider carefully which elements would help to achieve business objectives most effectively. Key influences on the decision include those below.

### Cost versus benefits

Promotion can cost a great deal of money and, regardless of the funds that are spent, there are no guarantees of success in increasing sales. In some cases, the effects of promotion may be immediate but last for only a short period. In other cases, a firm could find that a long-term promotional campaign is required to steadily raise awareness and persuade customers to buy. Although this may seem to be expensive, short-term costs can be justified by the long-term benefits of having a strong brand and a high degree of customer loyalty.

### Target market and exposure to media

For any promotional method to be effective, its message needs to be received by the intended audience, the target market. In many cases, there is a direct link between the cost of the method and the market coverage that it can claim. Firms with products that are aimed at mass markets, such as the major supermarket chains, need to use television and national newspaper advertising to achieve the coverage required. Businesses targeting small segments with highly specialised products are more likely to use promotional methods such as direct marketing and personal selling.

### Type of market

The type of market that a firm sells to is also a major consideration. Business to consumer (B2C) firms tend to rely to a large extent on mass advertising methods and sales promotions. This may be because their markets are relatively large or

## Enhancing corporate image at Marks and Spencer

In March 2010, UK retailer Marks and Spencer (M&S) issued a press release to launch a major new competition. 'Your Green Idea' invited people to make suggestions about 'new, positive green actions' that the company could implement under Plan A, its environmental and ethical initiative. The prize for the person with the best idea was £100,000 to spend on 'greening up' an organisation of their choice, such as a school, charity or local community group. A panel of experts was set up to choose the best three entries, with the winner chosen by public vote. The competition was supported by the use of national print advertising and in-store publicity.

At the competition launch, M&S chairman, Sir Stuart Rose, commented, 'We're looking for a groundbreaking green idea that we can implement across our stores so that all of our customers can get even more involved in Plan A. We want people to think creatively about actions that could really change people's behaviour and help us make a difference to the environment.'

The competition is the latest step taken by M&S in its bid to become the world's most sustainable retailer by 2015. According to the press release, the company's Plan A is 'encouraging M&S customers and employees to live "greener" lifestyles'.

**Source: www.marksandspencer.com**

### Questions

a) Describe the impact of activities such as the Your Green Idea competition and the Plan A campaign on the corporate image of M&S.

b) Examine the impact of this kind of promotional activity on the retailer's profits.

---

because the customers within them have, at least to some extent, similar needs and expectations. Businesses that sell to other businesses (known as B2B firms) are more likely to use personal selling, trade journals and direct marketing, as well as trade fairs and exhibitions. This allows more flexibility in terms of the information provided on the products available and, in many cases, the opportunity to build up a closer relationship with the customer.

## Market stability

The rate of change within the market, both in terms of the number of customers and the degree of competition, can influence both the amount of promotion and the methods used. The focus of promotion in a rapidly growing market is to maintain awareness, using high levels of advertising to attract the attention of new customers. Where the rate of growth is slower, firms may advertise less frequently, using sales promotions such as discounts and loyalty cards to maintain existing sales. Any advertising that is carried out can remain unchanged, also helping to keep costs down.

## Channel strategies

**Channel strategy** is a term used to describe the methods used for distributing products from the manufacturer or producer to the end user. The spread of the internet in recent years has led to a growing number of manufacturers selling direct to customers online. However, many continue to use intermediaries, such as wholesalers and retailers, to reach the consumer. The extent to which wholesalers and retailers are prepared to share the responsibility of promotion will also have an effect on the level and methods used by the producer. For example, book retailers such as WH Smith and Waterstone's run major advertising campaigns promoting book titles, as well as investing heavily in shop fittings and promotional materials, while book publishers concentrate on using methods such as personal selling.

## Objectives

The objectives of a business should influence every aspect of its planning and operations, including marketing and promotion. A business aiming to increase its share of an existing market needs to use frequent advertising to highlight the unique features of its products and their benefits over rivals, and sales promotions to attract new customers. A business that is struggling financially and attempting to reduce losses may avoid methods such as sponsorship and focus on more cost-effective methods.

## Branding and positioning

**Branding** is the process of creating a particular image for a product that makes it stand out from its competitors. **Product positioning** looks at the position of an individual product within a market, i.e. how it is viewed by customers relative to competitors. For example, Italian-restaurant chain Carluccio's has a more upmarket reputation than that of Nando's, but would be regarded as down-market in comparison with Gordon Ramsay's Pétrus restaurant in London's Knightsbridge. The choice of promotion depends on the image that is required. For example, a business wishing to develop or maintain an exclusive image is likely to avoid any mass advertising or promotions linked to price reductions, instead using methods that can be directed at a relatively small and carefully chosen group within the appropriate customer profile, based on factors such as income, professional status and lifestyle patterns.

## Competitors

Firms operating in the same market may feel obliged to adopt similar promotional methods in order to prevent rivals from gaining a competitive edge. For example, in late 2009, both Sainsbury's and Tesco announced plans to launch a 'Buy now, get one free later' scheme, to counter criticism of the waste generated by the traditional BOGOF sales promotion. Those businesses that attempt to differentiate themselves by using different promotional tactics are likely to find that they are copied if they are successful.

## Budget and timing requirements

Promotional activities are generally constrained by a budget, no matter how large the business is. This is to ensure that resources are used efficiently and not wasted, in order to keep a control over costs. There are a number of methods that can be used for budget setting. Some firms use previous years' budgets to guide them; others operate a **zero-budgeting** policy, where marketing managers have to justify all planned expenditure. This may be particularly difficult to do if the results of promotional expenditure are only likely to occur in the distant future.

Timing is also an important consideration. Some promotional activities, such as television advertising, can take many months – if not longer – to put together. Careful planning is necessary to ensure that these activities are timed appropriately. For example, the promotion used for products with highly seasonal demand needs to be in place at exactly the right time – too early and customers will have forgotten; too late and sales will have been lost to competitors.

## A model of communication

Communication involves sending a message from one individual or group (the sender) to another (the receiver). For communication to be effective, the message must be understood correctly and reach the target audience. The sender must **encode** the message appropriately by using a format and language that are suitable for the target audience. The message must also be sent using an appropriate medium. For example, the benefits of a new weight-loss drug might be described using technical language in a medical journal aimed at doctors, but described more simply when advertised on television in order to communicate with the general public. The message must also be decoded or understood by the receiver in the manner intended by the sender. In order to confirm this, a system for generating feedback is required. This could involve carrying out regular market research to survey customer opinions.

In 2010, Innocent ran a television campaign in the UK to promote its smoothie drinks. Figure 9.2 shows the communication process applied to the Innocent advertisement.

The term **noise** refers to any factors that can reduce the effectiveness of the communication process. In the Innocent example above, this could include a lack of interest among viewers in the benefits of a healthy diet or a reluctance to believe that a smoothie is an effective substitute for fresh fruit and vegetables.

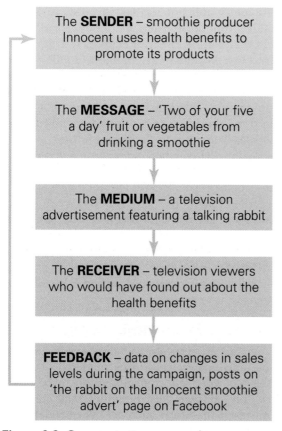

Figure 9.2 Communication process, Innocent advertisement

The Innocent rabbit

## Consumer response hierarchy

A great deal of research has been carried out into the complex process of consumer buying behaviour. AIDA is a well-known consumer response hierarchy model that is often used to help design advertisements and promotional campaigns. It sets out the key steps that consumers need to be taken through before committing themselves to buying a product. These steps are identified in Figure 9.3.

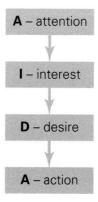

Figure 9.3 The AIDA model

The use of different promotional tools is timed to take the consumer through the process. The focus of the message communicated to the consumer also changes gradually. The four key AIDA steps are:

- **Step 1: attract attention** People have to be aware that a product exists before they can consider whether to buy it. Bold headlines on billboards or short advertisements that arouse curiosity are used to do this, along with sponsorship and public relations activities to boost the product's profile.
- **Step 2: create interest** Potential customers need to be encouraged to consider the various benefits of buying the product. Longer, more detailed advertisements and direct marketing can be used to give information on product features.
- **Step 3: generate desire** Customers need to become convinced that they want the product and are prepared to seek it out. At this stage, the focus of advertising is on showing people enjoying the product. Sales promotions offering price discounts and other special offers are used as tactics to persuade people to buy.
- **Step 4: ensure action** The final step focuses on securing the sale. Advertising and personal selling are used to pass on details about product availability, ordering and payment options, after-sales care and any other information relevant to the purchase.

## Key terms

**AIDA** A well-known consumer response hierarchy model that is often used to help design advertisements and promotional campaigns. The four steps are Attention, Interest, Desire and Action

**B2B firm** A business that sells its products to other businesses

**B2C firm** A business that sells its products to consumers

**Brand image** The identity created for a product that makes it stand out from its competitors

**Branding** The process of creating a particular image for a product that makes it stand out from its competitors

**Channel strategy** The term used to describe the methods used for distributing products from the manufacturer or producer to the end user

**Communication** The process of sending a message from one individual or group, known as the sender, to another, known as the receiver

**Corporate image** This refers to the public's perceptions about a particular business

**Product positioning** The position of an individual product within a market depends on how it is viewed by customers, relative to competitors

**Promotional mix** The term used to describe the different methods used to promote a good or service

## Q Re-cap questions

1　Outline the purpose of the promotional mix.

2　Explain why most businesses tend to use more than one method of promotion.

3　Identify four types of advertising media.

4　Explain the difference between personal selling and sales promotion.

5　Examine one benefit and one drawback of using public relations as a promotional tool.

6　Identify four influences on the choice of promotional mix for a product.

7　Describe how the promotional mix for a national supermarket chain might differ from that of a business manufacturing components for the car industry.

8　Describe the key stages involved in the process of communication.

9　Using examples, explain what is meant by 'noise' in the communication process.

10 State and briefly explain the stages of the AIDA model of consumer response.

## Grading tips

| P1 Describe the promotional mix used by two selected organisations for a selected product/service. You must identify and describe in detail all of the elements in the promotional mix for each product or service. | | |
|---|---|---|

See page 209 for suggestions for Assignments for Unit 9.

# Part 2: The role of promotion within the marketing mix

The promotional mix works together with the product and other key supporting elements, such as price and distribution, to form an **integrated marketing mix**. Therefore these elements must be taken into consideration when choosing how to promote a good or service. All businesses provide products. These consist of physical goods such as a car or a mobile phone, or intangible services such as insurance or interior design. A physical product's marketing mix typically consists of four key elements – product, price, promotion and place. Packaging can also play an important role in promoting a product, as well as providing protection. A service is a product that is intangible, which means that factors such as the people and processes responsible for delivering it are also significant.

## Products and services

### Product features, range and variations

Few firms provide only one basic product. Most offer a range of different products. This helps to increase sales levels and protect against a sudden fall in demand for one product line. For example, online store Amazon offers a huge variety of products, including books, CDs, DVDs and many other goods. Some businesses specialise in a certain type of product but produce many variations. Clothes retailers, such as Next, New Look and River Island, sell different ranges in a selection of different colours and sizes. Car manufacturers produce a number of versions of a basic model with different engine sizes and then offer customers a wide selection of optional features so that the resulting car can be customised to a high degree. Special features that differentiate products from others on the market can help to create a competitive edge. These special features are known as unique selling points (USPs) and help to provide a focus for promotion.

### Quantity and timing

Firms also need to take decisions about the quantity of products they intend to produce and sell, and the implications of this for its promotional mix. Large-scale production requires promotional methods that can communicate effectively in mass markets, such as television advertising. Lower levels of production aimed at small niches within the overall market will require a different promotional approach, perhaps using direct marketing and personal selling. Consideration also needs to be given to the timing of any new product launch or an expansion of existing product sales. In many cases, promotion is used to build customer awareness and raise interest before the launch takes place or greater quantities of an existing product are released. This might take the form of a press campaign in selected newspapers or magazines. Once this has occurred, promotion needs to be used to persuade customers to buy and to inform them about how to do so, again with the use of advertising supported by sales promotions and direct mailing of free samples.

### Product quality, style and associated benefits

All products are expected to be 'fit for purpose', i.e. to deliver what they promise to do. **Quality** can be seen as the combination of a number of factors, depending on the nature of the product and the expectations of its customers. Performance is central to the concept of quality. This refers to the extent to which a good or service actually meets or surpasses customer expectations. Out of the many different brands available within a given market, some may perform better than others. This superior performance acts as a USP and can be emphasised using promotion, as shown by Proctor & Gamble's long-running tagline 'The best a man can get' for its Gillette brand. Performance is also linked to reliability and durability. Customers expect products to continue to be useful and to meet expected performance standards each time they are required. They are also likely to be prepared to pay more for those that are longer lasting. Firms often provide guarantees, free after-sales care and other associated benefits to reassure customers about quality. Product design is also responsible for creating a style that is aesthetically appealing. This means that not only do products need to do what they claim to but they need to look good as well.

## New product development, including product and market trials

New product development is undertaken for a number of reasons. All products have a finite life cycle, which means that sooner or later they have to be replaced. Any business that fails to plan for this sufficiently far ahead runs the risk of falling revenues and even the chance of going out of business completely. Launching new products on a regular basis can generate marketing benefits, as well as helping to maintain sales. Companies like Apple, Microsoft and Sony have a reputation for product innovation and new product launches generally attract a great deal of media attention, leading to free publicity.

The costs of research and development and the high risk of new product failure often means that a **product trial** is carried out. This involves launching the product in a limited way – perhaps in a particular area of the country – so that consumer reaction can be gauged and adjustments made to the proposed marketing mix before the full product launch. Existing products may also be tested in a similar way prior to being launched in new markets. Although product and market trials inevitably add to development costs, they can help to avoid the damage caused by new product failure, including the loss of investment and reputation.

The iPad launch reconfirms Apple's reputation for innovation

## Price

Price has a major impact on the demand for goods and services. It determines not just how many people can afford to buy a product but also whether or not they see it as value for money and are, therefore, willing to pay. The price level chosen for a product can also have psychological effects. Many customers see price as an indicator of quality. If the price charged for a product is significantly lower than other rival brands on the market, customers may be suspicious rather than see it as a bargain.

## Factors affecting price

There are a number of influences on the price given to a product. The key factors are discussed below.

## Costs – development and production

The levels of revenue generated by a new product are likely to be low but the costs associated with developing and producing it will be high. In the short term, this may not be a problem as the business may have the resources to subsidise its losses. In the long term, however, the revenue generated from a product's sales needs to be sufficient to cover the costs of developing and producing it. If this is not the case, the business will fail to break even, will run out of resources and ultimately be forced to close.

## Consumer reactions

Price also has a significant impact on demand. If average incomes are rising, the level of demand is likely to increase even if prices remain constant. This is because more people can now afford to buy products and to buy them more frequently. Some goods and services are also more sensitive or responsive to changes in price than others. The price elasticity of demand measures this responsiveness. In some cases, even a relatively small reduction in price might lead to a major rise in demand (or vice versa). In other cases, substantial price increases can have little, if any, effect on sales.

## Competitors

Most firms will take into account the prices charged by their competitors when choosing their own pricing strategy. In some cases, there may be little, if any, variation in price from business to business. This is likely to be the case, for example, in markets where there are many firms all selling very similar products. Where a greater level of differentiation exists, firms price their products relative to others in order to achieve a particular position within the market.

## Channel strategy

Channel strategy refers to the way a manufacturer or service provider distributes its products to the final user (see Place, below). At each stage in the channel of distribution, the intermediary involved is likely to add a mark-up to the product's price. The manufacturer may therefore need to take the final retail price into account when setting its own prices.

## Pricing strategies

A pricing strategy sets out the level of prices a business intends to charge for its products over the medium to long term. The main types of pricing strategy used are identified in Figure 9.4 (refer to Unit 3.4 for a detailed discussion).

## Place

This aspect of the marketing mix is concerned with ensuring that products reach consumers via the most effective route. Goods and services must be available where and when customers expect them. If they are not, customers are likely to become dissatisfied and spend their money elsewhere. Improvements in technology and increasing use of the internet mean that many businesses – manufacturers, retailers and service providers – sell goods and services online. This offers customers the convenience of shopping from home at any time of the day. It also means that operating costs can be reduced, as businesses can locate their sales staff and warehouses in cheaper, out-of-town locations. Some businesses, including restaurants and beauty salons, still need a physical presence in order to deliver to customers. Although retailing, banking, insurance and other financial services can be provided online or over the telephone, many of these businesses recognise that some of their customers still prefer face-to-face contact and the opportunity to examine and compare products in front of them before they decide to buy.

The channel of distribution describes the method used to get a product from its producer to the end user. In some cases, the product may pass directly from the producer to the consumer. Some manufacturers sell their goods on to **intermediaries**, such as wholesalers and retailers. They may or may not sell directly to customers as well. A key reason for doing this is to maximise their exposure to the market, covering as many options as possible, to ensure that their goods are in place and waiting for customers to come and buy them. Of course, there is no guarantee that either wholesalers or retailers will stock a manufacturer's products. They may be reluctant, for example, to take established products off the shelves to make room for new goods unless they are confident that these will sell. Producers may therefore need to invest heavily in promotional campaigns,

**Figure 9.4** Types of pricing strategy

generating high levels of demand that are difficult for intermediaries to ignore. This is known as a **pull approach** or pull strategy. Another method used to persuade intermediaries to stock goods is to offer them incentives, such as point-of-sale materials and generous credit terms. This is known as a **push approach** or push strategy.

## Wholesalers

Wholesalers provide the link between the manufacturer and the retailer (or other business users). Their key function is to buy in large quantities of goods and then sell them on. This is known as **breaking bulk**. The manufacturer benefits from improved cash flow and reduced warehousing costs. Smaller retailers benefit from not tying up large amounts of working capital by having to buy in bulk from manufacturers. Wholesalers are likely to take some of the responsibility for promotion, particularly that directed at retailers, including discounts and special offers, to encourage them to buy.

## Retailers

Retailers are the final link in the distribution chain before the end user is reached. Large retailers, such as Tesco and Asda, buy direct from the manufacturer, whereas smaller stores are more likely to buy from wholesalers. Many retailers provide a range of services, including special ordering and delivery facilities, as part of their customer service. Retailers are also likely to carry out promotional activities, targeting the final consumer. This may include:

- Advertising campaigns, loyalty cards and other schemes
- Sales promotions, such as loyalty cards, 'buy one, get one free' and other sales promotions
- Point-of-sale displays, food and drink tastings and product demonstrations.

## Selling direct to the customer

Service providers, such as hairdressers, hotels and leisure centres, have always required direct contact so that the service can be experienced. However, as noted above, the spread of the internet has made it much easier for consumers to avoid the use of retailers and go straight to the producer. Large manufacturers have sophisticated websites that not only advertise product ranges and special offers, but also allow customers to order and arrange delivery online. The internet also gives much smaller businesses the opportunity

to communicate with customers all over the world. Removing intermediaries from the distribution chain may mean that manufacturers can raise their prices slightly but still reduce the price paid by customers by getting rid of the mark-up charged by the wholesaler and/or retailer. In such situations, however, the manufacturer is wholly responsible for promoting the product. This allows them to keep full control of the messages that are communicated but they have to bear all the costs of promotion, as well as distribution.

## Packaging

A product's packaging has to be carefully designed to carry out a number of functions. It must protect the product and allow it to be stored safely until it is ready for use. It may be some time before the product reaches the end user and it may have to pass through a number of stages in the distribution channel. Nevertheless, it must remain in good condition. This can present particular challenges for products that are fragile or perishable, that need to be transported over large distances and be subject to harsh conditions, such as extremes of heat. Packaging can also be designed to make a product more convenient to store and use once it has been purchased by the consumer. For example, many food and drink products come in cartons that are easy to reseal and keep the product fresh after the packaging has been first opened.

Packaging also plays an important promotional role for many goods. Its design can be used to attract customers' attention by making the product stand out from others on the shelves. The careful use of wording, logos and colour can help to develop a distinctive brand image. The packaging may also need to contain information on the product, such as its size, weight, ingredients and nutritional details.

## People

### Importance particularly in services

People are an essential ingredient in the marketing mix for services. The customer's experience is largely, if not wholly, based on their interaction with those employees involved with delivering the service in question. For example, the enjoyment gained from eating out at a restaurant is not just based on the quality and freshness of the ingredients that are used to create the dishes on the menu. The speed and friendliness of the initial greeting, the skills of the chef in preparing and presenting the food, the timing of the courses and the attitude of the waiting staff are also essential – the pleasure of eating a tasty three-course meal can be more than wiped out by a rude or inattentive waiter or waitress. Personal recommendation acts as an effective and low-cost method of promotion, but the damage caused to a business's reputation by poor customer experiences can be difficult to correct.

## Training and development

The ability of employees to carry out their roles as service providers can be enhanced by undergoing appropriate training. This can be used to develop not only specific technical skills, such as food preparation, sports coaching or beauty therapy, but also appropriate interpersonal skills including dealing effectively with customer enquiries and complaints.

## Consistency of image

Many businesses invest a great deal of time and money in creating a particular brand image for themselves and their products. Customer expectations are based around this image, making it vital to deliver a consistent service across the whole organisation, no matter how big it is. Even businesses such as McDonald's and Starbucks, operating on a global scale, must ensure that their standards of service are the same for all customers. Staff uniforms, common store layout, product menus, slogans and logos are used to deliver this consistency. The use of company-wide training programmes is also important.

## Processes

The processes used to organise resources also play a major part in how effectively a service is delivered to customers. The ability to offer variety by allowing customers to choose or combine a wide range of options helps to meet their needs more effectively. For example, Center Parcs gives its visitors different types of accommodation and activities during their stay. The processes need to be in place to ensure that these facilities are available as and when customers want to use them. Improvements in technology have made it easier to offer this level of choice. A high degree of service customisation can also be supported by options such as different methods of receiving information, booking, ordering or making reservations.

## Physical evidence

Although people are central to service provision, there are a number of other factors that also help to determine the customer's experience. Lighting, colour and sound are often used to create a specific atmosphere. This could be neutral colours, soft lights and calm music to create a relaxing hotel lounge or romantic restaurant; alternatively, spot lighting, vibrant colours and pop music could be used to appeal to young people in a clothes retailer or music store. The tone of voice used by sales staff and customer service is also important. It needs to convey interest in customer needs and confidence in the product for sale, but an aggressive tone that places pressure on customers to buy is likely to backfire and may also be against the law. Physical evidence needs to be chosen and combined with other elements in the marketing mix to support the overall image of the brand.

## Promotional objectives

Promotional objectives are the specific targets that an organisation's promotional activities set out to achieve. They should be designed in such a way as to support the marketing objectives, which are, in turn, derived from the overall objectives of the business. The business with the largest share of a saturated market might decide to pursue continued expansion by developing markets overseas. After extensive market research to assess market conditions, this is likely to require prolonged advertising campaigns to raise awareness and interest in the firm's products. Other common promotional objectives include creating a distinctive market presence, increasing market share, targeting relevant audiences, and market segmentation.

Promotional activity is not just aimed at consumers. As we have already seen, manufacturers often use promotional techniques to persuade wholesalers and retailers to stock their products. Other firms may produce equipment and machinery for business use or provide support services, such as IT, recruitment and accountancy. Promotion is just as important for business-to-business (B2B) firms as it is for business-to-consumer (B2C) firms. However, business customers' needs are likely to be wider ranging than those of consumers. In such cases, promotion is more likely to focus on personal selling to provide the level of advice and support required, and on advertising in trade journals and appearances at exhibitions and trade fairs.

**Figure 9.5** Promotional objectives

## Branding

Branding is used by firms to differentiate their products from those sold by competitors. It is a key marketing activity and, if done successfully, has major influence on customer buying behaviour. (Refer to Unit 3 for a more detailed discussion of branding.)

## Key terms

**Branding** The process of creating a particular image for a product that makes it stand out from its competitors

**Breaking bulk** Key function of wholesalers, involving buying-in large quantities of goods and then selling them on

**Channel strategy** This refers to the way a manufacturer or service provider distributes its products to the final user

**Integrated marketing mix** Where the elements such as price, promotion and place complement and support each other

**Intermediary** These are businesses, such as wholesalers and retailers, situated between the producer and the final consumer in the channel of distribution

**Product trial** This involves launching the product in a limited way in order to test consumer reaction and make adjustments to the proposed marketing mix before the full product launch

**Pull approach** Where producers invest heavily in promotional campaigns, generating high levels of demand that are difficult for intermediaries to ignore

**Push approach** Where manufacturers offer intermediaries incentives, such as point-of-sale materials and generous credit terms, in order to encourage them to stock their goods

**Re-cap questions**

1   Explain how the marketing mix for a service differs from that of a physical good.
2   State three factors that may contribute to a product's quality.
3   Describe one advantage and one disadvantage for a firm in carrying out product trials.
4   Outline three factors that might influence the price of a new games console launched by Sony.
5   Briefly compare the role carried out by a wholesaler to that of a retailer.
6   Examine one benefit and one drawback for a computer manufacturer selling directly to consumers rather than through retailers.
7   State two functions of a product's packaging.
8   Explain why people are a particularly important element in the provision of services.
9   Briefly examine how training can improve the quality of service provision.
10  Using examples, explain the link between a firm's overall objectives, its marketing objectives and its promotional objectives.

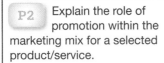

| **P2** Explain the role of promotion within the marketing mix for a selected product/service. | **M1** Explain how promotion is integrated with the rest of the marketing mix in a selected organisation to achieve its marketing aims and objectives. | **D1** Evaluate and justify the use of an appropriate promotional mix in relation to marketing objectives for the selected organisation. |
|---|---|---|
| You must describe the other key elements of the marketing mix, e.g. the product, its price, its distribution (place) and, in the case of a service, people, processes and physical evidence. | You need to develop the points raised in P2 and show how the promotional techniques used complement and support these elements to create a distinctive brand image. You must also show how this helps to achieve the firm's marketing aims and objectives, which should be clearly stated. | You must identify the marketing aims of the business, e.g. a target percentage increase in sales within a given period of time. You must then assess the extent to which these objectives have been met and balance this success against the costs of the promotional mix that has been used. |

See page 209 for Assignments for Unit 9.

# **Part 3:** The role of advertising agencies and the media

## Roles carried out by advertising agencies

Some businesses may lack the expertise or resources to organise their promotional activities in-house. They may decide, therefore, to outsource this particular marketing function to an advertising agency. This is a firm that specialises in designing advertising strategies on behalf of other businesses. Advertising agencies provide a range of services to their clients. Full-service agencies are those that offer all of the activities required to plan and execute an advertising campaign. Limited-service agencies specialise in a given area, such as graphic design or media planning. Using such an agency allows a business to carry out some of the functions itself, which may allow it greater control and confidentiality, especially where campaigns involve new and innovative products. Using suitably experienced employees from within the firm can also help to keep costs down. A business could also take this approach in order to use the top agencies in each area, in an attempt to produce the most effective campaign possible.

The services provided by advertising agencies include:

- **Media planning** This involves deciding where advertisements should appear in order to reach the audience being targeted in the most cost-effective way. It also involves buying time in media such as television, radio and cinema, or space in printed media such as newspapers and magazines.
- **Designing advertisements** This involves taking the initial promotional idea and developing it into a message that will be understood by the target audience. This is achieved by effective wording of the advertisement (**copywriting**) and enhancing this with appropriate type layout (**typography**) and use of visual images (**graphic design**).
- **Producing advertisements** Once the advertisement is designed, it needs to be turned into its final format. This may include choosing and briefing actors, booking recording studios, designing television sets and recording video clips and jingles.

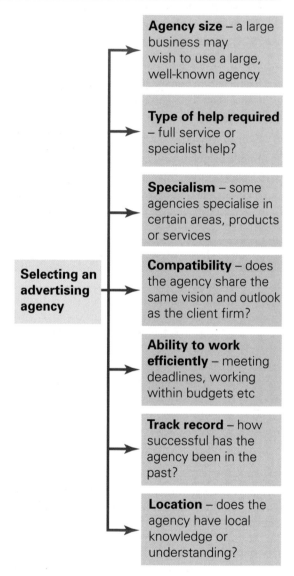

**Figure 9.6** Criteria for selecting an advertising agency

## Types of advertising media

Advertising media are the different channels used to communicate with customers. The choice of the media actually selected by an individual business or agency will depend on a number of criteria (see Criteria for media selection, below) but will be based on one or more of the following.

## Local, regional, national or international

Businesses need to consider not just the size but also the location of the target market for promotional campaigns, in order to determine the level of geographical coverage required. Mass media are needed to reach large-scale audiences. Television advertising is frequently used to do this, dubbing sound into different languages in some cases to cater for different markets around the world. This can be supported by national newspaper and radio advertising, as well as the use of magazines with an international audience, such as *The Economist*. Regional television channels and local radio and newspapers can be used to target smaller clusters of potential customers or to reinforce a national campaign. Generally, the coverage provided by the various media types is reflected in the cost of using them.

## Terrestrial versus satellite television

Despite increasing competition from other terrestrial channels and satellite television, the UK's major commercial television channel, ITV, still provides advertisers with the opportunity to communicate with huge audiences across the UK on a daily basis. TV programmes such as *Coronation Street*, *X Factor* and *Britain's Got Talent* consistently attract millions of viewers, making them prime time for advertisements. For those businesses targeting mass markets this means that, although the overall cost of advertising is very high, the cost per viewer (and, therefore, potential customer) is relatively low. However, the development of satellite and cable television has led to a large increase in the number of channels available. Many of these specialise in a particular type of programme, such as those relating to lifestyle and culture, sports, kids and music. This makes it easier for businesses to target segments within the overall market, making advertising potentially more effective.

## Digital

The UK began to switch to digital television – a process known as the digital switchover – in 2008. This means that by 2012 nearly all households in the UK will have access to a number of facilities unavailable under the previous analogue broadcast system, including the use of interactive television, allowing them to order goods directly, send feedback and participate in live programmes using a remote control.

## Internet

The internet has provided individuals and businesses with a fast and relatively cheap method of communication on a worldwide scale. Business websites serve two main purposes. Some are used simply as a means of promotion, providing information on products and contact details. More sophisticated websites can be used to order goods or post feedback online. Initial set-up costs depend on the complexity of the website and whether the information it contains needs to be updated regularly. However, these maintenance costs are likely to compare favourably with more traditional methods of reaching global audiences. There are a number of other ways in which the internet can be used as a promotional tool. Use of email, for example, is becoming an increasingly popular method for sending direct mail. Search engines, including Google, Bing and Ask.com, and social-networking sites, such as Facebook and Twitter, are used to promote businesses, products and, in some cases, the advertisements themselves.

## Specialist media

There are a large number of magazines, such as *Caterer and Hotelkeeper* and *The Grocer*, which are aimed at particular industries or sectors. Their readership numbers may be low compared with magazines aimed at the general public. Nevertheless, they can be a very effective means of promotion within the sector or industry concerned.

## Criteria for media selection

The actual combination of promotional media used will differ from business to business and from product to product. The selection criteria used to make the decision include:

- **Cost versus coverage** Cost is a key issue in determining the choice of advertising media for all businesses. Even those with large promotional budgets need to recognise the opportunity cost of any promotional expenditure: i.e. any money spent on promotion involves sacrifices elsewhere. However, it may also be useful to think in terms of cost per member of target audience that might actually see the promotion, particularly for businesses operating in mass markets, either national or international. This may help to justify spending on television advertising, because of its wide coverage.

## Coca-Cola's World Cup advertising campaign

Soft drinks multinational Coca-Cola used the 2010 FA Cup between Chelsea and Portsmouth to launch the UK element of a multi-million pound global advertising campaign, in the run-up to the FIFA 2010 World Cup. The company has been the official sponsor of the tournament since 1978 and the campaign is the largest that it has ever run.

The campaign was focused on a television advertisement featuring original footage of the goal celebration dance carried out by the legendary Cameroon player, Roger Milla. The TV advert was broadcast in the 150 countries around the world where Coca-Cola has a presence. Two other international adverts were only available online in the UK. One of them was a digital animation called 'Quest'. Aimed primarily at younger web users, it encouraged them to upload their own celebrations via YouTube.

### Questions

a) To what extent do you agree with Coca-Cola's choice of media for its World Cup advertising campaign?

b) Carry out your own research to find out the other key promotional activities carried out by Coca-Cola during the 2010 World Cup.

- **Promotional objectives** The choice of media is also likely to depend on what the business is attempting to achieve. For example, the launch of a new product requires initial promotional activity to create customer awareness. This may be done by using bold and colourful advertising on television, on billboards and in magazines.
- **Target audience** Effective promotion means that the message needs to be communicated to the intended customers. If a product is aimed at the majority, if not all of those, making up a market, then mass media such as national television and newspaper advertising are needed. Smaller segments and tiny niches require promotional methods that can cut through the market and seek out these groups, including direct mail and personal selling.
- **Focus of appeal** This is concerned with why customers are interested in buying a good or service. Some customers might choose to buy a car on the basis of rational decisions, such as reliability, extended warranties or economical fuel consumption, whereas others will choose models for their image, the status they confer and other emotional reasons.

- **Circulation/readership** As noted above, the cost per number of viewers or readers of an advertisement is often used as a key criterion, rather than the total cost of the campaign, in order to determine the effectiveness of a campaign. Obviously, the more people within a target audience that are exposed to a promotional message, the more effective the campaign is likely to be.

## Role of the internet

The increasing use of the internet as a promotional tool has been referred to on a number of occasions in this unit. In particular, its influence is felt in terms of the following:

- **Disintermediation** The development and increasing use of the internet have meant that manufacturers no longer need to rely on traditional chains of distribution, using wholesalers and retailers to get their products to the final consumer. Detailed and sophisticated business websites allow customers to identify the cheapest or most suitable suppliers and order goods online, thus cutting out intermediaries.

- **Direct marketing/one-to-one communications** The internet also allows businesses to use direct marketing to tailor their promotional campaigns by acquiring information regarding consumer purchasing patterns and contact details.

## Key terms

**Advertising agency** A firm that specialises in designing advertising strategies on behalf of other businesses

**Advertising media** The different channels used to communicate promotional messages with customers

**Copywriting** The process of wording advertisement, in order to convey the intended message effectively

**Disintermediation** The declining use of intermediaries, such as wholesalers and retailers, in the distribution process, resulting from the ability of manufacturers to communicate directly with consumers via the internet

**Promotional objectives** The specific targets or goals set for promotional activities, which should support the more widespread marketing and corporate objectives of a business

**Typography** The type of font and size used in an advertisement

## Q Re-cap questions

1 State three key functions carried out by an advertising agency.

2 Suggest one reason why a business might choose to use a number of limited-service advertising agencies rather than one full-service agency.

3 Using examples, explain what is meant by advertising media.

4 Give two reasons why a business might use local or regional media to advertise its products.

5 Examine one reason why a company organising activity holidays in the French Pyrenees might choose to advertise on a Sky lifestyle channel rather than on ITV1.

6 Identify two ways in which a business can use the internet as a promotional tool.

7 'Company websites can only be used for one-way communication.' True or false? Justify your answer.

8 Describe one advantage of digital television over analogue television when promoting products.

9 Explain why firms need to consider cost versus coverage when comparing different advertising media.

10 Outline two considerations, other than cost, that should be kept in mind when choosing which advertising media to use.

# Grading tips

| | | |
|---|---|---|
| **P3** Explain the role of advertising agencies in the development of a successful promotional campaign.<br><br>You must provide a clear explanation of the contribution that can be made by an advertising agency to the successful promotion of a selected product or service. | **M2** Explain the advantages and disadvantages of using professional agencies in ensuring promotional success.<br><br>You must develop the points made in P3, showing both advantages and disadvantages of using professional agencies, compared with carrying out promotion in-house. | |
| **P4** Explain the reasons behind the choice of media in a successful promotional campaign.<br><br>You must identify the media used during the campaign and show how it contributed to the campaign's success. | | |

See page 209 for suggestions for Assignments for Unit 9.

# Part 4: Creating a simple promotional campaign

## The campaign brief

The basis of any effective advertising campaign – whether designed in-house or by an agency – is a well-structured campaign brief. This should contain the following sections:

- **The project title and client's details** – and the names of those responsible for designing the campaign brief.
- A summary of the background to the campaign – including the reasons for the campaign, conditions in the market and any other information that could be useful to the team drawing up the campaign.
- The objectives of the campaign – i.e. what it is meant to achieve in terms of its effects on the target audience, on the level of sales or market share.
- A description of the target market – as much relevant information as possible on the people that the campaign is aimed at, including gender, age, income levels, professions/jobs, interests and opinions.
- A description of the product – including details about its key features, the benefits it provides to customers and the reasons why they are likely to buy it.
- The budget available – an indication of the funds available. This may be based on past advertising expenditure for similar campaigns, either by the firm or its competitors. Alternatively, it may be calculated as a percentage of the sales revenue that is expected to result from the campaign.
- The campaign schedule – setting out deadlines and timings of the planned promotional activities.

## The creative brief

This is a document that sets out the direction that the process of planning the promotional campaign should take. It contains details of the various ideas and concepts that should be explored – plus those that should be avoided – and identifies any research that needs to be completed. The creative brief acts as a set of guidelines to the team responsible for planning the campaign. Members of the team can use their expertise and experience to interpret its content and produce detailed and creative promotional support.

## Selection of content

An important step in the process of drawing up a promotional campaign is to decide what message will be conveyed to the target audience. The message needs to be informative and persuasive, highlighting key aspects of the product. Content may include one or more of the following:

- **Features** Information about key features that are unique to the product or are better than those of other products on the market.
- **Performance** Information regarding the speed or power of the product, which may also be compared with others on the market.
- **Benefits** The message is likely to convey a promise of the benefits – both rational and emotional – to be derived from using the product.
- **Quality** This may relate to the product's design, the high standard of materials used or the skills of the workers that produce it.
- **Reliability** It may also be useful to include the ability of the product to meet the same standards of performance again and again over time.

## Campaign tactics

Campaign tactics are the specific activities that are used during a promotional campaign in order to achieve its objectives. These tactics may include advertising, direct marketing, personal selling, sales promotions and the use of demonstrations and point-of-sale materials in stores. Issues that need to be considered before the final choice of promotional tactics is made include the following.

## Reach, given the target group

Reach refers to the total number of people within the target group that are able to see an advertisement or be exposed to a promotional activity. For example, advertising on daytime television may be effective in reaching certain groups, such as people who are retired or staying at home to look after young children, but less effective in communicating with others. Reach does not necessarily mean that the people concerned actually see the advertisement, let alone act upon it. However, a promotion that fails to reach a significant percentage of the target audience is unlikely to be effective.

## Selecting appropriate media

The choice of media is crucial to the success of promotional activity. A huge amount of time and money can be invested in the design of a campaign, only to find that the message failed to get through because the media used were inappropriate. Detailed research needs to be carried out into the behaviour of those within the target market, including what newspapers and magazines they read, what they watch on television (and when they watch it) and how regularly they listen to commercial radio or go to the cinema.

## Selecting or designing promotional materials

The design of promotional materials must also be carefully considered and fit in with the objectives of the promotional campaign. Whatever media are used, the chances are that the promotion will be competing against any number of competitors for the potential customer's attention and may easily become lost in a sea of information. Bold headlines and eye-catching images are used to make an impact and to attract initial interest, while colour and sound can be used to create a particular mood or style, and humour and pace can be used to maintain interest. The amount of text used needs to be sufficient to get the message across but not too detailed or the reader is likely to become bored.

## Target audience

From the outset, it must be clear as to who exactly the promotional campaign is aimed at. The target audience not only affects the design of promotional materials but also the media chosen to deliver them. For example, mobile phones may be an effective way to advertise to teenagers and young adults, as they tend to have a higher mobile usage than older people.

## Objectives

The objectives of the promotional campaign should be outlined in the campaign brief. The tactics chosen should support the achievement of these objectives within the timescales identified.

Mobile phones could be a way of targeting a younger audience

For example, the main objective of the campaign to promote a new upmarket holiday resort may well be to increase customer awareness about the facilities and services on offer. Suitable promotional tactics could include direct mail or email using mailing lists of people in the target group, along with advertisements and features in suitable lifestyle magazines, such as *Tatler* and *GQ*.

## Budget

Details of the promotional budget should also be contained in the campaign brief. The funds available may simply be insufficient to allow for some tactics, such as regular television advertising, to be used. The campaign team needs to ensure, however, that any funds that are made available are used as effectively as possible. This may mean, for example, that television advertising is used occasionally to keep a product in the public's eye, backed up with more regular use of sales promotions to encourage customers to keep buying.

## The use of focus groups

Focus groups are made up of a small number of individuals taken from the target audience and are used to provide qualitative market research data. They can be used to provide feedback on new promotional material before it is used as part of a campaign. This can help to identify and correct any possible problems, making the campaign more effective.

## Stages in developing a campaign advertisement

The process of developing an advertisement to be used in a promotional campaign includes the following key stages:

1 **Mock-up or storyboard** A mock-up is a drawing that illustrates how the finished printed advertisement will look. In the case of advertisements using moving images, a sequence of pictures, known as a storyboard, is used to show how the action will unfold, the dialogue that will be used and the actors that will be featured.

2 **Final proof** Once the initial designs have been agreed and approved by the client, the final version, or proof, can be produced, within the limits set by the budget, and the campaign can be put into action.

3 **Review** The effectiveness of the advertisement is assessed in terms of the extent to which it has met the campaign objectives. Measuring the effects on sales is difficult to do – any changes may take place gradually or could be caused by factors that are unconnected to the campaign. However, identifying the impact of the promotion on the target audience can help to inform future campaigns. Market research may, therefore, provide a means of generating feedback.

4 **Planning the next stage** Feedback from the review stage can be used to decide what happens next. For example, if the campaign has been successful in raising interest, customers need to be persuaded to begin buying with further campaigns, highlighting the benefits of using the product relative to others on the market.

## Developing a promotion plan

There are a number of key steps that need to be completed in order to develop a promotion plan. These are discussed below.

## Identify key objectives

It is essential that everyone involved in the campaign is clear as to what the campaign is supposed to do. The objectives of the promotion need to be expressed clearly, in SMART terms (refer to Unit 3). Doing this will help to ensure that everyone is working together, that progress can be measured and that the effectiveness of the campaign can be assessed.

## Clarify the target audience

It is also vital to identify who exactly the campaign is aimed at. A detailed picture of the target market needs to be established, along with the characteristics, needs and attitudes of those within it. This will help to ensure that the campaign message reaches its intended audience by helping the campaign team to choose an appropriate promotional mix and suitable media.

## Choose a suitable promotional and media mix

The possible elements that combine to form a product's promotional mix and the factors that influence their choice are discussed in detail earlier in this unit. Where advertising needs to be used, careful consideration is also required as to the most suitable media to choose (see Part 3). The choice will depend on a number of factors, including the product itself, the target audience and the budget available. The final promotional mix must also integrate into the wider marketing mix, complementing the good or service in question and the price and distribution methods chosen.

## Decide on frequency and timings

Promotion is not just about attracting customers to new products – they need regular reminders to encourage them to keep buying. The scheduling of promotional activity needs to be planned carefully. The demand for some products may be highly seasonal, so the timing of any promotion needs to support this by concentrating on the time immediately before and during the main sales period. Different elements of the promotional mix, such as mailshots and short-term sales promotions can be used to fill the gaps between major advertising campaigns.

## Set a promotional budget

Promotional activity uses up business resources, so controls need to be put in place to ensure that any funds allocated to promotion are used effectively. Some methods of promotion may be too expensive for smaller businesses and so the costs need to be considered from the outset.

## Using the promotion plan

Once the promotion plan has been drawn up, it needs to be put into action. Changes in consumer behaviour need to be monitored after the campaign is launched, by using market research techniques such as surveys and panels. The plan also needs to be flexible to respond to unplanned events affecting the market, such as an increase in competition or a downturn in the economy. Promotion is only one of a number of influences on demand for a product, so it is difficult to measure the direct effect of a campaign on sales. However, data can be collected on a regular basis to identify the main strengths and weaknesses of the campaign and to assess its success in meeting the objectives set at the beginning of the planning process.

## Creative campaigning from Walkers

In July 2008, snack manufacturer Walkers launched an innovative advertising campaign centred on the quest to discover a new crisp flavour. The £10 million campaign consisted of a series of television adverts featuring long-standing company ambassador, Gary Lineker. A range of other promotional techniques – including radio advertising, online promotions, public relations and in-store displays – were also part of the campaign, which ran for ten months. Six new flavour finalists were chosen from over 1.2 million competition entries by a panel of judges, headed by celebrity chef Heston Blumenthal. These flavours were turned into recipes and put on sale to the general public between January and May 2009. The eventual winner, receiving over 22 per cent of the 1 million votes cast, was Builder's Breakfast, winning its creator, Emma Rushin, a £50,000 cash prize and a 2 per cent royalty from sales.

**Source:** www.walkers.co.uk

### Questions

a) Suggest two possible objectives for the Walkers advertising campaign outlined above.

b) What do you think were the key strengths of the Walkers campaign?

c) Identify any possible weaknesses of the campaign and make suggestions as to how they could have been overcome.

## Key terms

**Advertisement mock-up** A drawing that illustrates how a printed advertisement will look

**Campaign brief** This provides the basis of any effective advertising campaign, identifying key aspects such as promotional objectives, the product and target market, the available budget and timescales

**Campaign schedule** An outline of the timings and frequency of the various promotional activities

**Creative brief** A document that sets out the direction that the process of planning the promotional campaign should take

**Focus group** A small number (typically between six and ten) of individuals, usually chosen from the target market to provide qualitative market research information

**Promotional budget** The funds available to finance the promotional campaign

**Storyboard** A sequence of pictures, used to show how the action will unfold, the dialogue that will be used and the actors who will be featured

## Re-cap questions

1   Identify the main sections of a campaign brief.

2   Briefly explain the role of the creative brief in promotion planning.

3   State four key areas that can be included in the content of an advertisement.

4   Explain what is meant by 'reach' in a promotional context.

5   Outline three influences on the choice of tactics used in a promotional campaign.

6   Briefly explain how focus groups can be used to improve the effectiveness of a promotional campaign.

7   Describe the four stages involved in the development of a campaign advertisement.

8   State the key sections contained in a promotional plan.

9   'It is impossible to accurately measure the direct effects of a promotional campaign on a firm's sales.' True or false? Justify your answer.

10  Explain why it is important to evaluate the effectiveness of a promotional campaign once it has been carried out.

## Grading tips

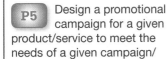 **P5** Design a promotional campaign for a given product/service to meet the needs of a given campaign/creative brief.

Your promotional campaign must be based on a campaign or creative brief, showing a clear understanding of the intended target market and relevant elements of the promotional mix.

 **M3** Provide a rationale for a promotional campaign.

You must give a clear explanation as to why you have chosen the elements of your promotional campaign and how it is expected to achieve the objectives set.

 **D2** Evaluate an existing national marketing campaign.

You must examine the strengths and weaknesses of an existing national campaign and assess the extent to which it has contributed to the success of the product and the organisation concerned.

## Assignments for Unit 9

### Assignment One

You are a freelance journalist who writes articles for a number of newspapers and business journals. You have been approached by a leading marketing magazine and asked to write a supplement for next month's edition, looking at the role of promotion within marketing. The magazine has hinted strongly that they will give you more work in the future if they are happy with the initial work.

**Note** – read through all the tasks, the relevant criteria and the assignment advice on pages 192 and 199 before deciding which organisations to choose. This will help to ensure that you are able to obtain all of the information needed.

**Criteria covered** – P1 P2 M1 D1

### Tasks

1. The first section of your work needs to contain a description of the promotional mix used by two selected organisations to promote a selected product or service. Do not simply identify the various promotional methods used, but provide sufficient detail and support this with the use of examples. (P1)

2. The second section should explain the role of promotion within the marketing mix for a selected product or service. You must include a description of the other elements of the marketing mix for the product in question. (P2)

3. The second section indicated in Task 2 can be extended to include a more detailed explanation of how promotion is integrated with the rest of the marketing mix in a selected organisation, in order to achieve its marketing aims and objectives. (M1)

4. The final section of your work should include an evaluation of promotional mix used within your selected organisation. This should consider the usefulness of the mix in achieving the organisation's marketing objectives. (D1)

### Assignment Two

Congratulations! Your first piece of work has been well received and you have now been commissioned to write an article for the magazine, explaining the role of advertising agencies in developing successful promotional campaigns.

**Note** – read through the tasks below, the relevant criteria and the assignment advice on page 204 to ensure that you generate all the necessary evidence.

**Criteria covered** – P3 P4 M2

### Tasks

1. The first section of your article must clearly explain the role of advertising agencies in the development of a successful promotional campaign. (P3)
2. The second section must explain the reasons for the choice of media used in a successful promotional campaign. (P4)
3. The final section needs to explain the main advantages and disadvantages of using professional agencies in ensuring promotional success. (M2)

### Assignment Three

You are part of the creative team at leading advertising agency, VCCP. The agency has been approached by a well-known manufacturer of soft drinks to produce a campaign designed to promote a new range of 'healthy' juices aimed at children aged between eleven and sixteen, which it plans to launch nationally in the UK within the coming year. The manufacturer wants the promotion to be eye-catching and humorous, but also emphasising the health benefits in order to appeal to both children and parents. The key marketing objectives are to achieve at least 70 per cent market awareness within three months of the start of the promotional campaign and a minimum market share of 10 per cent within 18 months of launch. The promotional budget set is in line with similar campaigns for national launches.

**Note** – read through the tasks below, the relevant criteria and the assignment advice on page 209, in order to ensure that you generate all the necessary evidence.

**Criteria covered** – P5 M3 D2

### Tasks

1. Design a promotional campaign for your product to meet the needs of a given campaign/brief. Refer to the scenario for this. (P5)
2. Produce a rationale for your promotional campaign in order to convince your boss at VCCP that the campaign should go ahead. This must explain why the various elements of the campaign have been chosen and how it is expected to achieve the objectives set. (M3)
3. Produce an evaluation of an existing national marketing campaign – you could, for example, log on to the VCCP website (www.vccp.com) and research one of their recent campaigns. Your evaluation should examine both the strengths and weaknesses of the campaign and make judgements about the extent to which it has contributed to the success of the product concerned. (D2)

**Unit 10:** Market research in business

# Part 1: The main types of market research used to make marketing decisions

There are two main types of market research that are used to gather information for decision making – **primary research** and **secondary research**.

## Primary research

It would be much easier and save a great deal of time if all the information required by a business had already been collected by someone else. Unfortunately, this is not always the case. Even if information does exist, it may be out of date or incomplete. In such cases, primary research will need to be carried out. This type of research involves gathering data for the first time. Although this can use up a considerable amount of time and resources, it should, in theory, provide information that is better suited to the specific needs of a business. There are a number of methods that can be used to carry out primary research, including **observation**, **surveys**, e-marketing research, **focus groups**, **panels**, **field trials** and **piloting**.

## Observation

This is a relatively cost-effective method of collecting data that involves simply watching and recording what happens. It could involve counting the number of people entering a supermarket during a given period of time (known as **footfall**), or noting down customer reactions to point-of-display promotions inside the store. The amount of time required to collect data using this method depends on what needs to be done to set up the observation, as well as carry it out and analyse the results.

One of the key advantages of this method is that, because it is usually undetected, it records what people actually do. If people are aware that their views and behaviour are being noted, they may be encouraged to act in a certain way, perhaps to create a more favourable impression of themselves. The lack of interaction also means that researchers cannot influence the behaviour of those being observed. This should result in a high degree of accuracy, assuming the results are correctly recorded. It should also lead to a high degree of validity, meaning that the results can be relied upon to reflect what is actually happening and are free from bias. However, observation can only help to reveal what people do – the lack of interaction means that it cannot establish the reasons for their reactions. Observation is, therefore, more suitable for collecting quantitative, rather than qualitative, data.

## Surveys

These are used to gather primary data, either quantitative or qualitative, from large numbers of people, known as **respondents**. Surveys are often based on a representative group or sample of people, if the number of potential respondents is very large. There are many ways of conducting a survey and the method chosen depends on the type and amount of information needed, as well as the cost and ease of obtaining it.

### Face-to-face surveys

These involve using trained interviewers to question respondents face-to-face, and are usually based on a pre-written **questionnaire**. This could take place on the street, within a shop, or by visiting households on a door-to-door basis. The salaries and travelling expenses involved make this method relatively expensive. This is also likely to mean that interviews are based on a relatively small geographical area, rather than being spread more widely. However, this method can give a good response rate, as trained interviewers can use their judgement to select appropriate respondents, encourage them to participate and clarify questions where necessary. It also creates the opportunity to use visual materials or carry out simple experiments, such as taste tests, and note respondents' reactions.

### Postal surveys

This involves sending out questionnaires to a selected group of people, along with a covering letter, outlining instructions for completion and return. This type of survey can be relatively cheap to conduct, as no interviewers are involved, making them particularly suitable for large-scale, national surveys. Respondents can complete the questionnaire in their own time, rather than being put on the spot. However, the response rate for postal questionnaires tends to be very low, so incentives such as free return postage, gifts and entry into competitions are often used to encourage a response.

A survey is a form of primary research

## Email surveys

The internet has become an important means of communication between businesses and their customers, providing a cheaper and faster means of conducting surveys than by sending question-naires through the post. One potential drawback is that it relies on people having access to the internet and using it regularly. However, this is becoming less of a problem as the use of laptops and mobile phones for internet access increases. Email surveys also share many of the drawbacks of postal surveys – for example, the people that actually complete them may not be the intended respondents but simply those with the necessary time to do it!

## Telephone surveys

This method involves the use of interviewers, but avoids the need for them to travel, meaning that data can be gathered on a national basis, if neces-sary, at a relatively low cost. Most households have at least one telephone, making it easier to access them and take representative samples. However, the length of questions and the over-all interview should be kept as short as possible. Apart from keeping costs down, this also helps to minimise the nuisance factor if disturbing people at home, in order to increase participation.

The accuracy and validity of the results are also dependent on the size and the method chosen to construct the sample used in the survey. The big-ger the sample, the more likely it is to reflect the overall population. Some sampling methods, known as probability samples, are designed to reduce the chances of selecting participants that are inappro-priate and can be tested to see the extent to which the results they produce are representative.

## E-marketing research

The methods available for conducting market research electronically are rapidly increasing, as consumers and businesses become more and more dependent on internet access, via PCs, laptops, mobile phones and digital television. Internet surveys using interactive questionnaires offer a much higher degree of flexibility than the traditional questionnaire format, where an in-dividual's response to one question dictates the next that appears. The launch of the UK's first directory service for mobile phones at the end of 2009 has made it much easier for firms to contact the country's 40 million mobile phone users for research purposes.

The factors affecting the appropriateness of e-marketing research are largely similar to those relating to the use of surveys to gather primary re-search. The global reach of the internet makes it a relatively cheap and fast method of communi-cating with potentially huge audiences. However, participants still need to be chosen carefully if the information produced is to be valid. Completing and returning an online questionnaire is free and more convenient than using the post, encour-aging a better response rate. However, it is not always possible to control who participates in the research – the person who actually completes the questionnaire may not be the one intended.

## Survey results prompt a 'fat tax' for Ryanair?

In April 2009, controversial budget airline Ryanair revealed that it was considering in-troducing an additional charge for its obese passengers. The proposal was announced fol-lowing a poll of passengers on the Ryanair web-site. According to the company, over 100,000 people (29% of those who participated in the on-line survey) voted for a so-called 'fat tax' to be levied on anyone large enough to 'invade the space of the passengers sitting beside them'. Around 24% of respondents to the survey also voted for a €3 charge for smoking in a converted lavatory cubicle, while 14% voted for an annual subscription for accessing the company's website and 9% for a €2 fee for passengers bringing their own food on-board.

Source: www.telegraph.co.uk

### Activity

Outline one benefit and one drawback for a company such as Ryanair from gathering market research data via its website.

## Focus groups

A focus group consists of a small number of people (typically between six and ten) who are brought together under the guidance of a trained moderator to talk about their attitudes towards a particular topic. Focus groups are commonly used to obtain more detailed, qualitative data than would normally be possible in much larger surveys. The group members are chosen on the basis that they represent the 'average' customer. Obtaining information in this way can be expensive, particularly if a large number of groups are used, because of the time taken to obtain and then analyse the data.

The role of the moderator is very important in ensuring that the views obtained genuinely reflect those of the group. Moderators need to have a good understanding of the discussion topic, but must remain neutral and not try to impose their own personal views on the group or lead them in any particular way, in order to ensure accuracy and validity. They also need to manage the discussions carefully, so that everyone participates, with no one individual dominating the group. Listening to other views can often encourage people to share their own, but participants may be reluctant to express opinions that contradict others or create an unfavourable impression.

## Panels

Panels gather data from individuals, households and other groups over a certain period. The main aim of this method of research is to identify any changes that might take place, including changing patterns of consumer expenditure, the kind of television programmes that are viewed or the reaction to the use of a particular product over time. Participants may be asked to keep an account of their behaviour by keeping a diary or filling in an online questionnaire regularly. Alternatively, they may be interviewed, either face-to-face or over the telephone.

The nature of panel research means that takes time to gather data. The cost involve depends to a large extent on how the data is collected. Participants need to be clear about data recording procedures, in order to ensure accuracy. The main problem with panels is that participants may be unable or unwilling to continue for the time required, leading to incomplete data which may affect the validity of the results.

## Field trials

A field trial involves limited testing of a new or modified product before it is fully launched within the market. For example, a sample of 1,000 men could be chosen to trial a new design of electric razor over a three-month period to provide feedback on the quality of the shave provided, as well as the ease and comfort of use.

Testing the physical properties of products in real conditions is expensive, as prototypes of the product have to be produced and used. It also needs to be done over a relatively long period, in order to assess the product's performance over time. However, this method of research can provide valuable data, allowing the manufacturer to make necessary adjustments before a full-scale launch. The accuracy and validity of the results obtained is usually very good, but may be affected by the fact that participants in the trials know that their views and experiences are being recorded.

## Piloting

This refers to a stage in the market-research process when a new questionnaire is tested out on a limited number of people to check its effectiveness. Inevitably, this adds to the cost of the research and the time taken to carry it out. However, by doing this, any problems relating to the wording or sequencing of questions can be identified and amended. This should improve the quality of the data collected when the questionnaire is eventually used as part of the survey, increasing the accuracy and validity of the results and helping to ensure that the objectives of the research are achieved.

## Choosing an appropriate method of primary research

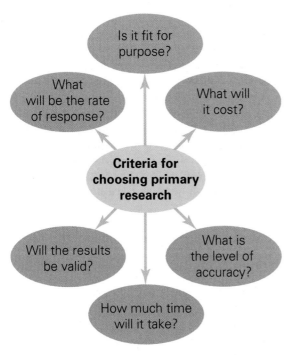

**Figure 10.1** Choosing primary research methods

## Secondary research

Secondary research involves selecting and using existing data, gathered at some point in the past either by the firm itself (internal sources) or by another organisation (external sources). Secondary data may have existed for some time, meaning that it could have become out of date. This may also make it difficult to check the original research procedures, casting doubt over its validity. Nevertheless, secondary data is an important starting point for most research. Some data is likely to still be relevant, providing information quickly and relatively cheaply. It also helps to highlight where primary research needs to be concentrated, so that marketing resources can be used more effectively.

### Internal sources

Firms hold a great deal of data that can be used in market research. It is free and quick to obtain and, unlike external secondary data, it is not likely to be available to other businesses. Secondary data can come from a number of sources within the firm:

- **Data records** – many firms keep detailed customer records that can be used to generate market-research information. For example, lists of customer addresses may reveal that the majority of them are concentrated in certain areas or regions, allowing the business to target its advertising more effectively.
- **Loyalty schemes** – a number of retailers offer loyalty or reward cards to customers. Points are accumulated each time that money is spent in the store, which can be redeemed against purchases in the future. These schemes help businesses to collect a great deal of data relating to customers' purchasing behaviour, including how often they visit the store and the products that they buy.
- **Electronic point of sale (EPOS)** – involves scanning the bar codes of products as they are bought by customers at cash tills in supermarkets and other retailers. The system automatically updates the business stock records but also provides a detailed breakdown of sales turnover, for example on an individual product, section or store basis.
- **Website monitoring and e-transactions** – firms that sell their products online can track customers' usage of their websites. For example, it is possible to identify what areas of the website are browsed most regularly, so that layout and design can be improved, if necessary. The

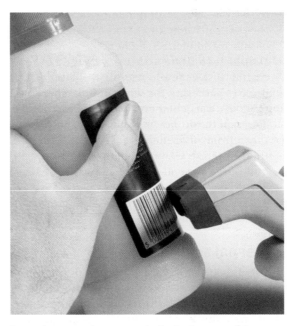

Barcodes provide a great deal of information for firms

**215**

buying patterns of customers can be studied to establish what products they buy and how frequently purchases are made. This allows firms to tailor promotions and make new product recommendations, based on previous purchases.

- **Accounting records** – firms are obliged to record and store large quantities of financial data in order to draw up accurate accounts and calculate profit levels. This financial data can also be useful to market researchers. For example, they will reveal which products generate the greatest sales revenue. They may also show the impact of past price changes on the level of demand.
- **Production records** – a firm's output figures can also contain useful data for researchers. They can reveal, for example, long-term trends or seasonal patterns in demand, which can act as the basis for further investigation.
- **Sales figures** – an examination of previous years' sales data can also contain important information. They can indicate trends in the market, such as changes in consumer tastes, the significance of individual products or different customer segments.
- **Sales personnel** – these staff have direct contact with the market, customers and competitors on a daily basis. They are well placed to note the effects of any changes that take place, such as the impact of a major advertising campaign or the launch of a new product by a rival. Their experience of such events in the past can, therefore, act as a valuable source of information for researchers.
- **Delphi technique** – this is a method of forecasting future developments in the market. It involves gathering the views of a number of experts in a particular area over a period of time. The experts do not meet in order to prevent them from influencing each other. Instead, their separate views are gathered in order to build up a general picture of possible events. For example, the technique could be used to predict the future growth in sales of environmentally-friendly hybrid cars.

## External sources

Internal data is unlikely to satisfy all of a firm's research needs. The next step is, therefore, to examine existing data from sources outside the business. The most frequently used external sources of data include:

- **Internet** – the importance of the internet as a research tool has grown significantly over the last decade. Firms use their websites for marketing purposes, but also post a great deal of information relating to their objectives, operations, human resources and financial performance. Professional bodies, such as the Chartered Institute of Personnel and Development (www.cipd.co.uk) and the Chartered Institute of Marketing (www.cim.co.uk) publish research on their websites. A number of organisations set up to support business start-up and development also produce useful information online (see www.startups.co.uk and www.realbusiness.co.uk). Although the amount of information available online is huge and growing ever bigger, search engines, such as Google and Ask Jeeves, are free to users to facilitate the research process and locate relevant information more quickly.
- **Government statistics** – the scale of certain kinds of data, such as those relating to the economy and social trends within the UK, may be too great for even the largest businesses to collect first hand. The Government publishes reports through the Office of National Statistics on a wide range of topics, including UK trade, retail sales and business investment, which it makes available online (www.ons.gov.uk and www.statistics.gov.uk).
- **Libraries** – these contain a number of potentially useful sources of reference, such as books on business topics, back copies of newspapers and journals and reports compiled by market-research agencies (see below).
- **Universities** – research articles and papers produced by academic staff and postgraduate students are often published and made available to the general public. Universities with large economics, business or sociology departments may well provide information on the state of the economy or consumer behaviour that could be useful to market researchers.
- **Company reports** – limited companies based in the UK are required by law to publish a set of financial accounts each year and submit them to Companies House. This means that the information they contain is available to other businesses and the general public. Not only do these reports contain a great deal of data on a firm's financial performance, but the Chairman's Statement usually provides a summary of the strategies employed by the company in the recent past, as well as those

intended for the future. Many larger companies also provide much of the financial information contained in the reports in the financial pages of their websites.

- **Specialist market-research agencies** – there are a number of organisations who carry out market research on different markets and sectors of the economy and then sell them to other interested businesses. The analysis produces data on key market characteristics, such as size, key players, market share and projected market growth. Three of the leading research agencies in the UK include:

  o **Mintel** – the UK's leading publisher of consumer market research, producing over 300 new reports each year, describing market size, structure and segmentation, as well as market forecasts, which are available online to subscribers (www.mintel.com). It also produces reports for individual clients.

  o **Thomson Reuters Datastream** – the world's largest financial statistical database, containing a vast range of current and historical financial data, including interest rates, exchange rates and share prices.

  o **Dun and Bradstreet (D&B)** – a major source of commercial information, providing reports on the financial well-being of different businesses, helping firms to build up detailed profiles of customers and the markets they operate in. D&B's database consists of information taken from over 130 million companies, spread over 190 countries.

- **Trade journals** – these are publications that target a particular sector or industry. For example, the *Grocer* magazine produces product news and reports for food and drink retailers, which subscribers can also access online at www.the-grocer.co.uk. The content is produced by experts who are able to analyse developments within a market and comment on future changes, providing valuable insight for researchers.

In addition to the sources listed above, researchers may obtain secondary data from trade associations, chambers of commerce and organisations such as Business Link, as well as using business directories and the general press. Sources of secondary data need to be selected carefully, in order to ensure that the objectives of the market research are met. For example, the data must be relevant to the investigation and available when it is needed. It may not be possible to check what research methods were used, so that the accuracy and validity of the data cannot be verified. Using reports produced by specialist agencies may be desirable, but the cost of obtaining them may prevent this from happening.

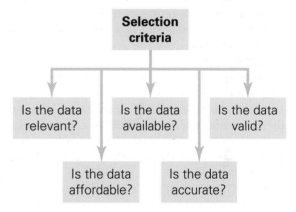

**Figure 10.2** Selecting secondary sources of data – useful criteria

## Survey shows that easyJet beats Ryanair

Market research carried out by consumer group Which? in 2008 claimed that the passengers of budget airline easyJet were more satisfied with the service they received than those of rival Ryanair. The research results were based on a survey carried out by Which? involving 30,000 of its members. Although neither airline scored particularly highly, easyJet received an overall customer satisfaction score of 59% to Ryanair's 47%. EasyJet also received reasonable individual scores for the helpfulness and efficiency of its cabin staff, cleanliness of its planes and how it dealt with delays. Ryanair was rated poorly in all of these areas.

The survey results did, however, confirm that budget airlines do not necessarily mean poor service. Germanwings and Hungary's Wizz Air were two of the highest scoring short-haul carriers, receiving scores of 79% and 69% respectively, despite offering a no-frills service.

In response to the results, Neil Fowler, editor of Which?, commented, 'You may think that you get what you pay for, but the best European no-frills airlines prove than you can offer a stripped down service at a good price and keep your customers happy. As for Ryanair and easyJet, they might be cheap, but if you want great customer service then look elsewhere.'

**Source: www.thetravelmagazine.net**

**Activities**

1 Explain whether the survey results outlined above would represent primary or secondary research data to managers at easyJet.

2 Comment on the usefulness of the results of the survey to easyJet's managers.

## Use of ICT applications in market research

In recent years, improvements in information and communications technology have made it much easier to access, store and process market research data. Modern computer databases have the ability to handle vast amounts of data at any given time, updating and modifying it as often as is necessary. Relevant data can be retrieved when needed, and compared and analysed more quickly and effectively. The results of this analysis can be summarised and presented in a variety of formats, tailored to the needs of the audience concerned. The software needed to carry out these tasks has become more affordable, so that even small businesses can access the necessary technology. Although sophisticated ICT applications cannot guarantee effective decision making, it can help to speed up the process by making it easier to acquire the information required.

## Quantitative and qualitative research

Before researchers can start gathering data, either from primary or secondary sources, they must also decide what kind of information they wish to collect. Market-research data can be either quantitative or qualitative. **Quantitative research** involves gathering numerical data, usually from large samples. This type of research concentrates on obtaining factual information that can be measured and be subjected to statistical analysis. Examples of quantitative data include the size of the UK economy, the number of people who regularly use a social-networking site or the rate of growth in average house prices in the last twelve months. One of the most commonly used methods of carrying out quantitative research is by survey, based on a questionnaire containing mostly **closed questions**, that is, those with a set number of responses.

**Qualitative research** is interested in finding out people's opinions, attitudes and beliefs. For example, researchers may want to find out why membership of Facebook grew more quickly than any other social-networking site, or why more people buy their groceries at Tesco than Sainsbury's or Asda. The data produced by qualitative research can help firms build up a detailed picture of the various reasons behind consumer behaviour. Interviews and focus groups are commonly used to gather qualitative data, as these methods are designed to encourage more detailed responses. This means that conducting and analysing qualitative research is usually a complex and time-consuming process.

## Triangulation

**Triangulation** involves using more than one type of research method. The main purpose of this is to help to ensure that the results obtained are accurate and valid. For example, researchers could conduct quantitative research using a survey, and then follow this up with qualitative research based on a number of focus groups. The results of both types of research could then be brought together and compared, to see if they supported each other and led to a more detailed understanding of the issue under investigation.

## Marketing strategies and activities

There are a number of ways in which market research can be planned and implemented, depending on the nature of the information under investigation:

- **Strategic research** – this involves gathering and analysing the data required to help senior managers formulate medium- and long-term planning and decision making within a business. Such strategies affect the whole organisation and could relate to growth by launching new products or expanding into new markets.

- **Technical market research** – this looks into the effects of an event or change on a specific aspect of a firm's marketing. For example, it might monitor the impact of launching a new advertising campaign or widening the number of distribution channels on sales.
- **Databank market research** – firms hold a great deal of information internally with respect to their customers and the markets in which they operate. This databank of information is regularly used as part of the market research process but needs to be kept up to date if it is to be effective.
- **Continuous market research** – this involves collecting data on an ongoing basis over a period of time. It is often used to identify gradual changes or long-term trends, such as the level of competition or patterns in consumer expenditure. A common method used to do this is by using consumer panels.
- **Ad hoc market research** – this involves collecting data on a one-off, rather than a continuous, basis. It aims to answer specific questions at a particular point in time. For example, Domino's Pizzas might be interested to find out the impact of the 2010 football World Cup on pizza home deliveries.

## Key terms

**Ad hoc research** A one-off collection and analysis of market-research data

**Continuous research** The collection and analysis of market-research data on a regular, ongoing basis

**Databank research** Carrying out market research in order to update information held internally within a business

**Delphi technique** Where a number of experts are consulted separately in order to gather their forecasts of developments in the market. Their separate views are brought together in order to try and reach a consensus

**Field trial** Involves carrying out tests on a new or modified product in a limited section of the market before it is fully launched

**Focus group** A commonly used method of gathering qualitative data, where a small group of people are brought together to discuss their views and attitudes on a particular product or topic

**Observation** A method of collecting primary data that involves watching behaviour and recording what happens

**Panels** Where data is gathered from a panel of individuals over a period of time in order to record their behaviour and any changes that take place

**Piloting** Involves testing a newly drafted questionnaire on a limited number of people to check its effectiveness and identify any problems before it is used in the market research process

**Primary research** Involves gathering data for the first time in order to meet the specific needs of the business involved

**Qualitative research** This involves using large samples to gather numerical, factual data that can be measured and subjected to statistical analysis

**Quantitative research** This involves finding out people's views, beliefs and attitudes regarding a particular product or topic

**Secondary research** Involves using existing data that has been gathered at some point in the past, either by the firm requesting the market research or another organisation

**Strategic research** Involves gathering and analysing data required to help senior managers decide on medium- to long-term planning and decision making within a business

**Surveys** Used to gather primary data from a large number of people, often using a sample

**Technical research** Research into the effects of an event or change on a particular aspect of a firm's marketing, such as a change in price

**Triangulation** Involves using quantitative and qualitative research to increase the accuracy and validity of market-research results

## Re-cap questions

1 Explain what is involved in primary research.
2 Outline one advantage and one disadvantage of collecting primary data.
3 Briefly explain the difference between observation and experimentation.
4 State three different ways of conducting a survey.
5 A breakfast cereals manufacturer wants to introduce two new flavours of its leading brand. Briefly outline two ways in which focus groups could be used to conduct market research.
6 Identify three criteria that should be considered when choosing an appropriate method of primary research.
7 Explain what is meant by secondary research.
8 Describe one advantage of using secondary research for a newly established business.
9 Outline one possible drawback for a firm operating in a rapidly changing market of relying on secondary data.
10 Give one reason why a business may begin its market research by looking at internal secondary data.
11 State three sources of external secondary data.
12 State three criteria that could be used to decide on whether sources of secondary data are suitable.
13 Using examples, briefly explain the difference between quantitative and qualitative research.
14 How can triangulation improve the quality of market-research findings?
15 Briefly explain the difference between ad hoc and continuous research.

## Grading tips

 **P1** Describe types of market research

You need to show that you have a clear understanding of the importance of market research to a firm and the different methods used to gather data including primary and secondary research, quantitative and qualitative research, and strategic, technical, databank, ad hoc and continuous research.

See p 243 for suggestions for Assignments for Unit 10.

# Part 2: Planning market research

## Stages in the planning process

Once the need to carry out market research has been identified, it is vital that the process is planned carefully. Effective planning should help to reduce the chances of spending time and money collecting unnecessary or irrelevant data and, therefore, help to ensure that the firm's objectives are achieved. Although the market-research process depends to some extent on the scope and nature of the information required, there are a number of stages that are likely to be carried out.

## Defining the issues and setting objectives

It is essential that everyone is agreed as to what the market research is setting out to achieve before any further steps are taken in the process. The managers responsible for instigating the investigation need to state clearly the nature of their concerns or issues. Once this has been done, specific **research objectives** can be established in order to provide direction as to exactly what action should be taken (see below). For example, a cosmetics company, wishing to investigate the reasons why a newly launched perfume brand has failed to achieve its targeted sales growth, may have the following objectives:

- Identify **sales trends** within the market
- Measure **brand awareness** of the new perfume
- Assess the effectiveness of competitors' promotional activities.

## Preparing the research brief

This sets out in writing the reasons why the market research is required and the problems or issues to be researched. It should state clearly the objectives of the research and contain a description of the product and market to be investigated. It should also provide details of any timing and financial budget requirements. The brief may be subject to amendment in the light of the findings of any initial research that is carried out.

## Planning and forecasting

This stage involves agreeing exactly what steps need to be carried out to obtain the necessary data. It requires a great deal of thought in order to ensure that the results obtained meet the research objectives, avoiding the need for further investigation, adding to the length and the costs of the project. A number of decisions need to be made regarding the type of data to be collected, the population to be targeted and the research methods to be used. The timing and format for reporting back any findings and the overall cost of the research will also need to be agreed.

## Collecting data

Relevant data needs to be collected according to the time and cost constraints already established by the research brief. The research may well begin by looking at any available **internal secondary data**, that is, existing data within the business requesting the research. Once this has been exhausted, researchers may turn to **external secondary data** sources. If, however, this proves to be insufficient to meet all of the research needs, primary research will then need to be conducted.

## Analysing and evaluating data

If successful, by the end of the collection stage, researchers will have generated sufficient amounts of data that is both accurate and valid. However, this raw data must now be turned into meaningful information upon which management decisions can be made. Quantitative data can be subjected to statistical analysis to identify average values or trends in sales figures over time. Statistical analysis may also reveal the degree of **correlation** between two variables, suggesting possible causes for changes in demand. If analysed carefully, qualitative data can be explored to reveal customers' opinions and feelings, allowing researchers to draw conclusions about the reasons or motivations for their behaviour. In both cases, however, great care has to be taken to avoid introducing bias into the process. For example, researchers may exaggerate the importance of opinions that they share and ignore those that they disagree with.

## Presenting findings

Once data has been analysed, the resulting information needs to be communicated to whoever is responsible for commissioning the research. This must be prepared and delivered in a format that is appropriate for the intended audience. Initially, this may involve delivering an oral report, outlining the process and summarising the key findings of the research. It may then be followed by a more detailed formal report.

## Making recommendations

This highlights any action that needs to be taken by the business, based on the findings of the research. These recommendations must be appropriate to the resources of the business and the circumstances in which it is operating. For example, suggesting an expensive national TV advertising campaign may not be an appropriate recommendation for a firm that is struggling financially.

## Re-evaluating marketing activities

The final stage of the process is for the business concerned to consider its current marketing activities and the extent to which they need to be adapted in the light of the findings and recommendations.

## Purpose of research objectives

Research objectives are the targets or goals which the market-research process is designed to achieve. The purpose of setting clear objectives is to give the process direction, helping researchers to stay on task and avoid wasting time and money gathering and analysing information that is not relevant. Setting clear objectives also allows any progress in completing the project to be measured and monitored.

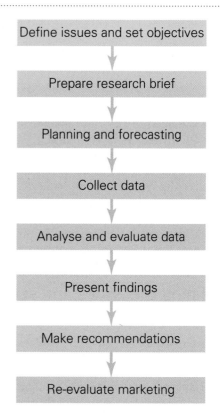

**Figure 10.3** Market research stages

Market-research objectives can relate to investigating any aspect of the market in which a business is operating, including the behaviour of its customers, its competitors or the wider economic environment. Although they are likely to vary from business to business, some typical research objectives are outlined in Figure 10.4.

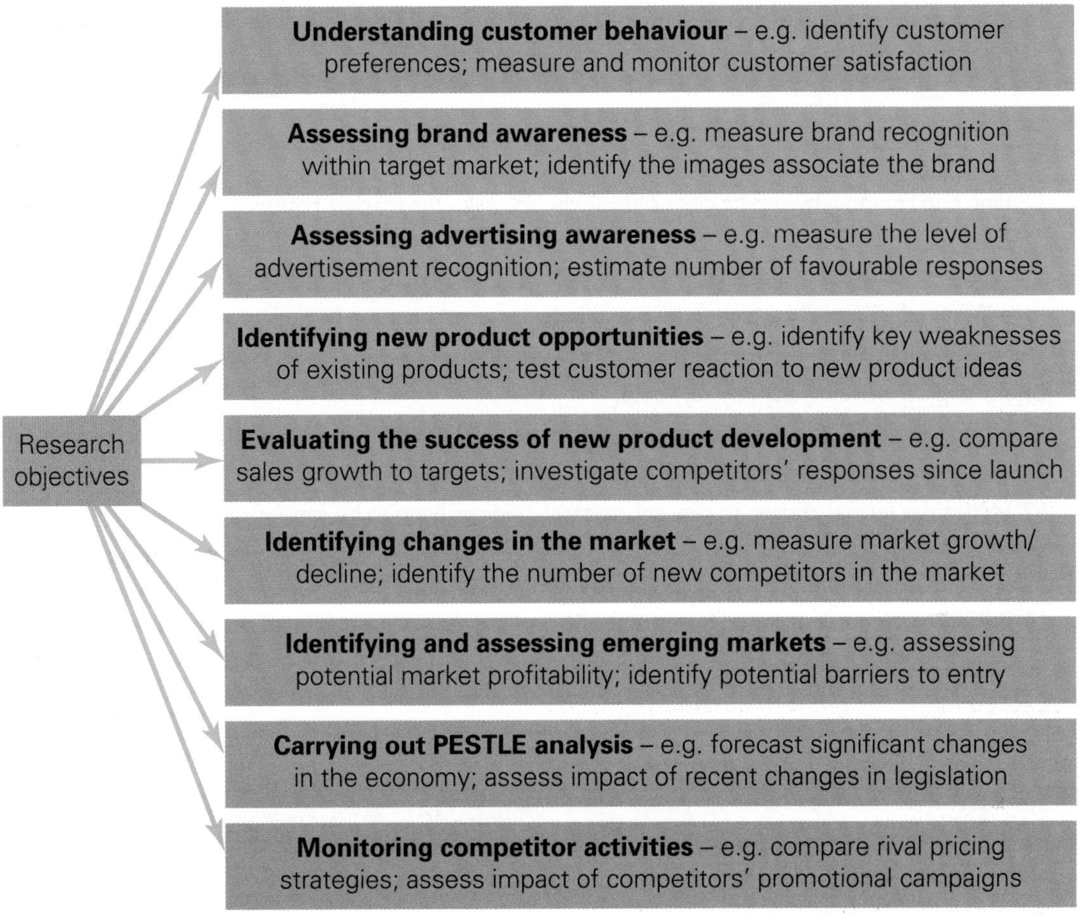

Understanding customer behaviour – e.g. identify customer preferences; measure and monitor customer satisfaction

Assessing brand awareness – e.g. measure brand recognition within target market; identify the images associate the brand

Assessing advertising awareness – e.g. measure the level of advertisement recognition; estimate number of favourable responses

Identifying new product opportunities – e.g. identify key weaknesses of existing products; test customer reaction to new product ideas

Evaluating the success of new product development – e.g. compare sales growth to targets; investigate competitors' responses since launch

Identifying changes in the market – e.g. measure market growth/decline; identify the number of new competitors in the market

Identifying and assessing emerging markets – e.g. assessing potential market profitability; identify potential barriers to entry

Carrying out PESTLE analysis – e.g. forecast significant changes in the economy; assess impact of recent changes in legislation

Monitoring competitor activities – e.g. compare rival pricing strategies; assess impact of competitors' promotional campaigns

Research objectives

**Figure 10.4** Typical research objectives

## Key terms

**Brand awareness** This involves measuring the percentage of people within the target population that are aware of the existence of a particular brand

**Emerging market** An economy – or section of it – where previously low demand has begun to grow in recent years and is forecast to continue in the future

**External data** Existing data that has been collected by other organisations

**Forecasting** The process of estimating the value of future outcomes, such as sales or costs

**Internal data** Existing data that has been collected and stored within a business

**PESTLE analysis** An examination of the political, economic, social, technological, legal and environmental factors within the business environment

**Primary data** New data that is collected for the first time for a specific purpose

**Research brief** A written document that sets out the reasons why a market-research project is taking place. It includes the objectives of the research, contains details of any timings and budget constraints

**Research objectives** The targets or goals that the market research process is designed to achieve

**Sales trends** The long-term patterns of change in sales, either increasing, declining or remaining stable

**Secondary data** Data that already exists and has been previously collected for another purpose

**Re-cap questions**

1 Explain why it is important to plan market research carefully.

2 Explain what is meant by a research objective.

3 Outline one reason why setting clear objectives can make the market-research process more effective.

4 What is a research brief and what information does it contain?

5 Identify two decisions that need to be made before researchers can begin to collect data.

6 Identify two influences on whether researchers use primary or secondary research to collect data.

7 Briefly explain what is meant by raw data.

8 Give two examples of how statistical analysis can be used to make quantitative data more meaningful.

9 Explain why bias can prevent qualitative data from being analysed and evaluated effectively.

10 Why does the format chosen to present research findings need to be carefully considered?

11 Why is it important for researchers to ensure that any recommendations made as a result of the market-research process are appropriate to the business concerned?

12 Market research commissioned by a major UK clothing retailer has revealed that, although the overall market is growing, it is losing market share to rivals. Suggest two ways in which the retailer's marketing activities might be re-evaluated, in light of these findings.

## Grading tips

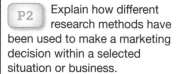

**P2** Explain how different research methods have been used to make a marketing decision within a selected situation or business.

You need to choose a business where you can access information regarding market research that has been carried out, and categorise this activity under the different market-research types described for P1. You must also show how the data gathered was used to inform and improve the decision-making process within the business; e.g. did it lead to the development of a new good or service, or to changes in the marketing mix of existing products?

**M1** Explain, with examples, how different market-research methods are appropriate to assist different marketing situations

You need to show that you understand which types of research are best suited for the collection of different types of data by giving reasons. For example, the use of secondary sources of information may be more suitable for a firm on a tight budget, or needing to make decisions quickly, because it is usually cheaper and faster to obtain. Think in terms of factors such as cost, time, accuracy and validity.

**D1** Evaluate the market-research method used by a selected organisation

You need to make a judgement on the effectiveness of the research methods used. For example, how well did the methods used meet the objectives of the research? Is there any evidence to suggest that using alternative methods would have been more effective?

**P3** **Plan market research for a selected product/service using appropriate methods of data collection**

You need to draw up a market-research plan for a product or service of your choice. Think very carefully about the specific issue you intend to investigate and set clear objectives for your research before you put together the remaining stages of the plan. You must plan to use both primary and secondary research (see P4) and be able to justify the specific methods of data collection that you choose by giving valid reasons.

# Part 3: Carrying out market research

## Census or sample

Ideally, market researchers would like to involve every member of the **population** in order to maximise the accuracy of any data collected. Conducting this type of research is known as a **census**. It could literally mean all of the people living in a particular region or country. Alternatively, the term could refer to all of the individuals, customers, products or firms making up the target group from which researchers wish to gain information. For example, Britax produces a range of products for babies and toddlers; it is likely, therefore, to focus its research on parents with young families.

In reality, however, it may not be possible for a firm to gain information from everyone in its chosen population. The population, for example, may consist of hundreds of thousands, if not millions, of members, spread across one or many countries. Contacting every single one may be prohibitively expensive and time consuming.

It may, therefore, be necessary to take a **sample**, consisting of a group chosen from the overall population. The members of the group must share the same characteristics, opinions and tastes as those of the population, in order for the process to be effective.

## Sample size

In theory, market researchers would try to create the biggest sample possible, in an attempt to ensure that it was representative. However, the size of the overall marketing budget acts as a constraint on this by limiting the amount of money available. Gathering information from the sample group involves incurring various costs, such as the costs of designing and printing questionnaires, interviewers' wages and processing the data that is collected. The bigger the sample, the greater the costs!

To some extent the size of the sample depends on the level of precision and accuracy required from the results – generally, the greater the degree of precision needed, the larger the sample size. The degree of variability within the population is also a consideration; for example, a relatively large sample would be required if the range of customer opinions is likely to be wide.

In fact, careful design and analysis should allow researchers to obtain useful results from relatively small samples. While it may not be possible to choose a sample that reflects the population exactly, estimating the likely margin of error attached to the sample data can make it more meaningful. Researchers can use statistical techniques to calculate the level of confidence of data collected using probability sampling methods, such as **random** or **stratified** samples. The **confidence level** gives the likelihood of sample results lying within the precision required. The higher the confidence level, the more certain researchers can be that the results obtained from the sample are typical of the population as a whole. A confidence level of 95 per cent is often used to obtain a strong degree of certainty. For example, market research into the popularity of different coffee retailers might be based on the responses of a sample of 1,000 coffee drinkers. The results of the research might show that 80 per cent of those questioned preferred Starbucks to Costa Coffee, with a 95 per cent confidence level. This means that researchers could be confident that, if the research was repeated over and over again, the same results would be produced 19 out of 20 (i.e. 95 per cent) times.

## Choosing the sample

Before a sample can be chosen, researchers must be clear as to exactly who makes up the population to be surveyed. This is known as the **sampling unit**. It is important that researchers have as clear and complete a picture as possible of the sampling unit, in order to ensure that the population is properly represented. Once this is done, researchers must decide how to select the respondents that will make up the sample. There are a number of sampling procedures that can be used. They can be categorised as either probability samples or non-probability samples.

### Probability sampling methods

These types of sampling method are designed to ensure that every member of the population has a chance of being chosen and the probability of their selection can be calculated mathematically. These methods produce samples that can be subjected to statistical analysis. For instance, levels of confidence can be calculated in order to determine sampling error and, therefore, the extent to which the results produced from the sample are representative of the population as a whole. However, ensuring that all the respondents chosen are included in the sample can be expensive and time-consuming.

## Random sampling

In its simplest form, random sampling gives everyone a known and equal chance of being selected. An example of this would be to gather the names of all of the people making up a group and pull out the number required for the sample.

## Systematic random sampling

This method of sampling involves randomly choosing a starting point from a list of the overall population group in which researchers are interested, then selecting sample members at regular intervals, for example picking every tenth name from a database of existing customers. There is no optimal interval size, but it is likely to be influenced by the size of the required sample and that of the overall population.

## Stratified random sampling

This method takes into account the fact that different groups within the population may be more significant than others by ensuring that they are adequately, rather than equally, represented. For example, if 70 per cent of a retailer's online customers were men, 70 per cent of any sample taken for research would need to be male customers, in order to ensure that the results reflected the views of the overall customer base.

## Multistage sampling

This involves carrying out a series of samples to reduce the potential size of the population and, therefore, the cost of the sampling procedure, but still retaining a large element of randomness. For example, the Government may be interested in finding out the reactions of high-school pupils to the idea of raising the school leaving age to 18. The starting point for a multi-stage sample would be to pick an education authority at random. The next stage would be to randomly select one high school from all of those within the education authority. Finally, one class or form would be randomly selected from the school and the views of all of the pupils within

the group would be taken to represent those of secondary pupils within the country.

## Cluster sampling

This involves dividing the overall population into groups or clusters. The characteristics of the members of each cluster must reflect those of the population. For example, the country could be split into regions, such as the south-east or the north-west, and one or more regions would be randomly chosen. This method is based on the assumption that each region's population would have similar views to the national population.

# Non-probability sampling methods

These samples do not have the element of randomness contained in probability samples. This means that the data produced by them cannot undergo any further statistical analysis and may be regarded, therefore, as less reliable. However, they are usually quicker and cheaper to carry out so that their use can be justified for these reasons.

## Quota sampling

This method involves identifying the key features of the population being investigated, such as gender or age and then setting quotas that reflect the make-up of the population. For example, if the number of women buying a particular brand of chocolate is five times greater than the number of men, an interviewer may be required to obtain the views of 50 men and 250 women. The interviewer will need to continue until the respective quotas have been reached, but is free to decide who to ask and to choose again if someone refuses to participate.

## Convenience sampling

This is where the choice of respondents is left entirely to the interviewer. This may be done on the basis of accessibility or willingness to volunteer. This method can provide useful results as long as researchers choose from a range of respondents, reflecting the population as a whole.

## Judgement sampling

This is where the interviewer chooses the respondents who he/she thinks will most accurately reflect the views of the overall population. There are a number of criteria that the interviewer could use to do this. For example, it could involve choosing people who resemble a 'typical' student, young mother or pensioner. However, such opinions are subjective and may introduce bias into the sampling procedure.

### Observation

This involves collecting data by simply watching people's behaviour and recording what they do. It could involve, for example, observing customers' buying patterns over a period of time and making a note of the brands that are purchased most frequently.

### Focus group

This involves putting together a small number of people under the guidance of a trained moderator to discuss their views on a particular topic. Focus groups are commonly used to obtain more detailed, qualitative data than would normally be possible in much larger surveys. The group members are chosen on the basis that they represent the 'average' customer.

## Questionnaires

Questionnaires are often used by market researchers to collect primary data. They form the basis of many different types of survey. They can either be completed by the respondent (known as self-completion), as would be the case in a postal or internet survey. Alternatively, the questions can be posed and the answers recorded by a researcher, which usually happens during face-to-face or telephone interviews.

## Questionnaire design

The structure of the questionnaire and the questions contained in it can have a significant impact on the quality of the data collected, so a great deal of thought needs to go into its design to make it effective. A number of decisions will need to be made, not just regarding the content of the questions, but their type, phrasing, layout and sequencing. Using clear and uncomplicated language throughout is important. Jargon or technical language should be avoided, as it may lead to misunderstanding and discourage completion. Providing further explanation may not be possible, particularly in the case of postal or internet surveys, or even desirable, as it can help to avoid any ambiguity or the need for further explanation. Care also needs to be taken to avoid questions that are irrelevant, offensive or too personal.

A questionnaire

## Questions to be asked

Before beginning to draw up a questionnaire, researchers must have a clear idea as to the objectives of the research, including the precise nature of the topic and the information that needs to be found out. Researchers also need to consider whether quantitative or qualitative data is required, as this will influence the style of question asked.

## Sequencing

**Sequencing** is concerned with structuring a questionnaire in a way that makes it as easy to use as possible. Doing so increases the chances of people completing it. The questionnaire should begin with questions that attract the interest of the respondent and that are short and easy to answer, followed by questions requiring more detail. All the questions relating to a particular topic should be asked before moving on to the next and the topics should follow in a logical order.

## Types of question

There are two main types of question used in market research – **closed questions** and **open questions**.

### Closed questions

Closed questions give respondents a limited range of answers to choose from – the idea being

| Sample type | Positive implications | Negative implications |
|---|---|---|
| **Probability** | | |
| Random | Relatively easy to design and implement; possible to calculate sampling error, creating a high degree of accuracy | A complete and accurate list of the whole population must be available; can be very costly and time consuming to implement, particularly if used with a large group |
| Systematic random | More likely to ensure sample is spread across the whole population, creating high degree of accuracy | Also needs a complete and accurate list of the whole population; relatively costly and time consuming |
| Stratified random | Eliminates the possibility that too many respondents from one group could be chosen, making results highly accurate | Detailed information on the whole population is required to identify the strata and to allow random selection; costly and time consuming |
| Multistage | Does not involve the whole population, making it quicker and more cost effective to design and implement | Inconveniently located groups can increase the time and cost of obtaining information; increased chance that the chosen group may not be representative |
| Cluster | Relatively quick to carry out, given that the group is concentrated in one location, making it more cost effective | Accuracy of results depends on the extent to which the characteristics of the cluster reflect those of the population |
| **Non-probability** | | |
| Quota | Relatively quick, easy and cheap to gather data that can be representative, as long as the quotas are satisfied | Sample members are not chosen randomly, so data cannot be used for statistical analysis |
| Convenience | Probably the quickest and cheapest way of gathering data, as little time is wasted trying to find suitable respondents | Very prone to bias; unlikely that the results will be representative |
| Observation | A relatively cost-effective method of obtaining information, due to the lack of interaction between researchers and those under observation | Little, if any, opportunities for finding out the reasons behind customer behaviour |
| Focus group | The opportunity for group discussion and listening to other people's ideas may encourage members to share their views | Can be expensive to obtain information in this way if a large number of groups are involved, due to the time needed to collect and analyse information |
| Judgement | Can provide data that is reasonably representative if interviewers are able to make objective judgements | Strong likelihood that the data produced will be biased and unrepresentative |

**Table 10.1** Implications of sampling methods

that one or more options are then chosen. Closed questions are often used to carry out quantitative research, as the data obtained is relatively easy to process. There are a number of different types of closed question, including

- **Dichotomous** – this is a type of question where the respondent is limited to choosing one of only two possible answers, such as 'Yes/No', 'True/False' or 'Male/Female'. Although the answers obtained lack detail, these questions are often used at the beginning of a questionnaire as a screening technique to identify suitable respondents and to see whether any further questions should be asked.
- **Multiple choice** – these questions provide a range of answers, usually limited to between four and five, and the respondent chooses the option that is most appropriate. For example, an online survey carried out by crisp manufacturer, Walkers, might contain the question 'Which one of the following is your favourite crisp flavour' followed by the following choices:
  - o Ready Salted
  - o Cheese and Onion
  - o Salt and Vinegar
  - o Roast Chicken
- The above example clearly does not include all of the potential options as it may be difficult to identify all of the potential responses, and the resulting list would be extremely long! In such cases, therefore, the question is likely to include the most popular choices, along with the additional option 'Others – please specify'.
- **Scaled** – there are a number of types of question that are specifically designed to measure the strength of customer views and opinions on a particular topic. A basic rating scale involves respondents choosing the most suitable option, from a limited list.

  For example – 'I would describe the standard of customer service at this McDonald's restaurant as':
  - o Excellent
  - o Very good
  - o Good
  - o Acceptable
  - o Poor
- **Likert scale** questions provide the respondent with a statement followed by a list of choices that reflect the extent of their agreement or disagreement.

For example – *the Government should introduce a ban on advertising during children's TV programmes:*

- o Strongly agree
- o Agree
- o Don't know/undecided
- o Disagree
- o Strongly disagree

Another approach, known as semantic differential scales, provides a relatively easy method of collecting qualitative data. Questions contain two key words or phrases that are at opposite ends of the scale, and respondents have to choose a point between the two extremes that best reflects their feelings.

For example: Ryanair

| Excellent reliability | [1] [2] [3] [4] [5] | Poor reliability |
| Excellent value for money | [1] [2] [3] [4] [5] | Poor value for money |

## Open-ended questions

Open-ended questions allow respondents to provide answers using their own words.

For example: What do you think of the Government's decision to ban smoking in public places?

They are designed to obtain more detailed, qualitative information, often on people's views and opinions on different subjects. They are also used in situations where it would be difficult to cover every possible response in a limited range of choices. However, giving respondents complete freedom in the choice and structure of their answers can make it very difficult to analyse the data that is collected.

# The length of the questionnaire

A questionnaire needs to be long enough to obtain the information required, but short enough to prevent respondents from completing it (or even starting it in the first place!). If the questionnaire contains some questions that may not be relevant to certain groups, the overall completion time can be reduced by instructing respondents to skip questions or sections.

## Avoiding bias

Bias is created when something causes data to be weighted towards one particular answer, rather than reflecting real opinions or views. For example, many people may not answer questions honestly in order to create a positive impression (or avoid being seen in a negative light). Bias can also be introduced by phrasing questions in a way that subconsciously leads respondents to certain answers. Careful wording and using a variety of question types can help to avoid this.

## The importance of relevance

Only questions that obtain information to satisfy the objectives of the market research should be included. Keeping questions relevant can help to reduce both the length of the questionnaire and the time taken to complete it, thereby increasing the rate of response. It also means that time and money is not wasted by researchers collating and analysing irrelevant data.

## Improving the rate of response

Researchers must bear in mind that respondents have to be prepared to give up their own time in order to provide the information being sought. The response rate can be measured in order to judge the effectiveness of the questionnaire design. This is done by calculating the number of actual responses as a percentage of the total number of people approached. The questionnaire must be designed, therefore, to retain the respondents' interest and to be as simple as possible to complete, in order to maximise the response rate. It should always begin with a brief statement explaining the purpose of the market research and containing any instructions for its completion. Not only is the length of the questionnaire important, but also different types of question should be used, to create variety and keep respondents focused. Firms will often use incentives, such as prizes or special offers, to encourage a better rate of response.

## Pilot stage

Pre-testing or piloting a questionnaire before actually putting it to use can help to identify any problems that may exist, which could prevent the survey from running smoothly. This involves putting together a small group of people to complete the questionnaire and provide feedback on the structure of the questionnaire, as well as the questions themselves. Although this inevitably adds to market-research costs, it can significantly improve the questionnaire's effectiveness in meeting research objectives.

## Surveys

Surveys are often used in market research to obtain primary data from a large number of people in order to inform the decision-making process.

## Difference between a survey and a questionnaire

A **survey** refers to the particular method or technique used to gather the required data from a specified number of people. This could, for example, involve face-to-face or telephone interviews requiring direct contact between the researcher and the respondent. However, not all surveys involve direct contact. In many situations, for example when the **target population** is large or geographically dispersed, this may be too costly and, therefore, undesirable. In these cases, researchers may decide to use a postal or internet survey.

A **questionnaire** is a document made up of a series of pre-printed questions, designed to uncover the information required to achieve a firm's research objectives. Questionnaires play an important role in carrying out surveys, particularly when there is no direct contact between researchers and respondents. Even when interviewers are used, questionnaires provide structure and help to ensure that the same questions are asked, in the same way, to everyone participating in the survey.

## The UK census

Since 1801 a census has taken place every ten years in the UK, with the exception of 1941 during the Second World War. Its basic principles have not changed over the years, although new questions are added and others taken out from time to time. The main purpose of the census is to provide population statistics on a national and local level for central government, local authorities, businesses and communities to use. The next census to be held in the UK is in March 2011 and will involve around 25 million households. A number of new approaches have been introduced to improve return rates. Printed questionnaires will be posted to all households using a newly developed national address register. People will also be able to complete and submit forms online. A questionnaire tracking and targeted field follow-up system will be used to identify and chase up households that have not returned their questionnaires.

**Source:** www.ons.gov.uk

### Activity

Why do you think that it is necessary for the Government to carry out a census to provide statistics on the population?

## Key terms

**Census** When market research is conducted using every member of a chosen population, rather than taking a sample

**Closed question** A question which has a limited range of responses to choose from

**Cluster sample** Where the population is organised into representative groups or clusters, and one or more is chosen at random to make up the sample

**Confidence level** Gives the likelihood of sample results being representative of the population as a whole

**Convenience sample** Where the decision as to who to include in a sample is left entirely to the interviewer

**Judgement sample** Where respondents are chosen to make up a sample on the basis that they are believed to be most likely to possess the characteristics and represent the views of the overall population

**Multistage sample** Where a series of samples are carried out randomly, gradually reducing the overall size of the population and, therefore, the cost of obtaining information

**Open-ended question** These allow respondents to provide answers using their own words, rather than choose from a list of predetermined responses

**Quota sample** Involves identifying the key features of the population under investigation, setting up quotas that reflect the distribution of these features within the overall population, and then choosing enough respondents to fill the quotas set

**Random sample** Where everyone in the population has a known and equal chance of being selected

**Sample** A representative group chosen from the overall population on which market research can be based

**Sampling unit** This consists of everyone within the overall population from which a sample is chosen

**Sequencing** Involves structuring a questionnaire in a logical way to make it as easy to use as possible

**Stratified random sample** Recognises that certain groups within the overall population may be larger or more important than others, and so attempts to reflect this in its composition

**Systematic random sample** Involves randomly choosing a starting point and then selecting sample members at regular intervals, e.g. every tenth name on a list

**Target population** The market or market segment at which a firm aims its marketing activities

# Re-cap questions

1   Suggest two reasons why it might not be possible for a firm conducting market research to use the entire target population.

2   Why is the size of a sample significant to the market-research process?

3   Briefly explain the difference between a probability sample and a non-probability sample.

4   What is the difference between a simple random sample, a systematic random sample and a stratified random sample?

5   Identify and briefly describe two other types of probability sample.

6   Describe how a quota sample is constructed.

7   Explain the difference between a convenience sample and a judgement sample.

8   Explain the difference between a survey and a questionnaire.

9   Outline two reasons why questionnaires are used in market research.

10   Explain the importance of effective sequencing in questionnaire design.

11   Identify three other factors that should be kept in mind when drawing up a questionnaire.

12   Explain what is meant by a closed question.

13   What is the difference between a dichtonomous question and a multiple-choice question?

14   Briefly explain why a questionnaire might use scaled questions, rather than open questions, to find out about respondents' opinions.

15   Outline one benefit and one drawback of piloting a questionnaire before using it in market research.

# Grading tips

 **P4** Conduct primary and secondary research for a selected product/service making use of identifiable sampling techniques

You need to put into action the market-research plan, using both primary and secondary research, and keep records of the data gathered. You may also wish to pilot any questionnaires that have been drawn up before they are used and amend them in light of the feedback received. You must be able to identify the sampling technique used to collect primary data, so think carefully about your choice beforehand. For example, will it be possible to obtain the information required to set up a genuine random sample?

 **M2** Explain the reasons for choosing the particular method of data collection for a selected product/service

You need to analyse your choice of primary and secondary research using criteria such as cost, availability and time, levels of accuracy and validity required.

 **D2** Evaluate the findings from the research undertaken

You need to justify any recommendations you make for changes in marketing strategy by highlighting their impact and showing how they should lead to an improvement in performance. You also need to make judgements on the quality of the research strategies carried out, pointing out any weaknesses and making suggestions regarding possible improvements.

See p 243 for suggestions for Assignments for Unit 10.

# Part 4: Interpreting market research findings

When data has first been collected and recorded, it may be no more than lists of numbers or observations. In this format, known as raw data, it is of little use. It needs to be processed further in order to draw conclusions and create meaningful information on which decisions can then be based. The results then need to be communicated effectively to those who commissioned the research. The methods of presentation chosen need to be appropriate for the audience.

> **Example**: A group of thirty people, aged between 18 and 25 were asked to keep a record of the number of times they visited the cinema over a three-month period. The following raw data was produced:
>
> 4 4 2 0 3 2 3 2 8 4 0 6 7 6 8 3 0 1 3 4 3 25 2 3 6 4 1 2 6 3

## Statistical procedures

There are a number of techniques that can be used to analyse data so that it can be used as a basis for marketing decisions.

## The arithmetic mean

It is often useful to produce a figure that represents the average or typical value from a set of data. For example, a hotel might wish to know the average rate of room occupancy over a 12-month period. The mean is the most commonly used average and is calculated by the following formula

> Arithmetic mean = the total value of all the results (x)/the number of results (n)

In the example below, the average number of visits to the cinema (measured by the mean) over the three-month period would be equal to 4.07 visits (122/30).

The mean is the most frequently used measure of an average, typically used to express figures such as the average increase in prices or average changes in consumer spending. However, it can be distorted by extreme individual results that make it unrepresentative of the majority of the results within the data set. For instance, the particularly keen cinema-goer in the example below, who made 25 visits in three months, is clearly not representative of the group overall. Nevertheless, this figure has pushed up the value of the mean, making it less representative of the data set overall.

## The mode

The **mode** is the value that occurs most frequently in a data set. The mode is often used to identify the most popular or typical choices, for instance consumers' favourite brands or the most popular tourist destinations in the UK. In the cinema example above, the modal value is three visits, as this was recorded by seven people – more than any other score. Unlike the mean and the **median**, there can be two or more values for the mode in a data set.

## The median

The median is the value at the midpoint of a data set, once this has been placed in order. Rearranging the data from the cinema example and starting with the lowest value would produce the following:

> 0 0 0 1 1 2 2 2 2 2 3 3 3 3 3 3 3 3 4 4 4 4 4 6 6 6 6 7 8 8 25

The middle value can be found by using the formula (n + 1)/2, where n is the number of results. In this case, the midpoint occurs between the fifteenth and sixteenth values, so the average number of visits, as given by the median, is three. Unlike the mean, the median is not affected by extreme values at either end of the data set, and so it may be a more suitable measure to use when such values are contained within a data set.

# Dealing with averages

Study the data in the table below and then complete the activity that follows:

| | Length of stay (nights) | Spend per trip (£) | Spend per night (£) |
|---|---|---|---|
| Scottish | 2.8 | 151.45 | 53.41 |
| English | 4.5 | 268.39 | 59.76 |
| Rest of UK | 4.1 | 388.52 | 94.80 |
| All UK | 3.7 | 219.41 | 59.38 |
| All overseas | 8.6 | 530.85 | 63.03 |

Table: Scottish tourism – average length of stay and spend (2009)

**Source: www.visitscotland.org**

## Activities

1 State the statistical procedure that has been used to calculate the average figures in the table above.

2 Suggest two ways in which the above data could be used by a small hotel situated in the Scottish highlands.

## Range

Calculating an average identifies the central value of a set of data, but it does not tell us how widely the data as a whole might be spread or dispersed around the average. The **range** is the simplest measure of dispersion to calculate and understand. It is found by working out the difference between the highest and the lowest value in the data set. In the previous cinema example, the range is 25 visits (25–0). However, the range is affected by extreme numbers that distort its value and affect decision making. For example, these results could tempt cinema managers into believing they would get more customers coming to see films than is likely to be the case in reality.

## Interquartile range

Rather than using the highest and lowest figures in a data set, the **interquartile range** concentrates on the central 50 per cent of values. By ignoring the lowest 25 per cent of values and the highest 25 per cent of values, the interquartile range is less likely to be affected by extremes.

In order to calculate the interquartile range, the data needs to be divided into four equal groups. The lowest 25 per cent of the data values will lie beneath Quartile 1 (Q1). In order to identify the value lying at Q1, the following formula is used:

Q1 = $(n + 1)/4$ – where n is the number of values in the data set

The highest 25 per cent of the data values will lie above Quartile 3 (Q3). The formula for finding Q3 is:

Q3 = $3(n + 1)/4$

The interquartile range is found by simply taking the value at Q3 and subtracting the value at Q1:

The interquartile range = Q3 – Q1

In the cinema example, the interquartile range is four visits. This is the difference between the Q1 or eighth value, which is 2, and the Q3 or twenty-third value, which is 6.

## Scatter diagrams

These diagrams are used to illustrate and compare two sets of data, in order to see whether there is any connection or **correlation** between them. For example, a business may have collected data on the level of sales of one of its products over a range of prices to measure the effects of any changes. The results could then be plotted on a graph to identify if a relationship exists between the two variables – price and sales level. The horizontal x axis of the graph is used to plot one set of data, known as the independent variable, while the vertical y axis is used to plot the other data set, known as the dependent variable. In this case, price would be the independent variable and the level of sales would be the dependent variable. This is because changes in price are likely to influence sales, rather than the other way around.

Plotting the data as a series of dots will reveal if any correlation exists. If the dots appear as a clear and closely compacted line sloping upwards, this suggests a strong and positive correlation: i.e. as one variable increases, the other increases. For example, there is likely to be a strong positive correlation between the average level of consumer incomes and the sale of luxury goods. If, on the other hand, the plotted data produces a clear downward-sloping line, this implies a strong, negative correlation – as one variable decreases, the other increases. Negative correlation exists

**235**

between the price of many goods and their volume of sales. Data sloping upwards or downwards, but which is more widely dispersed, suggests a weaker positive or negative correlation, whereas a lack of any discernable pattern implies that there is no correlation at all.

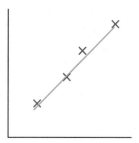

**Figure 10.5** Scatter diagram with strong positive correlation

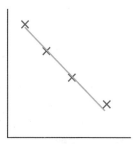

**Figure 10.6** Scatter diagram with strong negative correlation

**Figure 10.7** Scatter diagram with weak positive correlation

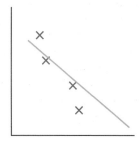

**Figure 10.8** Scatter diagram with weak negative correlation

**Figure 10.9** Scatter diagram with no correlation

## Time series analysis

Time series data is a set of figures, arranged in an order that is based on the time that they occurred. For example, the data set may consist of monthly sales figures for a restaurant based in a holiday resort, since it was established four years ago. Other businesses may find it more useful to use data that has been collected on a weekly or even a daily basis. Any past changes in the data can be easily illustrated with the use of a line graph.

## Trends

Demand for a firm's products can fluctuate signifi-cantly from one day, week or month to the next, making it difficult to spot whether the figures are moving in a particular direction over time. Despite these short-term fluctuations, managers need to know if, over a longer period of time, sales have been increasing, decreasing, or have remained relatively stable. The underlying pattern of growth or decline in a set of figures over a period of time is known as the **trend**. For example, looking at a firm's sales figures over the last ten years might reveal an average increase of 3 per cent per year. Making the assumption that this trend is likely to continue gives managers the ability to predict what will happen in the future. In this case, managers might assume that, as long as market conditions in the future are similar to those in the recent past, sales will continue to increase at around 3 per cent each year. Using past trends as an indication of future sales is known as extrapolation. The technique can produce accurate results in the short term, or where markets are stable. However, it is less likely to produce accurate sales forecasts in the longer term, or where markets are susceptible to dramatic changes in demand.

## Trends in Scottish tourism

Study the data in the table below and then complete the activity that follows:

| | 2007 £m | 2008 £m | 2009 £m |
|---|---|---|---|
| Australia | 52 | 64 | 66 |
| Canada | 83 | 86 | 55 |
| France | 57 | 74 | 97 |
| Germany | 187 | 93 | 146 |
| Irish Republic | 96 | 76 | 71 |
| Italy | 92 | 56 | 58 |
| Netherlands | 55 | 110 | 58 |
| Poland | 40 | 27 | 33 |
| Spain | 82 | 52 | 80 |
| USA | 257 | 260 | 225 |

Table: Origins of Top Overseas Visitors to Scotland 2007–2009 (by expenditure)

Source: www.visitscotland.org

### Activities

1 Comment on the trends illustrated in the table above.

2 Suggest two ways in which these trends could be used by firms operating in the Scottish tourism industry.

## Using spreadsheets for analysis

A spreadsheet is a way of inputting and storing data using a computer, often using formulae to calculate totals and subtotals. The effects of any changes to the data can be seen almost immediately, allowing managers to assess their effects, For example, the impact of an increase or decrease in price on revenue or profits over a range of sales levels can be quickly identified.

The data contained in spreadsheets can also be viewed diagrammatically. Figures can be converted into a number of different formats, such as line graphs, pie charts and bar charts, in order make information more meaningful.

## Presenting findings

Once data has been analysed, the results need to be summarised and communicated in an appropriate format. The main methods used are detailed below.

## Producing oral reports

Oral reports and presentations are widely used in business, but can be difficult to deliver effectively. The presenter needs to be clear as to the objectives of the presentation before beginning to put it together. Getting the structure of the report right is also essential, not only to present all the necessary information, but also to create and maintain interest.

Delivering an oral report

The key sections that should be included in any oral report are as follows:

- **An introduction** – the presenter should begin by greeting the audience and introducing him or herself, identifying the objectives of the presentation and outlining its structure. It may also be useful to include a brief explanation of how the research was carried out.

- **The main findings** – key points need to be addressed in a logical order and the presenter may find it useful to pause at the end of each section to check audience understanding. Diagrams, such as tables, charts or graphs, should be used to summarise information and highlight any patterns or trends.

- **A conclusion** – rather than simply repeating the key points of the previous section, the presenter needs to finish off by highlighting the implications of the research findings for future decision making and outline any recommended action to be taken.
- **A question and answer session** – a final opportunity should be given for members of the audience to seek clarification from the presenter of any of the points made during the report. Such interaction makes this style of presentation much more flexible than a written report, but highlights the need for the presenter to have an in-depth knowledge of the subject-matter.

The way that oral reports are delivered can have a significant influence on the understanding and response of the audience. The presenter's style of delivery needs be informed and confident, and he or she should attempt to interact with the audience, rather than simply read from a script.

## Producing written reports

A written report may be necessary when it is not possible to gather all those involved together in one place, or where a detailed, permanent copy of the research findings and recommendations is required. Written reports vary considerably in terms of size and structure. The following sections are, however, often included in a formal report:

- **Title page** – a short but comprehensive title, plus details of the client and the researcher (if separate organisations) and the date of the report.
- **List of contents** – details of the various sections and subsections, along with page numbers.
- **Executive summary** – this is a short summary, no more than one-page long, of the key points contained in the report; particularly useful if it is very long and detailed.
- **Procedure** – this explains how researchers collected the evidence on which the report is based, for example the sources of primary and secondary data used.
- **Findings** – this is where the results of the investigation are revealed in detail.
- **Conclusions** – this summarises the findings, linking them to the research objectives and highlighting any resulting issues.
- **Recommendations** – this outlines any action that may need to be taken, for example

> **Presenting oral reports – key tips**
>
> 1 Make effective eye contact – by looking at different members of the audience, rather than staring at one individual or the floor.
>
> 2 Use body language carefully – hands can be used to emphasise certain points, but constant repetition of gestures, such as messing with hair or pacing backwards and forwards, can be distracting and suggest a lack of confidence.
>
> 3 Avoid reading out notes or slides – speak directly to the audience, using slides or numbered cue cards as prompts.
>
> 4 Give out a report summary – this should follow the presentation and contain all of the key points, allowing the audience to concentrate fully on what is being said.
>
> 5 Use visual aids and flip charts – video clips and PowerPoint slides help to create variety, but the temptation to include too much information should be avoided. Flip charts can be used to record any questions or discussion points that arise. Remember to keep aids visible by not standing in front of them.
>
> 6 Reinforce understanding – by emphasising key points, summarising them on slides or handouts and pausing for questions.
>
> 7 Get pace and timing right – make sure the pace is slow enough for the audience to understand but fast enough to maintain interest and ensure that all points are covered, including time for questions.
>
> 8 Rehearse – this helps to build knowledge and confidence, as well as identifying any problems with content or timing.

suggested responses to falling sales caused by increased competition.
- **Appendices** – these are used to provide additional data, such as tables or charts, to act as supporting evidence for the points made in the findings section.

Informal reports might be drawn up for use within a department or as an initial step to producing something more formal in the future. They are likely to be much shorter and less detailed, simply containing an introduction, the main findings and conclusions or recommendations.

## Using visual aids

There are a variety of visual aids that can be used to enhance both oral and written reports, including tables, graphs and charts, computer graphics and video. They can often represent and summarise large quantities of data which would take much longer to explain using text or speech. They can also be used to create variety by breaking up presentations, helping to maintain interest. However, using visual aids inappropriately can reduce the quality of a report. Simple slides, graphs and tables are usually much easier to understand than those containing lots of information. Images can be very effective in conveying messages, but can also lead to confusion if included for decoration or to fill up space. Overuse of computer animation can also be very distracting. In short, visual aids should be used to highlight or reinforce the content of a report, not to replace it!

## Presenting conclusions and recommendations

The conclusions and recommendations of a report are likely to form the basis of any future decision making. It is important, therefore, that they relate directly to the objectives set for the research and they are based on the evidence gathered, even if the report conclusions do not support the course of action preferred by those that have commissioned it.

## Audience

Research presenters need to have a good understanding of the audience, in terms of their expectations and level of expertise, in order to make the content appropriate. For example, jargon or technical terms should be avoided and the level of detail kept to a minimum if the presentation is aimed at a general audience with little existing understanding of the issues being investigated. Written reports, in particular, are likely to be referred back to on many occasions, so the meaning of their findings must be just as clear in the future as in the present. Even though the information contained in the report should be presented as clearly as possible, audience members may still ask questions or seek further explanation, and presenters must be willing and able to do this.

## Effectiveness

There is a danger that, as reports are being prepared, presenters lose sight of both the original objectives of the research and the intended audience. A report can only be judged as effective if it is successful in meeting the research objectives and is understood by the audience to whom it is presented. There may be a temptation to include too much detail, especially if the report is based on a great deal of research that has taken a long time to compile. However, this should be resisted as this could mean that the key points within the report are lost or ignored.

## Quality of information

An effective presentation depends, ultimately, on what is being said, as well as how it is being delivered. Irrelevant details may be contained in the report, perhaps collected as a result of poorly designed research or in an attempt to increase its length to create a more favourable impression. However, this can also distract from the key points and lead to the wrong conclusions being drawn. It is also important that the recommendations contained in the report are based on the evidence and the capabilities of those with the responsibility of carrying them out.

## Facilities

The quality of an oral presentation will also depend, to a large extent, on the facilities used, so they must be checked in advance. Appropriate equipment has to be available and fully functional, and presenters must be confident about using it. For example, a well-designed PowerPoint presentation, full of relevant content, would be totally ineffective without access to a computer and a screen of a suitable size for the room and the audience. Gaps or pauses can also be caused by faulty equipment or a lack of technical knowledge from the presenter. They are likely to make it difficult for the audience to concentrate and can lead to boredom.

## Diagrammatic analysis and presentation

Diagrams are often used in reports and presentations in order to summarise data and make it easier and quicker to read and understand. The type of diagram chosen must be appropriate for the data and the intended audience. In all cases, diagrams should be clearly labelled, including a title and any measurements, such as the axes of a graph, must be accurately marked.

The most frequently used diagrams include:

- **Pictograms** – involve using simple images to present data. The picture or symbol chosen usually relates to the data or the business involved in some way. Pictograms can be used to present data in a very eye-catching way, making a presentation more attractive and holding the interest of the audience. It can, however, be difficult to represent complex or detailed information using this method.
- **Pie charts** – involve taking a circle (or pie) and breaking it up into segments. Each segment represents individual values, as a percentage of the total figure, and converted into degrees of a circle, using the following formula:

(Value of the part / total value) × 360 degrees

For example, pie charts are commonly used to represent the market shares of individual firms operating in the same industry or sector. They could also be used to illustrate the breakdown of total costs or sources of revenue of a business. However, they are less effective when lots of individual segments with similar values need to be shown.

- **Bar charts** – come in a variety of forms, all of which involve presenting data as a bar or bars. They allow data to be presented clearly, allowing the reader to make instant comparisons. For example, differences in the value or volume of different brands of a product could be illustrated and compared. The length of the bar represents a particular value or quantity. The bars are set out separately, either vertically or horizontally, as part of a graph. Alternatively, a component bar chart can be used, where one bar is divided into sections representing different values.
- **Histograms** – these are similar in appearance to bar charts, but each value is represented by the area of the bar, rather than its length or height. They are often used to represent continuous data, such as income or expenditure. However, they are often confused with bar charts and their meaning is misinterpreted.
- **Frequency curves** – these curves are drawn through the midpoints of the top of each bar of a histogram.

- **Line graphs** – these are frequently used to show how values change over time. This could be an individual firm's sales or costs, or economic data, such as the level of unemployment, output or interest rates. Time is usually shown on the horizontal (x) axis of the graph, with the changing variable illustrated on the vertical (y) axis.
- **Scattergrams** – are used to identify and illustrate the relationship between two variables, known as a correlation. The existence of a correlation would mean that changes in one variable, for example customers' incomes, would lead to a change in another variable, such as the demand for luxury goods. In some cases, however, even a strong correlation does not necessarily mean that changes in one variable automatically lead to changes in the other.

## Traveling to Scotland

Study the data in the table below and then complete the activity that follows:

|  | Holiday trips % | Business trips % |
|---|---|---|
| Car | 69 | 51 |
| Train | 12 | 18 |
| Coach tour | 4 | 0 |
| Regular bus/coach | 4 | 1 |
| Air | 7 | 19 |
| Other | 4 | 10 |

Table: Means of travel to Scotland by UK residents (2009)

### Activity

Choose a suitable diagram to present the data contained in the table above.

## Interpreting results

Gathering and analysing data can be a long drawn-out process. Once this has been done, managers can begin to examine the statistics that have been produced and consider their significance. For example, a number of market-research reports released at the end of 2008 and the beginning of

2009 clearly indicated that sales of organic food in the UK were set to fall significantly in 2009, after growing consistently for a number of years. The implications of this for food retailers across the country would have depended, to a large extent, on their interpretation as to the main reasons for the reversal of the trend in organic sales. Managers within these businesses would have been responsible for deciding on the most appropriate action to take. For example, some supermarkets may have decided to reduce the prices of organic foods or stock a greater range of cheaper, non-organic items, in order to attract customers cutting back on spending because of the recession. Others may decide to spend more on promotion to increase customer awareness and understanding of the issues relating to organic products.

## Limitations of research

The purpose of market research is to provide up-to-date and accurate information. This information can be of great value to a business, improving the quality of its decision making and giving it a competitive edge over other firms in the market. However, market research cannot guarantee that effective decisions are ever taken. There are many reasons why, in reality, the potential benefits of conducting market research may fail to materialise, for example sample reliability and accuracy, bias and subjectivity, the quality of the databases used and the problems associated with information obtained from e-business feedback.

## Sample reliability and accuracy

A great deal of market-research findings rely on the use of samples. It may simply not be possible – or necessary – to exactly replicate all of the characteristics of the population under investigation. However, the less representative the sample is, the less accurate will be the results obtained from it. Using probability sampling methods allows a researcher to calculate the sampling error, so that the difference between any results from the sample and those that would have been produced by using the whole population can be estimated. However, it is not possible to calculate sampling error when using non-probability sampling methods, such as quota or convenience sampling. Results produced in this way could, therefore, mislead managers into making poor decisions.

## Bias and subjectivity

Bias refers to any factors that influence research results towards any outcome, other than that which would have resulted if the influences had not been present. For example, a sample taken to represent the UK population as a whole might be made up of a disproportionate number of teenagers, meaning that the results will be biased towards their views. Subjectivity can affect results when researchers are required to interpret the responses gathered, particularly when dealing with qualitative research into people's opinions. For example, interviewers may make assumptions as to why people have certain views, based on the extent to which they resemble or differ from their own. Both bias and subjectivity can affect the quality of market-research data.

### Coke's big market research blunder

On 23 April 1985, global soft drinks giant Coca Cola launched New Coke. The move was a response to the growing challenge from rival Pepsi and was based on two years of research and taste tests carried out by the company's market research team. Despite the positive feedback, the new flavour launch was a disaster. The public reaction was overwhelmingly negative, provoking thousands of calls to the company's headquarters and customers protesting by pouring cans of New Coke down gutters. Within three months the new recipe was withdrawn and the classic formula was reintroduced. Coca Cola had committed a fundamental marketing mistake in failing to ask its customers if they wanted changes to be made to a well-established and much loved brand. The company's president, Donald R. Keough, said at the time 'We did not understand the deep emotions of so many of our customers for Coca Cola'. Since then, the company has successfully launched a number of variants, including Coca Cola Zero – a no calorie variation of Diet Coke – in 2006.

**Source:** msnbc.msn.com

### Activity

Briefly explain how a large, established company like Coca Cola could make marketing mistakes on the scale of New Coke, despite carrying out extensive market research.

## Customer databases

Improvements in the effectiveness and afford-ability of computer technology in recent years now means that even small businesses can gather, store and process a huge amount of data relating to their customers. However, managers may become overwhelmed by the amount of information available, much of which may not be particularly relevant to their needs. They may end up spending an increasing amount of time sorting through all the data presented to them, leaving less time to actually decide on the best course of action to take. Databases need to be updated regularly but this can also use up valuable time and money.

## E-business feedback

Email and online questionnaires are relatively low-cost ways for firms to gather potentially valuable market-research data. However, providing free and convenient methods for customers to communicate their views can also lead to information overload. Moreover, the opinions of the people that regularly use these methods may not be representative of customers overall, so any information obtained in this way may be of limited value.

## Key terms

**Arithmetic mean** Calculates the average value from a set of data by dividing the total sum of the values in a dataset by the number of values in the dataset

**Bar chart** A method of presenting data where a series of bars are used to represent the values of different quantities in a dataset

**Bias** Any factors that influence research results towards an outcome other than that which would have resulted if the influences had not been present

**Correlation** Measures the strength of the causal link between two sets of numerical data, such as advertising expenditure and demand for a product

**Frequency curve** A curve that is drawn through the midpoints of the top of each bar of a histogram

**Histogram** These involve presenting data as a series of bars where the area of each bar represents individual values or quantities

**Interquartile range** Difference between the first quartile (twenty-fifth percentile) and the third quartile (seventy-fifth percentile) of an ordered range of data

**Line graph** These are used to show how values change over time. The time period is usually indicated on the horizontal (x) axis of the graph, and the changing variable, such as a firm's sales or costs, is shown on the vertical (y) axis

**Median** This is the value that occurs at the midpoint of a set of data, once the data has been placed in ascending order

**Mode** This is the value that occurs most frequently in a set of data

**Pictogram** This is a diagram that uses images or symbols to represent the quantity of data involved

**Pie chart** This takes a circle or pie and breaks it up into segments, representing individual percentages or proportions of a total figure

**Range** The difference between the highest and lowest values in a set of data

**Scatter diagram** Used to identify and illustrate the relationship between two variables, which is known as a correlation

**Time series analysis** A set of figures, such as past sales figures, that are arranged in an order based on the time when they occurred

**Trend** The underlying pattern of growth or decline in a set of figures, such as sales, over a period of time

## Q Re-cap questions

1 Briefly explain what is meant by the average value in a set of data.

2 How is the mode identified?

3 Explain how the following average values are calculated: a) the arithmetic mean; b) the median.

4 Outline one reason why researchers might use the median, rather than the mean, to indicate the average value of a data set.

5 Explain why researchers might find it useful to calculate the degree of dispersion from the average for a dataset.

6 Outline one reason why managers of a business might wish to identify sales trends in recent years.

7 Using examples, explain what is meant by the term correlation.

8 State two benefits of using spreadsheets to store market-research data.

9 Briefly describe four factors that should be kept in mind when delivering an oral report.

10 Identify the main sections of a formal written report.

11 Outline one potential benefit and one potential drawback of using visual aids when presenting market-research findings.

12 Outline the difference between a bar chart and a histogram.

13 Explain what is meant by a pie chart and how it is constructed.

14 Suggest one reason why gathering and holding large amounts of data can actually reduce the effectiveness of market research.

15 State two possible ways in which bias can affect the validity of market-research findings.

## Grading tips

**P5** Interpret findings from the research presenting them clearly in an appropriate format

You need to summarise and present the findings of your research. You need to choose an appropriate format for your presentation, so consider whether a verbal or written presentation would be more suitable for your audience, as well as the most effective ways of using diagrams, graphs and text.

**M3** Analyse the research findings and make recommendations on how marketing strategies could be adapted or implemented

You need to examine the implications of the findings of your research by explaining how these findings could affect the business and the product involved. Make sure that you can justify any recommendations that you make for changes to marketing strategies from the evidence generated by your research.

### Assignments for Unit 10

#### Assignment One

The Head of Business at your school or college has asked you to produce a dictionary of market research for the department's virtual learning environment (VLE).

Note – read through the tasks below, the relevant criteria and the assignment advice on page 220, in order to ensure that you generate all the necessary evidence.

**Criteria covered** – P1

**Tasks**

1. Write a description of the different types of market research. This should include a definition of the term 'market research' and its importance to businesses. It should also provide explanations of the different methods used to gather data. (P1)

**Assignment Two**

Your school/college is keen to expand by increasing the number of students by 10 per cent in the next three years. You have, therefore, been asked to plan and carry out market research into possible ways of doing this, interpret the results and present them to the school/college's senior management team. Before you go ahead with this, you are advised to look into the different methods of market research used by organisations to make marketing decisions.

**Note** – read through the tasks below, the relevant criteria and the assignment advice on pages 220, 221, 225, 233 and 243 in order to ensure that you generate all the necessary evidence. You may be able to find a commercial business willing to give you access to market research that has already been carried out. If not, you may wish to use your own school or college.

**Criteria covered** – P2 P3 P4 P5 M1 M2 M3 D1 D2

**Tasks**

1. Write a case study explaining how different market-research methods were used within a selected situation or business to make a marketing decision. (P2)

2. Draw up a market-research plan for the scenario above using appropriate methods of data collection, including primary and secondary research. Make sure that you include all of the key stages in the planning process. (P3)

3. Using examples, explain how different market-research methods are appropriate to assist different marketing situations. This explanation could relate to Task 1 and/or Task 2. (M1)

4. Produce an evaluation of the market-research methods used by your selected organisation. This will require you to make judgements on how effective the methods were in obtaining the information required to make the marketing decisions in Task 1. (D1)

5. Put your plan into action by carrying out market research for the scenario above. Ensure that you use both primary and secondary methods and identifiable sampling techniques. (P4)

6. Write a report containing an explanation of the reasons why you chose the methods of data collection used in your market research in Task 5. (M2)

7. Produce a presentation interpreting the findings of your market research. (P5)

8. Develop Task 7 by producing an analysis of your research findings, making recommendations on how your organisation's marketing strategies could be adapted or implemented. (M3)

9. Develop Tasks 7 and 8 by producing an evaluation of the findings of the market research undertaken in Task 5. (D2)

# Part 1: The process of recruitment planning

People are a key resource for any business. Even in firms where production is carried out entirely by machines, human input is still required to plan operations and organise resources. Recruitment is the process of filling vacancies that arise within an organisation by attracting and appointing suitable people. This process includes a number of activities, such as defining the tasks and responsibilities involved in a job role, identifying the skills, qualifications and abilities needed to carry it out successfully and then attracting suitable people to apply for the post. Once this has been done, the selection process involves choosing the most appropriate applicant or applicants.

# Recruitment planning

Microsoft UK is the global IT giant's largest subsidiary, employing around 1,500 of its 91,000-strong total workforce worldwide, mainly in sales, marketing, service and support. The software company has won a string of 'best employer' awards in the UK and was ranked twenty-second in *The Times* Top 100 Graduate Employers listing for 2009. The prestigious Microsoft Academy for University Hires (MACH) looks to hire ambitious young people with a passion for technology. The two-year training programme has a starting salary of £26,000 plus a bonus of £1,000 and a number of additional benefits. New recruits complete two weeks of induction training in the USA, two weeks' professional skills training in Europe and attend a number of global MACH conferences. Unsurprisingly, Microsoft has been a very popular choice for UK graduate job seekers. In both 2008 and 2009, the company had over 6,000 applications for around 20 MACH vacancies in each year. Microsoft's recruitment and selection processes are, therefore, rigorous, involving the submission of application forms and CVs, telephone and face-to-face interviews, online aptitude and technical tests and assessment centres.

**Source: *The Times* Online, 26 January 2010**

Companies like Microsoft openly recognise that recruiting and retaining the right people is crucial to their current and future success. Fierce competition for customers and sales between firms, such as those operating in the global software market, mean they need to attract and appoint the most talented employees available in order to avoid falling behind their rivals.

The **recruitment** and selection process can be triggered within a business for a number of reasons. In some cases, it may be possible to foresee staff departure well in advance, for example when an employee retires or starts maternity leave. In other situations, a member of staff might leave their job relatively quickly, as a result of promotion internally or with a different employer. Staff sickness may create a sudden, totally unexpected need to recruit. Whatever the cause, it is important that managers respond to the imminent vacancy as quickly as possible. It can take a considerable amount of time to find a suitable replacement. During this time, productivity or the quality of service provided are likely to suffer and remaining staff placed under additional strain, as a result of unfilled vacancies.

Whenever an employee leaves, managers also need to stop and consider the contribution made to operations by the vacant job role, rather than automatically filling it. Changes within or outside of the business may mean that the post is no longer necessary, making the job redundant. For example, increases in productivity over time could mean that fewer workers are needed to meet production targets. Improvements in technology may make it possible to replace workers with more efficient machinery, leading to lower operating costs. If the job contains duties or responsibilities that are still required, it may be possible to allocate them to other employees via a programme of restructuring.

**Recruitment planning** also needs to consider the workforce needs of the business in the future. Job vacancies may also result from business expansion. Producing and selling more of an existing product may require a larger workforce. Developing new products or markets can create a need for employees with specific technical knowledge or skills, such as experience of working in a particular area or the ability to speak a foreign language.

Planning recruitment for future workforce needs is particularly difficult. As already noted, the recruitment process takes time to complete – during this time, the circumstances of the business may change significantly. Businesses merge with or take over other businesses, often leading to employees that are surplus to requirements. An unexpected downturn in the economy can lead to the postponement or even cancellation of expansion plans. Hiring staff on permanent contracts can prove to be a costly mistake if the size of the workforce needs to be reduced in the near future. Increasingly, businesses hire workers on temporary contracts, not only to cover for staff absences due to sickness or maternity leave, but also to create greater workforce flexibility.

The recruitment and selection process can be a costly exercise – in terms of both time and money. A great deal of planning and resources are required to try and ensure that the right workers with the right skills are in the right place at the time that they are needed. The responsibility for recruitment and selection in large firms is usually shared between the human resources department and individual managers involved in the areas where vacancies arise. In small businesses, the task of recruiting new employees is usually carried out by the owner, who may not have the skills and knowledge required to make the process effective. However, effective recruitment and selection adds great value to a business by creating a talented and motivated workforce. Ineffective recruitment, on the other hand, can damage productivity by hiring workers with inappropriate skills and attitudes, adding to costs when they eventually leave and have to be replaced by others.

## Sources of recruitment

Once managers have accepted that a vacancy does exist within the business, a decision has to be made regarding whether to recruit from the existing workforce (known as **internal recruitment**) or from outside the organisation (known as **external recruitment**).

## Internal recruitment

Existing employees can be used to fill vacancies by either redeploying or promoting them from their current positions within the business. There are a number of reasons why managers might consider internal recruitment. Vacancies can be advertised using internal communication systems, such as notice boards, staff bulletins and email, avoiding the need and the cost of using expensive recruitment agencies or the media. The abilities and work ethic of existing staff will already be known to some extent, meaning that selection can be completed in less time. Giving employees the opportunity to take on new roles and responsibilities can also raise motivation levels, by rewarding hard work and commitment. However, internal recruitment is inappropriate where businesses need to increase the total number of workers employed. Existing workers may lack the skills and experience required to carry out the duties of

more senior posts effectively. Even if internal recruitment is used in the first instance, it is likely to create a vacancy elsewhere in the business that will need to be filled from outside.

## External recruitment

Managers may decide to recruit new employees from outside the firm if no suitable internal candidates are available. External recruitment creates a wider pool for managers to choose from, increasing the chances of getting the best candidate for the job. It is also a way of bringing new ideas and practices into a business, which can help firms to remain competitive. External applicants may also already possess all of the sought after skills and qualifications, avoiding the need for training, and helping to control costs.

A business may choose to handle the process of external recruitment directly, particularly if it operates on a large enough scale to have specialist human-resources staff with the knowledge and experience required. Smaller businesses that are unable to dedicate all of the resources required may hand over at least some of the recruitment process to an external agency. There are a number of possibilities, including:

- **Job centres** – these are government-run organisations offering a number of services to people searching for jobs, including advice, training and help to claim benefits for the unemployed. Firms that advertise vacancies at job centres are not charged to do so and can receive £1,000 for every person recruited through the service who has been unemployed for over six months. Job vacancies are advertised on the Jobcentre Plus website (www.jobcentreplus.gov.uk), which receives around 1.5 million searches every working day. Vacancies are also advertised throughout Europe via the European Employment Services (EURES).
- **Commercial recruitment agencies** – these are private sector organisations that provide a number of personnel services to firms, including recruitment, in return for payment of a fee. For example, the agency collects details on people looking for employment in a particular area and attempts to match them up when firms notify them of vacancies. They may also carry out preliminary interviews in order to draw up a shortlist that can then be passed on to the potential employer. If the process results in a

successful appointment, the fee charged to the employer is usually calculated on the annual salary attached to the job vacancy in question.

- **Recruitment consultants** – these individuals also give advice and support to firms with job vacancies, usually those looking to recruit relatively senior managers or those with highly specialised skills. They may also offer to approach suitable individuals directly, effectively acting as 'headhunters'.

## Cost and time considerations of external sourcing

Despite the many potential benefits of attracting candidates from outside an organisation, there are also a number of costs that must be taken into consideration.

- **The financial costs** – the cost of both adverts placed in the media and agency or consultancy fees can be significant. Firms need to be able to find the resources and justify the costs, bearing in mind that resources could have had other uses within the business, such as training or marketing.
- **The time taken to hire suitable recruits** – recruiting the right person to fill a vacancy can be very time consuming and use up a lot of resources. The job vacancy needs to be analysed, relevant documentation needs to be drawn up, advertisements placed and the various stages of the selection process need to be carried out. It may take several months, therefore, to find the

right candidate. Once he or she has been chosen, they may have to serve a period of notice of up to six months with their current employer before they are ready to join the business. Any delay in filling a vacancy is likely to have a negative effect on business performance.

# Recruitment advertising

**Job advertisements** play a very important role in the recruitment process. The purpose of a job advertisement is to attract a range of suitably qualified people to apply for the job. It is important that advertisements are designed effectively, in order to attract candidates that are suitable and discourage those that are not. Applications from those who do not possess the right qualifications or aptitudes still need to be processed, wasting time and resources and adding to costs.

Some thought must, therefore, go into exactly where the advert should be placed to get it noticed by the right people. The methods used to advertise job vacancies depend on whether recruitment is internal or external.

## Internal advertising

This should be relatively straightforward, given that the target audience for internal recruitment is limited to existing employees of the business. The vacancy can be advertised through a number of channels, including internal notice boards, company newsletters or websites and email.

| Benefits of internal recruitment | Benefits of external recruitment |
|---|---|
| • Cheaper and quicker to advertise<br>• Already familiar with company policies and practices, so do not need induction<br>• Skills and working habits already known to managers<br>• Opportunities for promotion can be motivating | • Should result in a wider range of candidates to choose from<br>• Already possess necessary skills so can be effective immediately<br>• Bring in new ideas and approaches to work |
| **Drawbacks of internal recruitment** | **Drawbacks of external recruitment** |
| • May not have the skills required, making training necessary<br>• May lead to a shortage of new ideas and approaches to work<br>• Likely to create a vacancy elsewhere in the business, making external recruitment necessary at some point | • Can be expensive and time consuming<br>• More difficult to assess the knowledge and capabilities of the candidates<br>• Can demotivate the existing workforce |

Table 13.1 Internal and external recruitment: benefits and drawbacks

Examples of job adverts

## External advertising

For firms choosing to use job centres, agencies or consultants as part of the recruitment process, getting the details of a job advert is vital to make sure that only suitable candidates are considered. Firms that decide to recruit directly are faced with a wide choice of possible methods. Managers need to be clear as to whether they need to recruit on a local, national or even international basis, in order to create the best possible pool of candidates, while still keeping costs under control. The type of employee that is being sought is also likely to have a major influence on the methods used. For example, many retailers advertise part-time or temporary vacancies in shop windows or on in-store notice boards. A business may approach local schools and colleges to advertise relatively junior administrative jobs, requiring basic academic qualifications and little, if any, experience, but decide to take part in the university 'milk-round' to attract graduates to more demanding management training schemes. Employers also often use the media to advertise vacancies. This might involve placing advertisements on local radio, in the jobs sections of local and national newspapers or in specialist journals and magazines, aimed at a particular sector, such as retail or catering. In the case of some professions, such as teaching, nursing and the armed services, national recruitment campaigns are often run on television. The growing use of the internet in recent years means that many firms now advertise vacancies online, either using the 'careers' pages of their own websites or those of internet recruitment agencies, such as monster.co.uk.

## The format of an advertisement

Given that the cost of an advertisement is determined to a large extent by its length, it needs to be as concise as possible, but still contain enough information to give readers a clear impression of what the job requirements will be. The exact content will depend on the nature of the job vacancy. However, in most cases it is likely to include the following:

- The job title and a brief description of the role
- Details about the business, its name, location and the sector in which it operates
- Qualifications and experience required
- Details regarding the salary and any fringe benefits attached to the job
- Contact details, such as address, telephone and email, for applicants to use, along with the closing date for applications

Many firms choose to make their name or a well-known logo a central feature of printed advertisements to make them more easily recognisable. They also often choose to put a number of different job vacancies together to make the advertisement stand out.

## Cost and legal implications

Methods used for advertising job vacancies can vary greatly in terms of cost. For example, few businesses, other than the largest organisations, would consider using television to recruit new employees. However, recruitment to the police and other public sector services tends to take place on a national basis, justifying the costs involved in television advertising. The key point is to choose a method of advertising that is cost effective – there is little point spending thousands to use national media if cheaper methods are just as likely to reach the intended audience.

Firms must also ensure that any advertisements used in the recruitment process do not infringe any legislation relating to recruitment. There are a number of laws that have a direct impact on recruitment advertising (see 13.2). However, existing legislation means that all advertisements should be fair and allow equal access to everyone. Advertisements should be carefully worded to prevent discrimination on the grounds of gender, ethnicity, religion, age or sexual orientation. Costly fines can result from advertisements that are discriminatory. The publicity that would be likely to result from a prosecution could have a very damaging effect on the effectiveness of any future recruitment.

## Methods of applications

Before a job vacancy is advertised, managers need to decide on the method of application that candidates should use. Once the method has been chosen, clear instructions as to how to apply should be included in the job advertisement. There are a number of methods that can be used.

### Application by letter

Writing a letter of application gives candidates the opportunity to discuss in depth the reasons why they are applying for the vacancy and highlight any qualifications, past experience or attributes that would make them suitable. Letters are normally accompanied by a **curriculum vitae (CV)** or an application form, which are used to provide basic information such as personal details, qualifications and work history. However, the amount of information included in letters from different candidates can vary considerably, making comparisons difficult.

### Application by telephone

Candidates are often told to request information and application packs over the telephone, rather than post, in order to speed up the recruitment process. However, many large employers are also now using telephone interviews as part of the initial selection process. Candidates are asked a number of questions and those that respond correctly pass on to the next stage. Doing this means that a large number of applicants can be screened from all over the country at a relatively low cost, reducing the time and money spent by the employer on face-to-face interviews and focusing resources on assessing the most suitable candidates. It is also likely to be more convenient for those applying for the job.

## Application online

Sending an email to request information regarding a vacancy offers a quicker and cheaper alternative to making the request by letter or telephone call. Many firms also now ask candidates to complete online application forms. The information provided can be stored, retrieved and analysed more easily than is the case when forms are completed by hand. It also reduces the cost of having to print and post documentation in response to every request received.

**Figure 13.1** Methods of external advertising

## Key terms

**Commercial recruitment agency** A private sector organisation that provides personnel services, including recruitment, to other businesses

**Curriculum vitae** A factual summary of a person's personal details, qualifications, employment history and any other information that could be useful when applying for a job

**External recruitment** This takes place when people from outside the business are used to fill job vacancies

**Internal recruitment** This occurs when an existing employee is used to fill a vacancy that arises within a business, via promotion or redeployment

**Job advertisement** A document containing details about a job vacancy that is used to attract suitably qualified and experienced people to apply for it

**Job centre** A government-run organisation set up to assist people that are looking for work, which allows firms to advertise job vacancies for free

**Recruitment** The process of filling job vacancies that arise within a business

**Recruitment consultant** Individuals that, for a fee, give advice and support to firms with job vacancies. Also known as 'headhunters', they may also contact suitable people on the firm's behalf

**Recruitment planning** The process of ensuring that a business has enough suitably qualified employees to operate effectively by anticipating job vacancies and filling any when they arise

## Re-cap questions

1 Outline three reasons why a firm may need to consider recruiting new workers.
2 Describe two reasons why managers may decide not to recruit when an employee leaves the business.
3 Examine one advantage and one disadvantage of internal recruitment for a large, established company.
4 Analyse one advantage and one disadvantage for a small, new business from using external recruitment to fill a vacancy.
5 Briefly describe the service provided to businesses by government-funded job centres.
6 Describe one potential benefit and one potential drawback for businesses from using commercial recruitment agencies.
7 Outline the purpose of a job advertisement.
8 State two ways in which a job vacancy can be advertised a) internally and b) externally.
9 Identify five pieces of information that are usually included in a job advertisement.
10 List three ways commonly used by people to apply for job vacancies.

# Grading tips

| | | |
|---|---|---|
| **P1** Identify how two organisations plan recruitment using internal and external sources<br><br>You should be able to explain why the vacancies have occurred in both of the two organisations chosen and why, in each case, the decision was taken to recruit. You also need to make sure that one of the organisations has filled its vacancy using internal sources, and the other has used external sources, in order to give a detailed description of the processes used. | | |

See p 275 for suggestions for Assignments for Unit 13.

Firms are required by law to make every effort to ensure that they do not discriminate against individual candidates, including on the grounds of gender, ethnicity, disability, age or sexual orientation. **Equal opportunities legislation** is designed to ensure that people are employed purely on the basis of their skills and abilities. Treating all candidates equally and fairly throughout the recruitment process can have a number of additional benefits. Firms with a positive reputation are more likely to attract a wider field of applicants, increasing the chances of finding the most suitable people to fill its vacancies.

## Current UK and EU legislation

UK firms are not just affected by legislation created by the UK Government but also that passed by the European Union (EU). EU law is passed by the European Parliament and has a direct effect in all 27 member states. EU law always takes precedence, even if it clashes with national legislation. There are two main types of EU legislation. Regulations become law in all member states as soon as they are passed. Directives aim to achieve a specific result but the way this is done is left to member governments.

There are a number of pieces of legislation that attempt to promote equal opportunities in all aspects of employment, including recruitment and selection. This legislation is aimed both at **direct discrimination** and **indirect discrimination**. Direct discrimination occurs when the reason why one person receives unfavourable treatment results from factors that are unrelated to their ability to carry out a job. For example, a married female candidate in her 20s may not be appointed to a job, despite being the most suitably qualified, because of the expectation that she may soon start a family and take maternity leave. Indirect discrimination, on the other hand, occurs when existing rules, regulations or procedures within an organisation have a discriminating effect on certain groups. For example, insisting that female staff wear uniforms with short skirts may discriminate against women from certain ethnic groups. The **harassment** and **victimisation** of job candidates is also illegal under UK law. Harassment

may involve making derogatory remarks to individuals on the basis of their gender, race or disability. Victimisation would result if a person was treated less favourably as a result of complaining about discrimination or harassment.

The purpose and content of a number of laws that have a major effect on recruitment are outlined below.

Candidates for jobs are protected from discrimination by different laws

## Sex Discrimination Act 1975/1995/1997

The Sex Discrimination Act (SDA) of 1975 has been amended a number of times in recent years. Basically, the SDA states that it unlawful for firms to treat anyone unfavourably because of their gender, marital status or gender reassignment (where someone has had their gender changed under medical supervision). This means that firms must not discriminate against anyone on the grounds of gender during the recruitment process, for example, by inviting someone for interview purely on the basis of them either being a man or a woman. There are a limited number of exceptions to this, including organisations such as single sex prisons, schools or care centres, acting or modelling jobs where a man or woman is required, or where the job requires a high level of personal privacy, such as in the case of changing room attendants at leisure centres.

## Race Relations Act 1976/1992

The Race Relations Act (RRA) makes it unlawful for businesses to give unfavourable treatment to anyone on the grounds of race. Firms must not, therefore, discriminate against job applicants because of their colour, nationality, ethnic or national origin. The RRA also recognises a number of exceptions where, in certain cases, a job may require someone of a particular race, such as a black actor in a film or play, or waiters of a particular nationality to work in restaurants selling food from a particular area.

## Equal Pay Act 1970

This Act means that firms cannot legally discriminate either against men or women in terms of their pay and conditions when doing the same or similar work, work of equal value or work rated as equivalent by a job evaluation study carried out by the business. It would, therefore, be illegal for a business to advertise the same job vacancy with different rates of pay for men and women. This applies not just to wages or salary levels, but also to other terms, such as fringe benefits, company cars, holiday entitlement and sickness benefits.

## Disability Discrimination Act 1995/2005

A disabled worker is someone with either a physical or mental impairment that has a long-term effect on their ability to carry out work duties on a daily basis. Under the terms of the Disability Discrimination Act (DDA), it is unlawful for an employer to give unfavourable treatment to anyone as a result of their disability. In terms of recruitment, firms must ensure that disabled applicants are not treated unfairly at any time during the process, including the completion of application forms and arrangements for interview or other selection procedures.

## European Working Time Directive

This is an EU directive designed to protect the health and safety of people at work by creating a maximum working week of 48 hours. Working time is defined as any period that employees are working or at the disposal of their employer and carrying out duties. It also establishes minimum rest or break times during the working day and week, a minimum of four weeks paid leave and restrictions on the length of night shifts. Although this directive applies to workers already in employment, firms need to take the contents of the directive into account when setting out and advertising the details of job vacancies.

## Employment Act 2002

The provisions of this law extended workers rights in a number of areas of employment, which must be kept in mind throughout the recruitment process. The main points include:

- An increase in statutory maternity leave to up to six months' paid leave and six months' unpaid leave
- The introduction of maternity leave for adoptive parents of up to six months' paid leave and six months' unpaid leave
- The introduction of two weeks' paid paternity leave for working fathers
- The introduction of the right of parents of young or disabled children to request flexible working patterns, with the right to appeal against any refusals
- The requirement that employees on fixed-term contracts be given the same rights at work as those on permanent contracts
- The requirement that all firms, regardless of size, put in place minimum standard grievance and disciplinary procedures
- The creation of trade union learning representatives with a right to paid time off work.

## National Minimum Wage (NMW) legislation

The **national minimum wage (NMW)** was introduced in the UK in 1999. It gives a legal right to nearly all workers aged 16 or over to a minimum pay rate. The NMW applies to part-time, casual and agency workers, as well as those on permanent, full-time contracts. The rates paid depend on the age of the worker and are based on the recommendations of the Low Pay Commission. From October 2009, these hourly rates were as follows:

- The main rate (for workers aged 22 and over) – £5.80
- The rate for 18 to 21 year olds – £4.83
- The rate for 16 and 17 year olds – £3.57

# Data Protection Act 1998

The purpose of this law is to regulate the storage and use of personal information held by businesses on individuals, including employees and those applying for jobs. The recruitment process is likely to require a great deal of information on candidates, such as personal details, assessment grades and interview notes, to be kept on file. This can only be done if the candidate's consent has been obtained and, even then, must not be kept any longer than necessary. Candidates have the right to access information held about them and to insist that any incorrect information is amended. They also have the right to stop any information being used by businesses for marketing purposes.

## Ethical issues

Many businesses go beyond simply ensuring that they comply with the law when carrying out recruitment. Behaving ethically involves doing what is believed to be morally correct. Advertisements and job descriptions need to be honest in terms of what the job involves, to avoid misleading candidates. It also means that all candidates need to be treated equally and fairly, for example asking all candidates to carry out the same assessment activities and answer the same questions at interview. This should allow those in charge of the recruitment process to take an objective view of all of the candidates. The interviewers also need to be chosen carefully. There should be no personal connection between the interviewer and interviewee, that is, family or friends. If a panel is used, it should be a balance of men and women from different ethnic backgrounds.

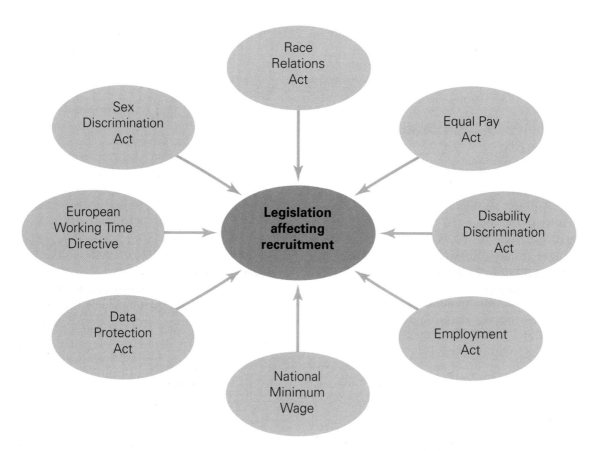

**Figure 13.2** Legislation affecting recruitment

# The Sainsbury's promise for online recruitment

Like many large organisations, UK retailer Sainsbury's uses its website as a major source of recruitment for a wide range of job vacancies, both within its stores and for support functions such as IT, finance and marketing. The company's online recruitment process requires applicants to provide a great deal of information about themselves, including their name and address, date of birth, national insurance number, qualifications and employment history. This information is stored for a number of reasons, including:

- To process applications for job vacancies
- To consider applicants for alternative positions
- To make up personnel records for applicants who are successful.

However, the company's recruitment privacy policy states that all information given by applicants is stored with 'the utmost care and security' and claims that it will not be used for any purposes for which candidates have not consented and will only be stored for a limited time in the case of unsuccessful candidates.

Source: www2.sainsburys.co.uk/aboutus/recruitment

## Questions

a) Identify the legislation that requires Sainsbury's to ensure that information supplied by job applicants is managed securely.

b) Explain two other reasons why Sainsbury's needs to handle the information provided by job applicants carefully.

# Key terms

**Direct discrimination** This occurs when a person receives unfavourable treatment as a direct result of factors that are unrelated to their ability to carry out a job, such as their sex, race or age

**Equal opportunities legislation** Laws designed to eliminate sex, racial, age and other types of discrimination in all aspects of employment, including recruitment and selection

**Ethical behaviour** Doing what is believed to be morally correct, rather than simply operating within the law

**EU legislation** Laws passed by the parliament of the European Union that take precedence over any national legislation that may exist in the member states

**Indirect discrimination** This occurs when the rules, regulations or procedures that exist within an organisation have a discriminating effect on certain groups

**Harassment** Making derogatory comments or remarks, either directly to individuals or about them to others, on the basis of their gender, race or disability

**National minimum wage** The legal right to nearly all UK workers aged 16 or over to a minimum rate of pay, which is based on the recommendations of the Low Pay Commission

**Victimisation** When a person is treated less favourably as a result of complaining about discrimination or harassment

**Re-cap questions**

1   Briefly describe two ways in which the existence of equal opportunities legislation affects the recruitment and selection process.

2   Outline two benefits for firms from ensuring that they adhere to equal opportunities legislation when they recruit new employees.

3   Explain, using examples, the difference between direct and indirect discrimination.

4   Using examples, explain what is meant by a) harassment and b) victimisation in the recruitment process.

5   Briefly explain how the existence of the following legislation affects a firm's recruitment:

  • The Sex Discrimination Act

  • The Race Relations Act

  • The Equal Pay Act

  • The Disability Discrimination Act

6   What is the purpose of the European Working Time Directive?

7   Outline three provisions introduced by the Employment Act of 2002.

8   The national minimum wage is only applicable to workers in full-time, permanent contracts – true or false?

9   Describe two ways in which the Data Protection Act affects firms' recruitment procedures.

10  Suggest two steps a firm could take to try and make its recruitment procedures more ethical.

## Grading tips

**P2** Explain the impact of the legal and regulatory framework on recruitment and selection activities

A good way of approaching this is to imagine that you are creating a leaflet or short handbook for those involved with the recruitment and selection process within an organisation. You should aim to provide a concise but sufficiently detailed explanation of the key legal and ethical issues that recruiters need to consider.

See p 275 for suggestions for Assignments for Unit 13.

# Part 3: Key recruitment documentation

The documentation used in the recruitment process has a major influence on the effectiveness of the recruitment and selection process. There are a number of key documents that will have to be drawn up if the vacancy involves a new job, or reviewed and possibly revised if the vacancy relates to an existing job. This is to try and ensure that they are up to date and reflect the current requirements of the job role. The two key documents that need to be drawn up when the vacancy is first identified are a **job description** and a **person specification**.

## Job descriptions

A job description does more that simply describing a particular job. This document sets out the overall purpose of the job and identifies the main tasks, duties and responsibilities that are involved. Every job role within the business needs to have its own, up-to-date job description. The precise format of the document will change from business to business, but a standard job description includes the following sections:

- **The job title** – this needs to give a clear indication of what the job involves.
- **The location of the job** and the department where it is situated – indicating where the job fits into the organisational structure.
- **Broad terms** – providing a brief outline of what the job involves, in terms of key tasks and duties.
- **Responsible to whom** – this identifies any supervisors or managers that the job holder will report to.
- **Responsibilities** – this identifies any staff or resources that the job holder will be in charge of.
- **Scope of the post** – this gives an indication of the level of authority attached to the job role.
- **Education and qualifications** – details of any experience or minimum academic or professional qualifications required, as stated in the job's person specification (see below).
- **Name of the compiler and the approver** – this refers to the members of staff who wrote the job description and agreed to the final draft.
- **Date of issue** – this states when the job description was written, or last updated.

## Person specifications

The purpose of this document is to set out the characteristics required by the job holder in order to perform the job's duties effectively. The person specification is particularly important during the selection stage, when it can be used to assess the extent to which the various candidates meet its requirements. Again, the exact format of this document will vary from business to business. However, a standard person specification will include at least some of the following points:

- **Job title and reference number** – this makes it easier to link the document to the relevant job description and any applications.
- **Location in management line** – this shows how the position fits into the organisational structure, who the job holder is responsible to and who they are responsible for.
- **Attainments and qualifications** – these give an indication of prior learning in both an academic or professional sense. Certain professional qualifications may be necessary, such as in teaching or medicine. In other situations, higher-level qualifications, such as a master's degree or a first-aid qualification, may be desirable, but not necessary to do the job.
- **Previous experience** – this may be important, especially if the company does not have the time or the resources to offer extensive training to the newly recruited employee. It may also be used to bring in staff with new ideas or approaches to work.
- **General intelligence** – this refers to basic level of ability in numeracy, IT and English language skills.
- **Attributes or special aptitudes** – this refers to personality characteristics or specific abilities, such as being outgoing, able to work well in a team, have good organisational skills or an ability to communicate effectively, perhaps in a foreign language.
- **Physical characteristics required** – this may be important in certain professions, such as the armed forces, acting or modelling.

- **Temperament and personality** – this may be particularly important for employees who have a lot of direct contact with customers, where they need to be friendly and polite at all times.
- **Hobbies and interests** – some hobbies may be particularly relevant and give a good indication of a person's ability to do a job.
- **Personal circumstances** – this could include the job holder having their own car, or being able to start employment immediately.

Many person specifications categorise skills and qualities as either essential or desirable. Anyone not possessing essential qualities would not be considered as suitable for the job. Desirable qualities are not absolutely necessary, but may be used to choose between candidates who possess all of the essential qualities.

| Job description | Person specification |
|---|---|
| • The job title<br>• The location of the job<br>• Broad terms<br>• Responsible to whom<br>• Responsibilities<br>• Scope of the post<br>• Education and qualifications<br>• Name of the compiler and the approver<br>• Date of issue | • Job title and reference number<br>• Location in management line<br>• Attainments and qualifications<br>• Previous experience<br>• General intelligence<br>• Attributes or special aptitudes<br>• Physical characteristics required<br>• Temperament and personality<br>• Hobbies and interests<br>• Personal circumstances |

**Figure 13.3** Comparing the contents of a job description and person specification

## Application documentation

These are the documents that are requested by the employer and completed by those applying for a job vacancy. The documents used are **letters of application**, **application forms** and the **curriculum vitae (CV)**.

## Letters of application

A business may decide to ask people interested in applying for a job to write a letter of application explaining the reasons why they feel they are suitable for the role and how they would go about carrying it out. Writing a letter, rather than filling in a form, allows the applicant to choose what information to include and focus on their strengths. It also can help to give the employer a clearer idea of the applicant's confidence, their ability to express themselves and their written communication skills, which may be important in some jobs. However, the lack of common format and possible differences in the detail or depth of information provided could make it difficult to compare candidates. This means that it is unlikely that they will be the only application documents used.

## Application forms

A carefully designed form can obtain all of the key information needed to sort through the applications for a vacancy and identify the most suitable, without having to waste time and resources processing irrelevant information. Sections requesting information, such as personal details, qualifications, current and previous employment, can be included, ensuring that such information is provided by all applicants and making it much easier to compare. Questions relating directly to the job role can also be included. Care must be taken, however, when designing application forms. There should be sufficient space for applicants to provide all the information required, without giving too much space, which may be intimidating. Forms should also not be too long or request sensitive information, as applicants may also be discouraged from filling them in.

## Curriculum vitae (CV)

This provides a factual summary of the personal details, qualifications, employment history and any other relevant information. CVs are often used to accompany letters of application because of this. There is no standard format for a CV so it may be difficult to compare individual CVs provided by different applicants and important information may be left out completely. It is also important that candidates update their CVs regularly and rewrite them to suit the requirements of different jobs.

## Recruitment and selection at Pret A Manger

Pret A Manger was founded in 1986 to make and sell sandwiches made from fresh, natural ingredients and free of preservatives, additives and chemicals. The company has grown steadily and now has around 225 shops, most of which are based within the UK, with 170 kitchens located nearby.

### Questions

a) Log on to the company's website – www.pret. com/jobs – and use the information provided to produce a job advertisement, job description and person specification for the post of a team member at one of its stores.

## Key terms

**Application form** A form designed by a business containing sections for personal details, qualifications, current and previous employment, and completed by people wishing to apply for a job vacancy

**Curriculum vitae (CV)** A factual summary of a person's personal details, qualifications, employment history and any other information that could be relevant when applying for a job

**Job description** A document that sets out the overall purpose of a job role, identifying the main tasks, duties and responsibilities that are involved

**Letter of application** A document used to apply for a job vacancy where the structure and content are usually decided by the applicant

**Person specification** A document that sets out the characteristics required by the job holder in order to perform the job's duties effectively, including qualifications, experience and general intelligence

**Re-cap questions**

1. Briefly explain why existing recruitment documentation should be reviewed regularly.

2. What is the purpose of a job description?

3. Identify and briefly describe the main sections that are typically included in a job description.

4. What is the purpose of a person specification?

5. Identify and briefly describe the main sections that are typically included in a person specification.

6. Briefly explain why some employers categorise the qualifications, skills and experience outlined on a person specification as either 'essential' or 'desirable'.

7. Explain one benefit and one drawback for a business of asking candidates to apply for a job vacancy by using a letter of application.

8. What is the purpose of a curriculum vitae?

9. Explain two reasons why many employers prefer candidates to complete application forms as part of the recruitment process.

10. Identify two factors that should be kept in mind when designing an application form for a job vacancy.

## Grading tips

**P3** Prepare the documents used in selection and recruitment activities

You need to choose a vacancy for which you are able to prepare the following documents:

- A job advertisement
- A job description
- A person specification

**M1** Compare the purposes of the different documents used in the selection and recruitment process of a given organisation

In addition to those identified above, you will also need to explain the different functions of any documents used during the selection process by your chosen organisation and compare how the information contained in these documents, once completed, is used by interviewers. These documents may include application forms, letters of application and CVs, as well as documents used to record candidates' answers or grade their performance during interviews or other assessments, such as test papers.

**D1** Evaluate the usefulness of the documents in the interview pack for a given organisation, in facilitating the interview process

You need to make judgements as to the usefulness of the documents you have provided. Try to provide examples of how the documents made the interview process more effective, how they helped interviewers to reach a decision, or how they could be changed and improved.

See p 275 for suggestions for Assignments for Unit 13.

# Part 4: Interviewing and selection

Strictly speaking, recruitment covers all of the activities involved in attracting candidates to apply for a job vacancy. Once this has been done, the process of selecting and appointing the most appropriate applicant or applicants has to begin. The managers and other employees responsible for recruitment and selection need to make a number of decisions as to how this selection should be made. For most businesses, the **interview** remains a key aspect of this process. However, a great deal of thought and work needs to occur beforehand in order to ensure that, when interviews do take place, they are effective in choosing the most suitable candidate for the job. The interview must provide sufficient information to make the selection decision, and those involved in the process need to be notified in an appropriate way.

## Pre-interview

There are a number of steps that have to be taken by the employer before interviews to fill job vacancies can take place. Firstly, all of the applications received by the deadline indicated in the job advertisement now need to be processed. The recruitment team has to carefully consider the information contained in them before deciding which of the applicants should proceed to the next stage.

## Application packs and information for candidates

The packs sent out to those people who wish to apply for a job vacancy often contain a great deal of information, in addition to the application form itself. For example, they are likely to contain instructions about how to complete the forms correctly, the deadline and the address to which they should be returned. There are also likely to be details given regarding the various stages of the recruitment process, what candidates can expect to happen if they are successful in passing from one stage to another and the time scale involved. The employer may also wish to take the opportunity to provide some general information on the business, its mission and the market or markets in which it operates. **Application packs** can provide

a good opportunity to communicate with the applicants, so they have a better understanding of the business and what it does. This can help to reduce the likelihood that candidates withdraw from the recruitment and selection process once they have applied, because they decide that they are no longer interested in working for the business.

## Selection criteria for shortlisting

The applications that are received by a business in relation to a job vacancy need to be sorted into those candidates that are suitable for further investigation and those that are not – a process known as **shortlisting**. In order to make this selection process as fair as possible, a set of criteria should be established beforehand and applied to each application received. The contents of the person specification drawn up when the vacancy is first identified usually act as the criteria for shortlisting. Each individual application can be compared to the qualifications, experience and other abilities needed to carry out the job role effectively. Those candidates that are the closest matches to the 'ideal' job holder, according to the person specification, are then chosen to proceed to the next stage. Adopting a consistent approach and keeping a written record of the selection criteria used for shortlisting should make the recruitment process more effective. It should also make it easier to justify any decisions made, should unsuccessful applicants challenge such decisions.

## References

A **reference** is a written account given by someone on the character of a job applicant and their suitability for the role. They are usually regarded as a very important element within the recruitment process and can have a significant influence on the outcome.

The person writing the reference can be a current or former employer, a school teacher or college principal. Guidance is usually given in the application instructions for a vacancy regarding the type of referee that should be chosen. Friends or family members are often not accepted as it may be felt that they are unlikely to make an independent and objective statement. Referees may be asked to make a general statement or to give specific details on areas such as competency in carrying out certain tasks or duties, time-keeping, sickness record and general attitude.

In some cases, references may be requested early in the recruitment process and before any interviews take place. This could be the case, for example, in situations where it is necessary to establish a candidate's suitability to work with groups that are particularly vulnerable, such as young children, the elderly or those with mental health problems. However, many employers do not request references until towards the end of the selection process when the decision as to who to appoint has been made. This reduces the level of paperwork and, therefore, the amount of time and resources spent on processing candidates' references. It can also avoid any problems that may result if a candidate's existing employer discovers he or she is looking for work elsewhere.

It is important that a written reference contains information that is factual and does not give an unfavourable impression of the candidate. In addition to having a significant influence, potentially, on the outcome of the recruitment process, job applicants have a right to see any reference written about them under the Data Protection Act. False or misleading comments could result in legal action and the requirement to pay compensation.

# Interviews

An interview is the process of obtaining information, either face-to-face or by telephone, for a specific purpose – in this case, in order to assess the suitability of candidates for a job vacancy. Interviews are a commonly used method of selection by employers. Holding interviews gives both the employer and potential employee the chance to question each other in a more flexible and detailed way.

A decision will need to be taken by the recruitment team as to what format the interviews for a job vacancy should take. There are a number of possibilities, including group interviews, individual interviews, team interviews, **multi-stage interviews**, **panel interviews** and telephone interviews.

## Group interviews

Group interviews involve the gathering together of a number of people for interview at the same time. The interviewees may be asked questions or invited to ask them, participate in group tasks and watch a presentation on the company, either on film or delivered by key staff, such as the human-resources manager. Group interviews are often held when a business is recruiting a relatively large number of people to carry out the same job role, such as when a retailer takes on temporary sales assistants in the autumn to work in the pre-Christmas and January sales period. They are also sometimes used at the beginning of the selection process when a large number of candidates have been shortlisted. However, it may be difficult to assess the suitability of some individuals in a group situation. It may also be an inappropriate method if the job role does not require the ability to work well as part of a group.

## Individual interviews

Individual interviews involve a one-to-one meeting between a job candidate and a member of the recruitment team. Candidates are expected to answer a number of questions relating to a range of topics, including their work experience, their knowledge of the business and their reasons for being interested in the job vacancy. They may also be asked to discuss aspects of their personal lives where they demonstrated a particular character trait, such as leadership, determination or the ability to solve a problem. If the interviewer is suitably skilled, the candidate can be encouraged to relax and perform to the best of their ability. However, there is a high risk that only using one interviewer may lead to **bias**, either against or in favour of the candidate, for reasons that are unlikely to have anything to do with their ability to perform the job.

## Team interviews

This involves using a group of people to interview the candidates. Each member of the group is likely to come from a different area of the organisation and their questions will focus on a particular aspect of the job. For example, an interview team for the post of a Business Studies teacher at a sixth-form college might consist of the head of department, asking questions on subject knowledge and teaching technique, the faculty head, who might be interested in areas such as classroom discipline and pastoral care, and the college principal, who might concentrate on finding out about the candidates' views on career progression. This type of interview can be very effective as each interviewer may be interested in finding out about different skills and abilities and it is also less

An individual interview

likely that any resulting decisions will be biased. However, using a number of people to conduct every interview is expensive, in terms of time, and likely to disrupt the normal work routine.

## Panel interviews

This type of interview is very similar to a team interview, where a group of staff representing the employer (and usually chaired by a senior manager) interviews candidates individually.

A team or panel interview

## Telephone interviews

Rather than meeting candidates face-to-face, interviewers may choose to question them over the telephone, at a time that is mutually convenient to both parties. This may be less intimidating for the candidates involved but makes it impossible to assess them by studying **body language** or reactions to certain situations. Because of this, they are often used at the early stages of the selection process. A range of standard questions are asked, so that any applicants who are clearly unsuitable can be immediately dismissed. This approach also means that less experienced interviewers can be used, speeding up the process.

## Multi-stage interviews

This involves the candidates having to complete a series of interviews. It may be the case that a number of applicants are rejected after each stage has been completed, with the successful candidates moving on to the next, and possibly harder stage. Interviewing in this way is time consuming and involves a high degree of inconvenience for both sides. However, it means that candidates can be exposed to different situations and environments, creating a more rounded picture of them. It also creates more opportunities for the interviewers to reflect on and discuss individual performance.

## Tasks and tests

In addition to interviews, candidates may also be asked to carry out one or more tasks or tests in order to assess their ability and suitability. These tests may be written, paper based or online, or may require the candidates to participate in role plays or simulations.

These might include:

- **Occupational preference tests** – these tests focus on skills that are required by a particular job role. For example, candidates applying for the role of a customer-service assistant may be presented with a number of different scenarios and asked to deal with them appropriately.
- **Attainment tests** – these tests measure the level at which candidates are able to perform a particular skill or ability, for example the speed of candidates' word-processing skills or the number of items that can be assembled within a given time limit.

- **Aptitude tests** – these tests assess candidates' skill levels in a number of general areas, such as numerical, verbal and non-verbal reasoning. Such skills may be required at a particular level in order to carry out certain job roles effectively.
- **Psychometric tests** – these tests are designed to assess people's personality type and its suitability for different types of career. For example, people applying for management positions would need to be confident and outgoing, with good leadership, communication and organisational skills and an ability to handle stress. The tests are designed to assess candidates using their responses to a series of multiple-choice questions, completed either on paper or online.

In addition to the above points, there are a number of other issues that need to be considered before a job interview takes place.

- **Use of specialists during the interview** – the experience and qualities of the interviewers are vitally important in ensuring that the correct candidates are chosen. Interviewers may be human-resource specialists, with an in-depth knowledge of interviewing techniques and employment law. Alternatively, the interviewer or interviewers may be specialists in the area of the job vacancy, with a clear idea of the skills and abilities that the 'ideal' candidates should possess.
- **Assessment and interview questions** – careful thought needs to be put into the type of assessment activities and interview questions that will be used before the selection process begins. The more activities and questions involved, the longer and more costly the process, so it is essential that both the activities and questions are relevant and relate to the job in question. However, the process also needs to be sufficiently thorough to develop a detailed picture of the candidates. The assessment activities and interview questions need to be designed and screened carefully to make sure that they are fair and do not discriminate against certain groups. In order to ensure fairness, many employers choose to ask the same questions of every candidate.

- **Procedure for informing candidates of interview decisions** – it is important to decide on the procedure for informing candidates of the results of the interviews before the process actually begins. This means that candidates can have a clear picture of how long they will need to wait before they are made aware of the outcome, so that they can plan appropriately.

## The interview

Interviewing candidates is a crucial part of the recruitment and selection process. Effective interview technique requires good communication skills from both the interviewer and the interviewee, both in terms of what is said and how it is said. An intimidating interviewer may make candidates nervous about expressing their ideas, making it difficult to judge their true potential. On the other hand, employers are unlikely to choose candidates who appear to be uninterested, aggressive or under-prepared.

From the employer's viewpoint, a number of points should be considered to try to ensure that the interview process is fair on all the candidates involved and effective in choosing the most appropriate one to fill the vacancy. These are interview protocol, fairness and confidentiality, creating an effective interview environment, agreed questions, checking of personal information and the interview checklist.

## Interview protocol

Interview protocol refers to the generally accepted standards of behaviour expected from both sides during the interview process. For example, candidates would be expected to arrive in good time for the interview and dress in a manner that is suitable for the job in question – in many cases, formal, rather than casual, dress is expected, but in all cases candidates should present a clean and well-groomed appearance. The employer should ensure that candidates have somewhere comfortable to wait, with access to refreshment and toilet facilities, particularly if the process is likely to take some time. The interview format and procedures such as health and safety should also be outlined and the candidates should be notified of any unforeseen changes as quickly as possible.

| What to do | What not to do |
|---|---|
| 1. Dress smartly, be keen and attentive, and speak clearly and confidently – the interviewer's opinion of you is formed on how you look, act and sound as well as what you say | 1. Don't be late |
| | 2. Don't swear or use slang words |
| | 3. Don't slouch in your seat or do anything else that makes you look uninterested |
| 2. Read over the contents of the person specification and your CV/application form, and think about what type of questions they will ask you | 4. Don't smoke |
| | 5. Don't lie – the interviewer may see through you, and you may be dismissed if you are found out, even if you get the job |
| 3. Prepare answers for the most likely questions, such as 'Why do you want this job?', 'What are your main strengths/weaknesses?' | 6. Don't let your nerves show too much. A few nerves are normal but extreme nerves will affect your performance |
| 4. Turn off your mobile, treat the interviewers respectfully and give them your full attention | 7. Don't be arrogant and assume you've got the job |
| 5. Think carefully and make sure you understand the question before you answer – ask for the question to be repeated if you didn't hear or understand | 8. Don't read from notes or your CV – make sure that you are able to discuss your own history and are able to talk about it unprompted |
| 6. Quote examples of when you've demonstrated the skills required by the job | 9. Don't criticise former employers or colleagues, as this is likely to create an impression of impatience or intolerance |
| 7. Be positive about yourself and your experiences | 10. Don't argue with the interviewer, no matter what is said, and try to remain positive at all times |
| 8. Keep your answers focused on what you can do for the employer, not what they can do for you | |
| 9. Prepare some questions to ask at the end – use it as an opportunity to find out more about the role and the company | |
| 10. Get feedback on your performance, whether you were successful or not, to help improve performance in future interviews | |

**Source: directgov**

**Figure 13.4** Advice for interviewees – ten top tips

## The importance of fairness and confidentiality

Any information supplied to a business by those applying for job vacancies should be treated in a fair and confidential manner. This means that all applications should be considered against the same criteria, stored securely and seen only by those directly involved in the recruitment process. In some cases, firms may choose to continue to hold information on at least some of the unsuccessful candidates, once the current recruitment process has finished, particularly if it intends to recruit for similar job positions in the future. Firms have a legal obligation to obtain the permission of the candidates in order to do this, or else the information should be destroyed.

## Creating an effective interview environment

The kind of environment chosen for the interview will depend to some extent on the activities the candidates will be required to complete. The room or space chosen needs to be of an appropriate size and suitably equipped so that these activities can take place. For example, if the candidates are expected to deliver a presentation as part of the interview, equipment such as flip charts, computers and screens need to be tested beforehand and put in place. The interview environment should also be free of distractions and interruptions, such as constantly ringing telephones, and be situated away from busy roads or noisy corridors.

## Agreed questions

A common approach to interviewing is to ask all candidates the same set of questions. This is one way of attempting to ensure that a firm's recruitment process is fair and treats everyone equally. However, in order to be effective and get the most out of candidates, these questions need to be considered carefully in advance and agreed by the interviewer or interviewers, with possible input from other members of the recruitment team. Interview questions can be designed in such a way as to be flexible and allow candidates to give more information and develop points where necessary.

## Checking of personal information

Personal information includes details such as the candidate's name, address and other contact details, national insurance number, age and date of birth. For legal and other reasons, it is important to check that the information supplied by candidates on application forms or CVs is accurate. For example, delays in contacting candidates regarding the outcome of an interview decision may result if the wrong address or telephone number is supplied. The beginning or end of the interview might be used, therefore, to check these details and ensure that they are accurate.

## Interview checklist

This consists of a list of the main areas or topics that the interviewer wishes to cover during the interview. It is particularly useful for conducting interviews where questions have not been agreed in advance. Even if this is the case, a checklist provides a plan of how the questioning is to take place to ensure that the interview runs smoothly and logically and that nothing is left out. A checklist can also act as an aide memoire, prompting the interviewer (or the chair of a panel) to greet the candidates, explain the format and tell them when they will be informed of the outcome.

An interview checklist is also useful in helping candidates to cover the key areas that they believe support their application for the job vacancy. It can also prompt them to behave confidently and to ask questions about the role and the business, helping to create a more favourable impression.

## Controlling the interview

Interviewing tends to be relatively time consuming, using up employees and resources that have usually been taken away from their usual tasks and duties. This means that, once the amount of time required to interview candidates has been agreed, this is controlled effectively. An interview that over-runs increases disruption and adds to the costs of the recruitment process. It may also mean that there is less time to spend interviewing other candidates, which could lead to accusations of unfair treatment. Interviewers need to be skilled in managing their time effectively, using questioning techniques that encourage answers that are sufficiently detailed but also relatively concise. Where team or panel interviews are held, it is the responsibility of the chairperson to ensure that each interviewer is given adequate time to put their questions to candidates within the overall time scale.

Candidates should also prepare adequately beforehand so that they remain controlled during the interview. This reduces the chances of becoming overly nervous and panicking and can help them to remain focused and relaxed and provide answers that are considered and appropriate.

## Communicating the decision to candidates

Candidates also need to be informed about the timing of the announcement of the outcome of the interview. Many will have several job interviews to attend over a relatively short space of time. It is in the interests of both sides, therefore, to reach a decision and make it known as quickly as possible, to avoid the possibility that candidates may turn down other offers or take up employment elsewhere. Although, it may not be possible to reach a decision quickly, candidates should be given some indication as to when the decision will be made, and informed if this changes at any point.

## Communication and listening skills

An interview is an example of two-way communication. Both the interviewer and the candidate need to be able to listen carefully, ask questions that are clear and unambiguous and make responses that are comprehensive and informative. The interviewee should concentrate fully and consider the meaning of each question carefully, resisting the temptation to merely repeat responses that have been practised beforehand. They should also feel confident enough to ask for questions to be repeated, if they have not been properly heard, or clarified if their meaning is not clear. The interviewer must also listen carefully to the responses made, checking and developing points to get as full a picture of the candidate as possible.

## Body language

**Body language** is a form of non-verbal communication, made up of the expressions and gestures made by people, either consciously or subconsciously. Body language plays an important role when people interact, particularly when people are forming initial impressions about each other, as is likely to be the case in an interview situation. For example, a candidate's fidgeting and failure to make eye contact could be interpreted by the interviewer as a lack of confidence or even that he or she is not telling the truth. Body posture is also important – crossed arms, for instance, give the impression of being defensive, whereas slouching in a chair might suggest a general lack of interest.

Examples of good and bad body language

The interviewer also needs to be aware of his or her body language, as this can be off-putting to the candidate, making them under-perform.

## Questioning techniques

The primary task of the interviewer (or interviewing team or panel) is to question the interview candidates and assess their suitability for the job vacancy. The interview environment is likely to be very different to the workplace and the amount of time available to question candidates is also likely to be limited. This means that the questioning techniques used during the interview need to be effective in creating a realistic picture of how each candidate would perform, if appointed. Using a variety of different questioning techniques is usually the best way of obtaining all the information needed, so this needs to be carefully planned beforehand.

Commonly used techniques include:

- **Closed questions** – these require candidates to give short, factual answers, usually from a limited range of choices. For example, 'Where did you go to college?', 'How many years did you work in your previous job?'
- **Open questions** – these are used to acquire more detailed answers from candidates. They may be used to get candidates to describe how they coped with a particular challenge or would tackle certain aspects of the job.

## Barriers to communication

There are a number of problems or barriers that may be present during the interview that can reduce the effectiveness of the process. Candidates

may struggle to express themselves clearly, due to nerves or poor verbal communication skills. Interviewers' assessment of candidates may be influenced – either positively or negatively – by factors that have little or nothing to do with their ability to carry out a job, which may include their appearance, their gender, their social or ethnic background. A number of measures can be used to attempt to reduce **bias** and discrimination, such as the use of panel interviews and common questions but, ultimately, this will depend on the skills and professionalism of the recruitment team.

## Analysing and summarising

Analysis involves breaking events down, examining the reasons behind them and the possible consequences leading from them. The interviewer also needs to be able to analyse the information provided by each candidate while the interview is actually taking place, in order to gain a good understanding of them and ask more questions where necessary. It is also helpful if the interviewer recounts and summarises the points made on a regular basis during the interview. This gives the candidate the opportunity to confirm the interviewer's view of what has been said or to clarify or correct any areas of misunderstanding.

## Decision criteria and documentation

The responses given by each candidate are used to create an overall impression of their suitability to carry out the vacant job. In some cases, interviewers may choose between candidates purely on the basis of instinct but this can introduce bias into the process. Agreeing and using a common set of decision criteria with all candidates helps to make the process fair and equal. The criteria used to assess suitability are usually drawn from the skills and abilities outlined in the person specification for the job, along with general characteristics, such as confidence or ability to show initiative. Candidates are scored or graded against the different criteria and the job offer is made to the individual with the best score. The documents used to record these decisions can then be stored and referred to at a later date. This may be necessary in the case of multi-stage interviews or if any unsuccessful candidates challenge the decision.

## Post interview

Once the interviews for a job vacancy have taken place, the recruitment team has to decide who to appoint and then inform everyone involved of the decision.

## Informing candidates

Once the decision has been made as to who to appoint to the job, the next step is to communicate the decision to all of the candidates involved. Contact with both successful and unsuccessful candidates is important, and the content of any communication should be considered carefully. The job offer needs to be made to the successful candidate quickly, otherwise they may accept an offer from an alternative employer (see below). This will mean that at least part of the recruitment and selection process will have to be repeated, wasting time and increasing costs. Constructive feedback should also be passed on to unsuccessful candidates, to help them to improve their performance at future interviews.

| Decision criteria | Grades | | | |
|---|---|---|---|---|
| | **Excellent** | **Good** | **Satisfactory** | **Weak** |
| **Relevant qualifications** | | | | |
| **Industry experience** | | | | |
| **Communication skills** | | | | |
| **Body language** | | | | |
| **Personal interests** | | | | |

**Figure 13.5** A typical interview evaluation checklist

# Making a job offer

Informing candidates of the outcome of the interview process needs to be carried out carefully. Many employers attempt to make contact with the person that has been chosen to see whether they will actually take up the job offer, before informing the other candidates that they have not been successful. The reason for this is that, if the first choice candidate is no longer interested, the job offer can then be made to another suitable applicant. The job offer may be made by the employer on a verbal basis in the first instance, either face-to-face or over the telephone, in order to save time. Once the candidate has accepted the offer verbally, a more formal written (or non-verbal) offer can be made. The contents of this offer, usually made by letter, is likely to include some basic information relating to the job, such as the start date, salary and working hours, along with a request for the candidate to confirm their acceptance in writing. The employer may attach certain conditions to the candidate's appointment, such as the outcome of police or medical checks or the provision of suitable references from previous employers (see below). If this is the case, these conditions will also be contained in the written job offer.

# Expense claims

Offering to pay candidates' expenses for travel, accommodation and meals is important in helping to attract a wide field of candidates, especially if the business needs to recruit on a national or even international basis. Candidates need to be given clear information as to the process involved in claiming back expenses before they are incurred, as most businesses require evidence, such as receipts, to be provided with any claims submitted.

# Candidates' feedback

Feedback from candidates to the firm can also be useful in helping to review the recruitment process, in order to make it fairer and more effective. They may be asked by the employer to give their opinions informally or by completing a questionnaire. However, candidates may be less likely to give an objective view unless they are allowed to do so anonymously. They may be concerned, for example, that making criticisms or negative comments before the decision is announced may affect the outcome of the interview. Once the outcome is known, unsuccessful candidates may be overly critical or simply not bother to return any questionnaires supplied.

# Taking up and checking references

References are a very important part of the recruitment and selection process. They can help provide details of how candidates actually behave at work, in terms of both their competency and their attitude, both of which may be difficult to assess accurately away from the workplace in an interview room. In some situations, references are taken up before interview, in order to reject any candidates that are unlikely to be suitable. However, this can be relatively expensive and time consuming given that, at this stage, there are likely to be a number of candidates still involved in the process. Because of this, many employers do not take up references until the successful candidate has been chosen. The candidate may then be informed that the taking up of suitable references may be made a condition of the job offer. The reference, once received, has to be checked carefully to see if it contains any information suggesting that the candidate may be unsuitable. If this is the case, the job offer may be withdrawn and another candidate chosen.

# Police and medical checks

A number of jobs, including those involving working with children or other vulnerable groups, require candidates to undergo a police check. In the UK, this involves the employer contacting the Criminal Records Bureau (CRB) to undertake a search to see whether the candidate has a police record which could mean that they are unsuitable for the position.

Some job roles also require candidates to undergo a medical or health check. For example, applicants for the fire services are required to complete a questionnaire on medical history and undergo an examination with the Fire and Rescue Service doctor, where they receive a number of tests, including hearing, lung function and physical stamina. In other situations, the medical may be carried out by the candidate's doctor and the results passed on to the employer. In either case, the candidate's permission must be obtained and they must be informed about the reasons for and the results of the examination. Care must be taken to comply with any relevant legislation, including the Disability Discrimination Act, the Access to Medical Records Act and the Data Protection Act.

## Rejecting unsuccessful candidates

Once a firm has received at least a verbal acceptance of a job offer from the preferred candidate, it can go about informing the others that their applications have not been successful. It is important that this is done as quickly as possible and in the correct manner. Any feedback given to unsuccessful candidates should be based on documented evidence of their performance during the interview and any other assessments. Giving constructive feedback can help candidates to understand the decision, reducing the chances of any claims of unfair treatment or discrimination and helping them to improve their performance at future interviews. Treating candidates fairly at this stage can help to create or maintain a positive image of the firm, encouraging people to apply for other job positions that may become vacant in the future.

## Key terms

**Application pack** The information and documents sent out to people interested in applying for a job vacancy, including the application form and instructions on how to complete the application process

**Bias** This occurs when someone gives favourable or unfavourable treatment to another person because of factors that are not related to their ability or performance, such as their gender, nationality or race

**Body language** A form of non-verbal communication, made up of the expressions and gestures made by people, either consciously or subconsciously

**Closed questioning** Where interviewees are required to give short, factual answers, usually from a limited range of choices

**Interview** The process of obtaining information, either face-to-face or by telephone, for a specific purpose – in this case, in order to assess the suitability of candidates for a job vacancy

**Multi-stage interview** A method of job selection where candidates are required to complete a series of interviews, with a number of applicants being rejected after each stage, and the successful candidates moving on to the next, and possibly harder stage

**Panel interview** Where a group of staff representing the employer (and usually chaired by a senior manager) interview candidates for a job vacancy individually

**References** This is a written account given by someone on the character of a job applicant and their suitability for the role

**Short listing** This is the process of sorting applications received by a business in relation to a job vacancy into the candidates that are suitable for further investigation and those that are not

# Re-cap questions

1. Identify two pieces of information often included in an application pack for a job vacancy, other than the application form itself.

2. Briefly explain what the process of shortlisting involves.

3. What is the purpose of a reference?

4. Explain two reasons why an employer may decide to take up references after, rather than before, an interview takes place.

5. What is the purpose of carrying out an interview?

6. What is the difference between a group interview and a team interview?

7. Using examples, explain the difference between an open question and a closed question.

8. Explain, using examples, how the body language of both the interviewer and interviewee can affect the outcome of an interview.

9. Identify and briefly describe two different tests that might be used to assess candidates' suitability for a job vacancy.

10. Give two reasons why many firms choose to provide unsuccessful candidates with interview feedback.

# Grading tips

 **P4** Plan to take part in a selection interview.

You need to prepare for the role of either the interviewer or the job applicant in a mock interview. You must ensure that you have prepared all the necessary documentation and you can supply this to the assessor who observes your role play for P5. For example, if you are playing the role of job applicant, you should ensure that you have completed an application form, or written a letter of application and produced an up-to-date CV, based on the job advertisement, job description and person specification provided. Pay careful attention to the spelling and presentation used in your documents.

**M2** Analyse your contribution to the selection process in a given situation.

The quality of your preparation for and participation in your mock interview will be assessed. It will help to think about what your assessor will be looking for, such as good organisation, effective questions, considered responses, professional appearance and behaviour.

**D2** Evaluate your experience of planning and participating in the recruitment and selection process.

You need to consider the strengths and weaknesses of the documentation that you have prepared and your contribution to the role play. For example, try to identify what you think you did well and what you could have improved on. You may be asked to produce a written analysis or be interviewed by your assessor who will write a witness statement as evidence.

|  **P5** Take part in a selection interview. | | |
|---|---|---|
| You need to take part in a mock interview, playing the role either of the interviewer or the job applicant, based on the documents that you have prepared for P4. Your performance will be observed and form the basis for your assessment, along with the documentation produced. You may also choose to swap roles with your partner to improve your understanding of the interview process, but this is not necessary to achieve this criterion. | | |

## Assignments for Unit 13

### Assignment One

You work as a consultant for Business Link and have been asked to produce some resources to help new businesses to improve their recruitment and selection procedures.

**Note** – read through the task, the relevant criteria and the assignment advice on pages 253 and 258 before choosing your organisations. You must make sure that you can obtain information on their procedures for recruiting internally and externally.

**Criteria covered** – P1, P2

**Tasks**

1. Select two organisations and describe how they plan recruitment using internal and external sources. In each case, explain how the vacancy occurred and describe the factors that influenced the organisations to recruit. For external recruitment in particular, look at the time and cost implications, as well as the choice of media used. (P1)
2. Produce a leaflet or factsheet for those involved in the recruitment and selection process in business organisations. This should identify the legal and regulatory framework affecting recruitment and selection, explaining its impact on the activities involved in the process. (P2)

### Assignment Two

Your next task is to assist a business in the process of recruiting and selecting a suitable candidate to fill a job vacancy. This will involve preparing the necessary documentation for recruiting candidates to an appropriate standard. It will also involve you preparing and participating in a mock interview, either as the interviewer or the interviewee, in order to demonstrate good technique.

**Note** – read through the task, the relevant criteria and the assignment advice on pages 263 and 274 before choosing your organisations.

**Criteria covered** – P3 P4 P5 M1 D1 D2

**Tasks**

1. Choose a job vacancy within an organisation and prepare an interview pack. This will contain the following documents:
   a) A job advertisement
   b) A job description
   c) A person specification.
   Make sure that you use a suitable layout, appropriate language and that all the necessary information is included (P3).
2. Write a comparison of the different documents used in the recruitment and selection process of your chosen organisation. (M1)
3. Produce an evaluation of the documents in the interview pack for your chosen organisation. (D1)
4. Plan to take part in a mock interview, either as the interviewee or the interviewer. Ensure that you have prepared all of the necessary documentation before the interview takes place and have copies ready for anyone observing you in Task 5. (P4)
5. Take part in a mock interview, either as the interviewee or the interviewer. The interview should be based on the documents prepared in Task 4. (P5)

6. Produce an analysis of your contribution to the selection process prepared for in Task 4 and carried out in Task 5, examining how well you performed and identifying any particular strengths and weaknesses. (M2)

7. Prepare an evaluation of your experience of planning and participating in the recruitment and selection process in Tasks 4 and 5. This can be in the form of a written statement, an interview or a presentation. It should include the key areas in which you feel you did well, giving evidence to justify this. You should also suggest how your performance could have been improved. (D2)

# Part I: The initial business idea

There are many reasons why people decide to start their own business. Some people believe that owning a business will earn them a fortune; others believe it will give them more flexibility and control over their lives. Many people set up businesses so that they can pursue a hobby or interest and generate an income at the same time. The term **entrepreneur** is often used to describe people who have a flair for spotting opportunities and are prepared to take risks in order to make a business succeed.

## Criteria

Often people begin new businesses without thinking through the idea. Although examining a start-up proposal, using a set of appropriate criteria, cannot guarantee business success, it can reduce the risk of failure. It can identify problems that need to be tackled, or may simply show that the chance of succeeding is too slim. Being able to produce evidence to justify sales and profit forecasts can also be useful in attracting investment or convincing banks to lend.

## The type of business

One of the first decisions that needs to be taken concerns the type of business that is going to be set up. The choice is between setting up a brand-new business, buying an existing business and buying a **franchise**.

## Setting up a brand-new business

This involves starting from scratch, either with a completely new idea or with a way of producing an existing good or service more cheaply or in some other way better than those already on the market. This option is likely to take time and involve a huge amount of work. A great deal of market research needs to be done, even before the business can be launched. This is needed to assess whether there would be sufficient interest or whether customers are already satisfied and could not be tempted to change their current behaviour. Initial research is also required to find out about customer tastes and requirements, allowing the good or service to be able to satisfy them successfully. Once the business is launched, further research will need to be conducted regularly to test customer reactions, identify and resolve any problems and come up with ways of developing the business further.

Further effort is needed to promote a brand-new business so that customers become aware of it and are attracted to it. This option involves most risk, incurring significant costs that will not be recouped if the business fails to become established. If the business is successful, however, this option has the potential to generate a great deal of personal satisfaction, as well as significant profits.

## Buying an existing business

The option of taking over an existing business has a number of benefits. As it is already established, there will be no need to spend time finding premises and equipment, obtaining permits and licences or recruiting staff. This means that the business should begin to generate revenues (and, hopefully, profits) immediately. Figures on past and present performance should be available and can be used to indicate likely future success. The business will already have an established reputation and customer base, avoiding the need to spend money raising customer awareness. It may also have an established credit record, making it easier to obtain loans and obtain credit from suppliers.

However, this reputation may be linked to the previous owner, and customer loyalty may disappear as soon as the sale has gone through. The reasons why the business has been put up for sale also need to be established. The reasons may not necessarily give cause for concern; for example, the owners may want to retire. However, it may be because of high stress or declining profits. Whatever the reason, financial details, such as past profits, future sales forecasts, the value of assets or existing debts, are likely to be presented in a way that puts the business in the most attractive light. Financial accounts need to be checked carefully, therefore, before any decisions are taken.

# Buying a franchise

This option involves one business (known as a **franchisee**) buying the right to sell the products of another business (known as the **franchisor**) and use its name, logos and methods of trading. In order to do this, the franchisee has to pay an initial purchase fee and then a share of any sales turnover generated in future. The size of the purchase fee will depend on a number of factors, such as expected levels of turnover and profits, the amount of support received and whether the franchisee will have exclusive rights to sell in a particular area. Many well-known businesses, including The Body Shop and McDonald's, operate on this basis.

There are many advantages for a new business in buying a franchise. In most cases, the franchisee gets the opportunity to sell a product that is already established in the market. The owners of the franchise have some control over how the business is run, but enjoy the support of a much larger organisation. Typically, this support includes benefiting from national marketing and promotional campaigns run by the franchisor, as well as providing supplies and help with staff training. These benefits mean that, in most cases, buying a franchise is less risky than setting up from scratch.

However, there are a number of potential drawbacks to operating as a franchise. The owners of a franchise have much less control than would be the case with an independent business. A proportion of any profits made must be paid to the franchisor, reducing the returns to the franchisee and the finance available for reinvestment in the business. The franchisor makes all of the decisions regarding product design, store layout, pricing and promotional strategies. The franchisee is also required to buy supplies from the franchisor, even if cheaper alternatives are available elsewhere, adding to operating costs. Despite paying what can be significant purchase fees, there are no guarantees that a franchise will be successful. The franchisor's idea may be new and, therefore, untried. Sales and profit forecasts may have been exaggerated in order to attract franchise buyers. In addition, bad publicity generated by the actions of the franchisor or another franchisee may well affect sales on a wider scale.

## Water Babies

Paul and Jess Thompson set up Water Babies in 2002. The inspiration for the business came from the couple's pleasure in teaching their own children to swim and their belief in the benefits of water exercise. Since then, it has grown into the world's biggest baby swimming company, teaching over 20,000 babies and children under four to swim every week. Lessons cost between £10.50 and £15.50. This premium price is justified by the levels of training given to instructors – 120 hours over ten days.

The company's expansion has been facilitated by selling franchises. There are now 27 operating across the UK. According to Paul Thompson, there are a number of advantages of buying a franchise over starting a new business from scratch. Two-thirds of Water Babies franchisees have succeeded in obtaining up to 75 per cent of the finance needed to buy their franchise. However, Thompson reckons that franchisees need to do their homework before signing any agreements. He suggests that they find out about the support that is in place, including correct documentation, a well-thought-out operating manual and the correct legal agreements.

**Source:** www.waterbabies.co.uk

### Questions

a) Is Water Babies a franchisee or a franchisor? Explain your answer.

b) Outline the key benefits and drawbacks for a new business taking out a Water Babies franchise.

## Aims for starting a business

Aims are the reasons why a business has been set up. Objectives are the specific goals that owners set out to achieve at some point in the future. Having aims and setting objectives are important at any stage of a business, but vital for a new firm, giving it a sense of direction and allowing it to measure and monitor progress. The specific aims and objectives vary considerably from business to business. Some owners may aim to generate a target level of profit by the end of the first year of trading; for others this may be an unrealistic target, with owners aiming to break even or simply survive during the first year.

For objectives to be effective, they need to be more than vague or general statements. They must be clearly expressed, relate to the business and take account of its circumstances. This can be achieved by setting objectives that are SMART, i.e. specific, measurable, achievable, resourced and time-bound. Becoming 'a successful business in the future' may be a desirable aim, but it is not an effective objective. Aiming to 'break even within six months, increase sales by 10 per cent each month in the first year and achieve an annual profit of £50,000 within two years' are all objectives that are specific, measurable and time-bound. It is clear what the business is trying to achieve and the deadlines that have been set for doing so. Whether these objectives are achievable and will be appropriately resourced depend on the individual circumstances of the business and the environment in which it operates – both now and in the future.

## Business planning

One of the most common causes of new business failure is a lack of detailed planning. Many owners rush to start trading without sufficient consideration of all of the set-up and operating costs involved. There is also often a tendency to be overly optimistic as to the speed and amount of cash flowing into the business from sales. Either of these factors can lead to inadequate levels of finance, which can force the business to close. The planning process needs to consider the business from every perspective. The results of the process can then be put together in a written report, known as a **business plan**. This document should contain any relevant information regarding the business and the market it is entering. It should clarify the objectives of the business and the resources and actions required to achieve them. A business plan is also likely to include:

### Ella's Kitchen

Paul Lindley wanted to do much more than simply be self-employed when he set up his own business in 2004. After years in a lucrative career in charge of marketing and communications at children's TV channel Nickelodeon, his decision was partly based on a desire to spend more time with his children. However, Paul had also become increasingly concerned about the increase in childhood obesity. By 2003, nearly one-third of UK children aged between two and seven years old were regarded as being medically overweight or obese. Paul became convinced that children should have the opportunity to eat food that is healthy but also fun. Eighteen months later, Paul was ready to launch his brand, Ella's Kitchen, onto the market. The product range, named after Paul's daughter, consists of a range of children's foods, including smoothies, baby foods and pasta sauces.

**Source: Ella's Kitchen**

### Questions

a) Outline Paul Lindley's key aims in establishing Ella's Kitchen.

- A marketing plan, describing the results of any market research into the business's likely customers and competitors
- A production or operating plan, identifying the scale and methods that will be used and any assets, such as buildings and machinery, which will be needed
- Detailed financial forecasts, including a cash flow forecast, a forecast profit and loss account and a forecast balance sheet
- Details of any finance invested by the owners and any borrowing required
- A SWOT analysis, outlining the strengths and possible weaknesses within the business, as well as any opportunities or threats that exist in the external environment.

One of the main advantages of drawing up a business plan at start-up is that it encourages owners to consider the whole picture, rather than focusing on the most attractive aspects of being in business. It should lead to more detailed and precise forecasts of sales and costs, which can be used to monitor the progress of the business once it begins to trade. Business plans can also be used to persuade investors and lenders to provide finance; for example, they are required in order to obtain a bank loan. However, producing a business plan is not, in itself, any guarantee of success. Cautious entrepreneurs may decide to understate sales and overestimate costs but, even so, unforeseen changes in the business environment can make the plan irrelevant. An increase in the level of competition or a downturn in the economy will mean that aspects of the plan have to be changed quickly in order to keep the business trading successfully. This means that the plan, once written, needs to be referred to and updated regularly.

## What makes a business idea attractive?

Setting up any new business involves stepping into a market and competing against established firms. These competitors will have had time to build a reputation and a degree of customer loyalty. New businesses therefore need to find ways of creating demand by attracting the interest of customers and persuading them to change their usual buying habits. This experience has to be good enough to make customers come back over and over again, remaining loyal even when rival firms try to tempt them away.

A **unique selling point (USP)** means something that gives a firm and its products a competitive edge, in order to stand out from rivals. Special features, higher standards of performance and quality and greater convenience can all be used to create product differentiation. For example, a jewellery or clothes shop could sell designs that are not available in other local shops; a grocery store could stay open on a 24-hour basis; or a pizza takeaway could offer a free delivery service. USPs help to add value to products, improving the customer experience. This not only increases the chances of repeat sales but may also mean that customers are willing to pay higher prices.

One of Superjam's USPs is that grape juice is used as a sweetener, rather than refined sugar, creating a healthier product

## Balancing personal and business needs

Having the opportunity to start a new business can seem like the answer to a dream – a way of earning money by doing things that are interesting, being your own boss and being able to work flexibly. However, the reality of getting a new business up and running usually involves having to work long hours and at weekends in order to generate sufficient sales during the day, and then dealing with the necessary administration and planning outside normal business hours. These demands leave little time for social activity or holidays – many entrepreneurs are even forced to work during periods of sickness in order to keep cash flowing into the business. In the long term, the pressures may ease, as the business grows and can afford to recruit additional staff. However, in the short term, the understanding and support of family and friends are necessary so that the effort required to establish the business can be made.

## Checking profitability

The ability to make profit is one of the main reasons why entrepreneurs set up businesses. Profit creates a source of income, acting as a reward for the risks taken and providing a source of funds for investment. Profitability refers to the ability of a business to generate revenues that are greater than the costs it incurs. It compares the basic level of profit to the resources that the business has at its disposal or the level of sales it is generating. It would be reasonable to expect a retailer operating on a national or international scale to generate a greater level of profit than a small independent. However, the relative success of the two in generating profits can still be compared. Their profitability can be calculated using an accounting ratio such as gross profit percentage of sales, net profit percentage of sales or return on capital employed (see Unit 5.4).

## Business and market trends

A trend is a change that takes place gradually over time. The business environment is not static but subject to constant change. Some trends produce regular fluctuations in sales, particularly where demand is likely to be seasonal. Some trends result in a long-term increase or decline.

One of the key factors driving this change is customer needs and wants. For example, the need for greater convenience has led to an increase in recent years in the number of people who shop regularly online. Technological innovation is also a key factor affecting consumers and businesses. These trends or changes can create opportunities for some businesses, leading to the development of new goods and services. However, they can also pose challenges. For example, there has been a significant increase in the number of budget airlines offering cheap flights within Europe in the last decade or so, many of which encourage customers to book online to keep operating costs low. This has led to a fall in demand for the traditional 'package' holiday and forced travel agents to rethink their product range in order to continue to attract customers.

## External influences

All businesses operate in an environment made up of other firms, consumers and the government. Few, if any, businesses are powerful enough to control this environment but all are affected by it. External influences can be:

- **Commercial** – e.g. the decision of a major competitor to cut its prices to gain a greater share of the market
- **Political** – e.g. a significant increase in the rate of VAT charged on goods and services in the UK
- **Local** – e.g. a council's decision to reduce the level of business rate charged to small firms
- **National** – e.g. the introduction of a ban on smoking in public places (introduced in Scotland in 2006 and in England, Wales and Northern Ireland in 2007)
- **International** – e.g. insistence by the European Union that the UK enforces the Working Time Directive of 48 hours per week for all employees.

The PESTLE framework is a tool often used by businesses to analyse external influences, looking specifically at any political, economic, social, technological, legal and environmental factors that could have either a positive or a negative effect on performance (see Unit 3.2 for more information on PESTLE analysis).

## Impact on self-esteem

Running a successful business can generate many benefits, in addition to the chance to earn a great deal of money. Unlike sales and profits, these benefits are hard to quantify or measure, but they explain why entrepreneurs are often willing to give up well-paid jobs and earn less running their own business. These benefits include:

- **Independence** Being your own boss means that you are free from the control of others
- **Power** The ability to do things in a particular way by 'being in the driving seat' can also act as the motivation for starting a business
- **A sense of achievement** Spotting an opportunity in the market and turning it into a successful business usually requires a great deal of effort and a certain amount of good luck. The satisfaction experienced in doing so explains why many entrepreneurs sell their businesses once they have become established, in order to pursue new ventures.

## Identifying the target market

The term '**target market**' refers to the group of customers to whom a business wishes to sell its goods or services. Some businesses aim their products at the whole market, but many decide to target a segment of customers within it. The customers within the target group will share certain characteristics, such as age, gender or income levels, that influence their purchasing behaviour. Building a detailed profile of the target market helps a firm to create products that meet customer needs precisely, giving it an edge over competitors. It will also influence the pricing strategy used and help in choosing effective methods of promotion and distribution.

Of course, there may be other customers who are attracted to the product. These customers do not share the same characteristics as those within the target market, so their needs and expectations are not taken into consideration to the same extent. For example, the BBC's Radio 1 may still attract listeners who are younger or older than the 16 to 24 year olds that the station targets, although many of its shows and features would not be considered as appropriate for other age groups.

Radio 1 is aimed at 16–24 year olds

## Market research

Building up a detailed profile of a firm's target market requires a great deal of market research. The market-research process involves gathering and analysing data in line with pre-defined objectives. Large businesses have the resources to carry out regular primary research, gathering new and up-to-date data that are relevant to their circumstances and needs. Although many new businesses also gather primary research, owners are likely to lack the expertise and the finance to carry out unbiased surveys on a large scale, relying instead on the opinions of friends and family members. However, there are a number of sources of secondary data that can be useful to new businesses. Secondary data already exists and may be published in newspapers, journals, books or on the internet. The government publishes the findings of its own research into a huge range of economic and social issues, much of which is available via the National Statistics website (www.statistics.gov.uk). Some of the past research of private market-research agencies such as Mintel on specific markets can be obtained free from the reference sections of public libraries. Trade journals, such as *The Grocer*, also carry out research into trends and changes in specific industries or sectors. All limited companies are required to produce yearly accounts, which can be obtained from Companies House and can provide useful information on competitor performance and behaviour.

Most of the sources outlined above focus on providing information on a national or regional level, whereas a small, newly established business may be more interested in events on a local level. Nevertheless, published research can be useful in giving a general idea of the state of the market that a new business is entering.

## Sales forecasts

A **sales forecast** is an estimate of the likely volume or value of a firm's sales at a future point in time. Producing accurate sales forecasts is a very important part of the planning process. The expected future level of sales will determine the level of production, the level of human resources and the quantity of supplies ordered. Established businesses can use internal data as a basis for predicting the future. For example, an analysis of past sales may reveal an increasing trend over a number of years and this can be extrapolated or projected, adjusting the figures to take into account any regular, seasonal fluctuations. New businesses are, however, unable to do this. They have yet to generate sufficient sales to be able to identify any trends or patterns. Examining trends in the overall market can provide insight and help to inform decision making. The results of carefully designed primary market research on the target market can also act as the basis for sales forecasting. Questionnaires can be used to try to find out a great deal of useful information, including:

- The number of people who are likely to purchase the product
- How much they are likely to buy at any one time
- How much they are likely to pay to buy the product
- How frequently they are likely to make their purchases.

Although the results of this kind of market research are unlikely to be that reliable, they can form the basis of some attempt to forecast sales.

## The effect on businesses of customers' actions and choices

Customers are fundamental to any business. Without them, no business can survive for long. New firms entering markets that already contain a number of competitors have to fight hard to get noticed. However, even when a business operates as a local monopoly with no immediate rivals, customers can still choose to spend their money on other goods and services. Once-popular products can go out of fashion quickly, leaving businesses with unsold stock that has to be heavily discounted or simply thrown away.

Customer actions with respect to choosing the goods and services they buy are influenced by many factors. In some cases, the price level will be a key influence, especially when choosing between products that, in every other respect, are very similar. However, many customers are prepared to pay higher prices in order to obtain better-quality products that are durable and reliable. Design and image have a major impact on demand for certain goods. Advertising campaigns and product endorsements by popular celebrities can cause demand for some products to soar, but it can be ineffective in other cases.

Even if a firm's target market is relatively small, the sheer number of possible influences on consumers makes it difficult, if not impossible, to predict their actions accurately. However, decisions still have to be taken in the present regarding future customer behaviour, so that the right products can be produced in the right quantities. Regular contact with customers through ongoing market research can help a business to maintain an up-to-date picture of the factors currently at work, taking some of the guesswork out of the decision-making process.

## Competitors

Keeping an eye on other firms in the market is also vital in maintaining competitiveness. Market research can be used to identify not just the number but also the behaviour of different rivals. It would be particularly hard for a new business to establish itself in a market where competition is very fierce. Established firms are likely to respond to the presence of a new competitor by undercutting prices or promoting their products heavily, in order to hold on to their market share. Being aware of the degree of competition should help to make a new business better prepared and more able to win – and then protect – a share of the market.

## Business strengths and weaknesses

Few entrepreneurs have all of the knowledge, experience and resources that they would wish for when setting up a new business. Furthermore, it is highly unlikely that conditions in the wider business environment are going to be completely positive. Taking time to examine internal and external conditions can, however, put the business in a stronger position. This can be done by conducting a **SWOT analysis**. This involves identifying the key internal strengths and weaknesses within the business in relation to its target market. It also requires consideration of the opportunities and threats that exist in the external environment that could affect the target market. Policies can then be put in place that allow the business to build on its strengths and take advantage, where possible, of the opportunities. Action can also be taken to deal with any weaknesses and to reduce – if not eliminate – the effects of any threats (see Unit 3.2 for more information on SWOT analysis).

## Environmental issues

Growing concern in recent years over issues such as global warming and the depletion of non-renewable resources, such as oil and gas, has led to increasing interest in the impact of business activity on the environment. Adopting a caring approach to the environment could involve recycling, reducing pollution, cutting down on the amount of packaging or using fuel-efficient technology. Many of these measures can help to reduce operating costs, as well as potentially giving a firm a competitive edge over its rivals.

## Key terms

**Business plan** A written document providing relevant information about the business and the market it is entering. It clarifies the objectives of the business and the resources and actions required to achieve them, including financial forecasts for cash flow and profit

**Entrepreneur** A person with a flair for spotting opportunities and who is prepared to take risks in order to make a business succeed

**Franchise** A type of business that buys the right to sell the products or service of another business and use the latter's name, logos and methods of trading

**Franchisee** The business that pays for the right to use another business's name, logo, etc. and sell its products or service

**Franchisor** The business that sells the right to use its name and sell its products or service to another business in return for an initial fee and a percentage of any profits made

**Sales forecast** An estimate of the likely volume or value of a firm's sales at a future point in time

**Target market** The group of customers to which a business aims to sell its goods or services

## Re-cap questions

1 Briefly explain why setting up a firm from scratch is seen as the most risky way of going into business.

2 Describe two possible benefits of buying an existing business.

3 Explain what is meant by a franchise.

4 Examine one advantage and one disadvantage of going into business by buying a franchise.

5 Explain the difference between a business aim and a business objective.

6 State two possible objectives that might be set by a new business.

7 Outline two ways in which a new business could benefit from writing a business plan.

8 Explain why it is important for a new business to have a clear idea about its target market.

## Grading tips

<table>
<tr>
<td>

**P1** Present the initial business idea, using relevant criteria.

Once you have come up with your idea for a business, you need to put together a presentation. Use the criteria discussed in this section of the book as guidelines, but remember that the criteria you use need to be appropriate for your particular business. For example, what are your objectives in setting up the business, what will be its unique selling point that will make it stand out from competitors, what are your expected levels of sales and profits? The presentation can be either a formal report or a visual presentation to a group.

</td>
<td>

**M1** Explain methods used to identify the target market for the proposed business.

You must show that you have a good understanding of market research. To do this, you need to use a range of research methods, describe each method chosen and explain why it was chosen. You also need to refer to your results, showing how the research method in question helped you to obtain them and how the results support your decision to go ahead with the launch of the new business and

</td>
<td></td>
</tr>
<tr>
<td>

**P2** Explain how to identify the target market.

The market that you will be targeting your business at needs to be included in your presentation. You need to give as much detail as possible, so you need to use market research to find this out.

</td>
<td></td>
<td></td>
</tr>
</table>

See page 308 for suggestions for Assignments for Unit 36.

# **Part 2:** The skills and development required to run a business successfully

Running a successful business requires a variety of knowledge, skills and abilities. Large businesses employ individuals with expertise in a particular area who can concentrate on performing particular functions, such as sales or accountancy. These skills are just as important for running a small business, but it is highly unlikely that one single entrepreneur will possess all of them. This does not necessarily make it impossible for one person to run a successful business. Being aware of the skills that are needed is important. It allows the owner to identify those skills that they already have and think about ways of developing or acquiring any others that will prove useful.

## Key business skills

The points below are not meant to form a comprehensive list of all of the skills and abilities that might come in useful at times when running a business. General qualities such as self-discipline, determination, enthusiasm and the ability to work under pressure are also very important. However, the skills identified and discussed over the following pages could act as a checklist for anyone considering setting up their own business.

Personal qualities that are useful in running a business

## Own contribution

In the early days, the owner of a small business usually carries out all of the work involved in running it. This may be necessary in order to control costs and because of a desire to build the business up gradually. However, this is likely to mean long days and working at weekends, which can be very stressful, particularly over long periods of time. Trying to do everything is also likely to have a negative effect on the performance of the business. At some point, therefore, the owner will need to consider handing over at least some of the work to others, by employing more staff or using consultants and other external support.

## Technical/operational

Many people set up a business based around a practical skill or craft that may have been developed at school, college or by working for someone else. For example, a plumber, a car mechanic or a hairdresser may choose to be self-employed rather than an employee within a business. This means that, in addition to managing their own business, they also play a technical or operational role. A key benefit of this is that the owner has a great deal of control over the quality of the work carried out, making sure that it is done to the standards required. Even as the business grows and the owner steps back from direct involvement in operations, a good understanding of the work involved will be useful in planning future developments and dealing with any problems that arise.

## Product knowledge

An in-depth understanding of the goods or services that are produced and/or sold is important for a number of reasons. From an operations point of view, the correct quantity and quality of materials need to be ordered, and the right machinery and worker skills need to be acquired. From a marketing viewpoint, customers may require information about the product and advice on how to use it. They are unlikely to have much confidence – and will therefore be reluctant to buy – if this information and advice are unavailable.

## Management ability

Management involves controlling and coordinating business resources (including human resources) to ensure effective performance. The process requires creative and communication skills, so that market opportunities can be turned into successful products and solutions can be provided to deal with any problems that arise. Managing a business successfully becomes even more of a challenge as the business starts to grow. However, people are not necessarily born as good managers and the skills involved can be acquired through experience, appropriate training, or a combination of both.

## Recording and checking business performance

Keeping detailed records of sales, costs and any other information relating to business may seem an unnecessary task to some owners already burdened with many other duties to perform and confident that the information will not be forgotten. However, checking performance on a regular basis is an essential management task. Entrepreneurs should have some idea of what they hope to achieve by running a business, and many will have set specific objectives in their business plans in relation to sales levels and growth, market share and profit. Progress in achieving these objectives needs to be monitored frequently. Recording all relevant information will build up a detailed picture of the firm's actual performance. It can then be compared with the targets that have been set and action can be taken if progress is considered to be too slow.

Accurate and detailed records are also needed to prepare financial accounts for tax purposes. Many small businesses do not need to have their accounts audited or to send them to Companies House. However, they must still produce accounting records if these are requested by the tax office and may be subject to substantial fines if they are unable to do so.

## Personal selling

Personal selling is one of the most common marketing methods used by small businesses to attract customers. It involves direct contact with customers, assessing their needs and proposing product or service solutions. Successful personal selling involves using a number of key skills, including excellent product knowledge, the ability to question and listen carefully to assess customer needs, and the ability to close a sale.

## Administration

Administration provides support for business operations. It involves keeping records and communicating with external groups, such as customers and suppliers, by sending letters, emails and invoices, and arranging payment. Administration is often overlooked because it does not contribute directly to generating sales. Nevertheless, ongoing business success requires effective administration. In turn, effective administration requires organisation and a logical approach.

## Previous experience

Many entrepreneurs go into business after being employed by other firms. During this employment, they will have acquired skills and experience that will be of benefit when running their own businesses. These could involve the ability to produce a good or provide a service. Alternatively, they could be in a supportive function, such as a knowledge of accountancy or bookkeeping, IT skills or a flair for administration.

## Strengths and weaknesses

The benefits of examining the strengths and weaknesses of a business and those responsible for running it have already been discussed. No individual can be expected to have all the necessary skills and abilities and no business is ever free of problems. However, an awareness of any weaknesses or problems that do exist means that action can be taken to deal with them, to prevent them from damaging performance. Strengths, on the other hand, can be exploited in order to support the business. One way of identifying strengths and weaknesses is to carry out a SWOT analysis.

## Development

### Identify skills gaps/shortages

The next step required by anyone preparing to set up a business is an appraisal or **skills audit** of their existing abilities. It is important to be completely honest when carrying out this process. If any gaps do exist, they need to be filled so that appropriate action can be taken to fill them.

However, being overly modest may mean that time and money are wasted on training or other support that is unnecessary.

## Seeking professional help

There are many sources of help from experts in particular areas of business, including advice on financial, legal and marketing issues, IT support and website design. Most banks now have specialist small business advisers who offer a range of services, as well as financial facilities such as loans and overdrafts. Accountants can not only be used to prepare business accounts but also give financial advice on areas such as reducing the amount of tax paid. It may also be necessary to contact a solicitor for advice on legal matters, such as the steps needed to set up a private limited company. Business consultants are experienced men and women who will examine an existing firm or a new business idea and give advice on how to run it effectively. It is important to find out at the outset whether the consultant has experience of working with small businesses. These sources of advice usually require the payment of a fee. The size of this fee is likely to depend on the amount of time involved but they can be substantial, adding to costs. It is essential, therefore, to discover whether the professional chosen is suitably qualified and experienced, to discuss in detail the work that needs to be carried out and to agree the fees that will be charged. It may also be sensible to choose someone who has been recommended or who can provide references.

In addition to the professionals identified above, there are a number of organisations that exist to provide support and advice to small firms. In some cases, this advice is provided free of charge: in others, a membership fee may be charged. Table 36.1 gives a list of the main organisations.

## Training

An entrepreneur could acquire at least some of the skills required for running a business by taking on a partner or hiring employees. However, there are a number of reasons why he or she may be reluctant to do so. A new partner would mean a smaller share of the profits and the possibility of disputes arising. Employing workers requires a good understanding of employment law, and employees may be hard to dismiss if sales start to dry up. One way of acquiring necessary business skills is to complete a training course. This could involve using the services of a specialist training consultant. A consultant with knowledge and experience of small businesses should be able to put together a tailored training programme to fit the owner's needs. However, these services are usually very expensive. A cheaper option might be to enrol on a course at a local college. This could be a general business course providing an overview of a number of topics and issues, or a more specific course on a topic such as marketing, bookkeeping or health and safety in the workplace. Such courses need to be chosen carefully to make sure they are relevant. They are also likely to take much longer to complete, as they will be spread over the college term, if not the whole academic year. Many of the organisations listed in Table 36.1 provide training courses as part of the support they offer to small businesses, so should also be investigated.

## Planning

Once the skills gaps have been identified and the various sources of support and training have been considered, the process of filling the gaps can begin. This stage needs to be planned carefully. Some support might be required immediately, whereas other help may not be required until a point in the future, helping to spread costs. It may not be possible to access some support immediately, perhaps because of a lack of finance, the existing workload of consultants and advisers or the lack of places available on a course. The plan will therefore need to consider costs, accessibility and timescales, and the impact these are likely to have on business performance.

| Organisation | Services provided |
|---|---|
| Business Link | A government-funded network providing advice on a wide range of business-related topics via its website www.businesslink.gov.uk. Support is also given by linking firms with locally based specialist advisers, who are employed on a freelance basis. Similar services are provided for businesses in Scotland by Business Gateway, for businesses in Northern Ireland by www.nibusinessinfo.co.uk and for businesses in Wales by Flexible Support for Business. |
| Enterprise agencies | Independent, not-for-profit bodies operating in England and Wales to provide support, including advice and training, in order to help businesses set up and grow. Many also offer subsidised workspace and secretarial and administrative support. |
| Federation of Small Businesses | A pressure group that works to protect and promote the interests of small businesses. It also offers expert information and guidance on a number of areas, including legal advice and help with taxation, employment law and health and safety. It charges a membership fee but this is based on the size of the business and its number of employees. |
| British Chambers of Commerce (BCC) | The BCC provide a number of services to their members, including publications, training courses and events. They also lobby local and national government over business matters. Membership fees depend on the size of the business. |
| The Forum of Private Business | Another leading pressure group, which aims to influence laws and government policies affecting business. Membership entitles firms to discounts on publications and a range of services. Membership fees depend on the nature and size of the business. |
| Shell LiveWIRE | This is a UK-wide investment programme aimed at 16 to 30 year olds wishing to start and develop a business. It offers free information via online mentors. The Shell LiveWIRE Young Entrepreneur of the Year Award provides a £10,000 top prize for the winner. |
| The Prince's Trust | Provides help and assistance to young unemployed people between 18 and 30 years of age in England, Wales or Northern Ireland to run their own business. The Trust's Enterprise Programme provides business skills training, help with planning, ongoing support from a mentor, start-up grants and low-interest loans. It also provides a range of free or discounted services, including a free legal helpline. The Trust also offers support to unemployed young people in Scotland aged between 16 and 25 years old. |

Table 36.1  Organisations providing support for small businesses in the UK

# Love Holistic Therapies

Carla Love set up Love Holistic Therapies in October 2008. The business is based in the village of Croft, near Warrington in the north-west of England. Carla is a qualified holistic therapist, trained to use reflexology, aromatherapy and a number of other treatments.

Carla had been a teacher for a number of years but had reached the decision that that career was not for her. She had been interested in holistic therapies for a number of years and wanted a job that would help people both physically and mentally. Working part-time in her last year of teaching allowed her to complete a VTCT diploma in Holistic Therapies at Sheffield College. Since then she has also gained qualifications in reiki, Russian honey and cupping massage and Tibetan acupressure head massage. Carla also has a diploma in sports remedial massage and is a member of the International Council of Holistic Therapists and the Federation of Holistic Therapists.

At first, Carla tried to gain some experience by getting a job in a salon but was unable to find suitable work, so she decided to set up on her own. She had to pay £100 to get a website created for the business, and a further £170 for equipment, including a massage bed and chair. According to her, the key skills required to run her business are bookkeeping, marketing and customer service. Carla received some advice from Business Link and Train 2000 but keeps up to date with business developments by networking and continuing to develop her skills and expertise.

## Questions

a) So far, Carla has chosen to expand the services offered by her business by training herself, rather than taking on a partner or employing additional staff. Examine the key advantages and disadvantages of this approach.

b) Suggest three sources of professional help and business advice that Carla could use in the future, other than those identified in the case study.

## Key terms

**Administration** The business function that provides support for operations by keeping records and communicating with external groups, such as customers and suppliers, by sending letters, emails and invoices and arranging payment

**Management** This involves controlling and coordinating business resources (including human resources) to ensure effective business performance

**Skills audit** An appraisal of the skills and abilities that already exist within the workforce in order to identify any gaps that need to be filled

**Training** The provision of work-related education in order to acquire new skills or develop existing ones

##  Re-cap questions

1  'Entrepreneurs are people who possess all the necessary skills to run a business successfully.' True or false? Justify your answer.

2  Outline one advantage and one disadvantage for an entrepreneur carrying out all the work and duties required for running a business.

3  Describe two benefits for an owner of playing a key operational role within his or her business.

4  Analyse two reasons why a new business should keep detailed financial records.

5  Briefly explain the role of administration within a business.

6  Outline one method that can be used to identify a firm's strengths and weaknesses.

7  Identify three sources of professional help for someone setting up a new business.

8  State four organisations that a new business could turn to for support and advice.

9  Explain why an entrepreneur might be reluctant to a) acquire a partner or b) recruit employees to access new skills.

10  Examine two sources of training that could be used by a business owner to acquire new skills.

## Grading tips

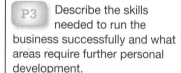 **P3** Describe the skills needed to run the business successfully and what areas require further personal development.

Think carefully about the different kinds of skills and abilities your business will need. Produce a skills audit that identifies those skills you already possess and those that you will need to acquire. Make sure that you are realistic about what will be needed (even though you will not actually be required to gain any of them).

**M2** Analyse the personal development needed to run the business successfully.

Analysis requires you to explain in detail exactly why the skills you have identified in P3 are needed and how they will help the business succeed. You also need to explain how you would go ahead with your personal development, e.g. sources of training, cost and timescales involved.

See page 308 for suggestions for Assignments for Unit 36.

# Part 3: Legal and financial aspects of business start-up

It is tempting to assume that setting up a business is simply about providing a good or service that people will want to buy. While this is certainly part of the process, there are a number of legal and financial considerations that also need to be addressed if the business is to be successful.

## Legal aspects of business start-up

There are a number of laws affecting the legal status, operations and trading conditions of businesses in the UK. Owners and managers must be aware of this legislation, as well as the implications for failing to operate within the law.

## Legal status of the business

There are many forms of ownership or legal structure that a business can take, so this is one of the first decisions that need to be taken. The main options include:

- **Sole trader** A business that is owned by one person who takes full responsibility for running the business.
- **Partnership** A business owned by two or more people who share the responsibility of running the business.
- **Limited company** A business that is owned by one or more shareholders who have **limited liability**.
- **Cooperative** A business that is owned and operated by either employees or customers (or a combination of both).

The main advantages and disadvantages of the above legal structures are outlined in Table 36.2.

| Legal status | Advantages | Disadvantages |
|---|---|---|
| Sole trader | • Requires little paperwork and finance to set up <br> • One person is in charge, meaning that decisions can be taken quickly <br> • Profits do not need to be shared with other owners | • One person has all the responsibility for running the business, meaning long hours and little opportunity to take time off for holidays or sickness <br> • The growth of the business may be constrained by a lack of skills and finance <br> • The owner has unlimited liability |
| Partnership | • Should introduce additional capital and skills into the business <br> • The responsibility of running the business can be shared, creating opportunities to take time off | • Profits have to be shared between more owners <br> • Disagreements between owners may slow down decision making <br> • Partners are still likely to have unlimited liability |
| Limited company | • Shareholders benefit from limited liability <br> • Easier to generate more finance from investment | • Setting up the business is more complicated and more expensive <br> • Accounts need to be published annually, adding to costs and giving competitors access to company information |
| Co-operative | • Worker-owners are likely to make more effort to make the business succeed | • Decision makers may have little, if any, knowledge of how to run a business |

Table 36.2 Key advantages and disadvantages of the main types of business legal structure

## Legal liabilities

The type of legal structure chosen for a business affects the liability of its owners for any losses that might be incurred from its operations. Sole traders and most partners are forced to accept **unlimited liability**. This means that they will be personally liable for any debts that the business generates, such as loans, overdrafts and payments to creditors, but is unable to repay from its own resources. In extreme cases, this could mean having to sell off possessions, such as a car or house, in order to raise the finance. However, not all business owners suffer from this degree of risk. The shareholders of a limited company – either private or public – enjoy **limited liability**. This means that their losses are limited to the amount they have invested in the business from buying its shares. If the business becomes insolvent, i.e. the value of its liabilities becomes greater than the value of its assets, shareholders are not personally liable to repay the debts. Limited liability makes it easier for limited companies to attract investment.

## Trading terms and conditions

It is important for a business to have a clear idea of the terms and conditions under which it trades, both in buying in goods and services from suppliers and in selling products to customers. Details such as sales price, discounts for paying early or buying in bulk, credit periods and delivery terms should be agreed by both sides and ideally be written down. This can help to avoid any future disputes or resolve any that do arise.

## Trading standards

Trading standards exist to try and ensure that all customers are treated fairly and not exploited when they buy goods and services. These standards are designed to protect businesses as well as the final consumer. All businesses have a responsibility to ensure that they are operating legally and that their actions do not infringe UK consumer protection law. It is therefore important for new business owners to have a clear idea of trading standards before they begin buying in and selling on. In the UK, the Trading Standards Institute (TSI) provides guidance on a wide range of areas, including product labelling, weights and measures and product safety (find out more about trading standards and the role of the TSI by visiting its website at www.tradingstandards.gov.uk).

## Licences

Many businesses also need to be licensed in order to operate. Whether or not a licence is necessary – and also the body responsible for issuing it – depends on the nature of the goods or services being sold. Businesses that need to be licensed include pubs, bars and nightclubs, cinemas, residential nursing homes, taxi firms, pet boarding kennels and child-minding services. (For a more comprehensive list, go to www.startinbusiness.co.uk.)

## Record keeping

The importance of record keeping has already been noted elsewhere in this unit. Accurate and detailed financial or accounting records are necessary to monitor and assess business performance. They are also required to calculate the correct levels of tax to be paid, as well as acting as evidence if these are challenged by HM Revenue and Customs. Traditionally, financial records were written in ledgers or day books, although accounting software is now widely used. Examples of the financial records that firms keep include:

- **The sales ledger** – records details of goods and services that have been provided to customers on credit
- **The purchases ledger** – records details of all the money owed by a business to its suppliers
- **The cash book** – records all of the cash and banking transactions made by a business
- **The nominal (or general) ledger** – includes details of any assets purchased and any expenses, including wages and petty cash. It also records the level of capital invested by the owners, as well as any money taken out of the business (known as drawings) by them
- **Stock records** – giving details such as the volume, cost and age of goods bought into the business.

In addition, firms are required by law to keep a record for a minimum of three years of any accidents or injuries that have occurred on their premises. Although it is not a legal requirement, it is also sensible to keep copies of documents that may help to avoid or resolve problems in the future. These documents include letters, emails and minutes of meetings, generated internally between partners, shareholders and employees, as well as external groups such as the bank, customers and suppliers.

# Resolving problems

Over time, it is possible that problems may occur with groups such as customers or employees. If and when this happens, it is important to have policies in place to resolve them as quickly as possible and in a way that treats everyone fairly. These policies include:

- **A customer complaints procedure** Customers should be informed about the steps they need to take if they are not completely satisfied with the goods or services they receive. Many firms choose to go beyond the minimum required by customer protection legislation in order to deal with customer dissatisfaction and maintain customer loyalty.
- **Employee discipline** and **grievance policies** Good employer–employee relations help a business to function effectively. A **disciplinary policy** sets out the standards of behaviour that are expected from employees and the consequences that will result from poor performance or misconduct in the workplace. **A grievance procedure**, on the other hand, clarifies the steps that employees should take if they have a complaint about the way that they have been treated by a colleague or manager. The Employment Act (2002) makes it a legal requirement for all businesses to have some kind of disciplinary and grievance procedures, which must be applied uniformly to ensure fair treatment for all employees. These procedures must be made available in writing to all employees.

# National and local laws

Over the years, governments have passed a great deal of legislation that affects the way businesses operate. It is the responsibility of business owners and managers to be aware of this legislation and any updates to it. Doing this may seem like a particularly daunting prospect for someone starting up a small new business, lacking the knowledge and resources to keep up with any changes. Nevertheless, ignorance of the law can lead to heavy fines, bad publicity and, in some cases, the business being forced to close down.

In particular, small businesses need to be aware of the following areas.

## Consumer protection legislation

The main UK laws that aim to protect the rights of consumers include the Sale of Goods Act (1979), the Consumer Protection from Unfair Trading Regulations (2008), the Consumer Credit Acts (1974 and 2006) and the Consumer Protection (Distance Selling) Regulations (2000 and 2005).

Refer to Unit 3 for more information on these laws.

## Individual labour law

This body of laws aims to protect the rights of individual employees and includes the Sex Discrimination Act (1975, 1995, 1997), the Equal Pay Act (1970), the Race Relations Act (1976/1992), the Disability Discrimination Act (1995/2005) and the Employment Act (2002).

Refer to Unit 13 for more information on these laws.

## Collective labour law

This legislation aims to influence the activities of trade unions and their impact on collective bargaining and industrial relations. During the 1980s and early 1990s, a number of laws were introduced by the government aimed at reducing trade union power, which many commentators believed had become excessive. Some of the key laws introduced in recent years include:

- The Trade Union Reform and Employment Rights Act (1993) – which states that trade unions must give at least seven days' notice to employers before taking official industrial action (i.e. that has been voted for by a majority of union members under a secret ballot)
- The Employment Relations Act (2000) – which states that an employer must recognise any union that has a membership of over 50 per cent of its employees and the right to introduce collective bargaining.

## Health and safety legislation

The Health and Safety at Work Act (1974) is the main piece of legislation in the UK that aims to prevent accidents and protect workers from dangerous practices. Under the Act, employers are legally obliged to safeguard the health, safety and welfare of their employees. In particular, they must:

- Carry out risk assessments to identify what aspects of the working environment could be harmful to workers and take precautions to prevent this
- Provide protective equipment, protective clothing, and health and safety training to workers free of charge

- Provide free toilets, washing facilities, drinking water and adequate first-aid facilities
- Have insurance covering workers who get hurt at work or become ill as a result of work
- Report any injuries, incidents or dangerous diseases that occur in the workplace to the Health and Safety Executive (HSE), the body that oversees the implementation of the Act and carries out investigations of any serious accidents.

Employers must legally keep their workers safe

In addition to employers' responsibilities, the Act also requires employees to take responsibility for cooperating with their employers and taking reasonable care of their own health and safety, and that of others. In particular, workers should:

- Use appropriately any health and safety equipment and training that they have received
- Pass on information about any risks to health and safety within the workplace to their employer, line manager or health and safety representative.

The Management of Health and Safety at Work (MHSW) Regulations came into force in 1999 and work alongside the Health and Safety at Work Act.

## Legislation to protect the environment

The government has passed a number of laws in recent years to protect the environment. These can have an effect on business. For example, the Environmental Protection Act (1991) and the Environment Act (1995) both aim to reduce pollution levels generated by businesses. Firms can face heavy fines if their activities are found to be causing damage to the environment.

Legal action can be taken against businesses that damage the environment

## By-laws and regulations

A by-law is a law made by a local authority in order to manage the area under its control. It is important, therefore, that the owner of a new business should find out from their local authority about any by-laws that could affect their operations. In addition, there are a number of regulations that businesses must consider, including:

- **Fire regulations** – all firms need to carry out fire risk assessments and put in place measures to deal with any risks identified, including the provision of fire safety equipment and appropriate training for staff in terms of using it
- **Planning permission** – any firm planning to build new premises or to extend existing buildings must seek permission from its local authority in order to do so.

## Contracts and other legal duties and responsibilities

The legal duties and responsibilities of businesses are wide-ranging and depend to some extent on the nature of the individual firm. It is advisable, therefore, for anyone about to set up a new business to contact a solicitor or seek advice from a reliable source (see below). Three areas that will be of particular concern are:

- **Employing workers** According to the law, a business must provide a written **contract of employment** to all employees within two months of them starting work. This must state the name of the employee, the name and address of the employer, the date that employment began, the job title and a description of the duties to be carried out and the place of work. It must also give details regarding the amount the employee will be paid, when payments will be made, paid holiday and sickness entitlements and notice periods for both the employee and employer. Firms are legally obliged to comply with national minimum wage legislation (see Unit 13.2 for details on current minimum wage rates) and make statutory payments for maternity, paternity and adoption leave. They are also legally required to provide employees with an itemised wage slip.
- **Insurance** Businesses are also required by law to take out certain forms of insurance. For example, any firm that employs staff must have employer's liability insurance, to provide cover against claims from staff who are injured as a result of doing their jobs.
- **VAT** Only businesses with sales turnover of at least £70,000 per year (figures for 2010) are required to register for VAT. If this is the case, it is important to keep detailed records of the VAT received from sales and that paid on purchases (see Unit 5, Part 2 for further information on VAT).

## Regulatory bodies

These are organisations that have been set up by the government to establish minimum standards of business behaviour. These bodies are responsible for monitoring business behaviour to ensure that these standards are met and also for dealing with those businesses that fail to do so. The Office of Fair Trading (OFT) is responsible for safeguarding consumer interests and therefore has a wide-reaching regulatory influence. Other regulatory bodies concerned with specific sectors include the Financial Services Authority, which regulates financial service providers, such as banks and insurance companies, and the Food Standards Agency, which is responsible for setting standards of hygiene and food preparation.

## Sources of advice

A number of organisations exist to provide advice and support to people in business and, in particular, those running small or new firms. Many of these sources of advice have already been identified earlier in this unit (see Seeking professional help in Part 2). In addition, the following organisations may also be helpful:

- All Business – www.allbusiness.com
- Business Wings – www.businesswings.co.uk
- Department for Business, Innovation and Skills – www.bis.gov.uk
- HM Revenue and Customs – www.hmrc.gov.uk
- Office of Fair Trading – www.oft.gov.uk
- Startups – www.startups.co.uk

## Financial aspects of business start-up

Effective financial management is crucial to the long-term survival and success of any business. Detailed and accurate financial planning is required from the outset in order to get a realistic idea of the level of finance needed for start-up and to keep the business up and running in the initial months of trading. A number of the many financial aspects of running a business are considered in the remainder of this section – some may be more relevant than others, depending on the nature of the business.

## Personal survival budget

One of the most common reasons for starting up a new business is the opportunity to be free of the restrictions of being employed by another firm and acquire greater control and independence. However, the downside of this is the loss of regular income in the form of a wage or salary. Starting a business inevitably means sacrifices – in terms of both time and money. Most entrepreneurs are prepared to make these sacrifices, particularly in the short term, in the hope of generating greater levels of satisfaction and the chance of becoming wealthy in the long term. Nevertheless, it is important to be realistic about how much money will be needed to support the business owner or owners and cover their living expenses. Drawing up a personal survival budget can be useful in estimating what will be required (a typical format for a personal survival budget is given in Table 36.3). The process involves identifying the likely sources of income over a period of time – perhaps the first 12 months of the business – along with the timings and amounts involved. The next step is to itemise any known expenses such as food, clothing, rent or mortgage repayments and other bills. It may also be prudent to allow an amount to be put aside to cover unforeseen expenses, such as car repairs.

## Cost of premises

The cost of the premises will have a significant influence on the choice of property. Keeping costs as low as possible is one of the reasons why many people decide to work from home initially. However, this may not be an ideal solution in the long term, meaning that at some point business premises will have to be found. It is important to be clear about all of the costs involved in the premises chosen, not just the purchase price or the cost of rent, but also business rates, insurance and other running costs, such as heating and lighting.

Cost is an important factor in the choice of location, particularly for new businesses with limited resources. However, the size, facilities and location of the premises can also have a major impact on the success of a start-up. The choice of premise must be considered carefully in relation to the requirements of the business on a high street or in a shopping mall. For example, a retailer may feel that the most important factor is being as close to as many customers as possible. However, the increasing trend for shoppers to buy online may have made this less relevant. Wholesalers and manufacturers are more likely to be concerned about the quality of the transport network in the area, so that supplies can be obtained quickly and reliably.

Once a business has identified its key location criteria, a list can be drawn up to compare the suitability of different sites. For example:

- How big do the premises need to be?
- What facilities are required, e.g. office space, storage space, workshops, kitchen, showroom, outside parking?

| (Months) | 1 | 2 | 3 | 4 | 5 | 6 | 7 | 8 | 9 | 10 | 11 | 12 | Total |
|---|---|---|---|---|---|---|---|---|---|---|---|---|---|
| **Estimated income** | | | | | | | | | | | | | |
| Wages/salaries | | | | | | | | | | | | | |
| Interest on savings | | | | | | | | | | | | | |
| Benefits received | | | | | | | | | | | | | |
| Other income | | | | | | | | | | | | | |
| **Total** | | | | | | | | | | | | | |
| **Estimated expenditure** | | | | | | | | | | | | | |
| Food | | | | | | | | | | | | | |
| Mortgage/rent | | | | | | | | | | | | | |
| Clothing | | | | | | | | | | | | | |
| Travel expenses | | | | | | | | | | | | | |
| Fuel bills | | | | | | | | | | | | | |
| Telephone | | | | | | | | | | | | | |
| Entertainment | | | | | | | | | | | | | |
| Other expenses | | | | | | | | | | | | | |
| **Total** | | | | | | | | | | | | | |

Table 36.3 A sample format for a personal survival budget

- Is the current layout suitable or does it require a significant amount of building work?
- Is there scope for expansion if this is needed in the future?
- Does the location need to be highly visible to customers and convenient for them to reach?
- Does the location need to be convenient for suppliers to reach?
- Is the appearance of the property important from a marketing point of view?
- What is the image of the area – e.g. upmarket – and is this important?
- What is the level of competition in the local area?
- Are there any grants, subsidies or other means of help available?

Finding premises that exactly match business requirements may not be possible, so the criteria used to make the choice will need to be ranked in terms of priority. The most suitable properties could well be too expensive for a small business. However, prime locations may also attract most customers, so that high costs can be offset by greater levels of sales income.

## Equipment and supplies

The type of equipment and supplies required by a business will obviously depend on the nature of its operations. Some businesses may need to invest heavily in capital equipment, such as machinery, vehicles, fixtures and fittings, before trading can begin. Although this may be seen as necessary, the money spent may not be recovered quickly if sales are slow to take off. This expenditure may also use up funds that are needed at a later point to keep cash flow positive. It is important, therefore, that a **capital needs budget** is produced, identifying exactly what is needed, when it is needed and how much it is likely to cost. Doing this may make it possible to spread capital expenditure over time, reducing the strain on finances. It may also be possible to lease some of the equipment needed, at least until the business becomes established.

The type and cost of supplies will also depend on the nature of the business. Manufacturers buy in supplies of raw materials and components; wholesalers and retailers buy goods that are sold on to customers; and other service providers buy in equipment and stationery and other supplies to support their operations. The cost of supplies is treated as a running expense. Keeping the cost of supplies as low as possible enables a business to charge lower prices and still make a profit. However, while cost is important, it is not the only consideration when choosing a supplier. The quality of the goods and willingness of suppliers to be flexible, in terms of the quantity and timing of delivery, may be just as, if not more, important. Supplies also need to be stored until they are needed, using up space and adding to costs. For example, food items may need to be stored in hygienic conditions at a particular temperature. Stocks may also need insuring against damage or theft.

## Running costs

It is important to have a clear and realistic idea of the other running costs that a business needs to cover. Again, the exact nature of the running costs involved will vary from firm to firm. Common running costs include rent, heating, lighting, wages, stationery and insurance.

## Employing staff

The owners of small businesses are often reluctant to employ staff, even when their business is becoming too big for one person to cope with. In some cases, this may be due to a reluctance to let go of any aspect of its operations. However, the financial implications of taking on employees can have a significant impact on running costs. In addition to wage costs, the employer is required to pay national insurance contributions for any employee earning at or over a certain rate of pay. Other staff costs may include providing uniforms, refreshments, company cars and pension contributions.

## Pricing policy

Another decision that needs to be taken before a new business begins trading involves the most appropriate pricing policy or strategy to adopt. The choice of pricing policy is significant for two main reasons. In the long term, the chosen price level needs to generate enough revenue to more than cover operating costs, if the business is to make a profit. The price of a good or service is a key determinant of demand. This does not necessarily mean that charging prices that are a lot lower than competitors' will necessarily win sales and lead to success. For some customers and some products, price may well be the most important influence on the decision to purchase. A number of price comparison websites now exist that allow customers to search online for the cheapest supplier of a particular brand. However, in other cases, price is taken as an indicator of quality. Many consumers are willing to pay higher prices for products with a strong brand image built on exclusivity or a reputation for high standards of quality.

Commonly used pricing policies include:

- **Penetration pricing** This involves using low prices initially to launch a new good or service onto the market. If successful, sales should increase quickly, helping a new business to recover the costs of setting up. There may be scope to increase prices in the longer term, once the product has become established. However, the level of competition and the likely reaction of customers may limit the scope for doing this.
- **Price skimming** This involves launching a product onto the market at a relatively high price. A new business may choose to do this in an attempt to create an exclusive image. In addition, a new business may plan to operate on a relatively small scale initially, perhaps due to a lack of investment funds or a desire to be cautious. Small-scale production is likely to mean that unit costs of production are relatively high. A successful price-skimming strategy should allow the business to generate a reasonable profit, despite high unit costs and low sales volumes. Prices can be reduced when the business is ready to expand in order to attract more customers.
- **Psychological pricing** This is designed to appeal to customers' emotional reactions rather than their rational decision making. For example, a price of 99p rather than £1.00 creates the impression, at least initially, of giving more value than a saving of 1p.
- **Competitive pricing** This policy involves pricing goods or services at the same level as other firms operating in the market. In markets with many competing firms selling products that are very similar, price is likely to be the main influence on demand. Charging a price that is above those of competitors will simply result in a lack of sales. However, undercutting rivals is likely to spark off a price war.

See Unit 3, Introduction to marketing, for more on pricing strategies.

## Break even

Breaking even is a common objective for many businesses in the early stages of trading. It means that, although a business may not be earning sufficient revenue to make a profit, it is earning enough to cover costs. Knowing the level of output and sales required to break even can be very helpful to a new business. The formula used for doing this is as follows:

$$\text{Break-even point} = \frac{\text{Fixed costs}}{\text{contribution per unit}^*}$$

$$^*\text{Contribution per unit} = \text{sales price} - \text{variable costs per unit}$$

In order to use this formula to calculate break even, a business needs to be able to classify its costs as either **fixed** or **variable**. A new business may find it particularly hard to estimate costs and revenues accurately, reducing the effectiveness of the technique. It also becomes increasingly difficult to apply the formula meaningfully when a business has several levels of prices and costs.

## Cash flow forecasting

Cash flows into a business from a number of sources over time. These include payments from customers as a result of sales, money invested in the business by owners, grants, bank loans and other borrowings. Cash is needed by a business to cover expenses, including payments for supplies, wages to employees and electricity and telephone bills. Managing cash flow effectively is essential. Insufficient levels of cash mean that bills cannot be paid when they fall due. This can damage a firm's reputation and make it difficult to obtain credit from suppliers in the future. If debts continue to go unpaid, the business may be taken to court and be forced to close down so that the money can be recovered.

It is helpful, therefore, for a business owner or manager to have a clear idea of the level and timing of cash inflows and cash outflows in the months ahead. This can be done by drawing up a cash flow forecast. Doing this helps to identify any points in time where cash outflows are likely to be greater than cash inflows, allowing corrective action to be taken. For example, more money could be invested by the owners or the firm's overdraft facility could be increased.

See Unit 5.2 for a more detailed discussion of cash flow forecasts.

## Profit and loss budgets/ accounts

A new business will also find it useful to produce a forecast profit and loss account and a forecast balance sheet relating to the first 12 months of trading. In addition to a cash flow forecast, these documents are usually included in the financial section of a new firm's business plan. A forecast profit and loss account gives details of estimated income, the various costs that are expected to be incurred and the resulting level of profit it is hoped will be produced. A forecast balance sheet gives estimates of the value of the assets owned and the level of liabilities owed by a business by the end of its first year of trading, along with figures for the amount of capital invested in the business.

See Unit 5.3 for more details on compiling profit and loss accounts and balance sheets.

## Sources of finance

Starting up a business requires finance, both to cover the initial cost of the capital required for premises, equipment, fixtures and fittings and also to pay for supplies and other expenses until the cash from sales begins to flow in. Understandably, most entrepreneurs are confident that they will succeed in generating the sales forecasted in their business plans within the planned timescales. However, taking a cautious approach and ensuring that back-up funds are available, should sales levels fail to meet initial targets, can ensure survival, at least in the short term. It is important to consider carefully how this necessary finance will be raised. Most entrepreneurs invest cash from personal sources, such as savings, into the business. This is important as it shows other potential investors and lenders that the owner is totally committed to the business. However, this may not be enough to cover all of the expenses incurred. There are many potential sources of finance available to support a new business start-up. Influences on the choice made include availability, cost, what the money will be used for and any loss of control over the business resulting from obtaining the finance.

### Short-term finance

This is needed to finance working capital, such as paying for supplies. The funds are usually repaid relatively quickly as money flows into the business from sales. Two commonly used forms of short term finance are:

- **Trade credit** This involves obtaining an agreement with suppliers that allows a business to receive supplies and pay for them at some

point in the future. Trade credit acts as a short-term, interest-free form of borrowing, allowing a business to narrow the gap between paying for supplies and receiving the cash from sales. However, failing to settle debts by the agreed date can damage supplier relationships and may lead to the credit agreement being withdrawn.

- **Overdraft** This involves a business having the facility to draw funds over and above those available in its bank account, up to a pre-agreed limit. The funds are available to be used as and when required and interest is calculated on the basis of the actual level and length of time of the borrowing. This provides a great deal of flexibility, allowing a business to cover short periods of negative cash flow, repaying the overdraft when cash flow becomes positive. Overdrafts can prove to be expensive in the long term, as the annual rate of interest is usually much higher than for other forms of borrowing. They are also repayable on demand, which means that the facility can be withdrawn immediately.

### Long-term finance

This is typically used to finance the purchase of fixed assets, such as premises, machinery or vehicles.

- **Loan** Borrowing funds to set up a business avoids the loss of control that usually results from taking on additional investors, but means that the money will have to be repaid, with interest, at an agreed point in the future. Most business loans are provided by banks. The amounts involved start from £1,000 with a minimum repayment period of 12 months. Interest rates charged can be fixed or variable and depend on the amount borrowed and the term of the loan, as well as the degree of risk perceived by the bank. Some form of security, such as an asset of a value comparable to the loan, may also be required, which can limit the amount that a small, new business is able to borrow. Local Enterprise Agencies may also provide **soft loans** to new businesses. These are loans that have lower rates of interest and more generous repayment terms than those offered by commercial lenders. They can be applied for if a business has tried and failed to obtain funding from a bank.
- **Mortgage** This is a specific type of loan used to purchase property. The sums of money involved are usually relatively large and the repayment

periods are typically between 10 and 25 years. The loan is secured against the property being purchased, which means that it could be seized by the lender if repayments are not maintained.

- **Hire purchase** This is an agreement to buy an asset, such as a computer or vehicle, by making agreed payments over a period of time. The key benefit of doing this is that the business gets to use the asset immediately but spreads the cost over a number of months or years.
- **Leasing** This involves setting up an agreement to make regular payments to use an asset, such as a photocopier or vehicle, without ever actually taking possession of it. Leasing also means that a business can reduce cash outgoings at start-up but still have access to the equipment required to operate effectively. Under the agreement, the leasing company may also be responsible for servicing the equipment and replacing any machinery that breaks down.
- **Grants** These are available from a variety of sources, including the government, the European Union and a variety of organisations such as the Prince's Trust (see 36.2). Grants are usually aimed at specific businesses, e.g. those set up by young people, the long-term unemployed, women, or people from ethnic minorities. They may also be provided to cover specific expenditure, such as building renovation, the purchase of equipment, training or research and development.
- **Venture capitalists and business angels** Venture capitalists are organisations or individuals that invest in businesses with the potential for high growth, in return for shares and a position on the board of directors. The sums of money involved are large – usually a minimum of £250,000 – making this type of funding inappropriate for the majority of small, new businesses. Business angels are private investors who provide money for businesses that have potential but are viewed as too risky by the banks and other lenders.

## Record keeping

Keeping detailed and accurate financial records from the beginning is vital if a new business is to be run successfully. These records are needed to calculate the correct amount of tax paid on any profits made. Inaccurate or incomplete records can lead to insufficient tax being paid, which could result in prosecution and hefty fines. Poor record keeping can also result in too much tax being paid, draining a firm's resources. Keeping accurate financial records is also necessary in order to measure and monitor the firm's performance. Details can be compared with the forecasts set out in the firm's business plan. This will help to identify whether the business is on track to achieve its objectives and highlight any areas where corrective action needs to be taken.

## Enterprise Finance Guarantee

The Enterprise Finance Guarantee (EFG) is a loan-guarantee scheme launched by the government in January 2009. The purpose of the EFG is to support small firms with a workable business proposal but who are unable to obtain funding from banks and other lenders. Under the scheme, firms with annual sales turnover of up to £25 million can apply for loans of between £1,000 and £1,000,000, which are repaid over a term of between one and ten years. The funds come from approved lenders, including many high-street banks, but 75 per cent of the borrowing is guaranteed against default by the Department for Business, Enterprise and Regulatory Reform (DBERR).

The EFG scheme is available both to new businesses in need of start-up capital and to existing firms needing finance to expand or to pay off existing overdrafts and free up working capital. It may also be possible to arrange a capital repayment holiday, where a business just pays the interest on a loan, for a period of up to two years. Firms who are successful in applying for the scheme have to pay an arrangement fee plus a 2.5 per cent government premium, in addition to any interest, on the outstanding balance of the loan.

### Questions

a) Explain why a new small business might struggle to obtain funding from a bank.
b) Outline one reason why the government would provide support to small businesses by offering loan guarantees.

## Key terms

**By-law** A law made by a local authority in order to manage the area under its control

**Capital needs budget** A breakdown of the buildings, machinery, vehicles and other equipment needed by a business, along with details of when they are needed and how much they are likely to cost

**Contract of employment** A written document that should be issued to all employees within two months of them starting work, giving key details such as the name of the employee, the name and address of the employer, the job title and a description of the duties to be carried out. It must also give details about pay, paid holiday and sickness entitlements and notice periods for both the employee and employer

**Discipline policy** A document that sets out the standards of behaviour that are expected from employees, and the procedures for dealing with poor performance or misconduct in the workplace

**Grievance policy** A document that sets out the procedures that should be followed if an employee has a complaint about the way that they have been treated by a colleague or a manager

**Legal liability** The extent to which an owner is personally liable for any of the debts generated by his or her business

**Ledger** Books that are used to record financial details, such as sales, purchases of stock and fixed assets and business expenses

**Personal survival budget** A document that identifies any known expenses, such as food, clothing, rent or mortgage repayments and other bills, that a business owner is likely to incur in the initial months of setting up a business, along with any income that may also be generated. This helps to determine how much money needs to be raised to support the owner until the business begins to generate sufficient profits for him or her to draw on

**Regulatory body** An organisation that has been set up by the government to establish minimum standards of business behaviour, e.g. the Office of Fair Trading

**Soft loan** A loan that has lower rates of interest and more generous repayment terms than those offered by commercial lenders. These loans are provided by local and national government, the European Union or organisations such as Enterprise Agencies or the Prince's Trust

**Trading standards** Legal standards that are created to try and ensure that all customers are treated fairly and not exploited when they buy goods and services

## Q Re-cap questions

1  Identify and briefly describe four types of legal structure commonly used to set up a new business.

2  Explain the difference between unlimited liability and limited liability.

3  State five types of business that require a licence to operate.

4  Identify four different areas of legislation that all businesses must be aware of and adhere to.

5  Outline three legal duties and responsibilities that a business has to its employees.

6  Identify five factors that a new specialist bookshop should take into account when choosing its premises.

7  Examine two pricing policies that a new firm might adopt when entering into a very competitive market.

8  Explain why a new business might find it difficult to use break-even analysis effectively.

9  Describe two likely sources of short-term finance and two sources of long-term finance for a small business.

10 Explain two reasons why accurate financial record keeping is important for a small business.

## Grading tips

**P4** Describe the legal and financial aspects that will affect the start-up of the business.

Use this section of the book as a checklist to guide you through the aspects that you need to cover. You must describe the legal status of your business and the kind of trading you intend to carry out. You also need to identify any particular legislation, regulations or responsibilities that are relevant to your business. For example, registering for VAT may not be necessary for a small-scale business but may become relevant as it grows. At this stage, you do not need to draw up any cost budgets or financial forecasts, but you do need to explain what they are and how they are used.

See page 308 for suggestions for Assignments for Unit 36.

# Part 4: Producing an outline business start-up proposal

## The business proposal

The purpose and benefits of business planning have already been discussed in Part 1 of this unit. The planning process involves setting targets and goals, and outlines the strategies that will be used to achieve them within given timescales. Drawing up a business plan can help to spot potential problems, so that action can be taken to prevent them from occurring. The written plan can then be used to monitor performance and progress in achieving objectives. Detailed plans also provide evidence that can be used to attract investment and loan finance.

There are many models or formats available that can be used as the basis for producing a business plan. They can be obtained from high street banks and organisations such as Business Link. The layout may vary from model to model, but they all include sections similar to those outlined below. A key point to remember is that a business plan is a living document, meaning that the initial draft needs to be updated regularly once the new business begins to trade.

## The components of a start-up business plan

### A summary of the plan

This section should provide a concise overview, giving key details and gaining the interest of the reader. It should include details on the following:

- The business
- The market
- Forecast profit
- The level of finance required
- Potential growth.

It may be easier to write this section once the rest of the plan is completed.

### Type of business

This section aims to give a clear idea of what the business is being set up to do. The following details should be included:

- The name and nature of the business and the sector in which it is situated
- The **legal structure** of the business and liability of the owners

- The date it was set up or, for an existing business, the date it was acquired from another owner
- The business vision, aims and objectives
- A basic description of the product or service and its **unique selling point (USP)**, i.e. what makes it different and why customers will buy it
- Anticipated levels of demand
- Details of any patents or trademarks that the business owns
- Details of any licences that must be obtained or specific laws that must be taken into consideration
- An outline of how the business and its products or services might be developed in the future.

## Marketing plan

This section is used to provide key details about the market in which the business will be operating, including:

- Market size and any trends, such as the rate of growth
- Details about the segment of the market that is to be targeted
- Information on customer characteristics, e.g. consumers or other businesses
- Information on likely competitors, e.g. numbers, market share, behaviour
- Details of the proposed pricing policy
- Activities that will be used to promote the business and sell its products or services, such as advertising, the internet, PR or direct marketing
- Ideas for new products or services that will support future business growth
- Details of the market research used to analyse the market, e.g. primary, secondary.

## Human resources plan

This section gives details on worker input into the business, including:

- The number of employees required, the duties they will carry out, the hours they will work, and the skills that they will need to possess
- The basis on which staff will be employed, e.g. part-time, full-time, temporary or permanent contracts
- Rates of pay, salary levels and an estimate of overall labour costs

- Details of any management structure, roles and responsibilities
- Information on how employees will be recruited
- Information on any training plans, including cost and timings
- Details of key HR policies, including equal opportunities, discipline and grievance procedures.

## Operations and physical resources plan

This section contains information outlining how goods or services will actually be produced, including:

- The location of the business, including any key benefits or drawbacks
- A description of the premises and whether they will be owned or rented
- Details of production facilities, whether they will be owned or leased and the costs involved
- Information on any planning permission that will be required
- Details of how the business will comply with fire and health and safety regulations
- Whether any production will be outsourced to other businesses
- Details of production capacity and forecasted capacity utilisation
- Names of suppliers and reasons for choice
- Details about procedures for stock and quality control
- Proposed use of IT to control operations.

## Financial resources plan

- Personal survival budget
- Breakdown of key sources of finance
- Details of how and when any borrowings will be repaid
- Capital needs budget
- Breakdown of running costs
- Monthly cash flow forecasts for at least the first three years of trading – many businesses

produce a series of these, reflecting more and less optimistic viewpoints
- Monthly profit and loss forecasts for the first three years of trading – again, a series of forecasts may be produced to reflect a range of scenarios
- Forecast balance sheets for at least the first two years of trading
- An explanation of the assumptions on which the forecasts are based
- A SWOT and PESTLE analysis.

## Growth and development plan

This section should outline how the business intends to develop in the medium and long term. It could include:

- An explanation of how the business's objectives may change over time
- Details of new products or services that may be developed
- Details of new markets that may be exploited
- Details of how any proposed expansion will be financed.

## Contingency plans

A **contingency plan** is a course of action that is drawn up to deal with any unforeseen and unwelcome events that could damage the performance of a business and prevent it from achieving its objectives. Possible risks might include:

- A significant increase in the level of competition
- A sudden and severe economic downturn
- The unexpected illness of a key employee
- A prolonged interruption in supplies
- An industrial dispute that halts production.

Identifying and planning responses to the main risks that a business faces is good practice. It can also help to convince lenders and investors that business owners are capable of managing the business successfully.

# Key terms

**Capacity utilisation** The percentage of a firm's maximum production or operational output that is actually being used at any given time. For example, a hotel with 30 of its 40 rooms occupied would have a capacity utilisation of 75 per cent

**Contingency plan** Course of action that is drawn up to deal with any unlikely and unwelcome events that could damage the performance of a business

**Executive summary** A concise overview of a business plan, giving key details of the plan and designed to gain the interest of the reader

**Patent** The right to be the only producer or user of a newly invented product or process, once it has been registered with the Patent Office

**Production capacity** The maximum level of output a firm can produce in a given period, given its current level of resources. For a service provider, this could relate to the maximum number of customers that could be served in a certain amount of time

**Trademark** A name, symbol or logo that is used to advertise a firm's products or services and differentiate them from those of rivals. The exclusive right to use a trademark can be obtained by registering it with the Patent Office

## Q Re-cap questions

1 Outline two benefits of business planning.

2 Explain the purpose of including an executive summary at the beginning of a business plan.

3 State the main sections that should be included in a business plan.

4 What is a contingency plan?

5 Explain two benefits for a new business of carrying out contingency planning.

# Grading tips

**P5** Produce a proposal containing the essential information for the start-up of a business.

You need to use a formal report format for your business proposal (these can be obtained online or from a high-street bank). Use this to ensure that you provide information on all of the key aspects of the business, as set out in this section of the unit. Your written proposal has to be supported by an oral discussion that explains the key points and justifies the decisions you have made.

**M3** Assess the implications of the legal and financial aspects that will affect the start-up of the business.

You need to discuss both the positive and negative ways in which the performance of your business will be affected. For example, taking out a loan or an overdraft can get the business up and running by providing the finance to obtain capital and supplies, but may lead to a significant increase in costs.

**D1** Present a comprehensive business proposal that addresses all relevant aspects of business start-up.

A comprehensive business proposal requires you to discuss in detail all the key aspects of the business start-up. You will have already generated much of the evidence you require by completing the pass and merit criteria. You now need to pull this together to create a convincing proposal. It would be helpful to get advice and guidance for doing this from someone with relevant experience, such as an existing business owner or adviser, or your teacher or lecturer.

## Assignments for Unit 36

### Assignment One

You have decided to set up your own business – a coffee shop based in the town where you live. Your idea was prompted by some research that you found on the internet that suggests that demand for independent cafés is growing in the UK (see below).

### Secondary research into the UK coffee shop industry

- According to the British Coffee Association, the UK consumes nearly 70 million cups of coffee a day. It also claims that around 11 million people visit coffee and tea shops at least once a week.
- The 2008–09 recession in the UK resulted in major chains such as Starbucks closing hundreds of branches.
- According to research carried out by Allegra Strategies in 2009, consumer expectations for cafés have increased as a result of the economic downturn, strengthening the demand for good-quality coffee shops.
- According to research carried out by The Independent, 20 per cent of all independent coffee shops operating in the UK in 2009 had started up within two years.

Source: www.startups.co.uk

You are currently in the initial planning stage of your business and have decided to present your idea to a business mentor in order to obtain some feedback.

**Note** – read through the tasks, the relevant criteria and the assignment advice on page 286 to ensure you generate sufficient evidence.

**Criteria covered** – P1, P2, M1

**Tasks**

1. Put together a presentation outlining your initial business idea. Make sure that the criteria you use to examine your initial idea are relevant to your business. (P1)
2. Explain how to identify the market your business will be targeting, describing it in detail. (P2)
3. Give a clear and detailed explanation of the methods that you used to identify the target market of your proposed business. Describe the research methods used and explain why you chose them. In addition, explain how your research results support your decision to go ahead with your business proposal. (M1)

### Assignment Two

Your business mentor is very supportive of your initial business proposal and has given you a great deal of feedback and advice. One of their suggestions is that you carry out an audit of your existing skills and abilities that will be useful in running your business. This should also help you identify any further skills that you should acquire.

**Note** – read through the tasks, the relevant criteria and the assignment advice on page 292 to ensure you generate sufficient evidence.

**Criteria covered** – P3 M2

### Tasks

1. Produce a checklist that identifies and briefly describes the skills and abilities that you think will be needed to run your business successfully. Some of these will be general skills and abilities but some will relate directly to your particular business. Distinguish those skills and abilities that you already have from those that you will need to acquire. (P3)
2. Analyse the personal development needed to run your business successfully. This can be done by explaining the reasons why the skills you currently lack will be needed. You should also explain how your personal development will be achieved. (M2)

### Assignment Three

Your mentor is confident that you are now ready to approach your bank with your proposal for your new business. This needs to contain all the information needed for the business start-up. Your mentor has also advised you to include an account of the legal and financial aspects affecting your start-up. For instance, you will need to comply with legislation relating to the preparation and serving of food (see the Food Standards Agency website for more information). Your business will also need to be registered with the local authorities and you are likely to face inspections from time to time.

**Note** – read through the tasks, the relevant criteria and the assignment advice on pages 304 and 308 to ensure you generate sufficient evidence.

**Criteria covered** – P4 P5 M3 D1

### Tasks

1. Produce a proposal containing the essential information for the start-up of your business. (P4)
2. Include within your proposal a description of the legal and financial aspects that are likely to affect the start-up of your business. (P5)
3. Extend Task 2 by assessing the implications of the legal and financial aspects that will affect the start-up of your business. This should include both the positive and negative effects on the business's performance. You must also explain the systems and procedures that you will put into place to ensure that these legal and financial requirements are met. (M3)
4. Present a comprehensive business proposal that addresses all aspects relevant to your business start-up. (D1)

# Index

The index is in word-by-word order, so 'communication skills' files before 'communications'. Page numbers in *italics* indicate diagrams and images; page numbers in **bold** indicate keyword definitions.

3i, investments 57
4 Ps *see* marketing mix
accessibility 139, **146**
accountability, lines of control 14
accounting 150–4, **154**, 294
accumulated depreciation 170
acid test ratio *69*, 70, 176
ACORN classification 101, **105**
ad hoc research 219, **219**
added value products 3
administration **291**
    costs 153
    departments 45
    small businesses 288
administrative records 125
adverse variances 63, **71**
advertisement mock-ups 207, **208**
advertisements *144*, 200, 205, 207
advertising 114, *115*, **117**
    campaigns 200–2
    communication techniques 129
    comparethemarket.com campaign 184, *184*
    content 205
    demography of audience 139
    ethical issues 134–5
    for jobs 248, 249–50, *250*, *251*
    language use 88
    in the promotional mix 185–6
    use of media 114, 185–6, 200–2, **203**, 206
    *see also* publicity materials
advertising agencies 200, *200*, **203**
advertising media 114, 185–6, 200–2, **203**, 206
Advertising Standards Authority 87–8, 134–5
aesthetics, product feature 109
affordability, and pricing 26, 194
aged debtor analysis 163, **164**
AIDA consumer response hierarchy 190, *190*, **191**
aims of businesses 17–18, 20–2, *21*, *22*, **22**, 49, 280
Ansoff's Matrix 82, *82*, **88**
application forms, jobs 260, *261*, **262**
application packs 263, **272**
applications, jobs 251
appraisals 48
Appropriation Account 66
aptitude tests 266
arithmetic mean 234, **242**
Articles of Association 5, **11**
asset turnover *70*, 71
assets *70*, **71**, 169
    *see also* current assets; fixed assets; intangible fixed assets;
        net assets; tangible fixed assets
attainment tests 265
audiences, presentations 127, 139–40, 145, 146, 238, 239

B2B firms 104, **105**, 188, **191**, 197
B2C firms 100, **105**, 187–8, **191**

B2G firms 105
backing up (computer data) 136
balance sheets *171*, **172**
    components 170–1
    description 64, **71**
    examples 66–7
    presentation 169–70
    publication 174
    purpose 169
bank loans 57, 67, 152, 154, **154**, 301
banks
    overdrafts and loans 56–7, **59**, 67, 152, **154**, 163, **164**, 301
    Payment Protection Insurance scam 87
bar charts 240, **242**
barcodes, data for research 215, *215*
BCAP Codes 88, 135
bias
    in interviews 270, **272**
    in research 231, 241, **242**
boards of directors 8
body language 146, **146**, 269, *269*, **272**
Body Shop, The 19
BOGOF offers 115, 116
BOGOFL offers 116
boom 24
brand awareness 79, 184
brand equity **88**
brand extension 85–6, **88**
brand image
    consistency 197
    description 84, *84*, 107, **191**
    and product placement 113, 189
brand-mapping 84, *84*
branding
    and marketing 83–6, *85*, **88**, 198, **198**
    and positioning 113, 189
    and pricing 29, 85
break-even analysis 61–2
break-even point 60, 61, 62, **71**, 78, 300
break-even position 20, 21, **22**
breaking bulk 196, **198**
Bridlington Pizzas, budget 64
British Chambers of Commerce *290*
British Code of Advertising, Sales Promotion and Direct
    Marketing 88, 135
broadcasting *see* digital broadcasting; media
Brompton Bikes 110
budgets
    decision making *62*
    description 63, **71**
    examples 64
    for personal living 297–8, *298*
    and promotion 189, 206, 207
buildings
    costs 153, 298

maintaining 51
security 53, **55**
business angels 302
business communications *see* communications
business continuance plans 136–7, **137**
business cycle 24, **30**
business documents 127–8, *128*, 139–40, 294
business environment 19, 282
*see also* economic environment
business functions 15–17, *16*
business letters 140–1, *141*
Business Link 33, *290*
business loans 57, **59**
*see also* loans
business markets 104–5, **105**
business memos 142, *142*, **146**
business objectives 4, 17–18, **22**, 42, 189, 197, *198*
business plans 280–1, **285**, 305–6
business proposals 305
business purposes 3–4
Business rate 32, **36**
business skills, small businesses 287–9, *287*, 291
business stakeholders *see* stakeholders
business types 4–7, 19, 278–9
buyers 100, **105**
by-laws 296, **303**

campaign briefs 205, **208**
campaign schedules **208**
candidates for jobs
information for 259–60, 263
interviews 264–6, *267*, 268, **272**
job offers and feedback 270–1
references 263–4, 271, **272**
rights 254–6
unsuccessful 272
capacity utilisation **307**
capital employed 67, **71**, 171, **172**, **179**
capital expenditure 152, **154**, 160, 163
capital income 151–2, **154**
capital needs budget 299, **303**
captive product pricing 112, **117**
Care Quality Commission, ensuring standards 21–2
carriage inwards 166, **172**
carriage outwards 168, **172**
cascading, business objectives 18, *18*
cash books 294
cash cycle 158, *158*
cash flow 157, *157*, 161–3, *162*
cash flow forecasting 157–60, *158, 160*, **164**, 300
cash purchases 159
cash sales 152, 158, **164**
catalogues, use of appropriate language *140*
census 226, 232, **232**
census data 101
chain of distribution 112–13, *112*
channel strategies 188, **191**, 195, **198**
channels of distribution
description 112–13, **117**
strategies 188, **191**, 195, **198**
charitable companies 7
charitable trusts 6–7, *7*, **11**
charities *see* not-for-profit organisations
Chocbox 54
cider tax proposal 20
circulation figures, advertising 202
clarification, seeking 145
climate change 10

closed questions 218, 228–9, **232**, 269, **272**
closing balance 158, **164**
closing stock 65, **71**, 166, 172
cluster samples 227, *229*, **232**
Coca Cola 202, 241
Codes of Practice 88, **88**, 135, **137**
commercial information providers 125
commercial mortgages 57, **59**
commercial recruitment agency **252**
commission received 152, **154**, 167
communication **126**, **191**
formal and informal 145, **146**
language use 139, *140*, 146
'noise' 140, 189
non-verbal 145, **146**
process 189
techniques in advertising 129
*see also* communications
communication problems 269–70
communication skills 145–6, 268–69
communications
audience requirements 139–40, 146
corporate 129–30, **131**
departmental 42–3
and equal opportunity 133–4, 139
methods 139–44
non-written 141–2, 143–4, *144*
online and digital 142–3
in organisations 14, 42–3, 135, 136
presentation methods 127–30
technological systems 112, 137, 142–3, 143, 144–5, 145, 186
two-way 122, *122*, 145, 268–69
written 123, 140–3, *144*, 238
*see also* communication
company reports 216–17
competition
EU policy 35
legislation encouraging 34–5
market research 124
and objectives 81
and planning 19
and pricing 195, 300
and promotion 189, 206
small businesses 281, 284
*see also* market penetration; product differentiation
Competition Commission 35
competitive insight 124, **126**
competitive pricing 195, 300
complaints procedures 295
computer backups 136
Computer Misuse Act 1990 133
computer viruses 133, **137**
computers
advantages 144
legislation on data 133
*see also* technological resources
concentration marketing 104
confidence level, sampling 226, **232**
confidentiality
and information 135–6
in job interviews 267
conflict
with customers 295
in teams 49
Consumer Credit Acts 86–7, 295
consumer markets 100–4
consumer protection 34, 86, 87, 295
Consumer Protection (Distance Selling) Regulations (DSRs) 87, 295

Consumer Protection from Unfair Trading Regulations (CPRs) 86, 295
consumer response hierarchy 190
consumerism 88, **89**
consumers 100, **105**
  buying behaviour 190
  changes in demand 81
  needs and aspirations 26–7
  protection 34, 86, 87, 295
  *see also* customers
contingency plans 52–3, 306, **307**
continuous research 219, **219**
contract workers, legislation 255
contracts of employment 34, 45–6, **49**, 297, **303**
convenience, product feature 108
convenience samples 227, *229*, **232**
cooperation, in team work 49
cooperatives 6, 7, **12**, 293, *293*
copyright 54, **55**, 135, **137**
copywriting **203**
corporate communications 129–30, **131**
corporate image *129*, 130, 187, **191**
corporate objectives 76–7, 104
Corporation tax 32, **36**
correlation 221, 235–6, *236*, **242**
correspondence, retention 294
cost of goods sold **172**
  *see also* cost of sales
cost limitation, public sector 21
cost of sales 65, **71**, 153, 166, *167*, **172**
costs 60
  administration 153
  advertising 201
  development and production 194
  distribution 113, 153
  market research 213, 214
  premises 153, 298
  promotion 116, 187
  raw materials 27
  recruitment 248, 249, 250–1
  revenue expenditure 153
  sales 65, **71**, 153, 166, **172**
  small businesses 297–8, 299
  starting a business 20
  stock purchase 153
  technological resources 137
CRB checks 271
creative briefs 205, **208**
creativity, employees 43
credit **30**
  and cash flow problems 162
  cost and availability 25
  legislation 86–7
  trade 301
credit period 158, **164**
credit purchases 159
credit sales 152, 159, **164**
creditors 67, **71**, 151, **179**
creditors' payment period 177, *178*
Criminal Records Bureau (CRB) 271
culture **49**
  *see also* professional culture
current assets 67, **71**, 170, **172**, 176, **179**
  examples 66, *171*
current liabilities 64, **71**, **172**, **179**
  examples 66, *171*
current ratio *69*, 70, 176
curriculum vitae (CVs) 251, **252**, 260, **262**

customer based structure 15
customer data 87, 133, 242
customer loyalty 85
customer satisfaction, importance 9
customer service 16–17, 41
customers 9
  complaints procedures 295
  data 87, 133, 242
  and disability 139
  information for 140
  and market segmentation 104
  relationship marketing 86
  of small businesses 284
  *see also* consumers
Cut Above, A 154
CVs 251, **252**, 260, **262**

data collection
  drawbacks 93–4, 242
  legislation 87, 133, 256
  reliability 125
  storage 145
  types of research *see* primary research; secondary research
  *see also* information for businesses
Data Protection Act 1998 87, 133, 256
databank research 215, *215*, 219, **219**
debt factoring 58
debtor collection period *70*, 71
debtors **71**, **164**
  in accounts 67, 151, 159, 176
  monitoring 163
debtors' payment period 177, *178*
debtors payment period ratio 171, 177
decision criteria, interviews 270
decision-making 124, 125
Decision Making Units (DMUs) 104, **105**
declining balance method, depreciation 168
deed of partnership 4–5, **11**
Delphi technique 216, **219**
demand **30**
  factors influencing 26–7, 27, *29*, 35, *36*, 81
  effect of fiscal policies 25
  and market price 28, *28*, 29, *29*
  and pricing 194
  ripple effect 24
demand curve 26, *26*, 27, *27*
demographic segmentation 100–1, *101–2*, **105**
demography **36**
  and business communications 139
  effect of change on demand 27, 35, *36*
depreciation 168, **172**
diagrams, in presentations 239–40
dichotomous questions 230
differentiated marketing 104, **105**
digital broadcasting 145, 201
digital television 201
direct discrimination 254, **257**
direct marketing 186, 187, 203
direct selling 196
directors, accountability 15
Disability Discrimination Act 1995/2005 139, 255
disciplinary policies 295, **303**
discounts received 167
discrimination *see* equal opportunities
disintermediation 202, **203**
distribution channels *see* channels of distribution
distribution costs 113, 153
distribution of goods 27, 112–13, *112*
diversification 83

dividend payments 56, 58, 66, 67, 152
division of work 14
DMUs 104, **105**
documents 127–8, *128*, 139–40, 294
drawings 171, **172**
DSRs 87, 295
Dun and Bradstreet 217
durability, product feature 109
DVDs, data storage 145
Dyson, innovation 80

e-business feedback 242
e-marketing research 213–14
easyJet 17, 217–18
economic cycle 24
economic environment
    effect of business cycle 24
    effect of changes 24–5
    demand fluctuations 26–7
    global influences 29–30
    effect of government policy 25–6
    effect on objectives 81
    price sensitivity 29
    product supply fluctuations 27–9
economic growth 21, 22, 24, **30**
economies of scale 79
economy pricing 111, **117**
efficiency **179**
efficiency measures 177–8, *178*
electronic point of sale (EPOS) data 215, *215*
Ella's Kitchen, new business 280
email *135*, 142, 186
email disclaimers *135*
email surveys 213
emergency planning 52–3, 306, **307**
emerging markets **223**
employability skills 46–7
employees 8, 9, *41*
    contracts 45–6, 297
    costs 153, 299
    creativity 43
    and disability 139
    discipline and grievance policies 295
    facilities 44, 51
    health and safety issues 136, 295–6
    legislation 34, 45–6, 133–4, 135, 136, 139, 254–5, 295–6
    monitoring performance 42
    as owners 7
    in promotion 196–7
    qualifications, skills and experience 46–9
    records 124
    rewards and incentives 43, 44, 153
    safety 52–3
    small businesses 305–6
    staffing needs 41–2
    temporary staff 41, **49**
    training 197
    *see also* staff
employer associations 9–10
employment *see* employees; job *entries*; recruitment
Employment Act 2002 255, 295
employment contracts 34, 45–6, **49**, 297, **303**
Employment Relations Act 2000 295
Employment Rights Act 1996 45–6
Enterprise Act 2003 35
enterprise agencies *290*
Enterprise Finance Guarantee 302
entrepreneurs 278, 282, **285**

environment,
    business 19, 282
        *see also* economic environment; government; political
            environment
    for customers 197
Environment Act 195 296
Environment Protection Act 1991 296
environmental issues 36, 284, 296
equal opportunities
    and business communications 133–4, 139
    legislation 34, 139, 255
    and recruitment 254–6, **257**
Equal Pay Act 1970 255
equilibrium price 28
equipment
    leasing 58
    for presentations 239
    purchase 51–2
    small businesses 299
established businesses 278
ethical behaviour 134, **137**
ethical issues
    advertising 134–5
    recruitment 256, 257
    social factors 36
EU Directives 34, 86, 87, 255, **257**
European Union 33, *33*, 35, 36, **36**
    *see also* EU Directives
European Working Time Directive 255
excise duty 32, **36**
executive summaries **307**
expansion 2, 21, 162, 197, 247
    *see also* growth
expense claims, interviews 271
Experian, retiree research 103
experiments, in market research 91, **98**
extension strategies (products) 110–11, **117**
external recruitment 248–9, *249*, **252**
external secondary data 216–17, 221, **223**
eye contact, in communication 145

face-to-face surveys 212
facial expressions, in communication 145–6
facilities, for staff 44, 51
factoring 58, **59**
family life-cycle classification 101, *102*
fashion, and demand 27
favourable variances 63, **71**
faxes 142, **146**
Fearnley-Whittingstall, Hugh 10
Federation of Small Businesses *290*
feedback, in communication 145
field trials 214, **219**
final accounts 64–7, 150–4
    *see also* balance sheets; profit and loss accounts
final proofs, advertisements 207
finance
    costs 153
    *see also* sources of finance
financial accounting 64–7, 150–4, 294
financial incentives 43
financial information 124
financial records 16, 294
financial resources plans 306
Financial Services Authority 297
financial statements 64–72
Firefly Tonics, growth strategies 83
fiscal policies 25, **30**, 32

fixed assets 67, **71**, 152, 162, 170, **172**
    examples 66, *153*, 171
fixed costs 21, 60, **71**
    examples 61, 66
fixed-interest loans 57
flexible working legislation 255
flip charts 129
flow charts 142
focus groups 91, **98**, 206, **208**, 214, 218, **219**, 228, *229*
footfall 212
forecasting **223**
formal communications 145, **146**
formulas
    accumulated depreciation 170
    acid test ratio *69*, 70, 176
    arithmetic mean 234
    break-even point 62
    cost of sales 65
    creditors' payment period 177
    current *69*, 70, 176
    debtors' payment period 171, 177
    depreciation 168
    interquartile range 235
    market share 79
    performance 70
    price elasticity of demand 29
    profitability *69*
    profits 65–6
    solvency *69*
    working capital 67
Forum of Private Business *290*
franchisees 279, **285**
franchises 279, **285**
franchisors 279, **285**
Freedom of Information Act 2000 133
frequency curves 240, **242**
full capacity 61, **71**
functional areas 14, 18
functional structure 15–16

general ledgers 294
geo-demographic segmentation 101–2, **105**
geographic segmentation 100, 101, **105**
geographic structure 15
geographical location 105, 298
global businesses 2, *3*, 29, 113, 127, 143
Global Ethics 8
global warming, impact of businesses 10
globalisation 2, *3*, 29, **30**, 113, 127, 143
goodwill 152, **154**, 170
government
    as customer 105
    effect of policies 11, 20, 25–6, 32–5
    skills training priorities 33
    standards for public sector 21–2
    support for businesses 27–8, 33
    taxation 25, 32–3
    *see also* political environment
government departments and agencies 6
government grants 159, 302
government statistics 216
government subsidies 27–8
grants 159, 302
grievance policies 295, **303**
Gross Domestic Product (GDP), and demand 26, **30**
gross profit margin *69*, 70, 174–5, *175*
gross profits 65, **71**, 151, **154**, 166–7, **172**, **179**
group interviews 264

growth and development 82–3, 306
    *see also* economic growth; expansion
growth strategies 82–3

hacking 133, **137**
harassment 254, **257**
Health and Safety at Work Act 1974 136, 295–6
health and safety policies 53, 136, 295–6, *296*
hierarchies, in business 14–15, **22**
hire purchase 57, **59**, 302
histograms 240, **242**
home workers, health and safety legislation 136
Honda, staffing problems 42
hot desking 44, *44*
human resources 16, 41–4, 305–6
    *see also* recruitment

ICT
    in market research 218
    *see also* internet; online *entries*; technological resources
image
    changes to 79–80, *79*
    corporate *129*, 130
    importance of consistency 197
incentives 43, 44, **49**, 153
income statements 166
    *see also* profit and loss accounts
income tax 32, **36**
indirect discrimination 254, **257**
individual interviews 264, *265*
industrial markets 104–5
inflation 24–5, **30**
informal communications 145, **146**
information for businesses
    from accounts 150–4
    backups 136
    ethical issues 134–5
    intellectual property issues 135
    legal issues 87, 133
    purposes 123
    reliability of data 125
    security 135–6
    sources 124–5, *125*, 283
    technological systems 137
    types 123–4
    *see also* market research; primary research; secondary data;
        secondary research
infrastructure 32–3, **36**
Innocent Drinks
    primary research 92
    promotion 189, *190*
    sales 150
innovation 80, **89**
insurance policies 53, **55**, 297
intangible fixed assets 152, **154**, 170
integrated marketing mix 193, **198**
intellectual property 54, **55**, 135, **137**
interest rates 19, 25
intermediaries 195, **198**
internal recruitment 248, *249*, **252**
internal secondary data 215–16, 221, **223**
internet
    for advertising 186, 201, 202–3
    for communication 142, 143
    for market research 143, 213–14, 215–16, 216
    for meetings 123
    for presentations 127
    sales 113, 195, 196
    *see also* online selling

internet surveys 213–14
interpersonal skills 48, *48*, 49
interquartile range 235, **242**
interview environment 267
interview protocol 266
interview tasks/tests 265–6
interview techniques 264–6, 268–69
interviewees
    communication problems 269–70
    tips *267*
    *see also* candidates for jobs
interviewers
    skills required 49, 266
    subjectivity 241
interviews
    for jobs 264–70, *267*, 268, **272**
    market research 212, 218
invoices 142, *143*, **146**

Jimmy Choo brand 108
job advertisements 249, 250, *250*, **252**
job analysis 45
job centres 248, **252**
job descriptions 45, *46*, **49**, 259, *260*, **262**
job offers 271
John Lewis Partnership 7, 43
Joseph Rowntree Charitable Trust 7
judgement sampling 227–8, **232**
just-in-time systems 27
justified text 128, **131**

labour resources, effect on supply 27
language use
    in advertising 88
    business communications 139, *140*, 146
large-scale production 193
layout, in communications 127–8
leasing, equipment 58, **59**, 302
ledgers **303**
legal liability **303**
legibility of documents 139–40, **146**
legislation
    constraints on marketing 86–7
    consumer protection 86, 87, 295
    data protection 87, 133, 256
    effect on businesses 33–4
    employee protection 45–6, 133–4, 135, 136, 254–5, 295–6
    environment 296
    equal opportunities 34, 139, 255
    recruitment 254–6, *254*, *256*
    small businesses 293–4, 295–7
letters of application 260, **262**
letters (business) 140–1, *141*
liabilities 67, **71**, 169
    examples 66
    *see also* current liabilities; long-term liabilities
liability
    limited 5, **11**
    unlimited 4, 5
licences 294
Likert scale 230
limited companies 5–6, **11**, 34, 56, 152, 293, *293*
    *see also* dividend payments; shareholders; shares
limited liability 5, **11**, 152, 294
limited liability partnerships (LLPs) 5
line graphs 240, **242**
lines of control/command 14, 15
liquidity **71**, 176–7, **179**

liquidity ratio *see* acid test ratio
listening skills 145, 268–69
livery 130, **131**
LLPs 5
loans **59**, 159
    from banks 57, 67, 152, 154, 301
    soft 301, **303**
local communities, business activities 10
location
    and market segmentation 105
    small businesses 298
logistics 27, **30**
logos 129–30, *130*, **131**
long-term finance 301
long-term liabilities 171
    examples 66
L'Oréal products, complaints 134
losses 3–4, 21, **71**
Love Holistic Therapies 291
loyalty scheme data 215

McDonald's, image 79–80, *79*
macroeconomic policies 25–6
magazine advertising 201
management 288, **291**
management accounting 150–1
Management of Health and Safety at Work (MHSW) Regulations 1999 296
Management Information Systems (MIS) 136
margin of safety 62, **71**
market development 82
market exposure 113
market leadership 79, **89**
market orientation 76
market penetration 82
market price
    and supply and demand 28, *28*, 29, *29*
    *see also* pricing
market research 76, **98**
    costs 213, 214
    crediting sources 135
    interpretation of results 240–1
    limitations 93–4, 241–2
    in marketing process 97–8
    methods 212–18
    in planning process 18
    presentation 221–2, 237–9
    process 221–3, *222*
    quality 239
    questionnaires 212, 214, 218, 228–31, *228*, 238–9
    reliability 241
    small businesses 283
    statistical procedures 226–8, 234–7
    surveys 91, **98**, 212–13, *213*, *217*, 218, **219**, 231
    types 91–3, 212–14, 215–17, 218–19
    use of internet 143, 213–14, 215–16, 216
    use for promotion 124
    *see also* information for businesses; primary research; secondary data; secondary research
market segmentation **105**
    benefits 100
    in business markets 104–5
    in consumer markets 100–4
    types 100–1
market share 79, **89**, 107
market-research agencies 217
marketing
    and branding 83–6, *85*, **88**, 198, **198**

constraints 86–8
description 16, 76, **89**
direct 186, 187, 203
objectives 78–81, *80*, **89**, 96–7, 107
planning process 94–7, 94–8, **98**, 305
strategies 82–3, 97
techniques 81–6
marketing audits 94–6, **98**
marketing mix *107*, **117**
objectives 107
placement 112–13
pricing 111–12, *111*
products 108–11
promotion 113–16
marketing objectives 78–81, *80*, **89**, 96–7, 107
marketing plans 94–7, 94–8, **98**, 305
marketing strategies
devising and implementing 97, 218–19
growth and survival 82–3
markets **89**
business and industrial 104–5
consumer 100–4
emerging **223**
and promotional methods 187–8
stability 188
targeting 283, **285**
Mars, product development 82
mass marketing 104, **105**
mass media 201, 202–3
mean 234
media, in advertising 114, 185–6, 200–2, **203**, 206
median 234, **242**
medical checks 271
memoranda 142, *142*, **146**
Memorandum of Association 5, **11**
memos 142, *142*, **146**
Microsoft, recruitment 247
migration, from EU 35, 36
Mintel 217
MIS 136
mission 17, **22**
mission statements 17, **22**, 129, **131**
mobile phones 112, 142–3, 143, 145, 186, 206
mock-ups 207, **208**
mode 234, **242**
monetary policies 26, **30**
monitoring
budgets 63, **71**
information for 124–5
team performance 42
through accounting 150
*see also* ratio analysis
Moonpig, card distribution 114
mortgages 57, 152, **154**, 301–2
MOSAIC classification 101, **105**
motivation 43, 44
multilingual communications 127
multimedia presentations 127, 128
multimedia resources 123
multinational corporations 2
*see also* global businesses
multiple choice questions 230
multiplier effect 24
multi-stage interview 265, **272**
multistage samples 227, *229*, **232**

National Insurance Contributions (NICs) 32, **36**
national minimum wage 255–6, **257**

National Statistics 125, 283
negotiating skills 49
neighbourhood classifications 101
Nestlé, product development 82–3
net assets 171, *171*
net book value 170
net cash flow 158, **164**
net migration 35, **36**
net profit before interest and tax 65
net profit margin *69*, 70, 175, *175*
net profits 65, **71**, 151, **154**, 167–8, *169*, 171, **172**, **179**
new businesses 20, 78, 278
New Deal 27–8
niche marketing 104, **105**
Nike 44
noise (communication interference) 140, 189
Nokia, diversification 83
nominal ledgers 294
non-financial rewards 43, 44
non-probability sampling methods 227–8, *229*
non-verbal communication 145, **146**
not-for-profit organisations 3, 4, 78
*see also* charitable trusts; social enterprises

objectives **22**, **49**
corporate 76–7, 104
market research 221, 222, *223*, **223**, 239
marketing 78–81, *80*, **89**, 96–7, 107
not-for-profit organisations 4, 78
promotional 185, 187, 197, *198*, 202, **203**
promotional campaigns 206, 207
small businesses 280
SMART 18, 96–7, *97*, **98**
*see also* business objectives
observation, primary research 91, **98**, 212, **219**, 228, *229*
occupational preference tests 265
Office of Fair Trading 297
Office of National Statistics (ONS) 125, 283
Olympic Delivery Authority, recycling 52
OMM equipment 58
One brand products 8
ONS 125, 283
online meetings 123
online presentations 127
online selling 113, 114, 195, 196
online surveys 213–14, 242
open questions 230, **232**, 269
opening balance 157, **164**
opening capital 171
opening stock 65, **71**, 166, **172**
operations plans 306
oral presentations 127, 146, 237–8, *237*
*see also* presentations
ordinary share dividends 67
organisational charts 15, *15*, **22**
organisations
structure 14–15, **22**
*see also* corporate *entries*
out-sourcing 43–4, **126**
overdrafts 56–7, **59**, 67, 152, 163, **164**, 301
overheads 168
overtrading 162, **164**
owners' capital 159
ownership of businesses 8, 19

packaging
corporate communication 129
functions 196

panel interviews 265, **272**
panels
    market research 214
    primary research **219**
partnerships 4–5, **11**, 152, 293
    advantages/disadvantages *293*
    investment 56
    taxation 34
patents 54, 135, **137**, 152, **154**, 170, **307**
paternity leave 255
penetration pricing 112, **117**, 300
performance 68, 70, 71
person specifications 45, *47*, **49**, 259–60, *260*, **262**
personal selling 114–15, *115*, **117**, 186, 187, 288
personal skills, employees 47–8
personal survival budgets 297–8, *298*, **303**
persuasion, in presentations 146
PESTLE framework 94–6, *95*, **98**, *223*, **223**, 282
phone communication 112, 142–3, *143*, 145, 186
phone interviews 265
phone surveys 213
physical resources plans 306
pictograms 240, **242**
pie charts 240, **242**
piloting, questionnaires 214, **219**, 231
placement 107, 108, 112–13, 189, 195
planning
    business continuance plans 136–7, **137**
    for contingencies 52–3, 306, **307**
    influence of competition 19
    information for 123
    for marketing 94–7, 94–8, **98**, 305
    for promotional campaigns 207–8
    small businesses 280–1, **285**, 305–6
plcs 6, 58
police checks 271
political environment 32–5
    *see also* government
population (demographic) changes, effect 27, 35–6, *36*
positioning 84
postal surveys 212
PR (public relations) 115, **117**, 186
premises *see* buildings
premium pricing 111
premiums **55**
presentation methods 127–30
presentation skills 146
presentations
    audience needs 140, 145, 146, 238
    flow charts 142
    market research 221–3, 237–9
    requirements 127–8, 237–8
    technological resources 129, 239
pressure groups 10, 88
Pret A Manger, recruitment *261*
price elasticity of demand 29, **30**, *117*, 194
price skimming 111–12, **117**, 300
pricing
    and affordability 26, 194
    and brands 29, 85
    and competition 195, 300
    products 111–12, *111*, 195, *195*, 299–300
    and quality 107, 194
    *see also* market price
pricing strategies 111–12, *111*, 195, *195*, 299–300
primary data **223**
primary research 91–2, 93, **98**, 212–15, *215*, **219**
    *see also* quantitative research

primary sector, description 3, **11**
Prince's Trust *290*
private limited companies 5–6, 58
private sector
    aims and objectives 20–1, 77–8
    definition 2, **11**
    organisations 4–6, *6*
probability sampling methods 226–7, *229*
problem solving 45
problems, resolution 45, 295
processed products 3
procurement 104
product awareness 79, 184
product based structure 15
product development *76*, 82–3, 107, 194, *194*
product differentiation
    and competition 26, 193
    and price sensitivity 29
    unique selling points 193, 281, *281*
product endorsements 130
product knowledge 287
product life cycle 109–11, *109*
product line pricing 112, **117**
product orientation 77
product placement 107, 108, 112–13, 189, 195
product positioning 84, 113, 189, **191**
product supply 3
product trials 194, **198**
production capacity **307**
production figures, in market research 216
production lines *51*
production orientation 77
products 107
    development *76*, 82–3, 107, 194, *194*
    differentiation 26, 29, 193
    features 108–11
    placement 107, 108, 112–13, 189, 195
    positioning 113, 189, **191**
    and promotion *see* promotion
    *see also* product *entries*
professional culture 43
professional support 124, 289, *290*, 297
profit and loss accounts 64, **72**, 166, 167–9, **172**
    examples 65–6, 169
    publication 174
    small businesses 300–1
profit maximisation 21, **22**, 77, **89**
profitability 68, 103, 174–5, **179**, 282
profits 3, **72**, **164**
    accounting records 150–1
    calculations *60*, 65–6
    effect on supply 27
    maximisation 21
    reserves 67, **72**
    retained for investment 56
    and survival 78
promotion 107, 113–16
    and brand image 107, 184, 197
    and budgets 189, 206, 207, **208**
    and business objectives 189, 197, *198*
    campaigns *184*, 205–8
    costs 116, 187
    decision making 124
    importance of employees 196–7
    materials 206
    planning 207–8
    PR 115, **117**, 186
    services 193–4
    *see also* advertising; promotional mix; publicity materials

promotion plans 207–8
promotional budgets 189, 206, 207, **208**
promotional campaigns *184*, 205–8
promotional materials 206
promotional mix 113, *113*, **117**, 185–7, *185*, **191**
    brand image importance 184, 197
    employees' role 196–7
    factors affecting decisions 187–90, 207
    purpose and objectives 185, 187, 197, *198*
promotional objectives 202, **203**
Prompt Payment Code 163
psychographic segmentation 101, **105**
psychological pricing 112, **117**, 300
psychometric tests 266
Public Interest Disclosure Act 1997 135
public limited companies (plcs) 6, 58
public relations (PR), in promotion 115, *115*, **117**, 186
public sector 2, **11**
    aims 21–2
    objectives 78
    organisations 6, *6*
public spending 25
publicity materials 142
pubs, change in popularity 81
pull approach/strategy 196, **198**
purchase returns 166
purchases 65, **72**, 166
purchases ledgers 294
push approach/strategy 196, **198**

qualifications 46–7
qualitative research 93, **98**, 218, **219**, 241
quality, in promotional mix 107, 193, 194
quantitative data, observation techniques 212
quantitative research 93, **98**, 218, **219**
questionnaires 212, 214, 218, 228–31, *228*, 238–9
questions
    for interviews 266, 268, 269
    in questionnaires 228–9
quota samples 217, *229*, **232**
quota sampling 227

R&D 77
Race Relations Act 1976/1992 255
random samples 227, *229*, **232**
range 235, **242**
rate of stock turnover 177–8, *178*
ratio analysis 68–71, 174–9, **179**, 282
raw materials, cost and supply 27, 52
RDAs 33
reach, promotional campaigns 205–6
readability of documents 139, *140*
recession 24, **30**, 47, 83
record keeping, small businesses 288, 294, 302
recovery, after recession/slump 24
recruitment **252**
    advertising jobs 248, 249–51, *250*, *251*
    application packs 263, **272**
    application process 251, 260, *261*
    costs 248, 249, 250–1
    ethical issues 256, 257
    feedback from candidates 271
    informing candidates 268, 270
    interview tests 265–6
    interviews 264–5, 266, 267–8, 269, *270*
    job descriptions 259
    job offers 270
    legislation 254–6, *254*, *256*
    need for 247
    person specifications 259–60
    planning process 247–8
    references and checks 263–4, 271, **272**
    sources 248–9
    unsuccessful candidates 272
recruitment agencies 248–9
recruitment consultants 249, **252**
recruitment planning 247–8, **252**
references, for jobs 263–4, 271, **272**
Regional Development Agencies (RDAs) 33
regulations 296
regulatory bodies 297, **303**
Relapse, break-even analysis 61
relationship marketing 86
reliability
    data 125
    in market research 241
    product feature 109
rent received 152, 167
reports
    company 216–17
    oral 237–8
    written 238
repositioning 84
research *see* market research; primary research; secondary
    research
research brief 221, **223**
research and development (R&D) 77
research objectives 221, 222, *223*, **223**
reserves 67, **72**
resources 40
    buildings and facilities 51
    employees *see* employees
    equipment *see* equipment
    influence on objectives 81
    raw materials 27, 52
    stock 52
    technology 52, 54
    *see also* sources of finance
respondents, surveys 212
response rate, questionnaires 231
retailers 113, **117**, 196
return on capital employed (ROCE) *69*, 70–1, 171, 175, *175*
revenue expenditure 153–4, **154**, 159
revenue income 152, **154**
    *see also* sales
revenue targets 78
rewards 43, 44, **49**, 153
ROCE *69*, 70–1, 171, 175, *175*
role plays 127, **131**
Ryanair, surveys 213–14, 217–18

safety, product feature 109
Safeway takeover 35
Sainsbury's
    online recruitment 257
    profits and expansion 151
salaries 255
Sale of Goods Act 1979 86, 295
sales 16
    costs 65, **71**, 153
    use of data in research 216
    fall in level 162
    information on 124
    trends **223**, 236
sales forecasts 283–4, **285**
sales growth, and brands 85

sales ledgers 294
sales orientation 77
sales promotion 115, *115*, **117**, 124, 186
sales returns 166
sales revenue **179**
sales targets 78
sales trends **223**, 236
sales turnover/revenue 166, **172**
sample size 226
samples **232**, 241
sampling methods 213, 226–8, *229*
sampling units 226, **232**
scaled questions 230
scattergrams (diagrams) 235, *236*, 240, **242**
Scotland, tourism trends 237
screen-based communication 142
seasonal workers 41
secondary data 92–3, *92*, *217*, 221, **223**, 283
secondary research 92–3, **98**, 215–18, *217*, **219**
secondary sector, description 3, **11**
security
    of information 135–6
    for loans 57
    premises 53, **55**
selection criteria, jobs 263, 270
self-regulation 134, **137**
sequencing **232**
service provision, public sector 21
services
    flexibility 197
    and promotion 193–4
Sex Discrimination Act 1975/1995/1997 254–5
share capital 58, **59**
share issue 58, **59**
shareholders 4, 5, 6, 8, **11**
shares, selling 56, 58, 59
Shell LiveWIRE *290*
Short Message Service 142–3, **146**
short-term finance 301
shortlisting 263, **272**
size of company, and procurement of supplies 104
size of market, and promotion 116
skilled workforce 33
skills
    communication 145–6, 268–69
    interpersonal 48, *48*, 49
    interviewing 266–69
    listening 145, 268–69
    management 288
    negotiating 49
    small businesses 287–9, *287*, 291
    suitability for jobs 46–7
skills audit 288, **291**
slumps 24
small businesses
    aims and objectives 280
    business plans 280–1, **284**, 305–6
    cash-flow forecasting 300–1
    competition 281, 284
    contingency plans 52–3, 306
    costs 297–8, 299
    customers 283, 284
    equipment and supplies 299
    establishment and expansion 2
    external influences 282
    finance 297–9, 301–2
    initial start-up 278–9
    legislation and regulation 293–4, 295–7

pricing policies 299–300
professional support 124
profitability 282
record keeping 288, 294, 302
recruitment 248
sales forecasts 283–4
skills and knowledge required 287–9, *287*, 291
staffing 287, 295–6, 299
support for *290*, 297
SWOT analysis 284
time commitment 281–2
small-scale production 193
SMART objectives 18, 96–7, *97*, **98**
SMS communication 142–3, **146**
social enterprises 7, 8, 19, 78
social environment 35, 36
socio-economic groups *101*
soft loans 301, **303**
software licences 54, **55**
sole traders 4, *4*, 293
    accounts *167*, *169*, *171*
    advantages/disadvantages *293*
    examples 154
    investment 56
    sources of finance 151
    taxation 34
solvency 68, *69*, 70
sources of finance 56–9, 151–2, 177, 301–2
sources of information 124–5, *125*, 283
span of control 14, **22**
sponsorship
    as communication 130, **131**
    for promotion 10, 186, *187*
spreadsheets, in analysis 237
staff records 124
staff training 197
staffing
    costs 153, 299
    levels 41–2, **49**
    *see also* employees; recruitment
stakeholders 7–8, 8, *9*, **11**, 19
start-up costs 20
statistical analysis 221
statistics, procedures 234–7
statutory maternity leave 255
stock 153, 176, **179**
stock ordering 52
stock records 294
stock turnover *70*, 71, 177–8
storyboards 207, **208**
straight line method 168
strap lines 130, **131**
strategic aims and objectives 17–18
strategic planning 17, 18–19, *19*
strategic research 218, **219**
strategies 97, **98**, **126**
    channels of distribution 188, **191**, 195, **198**
    growth 82–3
    information for 123
    marketing 82–3, 97
    pricing 111–12, *111*, 195, *195*, 299–300
    product extension 110–11, **117**
    survival 83
strategy **22**
stratified random samples 227, *229*, **232**
strengths and weaknesses 288
    *see also* SWOT analysis
subjectivity in research 241

substitute goods 26
suppliers 9, 143, 159, 163, 301
supplies, small businesses 299
supply 27–8, *28*, *29*, **30**
supply curve *28*
surveys 91, **98**, 212–13, *213*, 217–18, 218, **219**, 231
survival 21, 78, 83
SWOT analysis 96, *96*, **98**, 124, **126**, 284
systematic random samples 227, *229*, **232**

tables, in documents 128
tactics 97, **98**
tangible fixed assets 152, *153*, **155**, 170
target markets 283, *283*, **285**
    *see also* targeting
target populations **232**
targeting
    and advertising 185–6, 202
    consumer groups 103–4
    and promotion 187, 206
targets 42
    monitoring 45
    sales and revenue 78
    setting 18
    and team working 47
taxation 25, 32–3, 297
team interviews 264–5
team working 42–3, *43*, 47, 48, 49
technical market research 219, **219**
technical obsolescence 137, **137**
technological resources 52, 53
    for communication 137, 142–3, 144–5, 186
    effect on product supply 28
    legislation on data 87, 133
    in market research 218
    for presentations 129, 239
teleconferencing 123
telephone interviews 265
telephone surveys 213
telesales *see* personal selling
television advertising 201
temporary staff 41, **49**
terms and conditions, trading 294
tertiary sector, description 3, **11**
Tesco, factory farming 10
text formatting 128, *128*, **131**
Thomson Reuters Datastream 217
time series analysis 236, **242**
total expenses 157
total receipts 157
total revenue **72**
touch screens 144–5
trade (business) cycle 24, **30**
trade credit 301
trade journals 217
trade organisations 125
Trade Union Reform and Employment Rights Act 1993 295
trade unions 9, 295
trademarks 135, **137**, 152, **155**, 170
Trades Descriptions Act 1968 *see* Consumer Protection from
    Unfair Trading Regulations
trading accounts 166–7, *167*, 17?
trading standards 294, **303**
trading terms and conditions 294
training **291**

employees 197
    for small business owners 289
transactional marketing 86
trends 236, **242**, 282
triangulation 218, **219**
Triframes 59
troubleshooting 45, **49**
two-way communication 122, *122*, 145, 268–69
types of business 4–7, 19, 278–9
typography **203**

UK census 232
undifferentiated marketing 104
Unfair Commercial Practices Directive (UCPD) 86
uniforms 130, **131**
unique selling points 193, 281, *281*
    *see also* product differentiation
university research 216
unlimited liability 4, 5, **12**, 152, 294

Value Added Tax (VAT) 32, **36**, 94, 161, *161*, **164**, 297
value for money, public sector 21
value owed 151
variable costs 60, 61, **72**
variable-rate loans 57
variances 63, **72**
VAT *see* Value Added Tax
venture capital 57, 59
venture capitalists **59**, 302
verbal communications 145, **147**
verbal information 123
verbal presentations 127, 146
vertical format balance sheets 169, *170*
Vertu mobiles 112
victimisation 254, **257**
video conferencing 144, **147**
Vintage Choice 53
viruses, computer 133, **137**
visual aids, in presentations 238, 239, 240
voluntary organisations *see* not-for-profit organisations

Walkers, advertising campaign 208
WAP 145, **147**
waste recycling 52
Water Babies, franchise 279
websites 123, *123*, 127, 215
    *see also* internet; online *entries*
whistle blowing 135, **137**
wholesalers, in marketing mix 113, **117**, 196
wireless application protocol (WAP) 145, **147**
work experience, previous 47–8
work-related skills 46–7
worker cooperatives 6, 7, **12**, 293
    advantages/disadvantages *293*
working capital
    description **49**, 64, 67, 170, **172**
    indicator 176
Working Time Directive, The 34
World Trade Organisation (WTO) 33, **36**
worldwide web *see* internet; online *entries*
written communications 123, 140–3, *141*, *144*, 238
WTO 33, **36**

zero-budgeting policy 189